GOVERNOR ROCKEFELLER IN NEW YORK

Recent titles in Contributions in Political Science
Series Editor: Bernard K. Johnpoll

Eurocommunism: The Ideological and Political-Theoretical Foundations
George Schwab, editor

American-Soviet Relations: From 1947 to the Nixon-Kissinger Grand Design
Dan Caldwell

The First Amendment Under Siege: The Politics of Broadcast Regulation
Richard E. Labunski

Political Culture, Foreign Policy, and Conflict: The Palestine
Area Conflict System
Basheer Meibar

The Politics of Wilderness Preservation
Craig Willard Allin

Nationalism: Essays in Honor of Louis L. Snyder
Michael Palumbo and William O. Shanahan, editors

Compromised Compliance: Implementation of the 1965 Voting Rights Act
Howard Ball, Dale Krane, and Thomas Lauth

City of the Right: Urban Applications of American Conservative Thought
Gerald L. Houseman

The Conservation of Enemies: A Study in Enmity
Frederick H. Hartmann

The American Governorship
Coleman B. Ransone, Jr.

Strategic Studies: A Critical Assessment
Colin S. Gray

Keeping a Finger on the Public Pulse: Private Polling and Presidential Elections
Bruce E. Altschuler

The Quest for Nuclear Stability: John F. Kennedy and the Soviet Union
Bernard J. Firestone

The Solzhenitsyn-Sakharov Dialogue: Politics, Society, and the Future
Donald R. Kelley

GOVERNOR ROCKEFELLER IN NEW YORK

The Apex of Pragmatic Liberalism in the United States

James E. Underwood
and
William J. Daniels

Contributions in Political Science, Number 75

GREENWOOD PRESS
Westport, Connecticut • London, England

Library of Congress Cataloging in Publication Data

Underwood, James E.
Governor Rockefeller in New York.

(Contributions in political science, ISSN 0147-1066 ;
no. 75)
Bibliography: p.
Includes index.
1. New York (State)—Politics and government—1951-
2. Rockefeller, Nelson A. (Nelson Aldrich), 1908-1979.
I. Daniels, William J. II. Title. III. Series.
JK3425 1982.U52 353.974703'1'0924 81-13259
ISBN 0-313-21335-6 (lib. bdg.) AACR2

Copyright Acknowledgments:

Grateful acknowledgment is given for permission to use
the following:

Excerpts from *"I Never Wanted To Be Vice-President of Anything!" An Investigative Biography of Nelson Rockefeller*, by Michael Kramer and Sam Roberts. Reprinted by permission of Basic Books, Inc.

Excerpts from *The Rockefellers* by Peter Collier and David Horowitz. Reprinted by permission of Holt, Rinehart and Winston, Publishers, and Jonathan Cape, Ltd.

Library of Congress Catalog Card Number: 81-13259
ISBN: 0-313-21335-6
ISSN: 0147-1066

First published in 1982

Greenwood Press
A division of Congressional Information Service, Inc.
88 Post Road West, Westport, Connecticut 06881

Printed in the United States of America

10 9 8 7 6 5 4 3 2 1

To
our parents
GRACE AND JAMES P. UNDERWOOD
and
ETHEL D. AND WILLIAM H. MC COY

Contents

Illustrations

Tables

Figures

Preface

Our purpose in writing this book is threefold. First, we seek to examine Nelson Rockefeller as a case study in executive leadership, describing aspects of his personality, his political beliefs, and his executive style. Second, we seek to describe and analyze the Rockefeller administration in New York as a case study of policy making at the state level. Third, we seek to determine the degree to which the Rockefeller administration reflects the public philosophy of "pragmatic liberalism," a public philosophy that we see as dominant among political elites through much of the period since World War II. Although we make no explicit attempt to compare the Rockefeller administration to other modern administrations at the state or national level, we do seek to build an argument that places the burden of proof upon those who might argue that some other administration is a more accurate reflection of modern liberalism.

Because our purpose is threefold, we have been forced to be selective in our examination of Nelson Rockefeller and his administration. Thus, for example, our biographical information is not exhaustive, nor do we attempt a comprehensive analysis of all important decisions and policies in his administration. Rather, we seek to capture the essence of Rockefeller as a political personality and political executive and the essence of his administration as it is reflected in what we believe reasonable observers would agree are key elements in both the means and ends of that administration.

Acknowledgments

We owe thanks to a long list of people who helped us in one way or another. First, there were those many who generously submitted to interviews, including the late Nelson A. Rockefeller and many of his associates and staff aides. Furthermore, many of those interviewed helped us by identifying others with whom we could talk. It should be noted that those interviewed were usually willing to be quoted "on the record." However, in those instances in which an individual requested that particular remarks not be attributed to him, we have abided by that request. We are also indebted to those many persons in and out of state government who provided us with valuable materials. Among those persons were Perry B. Duryea, former speaker of the New York State Assembly, Hugh Morrow, former director of communications for Governor Rockefeller; William Stevens, bureau chief of United Press International in Albany, New York; and Thomas W. Wallace, Jr., executive director of the New York State Board of Elections.

Several students performed valuable services as research assistants during the course of our work. Among them were Cathy Carew, Phyllis Edelman, Judy Ratner, Diane Rosse, and Gail Sunderlin. Research assistants who played especially valuable roles in developing crucial data were Doug Arnold, Laurie Brecher, and Gary Haber. In addition, Gary Haber conducted several interviews. Among the student theses and papers which proved valuable were those by Mark Blackstone and Gary Haber.

Among those who were always willing to clarify a complex matter involving state government and state programs or provide the name of someone who might were Cornelius Foley, Lloyd Nurick, Eric Markell, and Frank Mauro.

We are indebted for institutional support to a number of individuals and groups at Union College. The staff of Schaffer Library has invariably provided service of the highest professional quality. The Faculty Research

Committee has supported us with a series of research grants during the course of our work. We are indebted to Paula Brownlee and Martin Lichterman, former deans of Union College, for their support. Finally, we have had the encouragement and enthusiastic support of those two colleagues who have chaired the Department of Political Science while our research was in progress, Charles Gati and Robert Sharlet.

Authors are always indebted to those who act as sounding boards for ideas and offer criticism and advice. Whether in casual conversations or more structured settings, all our colleagues in the Department of Political Science helped fulfill this function. However, we express our special thanks to Charles Tidmarch for the quantity and the quality of his assistance. His extensive knowledge of state politics, campaigns, and American politics in general and his constant willingness to lend a hand made him all but indispensable to us.

Typing of drafts and our final manuscript was done with skill and dispatch by Claire Covey and Jean Kozel. Our department secretary Jean Kozel has provided service above and beyond the call of duty from the very beginning of this project. More than once she rescued us from impending disaster.

Only our families can fully appreciate the labor that went into this project. We thank our wives, Jean Underwood and Fannie Daniels, for indispensable support, assistance, and forbearance. Our greatest debt is to them.

James E. Underwood
William J. Daniels

GOVERNOR ROCKEFELLER IN NEW YORK

1 The Emergence of Pragmatic Liberalism

There is wide agreement that liberalism has been the dominant public philosophy throughout America's history, but it is generally acknowledged that developments beginning with the New Deal have altered its meaning.[1] According to most interpretations, classical liberalism, with its emphasis on individualism and a free-market economy, lost ground to a newer version of liberalism. The new version accepted the idea of positive government and tended to place somewhat less emphasis on property and equality of opportunity and more on equality of condition. Two political scientists, Kenneth and Patricia Dolbeare, use the term reform liberalism to denote the latter variant.[2]

Arguing that there have always been significant illiberal elements in American thought, Garry Wills agrees that liberalism suffered a schism in the 1930s. Deserting those who emphasized economic freedoms, those who emphasized human and political rights joined the growing ranks of people like Franklin D. Roosevelt who emphasized a larger role for government in dealing with social and economic problems.[3] In Wills's view, the resulting merger became the "left" in American politics. At the same time, a second merger took place as the deserted believers in economic freedoms and a minimal role for government vis-a-vis private enterprise joined in a political alliance with those who favored greater social control by government, control aimed at "deviant" social or political behavior. According to Wills's interpretation, the product of this merger has since constituted the "right" in American politics.[4]

Following World War II, the dominant liberals, the left in American politics, faced a severe challenge. With the end of a hot war and the beginning of a cold war, many liberals were eager to put as much distance as possible between themselves and those with radical, socialist, or communist leanings. The Democratic party was the main arena in which liberals struggled with each other. As history records, those sympathetic to Henry Wallace lost out to those who rallied around President Harry S. Truman.[5]

Following World War II, liberalism in the United States became "harder" in style and more pragmatic in substance. It is notable that Americans for Democratic Action (ADA) was founded in 1948 by liberals who were aggressively anti-Communist. One of ADA's founders and leading spokesmen, Arthur Schlesinger, Jr., provides a nice illustration of the direction that the dominant liberalism took after the war. In *The Vital Center* (1949), Schlesinger makes explicit the liberal's rejection of socialism and at the same time underscores support for the idea of positive government.

> Big government, for all its dangers, remains democracy's only effective response to big business. . . . [But] the lesson of the experiments with democratic socialism is plainly that the state should aim at establishing conditions for economic decisions, not at making all the decisions itself. It should create an economic environment favorable to private business policies which increase production; and then let the free market carry the ball as far as it can. Keynes not Marx is the prophet of the new radicalism.[6]

In *The Vital Center* Schlesinger is particularly contemptuous of "soft-headed progressives." The message seems clear; no one should mistake a liberal for a communist sympathizer. He writes that "the type of the progressive today is the fellow traveler or the fellow traveler of the fellow traveler: see the Wallace movement or (until fairly recently) the columns of the *New Republic* and the *Nation.* His sentimentality has softened up the progressive for Communist permeation and conquest."[7]

The "hardening" of liberalism that took place after the war was reflected in some of the policies and decisions of the Truman administration. Among them were the federal-employee loyalty program and the Smith Act prosecutions, both of which were begun in 1947, well before the emergence of Senator Joseph McCarthy as a major political force. Although a majority of liberal spokesmen and organizations opposed these initiatives by the Truman administration, it is widely accepted that the aggressive anti-Communist stance of many liberals tended to make them less vigilant defenders of civil liberties than might have been expected.[8]

To the casual observer, the decade of the 1950s may seem irrelevant to the development of modern liberalism. It is true that a "conservative" president, Dwight D. Eisenhower, beat a "liberal" candidate, Adlai Stevenson, in two landslide elections. But it is also true that the more conservative victor did little or nothing to reverse the "big-government" trend established during the New Deal. And while Eisenhower and the Republican party showed that they could live with the results of the New Deal on pragmatic grounds, leading liberal spokesmen, most notably Kenneth Galbraith, showed that they could in turn live with "capitalism."[9] Thus Galbraith could argue that government need not intervene in the affairs of the private sector as long as the mechanism of "countervailing power" operated effectively.[10]

If post-New Deal liberalism had become "harder" and less ideological during the 1950s, it had not abandoned its taste for problem solving. Looking back upon the decade, one can find indications of political elites preparing for a period of problem solving. The blandness of the Eisenhower years had offended liberal Republicans as well as Democrats. Furthermore, liberals and nonliberals had been frightened by the thought that we might be outstripped in technological, educational, economic, and military spheres by the better organized and more tightly indoctrinated "totalitarian nations,"in particular the Soviet Union. (The Soviet launching of *Sputnik* in October 1957 served to confirm some of our worst fears.) As a consequence we set out to define our national goals and the problems we faced and to conduct systematic searches for ways of achieving goals and solving problems. One manifestation of this course of action was the Special Studies Project of the Rockefeller Brothers Fund, a project begun in 1956. Chaired by Nelson Rockefeller and directed by Henry Kissinger, this undertaking is probably the best expression of a rapidly developing consensus among "establishment" figures that the time was ripe for showing that democracy in the United States could meet challenges and solve problems. As one of the six reports that were eventually published put it,

> [Democracy] needs excitement.... There is more than enough excitement in the problems it faces to keep American democracy occupied for some time.
>
> Is American democracy capable of dealing with these issues? Is democracy too loose, too slow, too inefficient, to move with the speed, concentration, and daring these problems demand? Can it set definite goals, follow long-range plans, and pull its citizens together for a concerted effort to achieve clearly formulated objectives?[11]

In the best liberal tradition, those involved in the project were optimistic about solving problems. Furthermore, the problem-solving process was seen as valuable and inspiring in itself. As the sixth report said, "Most men want a sense that large projects are under way and that they are part of some significant and enduring human enterprise.... A society that is moved by an image of what it can be and that translates this image into definite programs of action can also satisfy the human impulse to idealism."[12]

The trustees of the Rockefeller Brothers Fund maintained that the thirty members of the "overall panel" that supervised the production of reports represented "many shades of opinion."[13] However, an inspection of the membership reveals that it included a number of individuals who were generally identified as liberals while including few, if any, generally identified as conservatives. (Prominent liberals included Adolf Berle, Jr., Chester Bowles, and Theodore Hesburgh.) This is so despite the fact that the panel included representatives from labor, foundations, and universities. The fact that six members of the overall panel and four members of subpanels eventually came to serve in the Kennedy administration can be taken to illustrate the ease with which liberal problem solvers could move from serving a Republican leader, Nelson Rockefeller, to serving a Democratic leader, John Kennedy.[14]

The reports produced by the Special Studies Project had some influence on setting the public agenda for the 1960s. In particular, the great concern expressed over the adequacy of America's military posture foreshadowed some of the positions John Kennedy was to take as candidate and president. But more important for our argument is that the Rockefeller project symbolized a readiness among liberals, whether from the academic, corporate, or political worlds, to embark on an activist, problem-solving approach to tackling the nation's problems, an approach that would be untinged by ideology or partisanship. As the reports made clear, the project was aimed at defining goals and suggesting directions around which a consensus could be achieved. The product was to be an American product, not the product of any particular segment of America.

Ironically, even President Eisenhower, criticized by many for not offering firm direction, seemed to succumb to the desire to define goals that all America could pursue. In 1959 he established his own President's Commission on National Goals, a body which eventually produced a report entitled *Goals for Americans.*[15] Although commission members had difficulty agreeing on a proper role for the federal government, they produced a set of ambitious goals for the resolution of a wide variety of domestic and foreign problems.

At the same time that the Rockefeller project was in progress, the liberal wing of the Democratic party was busy preparing a program much of which would be enacted in the 1960s. As James Sundquist points out, an alliance of liberal Democratic senators, liberal Democratic congressmen (organized in the Democratic Study Group), and the Democratic Advisory Committee worked independently of the party's congressional leadership to develop and advance activist positions that could later be incorporated in a Democratic platform for a presidential election.[16] The advisory committee, founded by Democratic party chairman Paul Butler in 1956, was particularly influential in the areas of civil rights and economic policy, the latter being the province of one of the leading liberal thinkers, John Kenneth Galbraith.[17]

In general, the kinds of domestic social programs that were being advocated by Democratic activists, medicare, for example, were based on ideas that had been advanced initially in the 1930s and resurrected by the Truman administration. One might argue that the Democratic activists of the latter part of the 1950s combined the New Deal concern for social needs with a pragmatic attitude toward questions of economic policy and an appropriate stance toward business.[18] Thus the groundwork was laid for the tax policies that were to be pursued by the Kennedy and Johnson administrations and eventually culminate in the Tax Reduction Act of 1964, an act that received widespread support from business groups in congressional hearings prior to passage in 1963.[19] Perhaps nothing more clearly symbolizes modern liberalism's ability to accommodate itself to business than does the list of "conservative" groups that supported the tax-cut bill. Such groups included the Chamber of Commerce, the National Association of Manufacturers, the American Bankers Association, and numerous trade associations.[20]

In addition to the support of elites for a more activist approach by government toward solving domestic problems (as demonstrated by the Rockefeller Brothers study), growing business support for deficit financing, and the program-building activities of Democratic party leaders and their academic advisers, there is considerable evidence that the general public was favorably disposed toward governmental activism by the second half of the 1950s. As one analysis of public opinion polls during this period shows, there was strong support for a larger federal role in dealing with domestic problems.[21] Partly because of his analysis of public opinion data, James Sundquist argues that the election of John F. Kennedy in 1960 represented a mandate to the president for activism on domestic issues. Sundquist's conclusion is worth quoting in full:

> The Democratic tradition the voters endorsed was, in a word, one of activism. It was the activist approach to public problems—open-minded, innovative, willing to employ the powers of government (or, as seen from the opposing point of view, rash)—that characterized the Democratic program developed in the 1950's and both the attitude and substance of the Kennedy campaign. The election cannot be interpreted as a clear endorsement of all of the specific policy proposals in the Democratic program. But it was a clear endorsement of an approach to domestic problems, of a governing temper—and tempo. That was the mandate Kennedy asked for. That was the mandate he was given.[22]

Given the nature of presidential elections and the American party system, one might well have reservations about the idea that an election confers a mandate on any president, especially one who, like Kennedy, wins office by a bare plurality. But one need not adopt Sundquist's claim of a mandate in order to concede that the outcome of the 1960 election was consistent with public attitudes toward governmental activism in the domestic arena. One can also point to additional evidence supporting that conclusion. For example, political scientist V. O. Key concluded that "prospective voters who were preoccupied with domestic problems.... were strongly for Kennedy."[23]

A key point for our argument is that the activist approach to domestic problems was an important element in modern liberalism as well as a part of the Democratic party tradition. Thus one night expect this approach to be reflected in the behavior of some Republican as well as Democratic leaders. Without a doubt Nelson Rockefeller was one such Republican leader.[24]

The Democratic nominee for the presidency in the 1950s, Adlai Stevenson, was perhaps the leading politician spokesman for liberalism in that decade. In 1952 and 1956 both Galbraith and Schlesinger as well as almost all liberal intellectuals had supported Stevenson. In fact, they and many other academics played key roles as advisers. The switch by Galbraith and Schlesinger from the Stevenson camp to the Kennedy camp in 1960 symbolized a turning away from a "softer," more idealistic liberal to a pragmatic "winner" who had never been particularly identified with traditional liberal positions.[25] Both Galbraith and Schlesinger assisted Kennedy in forming a brain trust during his quest for the nomination. They also tried to sell Kennedy to liberals who preferred Stevenson or Hubert H. Humphrey. After Humphrey withdrew from the race following the West Virginia primary, Galbraith and Schlesinger were among the authors of a statement endorsing Kennedy as the preferred Democratic nominee. Among other things the statement characterized Kennedy as "a man of whom liberals can be proud."[26]

The Kennedy administration has sometimes been criticized for emphasizing style at the expense of, or as a substitute for, substance. But it is not necessary to accept this charge to acknowledge that there was a style peculiar to the Kennedy administration and that it seemed to be in tune with certain popular needs and expectations present at the end of the 1950s. In contrast to the style of Eisenhower, low-key and somewhat bumbling in appearance, the Kennedy style included wit, grace, and "toughness." Perhaps Garry Wills best captured the toughness aspect of the Kennedy style.

> Jack Kennedy would out-tough Khrushchev politically as Arthur Schlesinger had out-toughed domestic leftists. . . . The Kennedy team could take on the world. It would even take on the Pentagon, where Republican Robert McNamara seemed the essence of non-partisan hardheadedness—the wire hair bent around his iron ball of a head, his body kept lean in murderous squash games, his blazing eyeglasses wired to receive computer data.[27]

One could easily cite examples of Kennedy's toughness, including his celebrated confrontation with the steel industry in 1962. Notable among Kennedy's tactics aimed at forcing the industry to rescind price increases was a discretely delivered threat to corporate executives that their personal income tax returns would be subject to audits by the Internal Revenue Service. It should be obvious that the toughness of the Kennedy style found an appreciative audience in the America of the 1960s. For example, his handling of the steel industry price increase met with widespread approval, including that of the liberal press.

In the late fifties there appeared a virtual manual for instructing presidents in the acquisition and use of power. Implicitly, and sometimes explicitly, a celebration of presidential power, the book of the same title was written by Richard Neustadt, an "in-and-outer" who had served on President Truman's staff and later as consultant to President Kennedy during the transition period. Neustadt's book epitomized the view of modern liberalism regarding executive leadership.

The contributions that a President can make to government are indispensable. Assuming that he knows what power is and wants it, those contributions cannot help but be forthcoming in some measure as by-products of his search for personal influence. In a relative but real sense one can say of a President what Eisenhower's first Secretary of Defense once said of General Motors: What is good for the country is good for the President, and *vice versa.*[28]

Neustadt does not go so far as to say that the presidential power is in itself a desirable end, but neither is he much concerned about any dangers inherent in a powerful chief executive. "If skill in maximizing power for himself served purposes no larger than man's own pride or pleasure, there would be no reason for the rest of us to care whether he were skillful or not. More precisely there would be no reason except sentiment or partisanship."[29] As fits one who was an insider in the problem-solving world of modern liberalism, Neustadt sees presidential power in positive terms. "Energetic government and viable public policy are at a premium as we begin the seventh decade of the twentieth century. Expertise in presidential power adds to both."[30] One is reminded of Schlesinger's memorandum to Kennedy arguing that "vigorous public leadership would be the essence of the coming new era in politics, an era which would arise out of spiritual rather than economic discontent."[31]

As a consequence of Watergate, there has been a widespread reevaluation of the presidency and the permissible boundries of presidential conduct. It is true that some, most notably Theodore H. White, see the Watergate evils as almost exclusively the product of the personal failing of a particular president.[32] However, many observers, correctly we think, have noted that the Nixon administration inherited in the presidency an institution whose norms legitimated practices that were inconsistent with ideals often professed as part of our democratic tradition. Such practices were often justified on the gounds that national survival in the modern world requires that political leaders be allowed to violate normal standards of morality applying to private behavior.[33] Some leading examples include manipulating public opinion through dissembling, outright lying and secrecy, and using dirty tricks such as wiretapping citizens of the United States and harassing leaders of foreign countries with a variety of devices and schemes, even including assassination. The fact that such practices occurred under a variety of presidents before Nixon, including Kennedy and Johnson, suggests that more than just the personality of one bad apple was at fault. Specifically, we agree with those who suggest that the modern liberal's excessive promotion of strong executive leadership as both necessary and desirable provides a context in which such practices were likely to be employed.[34]

Components of Pragmatic Liberalism

Our brief account of the evolution of liberalism in the period from the end of World War II into the decade of the sixties provides some sense of the political mood of the times as reflected in both elite attitudes and, in lesser degree, public attitudes. Most relevant to our purposes is that Nelson Rockefeller emerged as a force in national politics in this era.

Before discussing in any detail the various components of liberalism as it had evolved, the question of an appropriate label for that liberalism deserves some attention. The term pragmatic liberalism has been chosen to describe the public philosophy which we believe dominated the thinking of most political leaders in the latter half of the fifties and all of the sixties.[35] By public philosophy we mean that set of ideas that provides assumptions regarding the possibility of solving societal problems, beliefs regarding the proper role for government in solving societal problems, values underlying choices of both the ends and means of government policy, and criteria for choosing strategies and tactics appropriate to ensuring that one's policy choices prevail.

We think the label pragmatic liberalism preferable to others even though we are aware of possible objections to our choice. For example, it can easily be argued that a pragmatic outlook has long been one of the components of American liberalism. However, we choose the term pragmatic liberalism in order to emphasize our belief that the most notable change in liberalism after World War II was that it became even more pragmatic and even less committed to principles and ideals.[36]

It should be obvious that pragmatic liberalism as a public philosophy does not represent the kind of comprehensive and self-conscious ideology such as Marxism-Leninism which guides leaders in some political systems. However, we do argue that pragmatic liberalism was, in fact, implicit in the decisions and policies of most American political leaders of the late fifties and sixties including Presidents Kennedy and Johnson.

(It should be obvious our pragmatic liberalism has elements in common with formulations by other scholars. Perhaps the most prominent is Theodore Lowi's interest group liberalism. However, although there are some common elements, his conception clearly differs from our pragmatic liberalism.)[37]

The components of pragmatic liberalism as we conceive it are as follows:

1. A belief that all problems can be solved with sufficient determination and effort;

2. A belief that solving societal problems requires big government that employs an activist approach (as opposed to the extremes of either laissez-faire or socialism);
3. A belief that the primary test of good policy is the pragmatic consideration of workability and practicality as opposed to considerations of abstract principle;
4. A belief that government and the private sector should cooperate in solving societal problems;
5. A belief that government should place high priority on meeting human needs, including those such as housing, education, and an adequate standard of living;
6. A belief that all major segments of society should receive an equitable share of the benefits allocated by government;
7. A belief that science and technology provide the key to solving many of society's problems;
8. A belief that the executive branch of government has the main responsibility for leadership and direction in attacking public problems;
9. A belief that it is sometimes desirable to manipulate public opinion and outflank widespread public and legislative resistance in order to accomplish what one perceives to be in the best interests of society;
10. A belief that political leaders must be willing to put aside idealistic and humane considerations in order to accomplish what one perceives as fundamental purposes such as the protection of the national interest or the legitimacy of the state;
11. A belief that actions normally considered unethical or illegal are often acceptable in the political arena.

This listing represents our interpretation of history in the period following World War II, and it is based on three kinds of sources. The first includes works by leading liberal spokesmen, most notably Schlesinger and Galbraith. The second includes works describing and interpreting American political beliefs during the period, especially those of Lowi and Wills. And the third includes descriptions of the policies and actions of political leaders and their administrations.[38]

The examination of the Rockefeller administration in New York which constitutes the greater portion of this book is directed in part at providing a basis for determining the extent to which that administration reflected the public philosophy of pragmatic liberalism. This examination gives attention to both the style and substance of the administration as it was reflected in programs, specific decisions and actions, rhetoric, and the decision-making process itself.[39] However, before commencing our examination of the Rockefeller administration, it is essential to discuss in some detail the man who put his imprint on every aspect of that administration. Chapter 2 examines certain elements of Nelson Rockefeller's personality and political beliefs, his "life strategy," and the evolution of his style as an executive.

2 Nelson Rockefeller before New York

Nelson Rockefeller became coordinator of Inter-American Affairs in 1940 and remained in that position until 1944. The significance of his service was that it enabled him to develop what we term a *life strategy* and form the essential elements of what we term *executive style*. We see that executive style as being well-suited for carrying out the particular life strategy chosen by Nelson Rockefeller. However, this is not to say that the choice of life strategy was the only determinant of his executive style. Rather, we would argue that both were shaped by the same forces. But before proceeding to a brief discussion of those forces, a few remarks regarding definitions are in order.

By the term life strategy we mean a consciously chosen role by which certain politicians seek to achieve their larger goals in life.[1] (We would argue that family forces, both direct and indirect, influenced Nelson Rockefeller and his brothers toward a self-conscious choice of both goals and life strategy.) The particular life strategy that Nelson Rockefeller adopted was that of identifier and seller of solutions to problems deemed significant for the survival and well-being of the United States. (As used here , the role of seller includes tasks related to achieving adoption on one's solutions.)

Unlike the concept of life strategy, the concept of executive style is one which, under one name or another, has been much discussed in the literature of political science and other fields.[2] While not borrowed from any other definition, our definition is sufficiently comprehensive so that it is capable of subsuming most elements in other definitions. We define executive style as the pattern of behavior an executive uses in structuring the decision process and in influencing and making decisions.[3] As we use the term, executive style involves and executive's dealing with information, including both ideas and facts, as well as with people. However, we do not see these as mutually exclusive categories, for dealing with people often involves handling information, and handling information often involves dealing with people.

There are many ways in which one could distinguish among executive styles.[4] One distinction that we see as significant is based on three factors: 1) the degree to which an executive works in the company of others; 2) the amount of structure and regularity that an executive incorporates into his activities and those of his subordinates; and 3) the level of involvement by an executive in his job.[5] All three are closely related to his ability to control the outcome of decisions in which he has a stake, whether they are decisions regarding policies, campaigns, the survival of his organization, or other relevant matters.

As Downs and others have pointed out, any executive must solve the twin problems of finding out what is really going on inside his organization and controlling the behavior of people in it.[6] One reason why executives have difficulty in these respects relates to the peculiar characteristics of large organizations, especially bureaucratic organizations. Most important, it is widely accepted that information tends to be distorted as it rises through a hierarchy and that subordinates in large organizations have many incentives to resist control by superiors. Our assumption is that an executive's level of involvement in his job, the degree to which he works in the company of others, and the degree to which he incorporates structure and regularity into his activities and those of his associates will have an impact on his ability to deal with the problems of coping with distorted information and controlling the behavior of subordinates.

A third problem which political executives face is that of assuring the survival and well-being of their organizations in the face of changing conditions in a sometimes hostile environment, an environment consisting of many other organizations, including legislatures, bureaucracies, and interest groups, as well as public opinion.[7] In order to function as an effective advocate for, and protector of, his organization, an executive must have the ability to gather and use accurate "external" information and to engage in personal diplomacy as well as bureaucratic infighting. We contend that the three factors we identify all affect an executive's capacity to conduct "external relations" for his organization.

A fourth problem that executives face is dealing with the syndrome that Irving Janis has termed "groupthink." Basically, Janis identifies this as the phenomenon that occurs when members of a small cohesive group allow an urge toward unanimity to interfere with their capacity to engage in more-or-less rational problem solving.[8] We assume that the ability of an executive to avoid groupthink is also dependent upon his level of involvement, the degree to which he works in the company of others and the degree of structure and regularity in his activities and those of subordinates. For example, one might expect that an executive who interacts with a significant number of outsiders will be more likely to challenge the assumptions of his top staff personnel. To the contrary, a very high degree of structure and regularity as expressed in the form of reliance on deliberations by a staff in which there is little turnover may promote the type of cohesion leading to groupthink.

Before proceeding to a discussion of the formation of Nelson Rockefeller's life strategy and the evolution of his executive style, it is appropriate to offer a few words about determinants of executive style. We suggest that a particular individual's executive style will have been shaped by the following factors:

1. emotional needs, for example, needs for domination or affection;
2. cognitive needs, for example, needs for objective information necessary for problem solving and concepts needed to order facts;
3. the nature of one's belief system, for example, one's views regarding the appropriate role for a political executive, and one's views regarding appropriate approaches for dealing with public problems;
4. the nature of one's relevant experience, for example, one's notable successes and failures;
5. one's basic physical and mental capabilities, for example, one's level of energy and degree of analytical ability.[9]

We also assume that these same factors would influence the particular life strategy adopted by those who do, in fact, develop a life strategy.

Our definition of executive style, the three dimensions of style set forth above, and our brief remarks on determinants of style are intended to provide some helpful keys to understanding the evolution of Nelson Rockefeller's executive style and life strategy. We now proceed to a consideration of certain characteristics of Rockefeller which most observers would place in the category of personality.

Nelson Rockefeller as Problem Solver

Although there are differences in their respective positions, many students of political personality seem to agree that the behavior of political leaders is directly or indirectly shaped by what might be termed basic personality needs. For example, Fred Greenstein sees what we would term a leader's belief system as being determined in part by "basic personality needs" or "basic personality structures."[10] He sees the belief system in turn as having an impact on political actions.

For Greenstein, there are three kinds of needs, the first being "unconscious" needs which spring from inner emotional conflicts such as the inability to resolve a conflict with a parent. (Such needs are dealt with by what are normally labeled ego defenses.) The second kind consists of "social needs," for example, the need to "stand out from the crowd," and the third consists of cognitive needs, needs to "screen and canvass the environment."[11]

In their now classic study of Woodrow Wilson, Alexander and Juliette George interpret much of Wilson's behavior, often self-defeating, as the product of a childhood that left him with a damaged self-esteem, one that could be bolstered only by fulfilling strong needs for affection, power, and achievement.[12] Similar to the Georges, James Barber argues that all politicians are motivated by the need to enhance and maintain self-esteem. He argues further that presidents seek to maintain self-esteem by fulfilling needs for achievement, affection, power, or duty.[13]

Although we accept as valid much of the work that analyzes political leaders behavior in terms of basic personality needs, we are attempting no deep analysis of Nelson Rockefeller's personality. We are content to leave that task to psychologists and psychobiographers. However, some discussion of certain aspects of his needs and other personal characteristics is essential if one is to understand anything at all about the development of his life strategy and his style as an executive.

Although their work is generally consistent with that of the authors we cite above, Payne and Woshinsky add a dimension that strikes us as particularly helpful in analyzing Nelson Rockefeller's life strategy in the context of his personality. In carrying out field research into the motivation of politicians, research based on interviews, the authors came to think of motivation in terms of fundamental emotional needs. As they say, "Our respondents, it appeared, engaged in politics because they gained deep personal satisfaction from such activity. Or conversely, if they could not engage in politics, they would have feelings of anxiety or unhappiness. Their motives were not intellectual 'reasons' but 'drives' or 'needs.'"[14] Reacting to what they found in their research, Payne and Woshinsky defined motives or incentives as "the emotional needs which individuals seek to fill, or the satisfactions they get, through political participation."[15] They go on to identify six incentive types, consisting of those who are motivated by adulation, status, programs, mission, obligation, and game respectively.[16]

Without arguing that the typology developed by Payne and Woshinsky represents the last word, we are, nevertheless, struck by the close fit between their "program type" and Nelson Rockefeller. Based on a variety of sources, including our own interview with the Governor, published interviews with other authors, and biographical material, we conclude that the following description of a program type is a generally apt description of Rockefeller, and it is consistent with what we define as the latter's life strategy.

This participant gains satisfaction from devising and managing public policy. He enjoys learning about substantive issues, piecing together his preferred policies and shepherding their implementation and work-a-day operation. He is a problem-solver, but, it must be emphasized, his incentive is not the solution itself (which is simply a goal) but the satisfaction of engaging in the solving. The main identifying characteristic of this type is an expressed interest in the substance of policy and the policy-making processes. This interest goes well beyond the broad clichés which other participants utter. The program politician talks at length about specific policy issues, the details and side issues. . . . The program participant enjoys describing the complexities of social problems and measures to tackle those problems.[17]

(The only reservation we have in categorizing Rockefeller as a program type is our knowledge that he was not always attentive to the implementation of policies or the everyday operation of state government. His instinct and his philosophy of management were to leave such matters to his subordinates. Indeed, one of the few criticisms of the Governor made by former members of the Rockefeller administration in that he failed to pay enough attention to the day-to-day administration of his programs. However, there were some instances in which the Governor remained involved in the implementation of a program on a day-to-day basis.)[18]

Nelson Rockefeller was firmly committed to the view that leaders must act as problem solvers. And on numerous occasions he confirmed his own central interest as being involved in solving society's problems. But, in terms of his emotional needs, perhaps his explanation of what problem solving meant to him in personal terms is most to the point.

I think most people don't like problems and they are worried by problems in life, that they try to avoid and get rid of problems and they think that when they have no problems then they are happy. Then they go and play tennis, or play bridge, or play some other game and create problems for themselves. They really are all sort of little problems that they artificially create of how you play this hand, or how you play golf, or how do you do this, see. Now, I happen to like problems very much. I love people, I am interested in people and their problems, and if anybody comes to me with a problem I immediately start thinking what is the solution.

I don't say "Oh my God, another problem," or, "How can I get rid of this person or this question?" or, pass it to somebody. I am immediately interested myself, and my mind goes without emotional opposition responsively to the individual, or the group, or the problem to wrap myself around it and try to understand so that I am not resenting it, or resisting it. I am embracing it, and I ask questions and then start thinking immediately, creatively . . . how do you solve it?[19]

Rockefeller's description of his commitment to problem solving is interesting for its use of physical metaphors, its intensity, and the way in which it serves to mark him off from other people, many of whom he implies are engaged in trivial and unworthy pursuits.

As is well known, the Governor had a deep interest in art as well as in government. Significantly, even his approach to art had some of the characteristics of problem solving. For example, only a few years after having retired from public office, he was engaged in a major project to bring great art in the form of relatively inexpensive reproductions to a larger audience. The works to be reproduced were to come from his personal collection. (By the time of Rockefeller's death in January 1979, the business had reputedly grossed more than $900,000.)[20]

Nelson Rockefeller as Child and Young Adult

There remains the question of the origins of Rockefeller's need to engage in problem solving. Although there may be no definitive answer to this question, an examination of some aspects of his life as a child and young adult can provide some partial answers.

There is nothing to suggest that as a child Rockefeller was deprived of any basic emotional needs, including those of love and affection. Certainly he was not subject to anything like the humiliation that Woodrow Wilson suffered at the hands of his father, or even the austere and depressing childhood atmosphere in which Richard Nixon grew up.[21]

By all accounts John D. Rockefeller II, Nelson Rockefeller's father, was a somewhat formal man who found it difficult to express his feelings to his children. While he was not especially harsh with them, he did try hard to impose discipline, order, and responsibility into their lives. However, their mother Abby was a warm and affectionate woman who, according to Collier and Horowitz, established "a reign of domestic liberality unknown in either of the two previous Rockefeller generations."[22]

The consequence of Abby Rockefeller's liberality was that "the Baptist authoritarianism of Junior's youth so deteriorated . . . that when he tried to secure pledges of abstinence from cigarettes and spirits from his sons until they reached twenty-one, he had to rely on bribes of $2,500."[23] (John D. Rockefeller II was known as "Junior.")

It is clear that Nelson was the most energetic as well as the most aggressive and competitive of all the boys. According to Collier and Horowitz, he only rarely failed in his constant attempts to outdo his brothers at games and other endeavors. Because of his energy, childish charm, and ebullient personality,[24] Nelson inevitably became the center of things, even though John D. III was the eldest brother, the one with first claim on the leadership of his generation of Rockefeller's. One long-time family employee explained that the way in which Nelson as a young man inevitably superseded John D. III as the dominant figure in the family. "John was removed and aloof. . . . Now Nelson, on the other hand—he would come into the room and slap you on the back and ask you how you were doing. He was different. And he muscled John out by the sheer force of his personality, without even trying."[25]

Being at the center of things is something that young Nelson Rockefeller enjoyed. Unlike John, he had no tendencies toward aloofness or shyness.

Even more than the typical boy, he enjoyed all the heady benefits of companionship with brothers, cousins, and friends. His later experiences in high school were in the same mold. As a former classmate noted, "Nelson . . . was always clasping people and laughing with them. He was terribly popular always running for class chairman and winning."[26]

One of the consequences of Nelson's high spirits and aggressiveness was that he sometimes came into conflict with his father. Without providing the kind of supporting evidence one would like to have, Collier and Horowitz, nevertheless, refer to "a deep, almost irresolvable conflict" between Nelson and his father. Perhaps the best illustration of this conflict consisted of the father's attempt to "cure" Nelson of his left-handedness. At mealtimes John D. II would tie a string to a rubber band around the boy's wrist. He would then jerk the string each time Nelson tried to use his left hand instead of his right and the rubber band would then snap against the boy's wrist.[27]

Although Nelson's father partially succeeded in making his son right-handed, his victory seems to be one of the few that he achieved over his impetuous son. Clearly, Nelson was far from being the submissive son that Woodrow Wilson was. In addition, there is no indication of the repressed hostility toward a father that the Georges attribute to Wilson.[28] Headstrong and stubborn, Nelson openly chafed at discipline and often went directly against his father's wishes, even in very important matters, including becoming engaged during his senior year at Dartmouth, a time his father thought too early.[29] Although he was an aggressive child and young adult, one who clearly resisted attempts to be dominated, there is no evidence that he hid away any feelings of hostility against his father in some dark recess of the mind where they might later interfere with his ability to deal effectively with adult men.[30]

Perhaps the one problem that might have seriously damaged the ego of the young Nelson Rockefeller was the considerable difficulty he had in school. As children, Nelson and his brothers (with the exception of the eldest, John D. III) were sent to the progressive Lincoln School, supported generously by the Rockefeller family and staffed by Columbia Teachers College. Unlike Laurance and David, who were excellent students, Nelson had great difficulty, especially with reading and spelling. The problem, according to him, is that he had dyslexia, a learning disability that makes reading especially difficult. As he later wrote, "I remember vividly the pain and mortification I felt as a boy of 8 when I was assigned to read a short passage of Scripture at a community vesper service during summer vacation in Maine—and did a thoroughly miserable job of it."[31]

Given his innate curiosity, it must have been very frustrating for the young Nelson Rockefeller to have faced reading difficulties that interfered with his ability to understand his environment and impose some order on it. Assuming that everyone has a fundamental need to "make sense of" his environment, the ability to gather facts and discover concepts through reading is indeed an invaluable asset.[32] (It seems to have been in compensation for his reading difficulty that Rockefeller later came to depend heavily on visual aids such as charts, graphs, and maps for both absorbing and presenting information. His lifelong passion for art and his earliest career interest, architecture, suggest that Rockefeller may have had in common with other dyslexics unimpaired, or even superior, spatial abilities.)[33]

Early in his life Rockefeller became an inveterate information seeker. For example, he was impatient with rambling college bull sessions, partly because they did not satisfy his prodigious appetite for "the facts."[34] Moreover, he had a lifelong fascination with collecting new concepts that enabled him to see how facts fit together, the "big picture."[35]

In terms of his later development, Rockefeller's reaction to his learning problems is surely most significant. More than once, he testified to the fact that he turned a seeming disadvantage into an advantage. Explaining that he took his headmaster's advice to work harder in order to compensate for "a low I.Q.," he said:

> Well, I thought he sounded reasonable, and I did it. And I worked very hard because I was ambitious and competitive. And I had to discipline myself in order to read and do mathematics so that I didn't see everything backwards.... But out of that discipline I learned; I mean out of that desire I learned tremendous discipline in order to correct my eyes or whatever it is, dyslexia, that is the problem. So I had tremendous concentration; so I can listen to you and concentrate on what you are thinking and feeling and focus on it, and this helps me very much in understanding people and in coming up with problem-solving. Plus I have an ability to sustain concentration almost indefinitely. I can go for hours with sustained concentration.[36]

By sheer hard work at Lincoln, he managed to do well enough to be admitted to Dartmouth College. And by continuing to work hard there, often arising at 5:00 A.M. to study, he eventually achieved election to Phi Beta Kappa.[37]

Rockefeller never allowed himself to succumb to the illusion that his academic success was due to brilliance. He remained very conscious of the facy that success came harder to him than to those more gifted. In fact, both he and his brother Laurance have commented on the fact that Nelson profited from rooming with, and competing with, a very brilliant student. As Laurance put it,

> "He [Nelson] happened to room with my brother-in-law, John French, Jr. John was a superb scholar, was elected to Phi Beta Kappa in his junior year, was editor of the college newspaper, and at one point was class president. John set a fast pace in terms of campus relationships and campus political leadership. He and Nelson were quite different but also quite competitive. Trying to keep up with my brother-in-law on all fronts, I think, was the source of a great competitive challenge to Nelson. I believe that right in this area is where he first had to meet really tough competition and learn to lose as well as to win."[38]

His experiences at Lincoln School and Dartmouth College seem to have convinced Nelson Rockefeller that he could compete and hold his own even with those who had more ability than he did. In short, his academic experience was a confidence-building experience rather than the confidence-shattering experience that it could have been, given the learning disability that handicapped him.

It is important to note that Rockefeller succeeded at school not only in the academic sphere but in the social and political spheres. True, he failed in an attempt to be elected president of his class at Dartmouth, but that was one of his few real failures outside the academic sphere.

In addition to playing varsity soccer at Dartmouth, he engaged in numerous extracurricular activities. He edited and contributed photographs to the college magazine, took a leading role in his fraternity, and reorganized the campus arts group, bringing in numerous literary personalities.[39] Furthermore, he led an active social life. It seems clear that he could only have maintained such a heavy load of study and activity by the exercise of considerable self-discipline and the ability to effectively organize his time.

There is considerable evidence that Rockefeller engaged in a struggle with himself to keep under control the impulsiveness that had been from childhood an important part of his personality. For example, as a student at Dartmouth, he occasionally wrote letters to his parents in which he pledged to bring himself under control and to do better at living within his allowance and to work harder at his studies.[40] But it was never easy for him to live within the bounds of the allowance he received as a child and later as a student at Dartmouth. Although his father required all his sons to maintain accounts of their spending, that regimen did not prevent Nelson from habitually overspending. His spending habits at Dartmouth were such that he often borrowed from his roommate. At one time he considered taking a part-time job as a waiter in a college dining hall. Whether his father vetoed that idea as inappropriate for a Rockefeller is not quite clear.[41]

In general, Rockefeller's career at Dartmouth confirms that he was a person displaying unusually high levels of energy, one given to throwing himself into an extraordinary number of activities, but a person capable of channeling his energy and controlling his impulsiveness through the devices of discipline, organization, and plain hard work. The scope of his activities is illustrated in a letter to his mother written in December of his junior year. "This is the 52nd letter I've written since I got back from Thanksgiving.... I planned to do nothing but work when I got back and I've done everything but. This afternoon I had six meetings of various committees and organizations and I have three tomorrow afternoon."[42] His ability to channel his energy, set priorities, and exert self-discipline are shown by the fact that during his junior year he gave up all but two or three of his activities, even soccer, in order to concentrate his energies on the honors program for which he had become eligible.[43]

The young Nelson Rockefeller's concern with order and discipline in his own life extended to a concern with bringing order to the world external to him. This was reflected in his determination to "know and understand" his environment and later in a concern with protecting American society against potential breakdown from either internal or external causes. And years later when his brother Laurance, perhaps his closest friend, delivered his eulogy, it was this concern for order that he chose to address. "Nelson dramatically demonstrated this fantastic ability to be both statesman and artist; to endlessly bring order out of chaos, whether it be within the family, the state, the nation, or the world itself."[44]

In terms of the role he would evenually come to play in American politics, the most important aspect of Nelson Rockefeller's adolescence and young adulthood was probably his identification with his paternal grandfather's grandiose role in American life. He regarded as a portent his having the same birthday as his grandfather.[45] Not surprisingly, he chose as a topic for his honors thesis his grandfather's company, Standard Oil. After reading a friendly, unpublished history of the life of John D. Rockefeller, he wrote to his parents to express the great impression that the exercise had left.

> I don't know when anything has interested me more than this study of the Standard Oil Company—it really was thrilling! For the first time I felt that I really knew Grandfather a little—got a glimpse into the power and grandeur of his life.... For the first time, I realize the significance of his life and its influence for good on this earth and I was just left speechless.[46]

As do many young men, Rockefeller went through a period of searching in which he reflected upon what sort of career he might enter. However, unlike most individuals, he was part of a family that deliberately sought to inculcate a sense of family responsibility and, indeed, mission. His father had spent a lifetime trying to rationalize and make acceptable to the world his own father's acquisition of great wealth. As Collier and Horowitz point out, John D. II or "Junior," succeeded in changing the family's public image from that of avaricious capitalist to that of responsible philanthropist.[47] For all his sons, the question was what sort of role could each play that would be worthy of the Rockefeller name and fortune. In the context of their socialization, that question was simply impossible to avoid, painful as wrestling with it was for some of them, namely John D. III and Winthrop.[48]

Nelson's period of searching appears to have begun in earnest during his junior year at college. It is clear that above all else his choice of career had to be one that had some broader significance. Being the grandson of John D. Rockefeller, he could not choose a career just because it would provide him with satisfying work. As he explained when he was past sixty,

> What I really wanted to be was an architect. If you want to know why I wasn't, it's because I didn't feel I could justify [it] in terms of service. I thought what would hap-

pen, would be I'd get projects that the family was doing. It wouldn't be a genuine operation. I wanted to go out on my own. I've always wanted to go out on my own.[49]

If one examines the above statement, it is clear that there are at least two reasons why Rockefeller decided not to be an architect. One is that he felt it could not be justified in terms of service, or "significance." Indeed, his close friend Wallace Harrison, himself an architect, claims that Nelson's mother vetoed architecture as a profession on the grounds that it was not significant enough. The second reason is that he would be too closely dependent upon his family regardless of what career he chose. He expressed this sentiment to his parents in a letter from Dartmouth that must have struck his father as somewhat insulting since it rejected as unworthy a role similar to the one John D. II had himself played. "Just to work my way up in a business that another man has built, stepping from the shoes of one to those of another, making a few minor changes here and there and then, finally, perhaps at the age of sixty, getting to the top when I would have real control for a few years. No, that isn't my idea of living a real life."[50]

There is every reason to believe that Nelson Rockefeller's commitment to a "significant" career was strongly influenced by a desire to follow in some way in his grandfather's footsteps, to live up to the heritage that the old man left. At the end of his junior year at Dartmouth he wrote to his parents. "It seems funny to think that today is Grandfather's 90th birthday and my 21st birthday. The 90 makes my 21 seem mighty small and insignificant, just like a little sapling standing by a mighty fir. But the sapling still has time to grow and develop and someday it might itself turn into a tree of some merit. Who knows?"[51]

Convinced that his grandfather had made a great contribution to the world, Nelson was determined to make an equally impressive contribution, although not necessarily in the field of business. As Garry Wills put it, "Rockefeller came out of college determined to 'do good' with all the zeal and fire that had made his grandfather 'do business'. There was a natural attrition of the family's Baptist fundamentalism.... But the consequence of this was to displace the ardor, not extinguish it—to channel it toward a secular religion of work and philanthropy."[52]

It is clear that by the end of his college career Nelson Rockefeller knew that he must pursue some grand goal. What he had not yet done was to develop a particular strategy for achieving the significance that he demanded of himself and he spent the first few years after graduation trying to "find himself." Frustrated by the scope of his role in the family office, he tried some semi-independent ventures, including formation of a small company involved in the renting of office space. Eventually the company limited itself to the renting of space in the Rockefeller Center.[53] Late in 1933, in a letter to his father, he declared his intention to give up his semi-independent ventures and concentrate on becoming more familiar with family interests. Collier and Horowitz conclude that at this point in his life

Nelson, "like Junior, . . . felt the Rockefellers had a manifest destiny and that it was his duty to further it."[54] Thus motivated, he went to work at Chase Manhattan Bank, concentrating on "the foreign department and its relations with international politics and the oil companies."[55]

By 1933 his father had dispersed most of his fortune to his children and grandchildren by setting up a trust for each. By becoming actively involved in a number of family interests, including Rockefeller Center, the Museum of Modern Art, Chase Manhattan, and Standard Oil, and by cooperating with his father as the dominant personality among the sons, Nelson had put himself in a position from which he could exercise considerable control over the destiny of the family. As Collier and Horowitz remark, "He reveled in the image, already in the process of creation, of five remarkable young men: selfless, unspoiled by wealth, and dedicated to the common good, a conspicious national resource."[56] Many years later, in the prepared statement he submitted to the House Judiciary Committee, he put into his own words his conception of that role and its source: "And so we as children grew up in a closely-knit religious family, involved in human concerns, influenced by cultural forces and inspired by father's credo that 'Every right implies a responsibility; every opportunity an obligation; every possession a duty.' Here are the influences that inspired *my life of concern for the effective functioning of society* and the well-being of others." [authors' emphasis][57]

Striking Out on His Own: Latin America and O.I.A.A.

Assuming Nelson Rockefeller's life strategy to be one of indentifying public problems and offering solutions to these problems, the manner in which he became coordinator of Inter-American Affairs is instructive. With his entry into the Chase Bank in 1934, he began to develop an interest in the oil business, especially in Latin America. After becoming a member of the board of directors of Creole Petroleum Company, owned jointly by Jersey Standard and the biggest oil producer in Venezuela, he completed a tour of twenty Latin American countries in 1937. Collier and Horowitz refer to this experience as "a turning point in his life," the moment when "he found that 'something big' he had been looking for."[58]

As was characteristic of Rockefeller, he sensed both risk and opportunity in Latin America, the kind of worthy challenge for which he later showed an appetite. As was also characteristic, he plunged ahead with great energy and enthusiasm, even learning Spanish by the Berlitz method. His own formulation of problems in Latin America reflected a blend of realism and idealism that stayed with him throughout his career. He embarked on a campaign in which "he urged upon [Jersey executives] a more active policy of social responsibility, pointing out that the corporation held property only by the will of the people and the laws of its governments. If the corporations didn't recognize its social responsibilities, he said, 'they will take away our ownership'."[59] According to Collier and Horowitz, Rockefeller "spent weeks on end touring their [Creole] operations and trying to explain that the changes he had in mind had less to do with fuzzy idealism than making sure they did not create an opening for the Communists and thus lose everything, as in Mexico."[60] (In 1938 the Mexican government had announced the expropriation of Western oil interests.) Greatly concerned with the dangers of communism, he sometimes carried a copy of *Das Kapital*, urging aides to become familiar with the ideas of Marx.[61] Eventually, in 1940, he formed the Venezuelan Development Company to demonstrate that economic diversification could be achieved in Venezuela.

Rockefeller's involvement with Latin America led him to bring together a small group of men who met to discuss developments in that area.[62] The immediate object of the group was to formulate a policy to prevent Nazi Germany from dominating Latin America in the event the former was victorious in Europe. The "intellectual" within the group, Beardsley Ruml, drafted a short paper entitled "Hemisphere Economic Policy" which represented the thinking that emerged from the group's many discussions.[63]

The job of selling his group's ideas fell to Rockefeller, who, by virtue of his facility in dealing with people, seemed ideally suited for such a role. As chance would have it, he had already met President Franklin D. Roosevelt. As president of the Museum of Modern Art, Rockefeller had earlier persuaded FDR to speak on a national radio show that would focus on the museum. Quick to sense any opportunity, Rockefeller talked with the president before the show about the problem of growing German influence in Latin America. When the president said he would be interested in hearing more, the way was prepared for forwarding a memorandum to him.[64]

Harry Hopkins, Roosevelt's right-hand man, had already met Rockefeller. As did FDR, he found the latter an engaging young man (Rockefeller was then a mere thirty-two). Thus, in June of 1940, Rockefeller was able to meet with Hopkins and deliver a three-page memo, his group's "Hemisphere Economic Policy." One suggestion he made to Hopkins was that a position be created for the purpose of giving focus to efforts to prevent German domination in Latin America. As the memo began, "Regardless of whether the outcome of the war is a German or Allied victory, the United States must protect its international position through the use of economic measures that are competitively effective against totalitarian regimes."[65]

Within a month, James Forrestal, special assistant to the president, offered Rockefeller the position of coordinator of Inter-American Affairs. Upon accepting, Rockefeller was in a position to try to implement the solutions to the problems he and his group had identified. Thus his memorandum had been a success. As he was later to tell two interviewers, "Most of the things I've done in my life have been because I've written a memo to someone suggesting someone ought to do something."[66]

The stage was now set for Nelson Rockefeller to embark on the first venture of his life that was not in some way related to enterprises in which his family had some involvement. Thus, OIAA would present him with the opportunity to achieve what James Barber would term his "first independent political success," an event which Barber believes helps to determine the shape of an executive's style.[67]

When Rockefeller took over as coordinator of Inter-American Affairs, head of what was officially labeled in the executive order creating it as the Office for Coordination of Commercial and Cultural Relations between the American Republics, there was no guarantee of his success.[68] Having only a vague charge which gave it "liason" and "coordination" functions as an independent body and headed by a director who was to serve without compensation, the office could very easily have been swallowed up in bureaucratic infighting. Instructed to "cooperate" with the State Department, the office did have one advantage: its director reported directly to the president himself. And more than once, Rockefeller had to appeal directly or indirectly to the president to avoid having his office's functions taken over by other agencies. The mission of OIAA, as Rockefeller saw it, was to save an entire continent from foreign influence. That mission was tailor-made for Rockefeller in almost every respect. First, it was grandiose enough to constitute a role that would satisfy his thirst for doing something fit for a Rockefeller, a Rockefeller who in some way wanted to follow in the footsteps of his grandfather. Second, it was consistent with his belief system, one that drew black and white distinctions between "them and us," totalitarian regimes as opposed to the "free world."[69] Third, it reflected his close identity with the maintenance of the United States as the dominant economic force in the Western Hemisphere, a goal that happened also to involve the best interests of American capitalism in general and the Rockefeller oil interests in particular.[70] Fourth, the mission embodied a positive problem-solving approach that would try to improve the human condition and give other nations a "piece of the pie." As his memo to President Roosevelt had argued, if the United States were to maintain its position in the hemisphere, it must take measures to bring economic prosperity to Latin America "in the frame of hemisphere economic cooperation and dependence."[71] By insuring economic prosperity, Rockefeller believed that change could be managed in an acceptable way.

If the OIAA offered a perfect challenge for Nelson Rockefeller, it also offered him the opportunity to develop a clear-cut life strategy, one based on the belief that political leaders have the responsibility for guiding a society past the hazards that history offers. For the first time in his life, Nelson Rockefeller had said, "Here is a major problem facing the United States and here is how I propose to solve it." But this was not to be the last time that he would say it, for it was to become the strategy through which he was to fulfill the role of significance that he demanded of himself. Having taken the first steps with the creation of OIAA, he was now in a position to put his proposals into operation.[72]

Nelson Rockefeller's performance at OIAA was characterized by a level of energy, enthusiasm, and emotional commitment difficult to imagine. (David Lilienthal, eventually to become chairman of the Atomic Energy Commission, termed him "the Eager Beaver to end all E B's.")[73] On many days he arose at 6:00 A.M. and went to sleep only at midnight, having spent most of the day working.

One of the striking aspects of Rockefeller's performance as coordinator is that there was little distinction between his personal life and his business life. The Rockefeller residence housed not only his wife and five children but in addition many OIAA staffers boarded there at one time or another. Indeed, his close friend and deputy Carl Spaeth moved into the house along with his wife. In truth, Rockefeller was rarely alone. When he left home in the morning in his car, he picked up three or four aides on the way to his office. And when he returned in the evening, he often brought several home with him.

Rockefeller brought with him to the OIAA a group of experts some of whom were personal friends and some of whom he had worked with in other South American ventures, including the Venezuelan Development Company.[74] Three who came with him had been members of the study group that had proposed creation of OIAA. (They were Joseph Rovensky, Wallace Harrison, and Jay Crane.) The fourth member of the group, Beardsley Ruml, agreed to consult on a part-time basis. In addition to these men and Carl Spaeth, other top aides included family friend John Hay Whitney, John Lockwood, an attorney with Milbank and Tweed and later the family's main legal adviser, and Frank Jamieson, a former newspaper man who had won the Pulitzer Prize and had been actively involved in several political campaigns. One result of bringing his own people to Washington as top aides was that it tended to insure that he would command the utmost loyalty from staff. His reaction when he did not receive what he felt was the loyalty owed him is illustrated by his dispute with Carl Spaeth.

Rockefeller came to believe that Spaeth, his friend and number-one aide, was making decisions on his own without consulting the top man. The result was that Spaeth and his wife, she in tears, hastily left the Rockefeller home, after which he got a new job with the South American Division of the State Department. According to Stewart Alsop, Rockefeller vowed that as a result of this experience, he would "never again have a single 'deputy' whose title and position imply the right to move independently."[75] (Showing little inclination to forgive and forget, Rockefeller later asked that Spaeth be fired before agreeing to take the position of assistant secretary of state for South American Affairs. After leaving OIAA for the State Department, Spaeth had further angered Rockefeller by proposing that a committee of South Americans he was working with should have a role in counteracting Nazi propaganda, a role Rockefeller saw as a threat to OIAA.)[76]

Although Rockefeller relied heavily on informal gatherings and discussions as head of OIAA and regularly mixed business with social functions, it would be inaccurate to picture him as another Franklin Roosevelt, a president notorious for his use of ad hoc arrangements, informal understandings, fuzzy lines of authority, and deliberately-instigated conflict among his subordinates. In fact, the coordinator was on one plane a highly organized administrator. One manifestation of the regularity to which Rockefeller was committed was his daily conference of top staff. This meeting was built around an agenda prepared by the coordinator himself. In addition to these daily meetings, there was a weekly briefing in an elaborately equipped chart room. Designed and operated by George Dudley, an architect from Wallace Harrison's firm, the room could hold over two dozen people. Large charts and maps could be placed three high, wall-to-wall, on all four walls. Charts were updated to reflect developments in each country and other charts prepared to illustrate particular problems, for example, the rubber shortage. Dudley would explain the charts and Rockefeller would point out the highlights to those attending, OIAA staff and relevant officials from other agencies.[77] (Morris compares the operation of the chart room to a performance at Rockefeller Center and says that it was eventually staffed by several research directors, about two dozen designers of visual aides, and other "administrative helpers.")[78]

It would apppear that the primary purpose of the briefings was to inform people rather than to solicit suggestions. The latter process went on in other forms, including daily staff meetings and Rockefeller's endless round of informal interchanges with people both inside and outside OIAA. His own conception of the function of the visually-aided briefing has been reported by Morris as being motivated by a desire to keep personnel from OIAA and other agencies informed and to enable them to achieve coordination and avoid interfering in each other's responsibilities.[79] Again, this tends to confirm an important distinction between Rockefeller and Roosevelt as administrators. Unlike Roosevelt, Rockefeller did not consciously set out to have subordinates work at cross-purposes.

Although his personal energy and his resources as a Rockefeller enabled him to draw upon numerous sources for analyses of problems and ideas for solutions, the coordinator relied heavily upon a small group of trusted advisers for developing ideas into programs for OIAA. As benefits an executive with Rockefeller's personality and belief in the efficiency of problem-solving efforts, his emphasis was on how to get things done. As one of his advisers later said,

> Most of us figured that it was Nelson's show. We wanted him to run it and we wanted to go along with him as far as possible. His ideas and plans were formulated in long bull sessions and conferences and he had a pretty good idea of what each of us thought by the time he made up his mind. Then he would tell us to do it and he would not worry much about what obstacles had to be overcome. Frequently, it took a lot of doing, and sometimes, of course, his ideas were complete busts.[80]

Although the emphasis was on "getting things done," this does not mean that Rockefeller made no attempt at all to perfect his ideas before putting them into operation or that he consciously suppressed criticisms of his ideas. For example, Collier and Horowitz report that Frank Jamieson "was known as the devil's advocate in the coordinator's office, arguing that 'no' position as a way of testing the depth and resilience of Rockefeller's sudden enthusiasms."[81] And a former OIAA staffer explained that Rockefeller could sense when advisers might oppose a program even when they would not put their opposition in so many words. He explained that when close advisers would cite basic problems with a proposal, Rockefeller might well say, "What you are really saying is that we shouldn't do it. He pulled forth the no's, but he didn't like to have them prematurely."[82]

Rockefeller's taste in advisers reflected his emphasis on "getting things done." Again, according to the same OIAA aide, the coordinator wanted "effective, professional people; positive people...; he was restless with people who emphasized the negative"; he wanted "positive critisism"; he wanted people who were "energetic, guys who would work and not whine."[83] This taste was to stay with him throughout his career.

As Anthony Downs has pointed out, those who head agencies are expected to play the role of advocate for the agency.[84] Rockefeller's personality and his beliefs suited him for such a role, and most accounts agree that he performed the role well. His performance was marked by a number of characteristics including an intuitive understanding of power relations, a sensitivity to potential dangers to OIAA, an incredible amount of energy and tenacity, considerable skill at making and using friends and allies, and a willingness to be tough and make enemies when necessary.

As any bureaucrat can testify, congressional relationships present a very important challenge, especially those relationships with chairmen of the subcommittees that control agency budgets. Early in his career as coordinator, Rockefeller severely embarrased himself by being unprepared when he appeared before such a chairman, Senator McKellar, a man with a reputation for being tough with agency heads. Profiting from the experience, Rockefeller vowed never again to be unprepared. From then on, he was an informed and aggressive witness and one who made heavy use of elaborate visual aides to buttress his case.[85]

By being an informed witness, by being solicitous and charming, and by keeping relevant congressmen well-informed, Rockefeller managed to gain support for OIAA in general and its budgets in particular. For example, Senator McKellar defended the coordinator as "a young man of unimpeachable integrity, honesty and excellent ability.... He has indomitable energy, is a fine personality and is one of the best witnesses of those who appear from time to time before the Senate Appropriations Committee. The President could not have found a better man...."[86]

OIAA survived serious threats to its autonomy because of Rockefeller's willingness and ability to fight hard against formidable opponents. As Alsop reports, both critics and admirers agreed that

> In the fierce and bloody battles which took place continually within the richly proliferating wartime bureaucracy, the fledgling Rockefeller held his own remarkably well. He defended his own empire with single-minded ferocity, and he was not at all averse to carving a slice or two out of someone else's empire. In the process he made enemies, for the first time in his young life.[87]

One serious challenge to OIAA's autonomy was the proposal (in 1942) by the Bureau of the Budget that all information activities be centralized in the Office of Facts and Figures, headed by Archibald MacLeish. As the president's most powerful staff agency, the Bureau of the Budget could normally have been expected to prevail in any executive branch dispute with OIAA.[88] However, by dint of great effort, including a virtual threat to resign, Rockefeller managed to prevail against the proposal by the Budget Bureau. Although he failed to sway Budget Director Harold Smith and Presidential Advisor Samuel Rosenman in a meeting that included some nasty exchanges, Rockefeller won the president to his side by enlisting the assistance of numerous top officials, including Undersecretary of State Sumner Welles, Secretary of the Navy Frank Knox, and Vice-president Henry Wallace. As coordinator, he had developed good working relationships with both Wells and Knox, and Henry Wallace was his tennis partner and frequent dinner companion. When Roosevelt finally signed the Budget Bureau order centralizing information activities in June of 1942, the order specified that the authority of the new Office of War Information should not extend to Latin America.[89] The OIAA's autonomy had been preserved.

The fact that Rockefeller knew how to influence the president through the use of intermediaries should not obscure the additional fact that he was capable of using his charm and enthusiasm to deal successfully with superiors on a personal basis. Shortly after Pearl Harbor, he decided to expand his agency's operation to meet, and to take advantage of, the new wartime situation. In order to do so, he needed more money, having begun at OIAA with the expectation of about $3.5 million per year in funding.[90] His argument was to be that initiation of social and health programs in South America would help the war effort by assuring a labor force adequate for producing and transporting the raw materials available in Latin America. Armed with a book of transparencies, including maps with appropriate overlays, he went to the White House to make his case. Fascinated with the transparencies, the president called for his famous guest Winston Churchill to "come look at this." The end result was that Rockefeller received a presidential pledge for about fifty million in additional funding.[91]

As coordinator, Rockefeller, was an avid collector of all kinds of information relevant both to conditions in South America and to the continued well-being of OIAA. His endless round of staff meetings and interagency meetings, visits to cabinet members and congressmen, OIAA briefings, informal conversations at luncheons, dinners, and other social gatherings, and meetings with South American diplomats all helped to satisfy his appetite for "knowing what was going on." Never a great reader, he gathered the bulk of information from short memos, face-to-face conversations, and visual displays.

The staff that Rockefeller built at OIAA helped him to stay abreast of developments in South America as did his use of public opinion polls. But he was never a captive of what the experts found or advised. As James Desmond put it, "He relied on the experts for the facts, and he would take an idea from any source if it fit his general scheme, but when the chips were down he put his faith in his own intuitions."[92]

Initially, the OIAA was to carry out programs in South America that would fall into either the "cultural" realm or the "economic" realm. The overriding goal was to advance United States interest in Latin America regardless of whether Germany was victorious. In typical fashion, Rockefeller mounted an all-out effort to rid the continent of German influence. Temporarily, the threat of socialism and communism was superseded in his view by the threat of Nazism.

One effort undertaken initially was that of utilizing personal pressure and propaganda to force U.S. companies in Latin America to rid themselves of German and Italian citizens.[93] It was undoubtedly clear to Rockefeller and his staff that the Nazi challenge offered economic opportunities for the United States as well as dangers. For example, if United States firms could take over the markets and access to raw materials previously dominated by Britain and Germany, OIAA's efforts could be justified in terms of economic self-interest alone. A second aspect of OIAA's economic activities involved promotion of long-term economic development. Such a goal had been seen as desirable by Rockefeller during his earliest involvement in South America as a means of insuring against the emergence of socialist or Communist regimes. However, for a variety of reasons OIAA made little progress in promoting economic development. One of those reasons is discussed by Collier and Horowitz.

> Much of the resistance to an attack against feudal living conditions, in fact, had come from the coordinating committees that Nelson set up in each of the Latin American countries. They were "composed of the biggest businessmen" (as one senior American diplomat complained in a letter to the Undersecretary of State), including executives of Standard Oil, Guggenheim, General Electric, and United Fruit. "They have very definite ideas as to what the general policy should be, and in general their ideas have been the most reactionary."[94]

Aware that the United States motives with regard to South America were viewed primarily as involving narrow self-interest, Rockefeller wanted to use OIAA to "develop closer cultural and spiritual ties" between the United States and South America.[95] To this end OIAA sponsored a vast array of tours and exchanges involving ballet companies, athletic teams, art shows, newspaper editors, and political leaders.

Although economic and cultural activities as well as social and health programs were important parts of OIAA's efforts, the keystone of its endeavors was an attempt to foster hemispheric unity and improve the image of the United States through influencing the dissemination of information throughout the southern continent. First and foremost, the OIAA became a propaganda agency. The key man in this effort was Frank Jamieson, head of OIAA's Publications and Information Division.[96] Among the publications produced were a Spanish language equivalent of *Life* magazine which eventually reached a circulation of 500,000 and a weekly edition of the *New York Times* printed in Chile and distributed throughout Latin America.[97]

In order to help guide OIAA's propaganda activities, the office developed an information-gathering capacity to supplement the personal contacts it had initially developed.[98] After the war had begun, activities were expanded to include public opinion surveys in Brazil (conducted by George Gallup and a group of social scientists) and use of personnel from the Export Bureau of the American Association of Advertising Agencies in Latin America to supply data on the "ownership, editorial policy, and personal opinions of the owners and editors of the newspapers" in Latin America.[99]

Economic pressure was applied to the media in order to assure favorable handling of news. At the coordinator's request, the Treasury Department exempted from taxation the cost of ads placed in Latin American news media by American corporations that were cooperating with OIAA. Rockefeller helped direct this advertising and the valuable revenue from it to those newspapers and radio stations that were anti-Nazi or pro-United States. The resulting leverage was considerable since tax-exempt advertising eventually constituted more than 40 percent of all such advertising in Latin America.[100] In related action, OIAA saw to it that export licenses for newsprint sources were allocated only to benefit those newspapers that were friendly to the United States.

Generally speaking, the information activities of OIAA were considered a great success. Specifically, by the end of the war OIAA estimated that 75 percent of the world news reaching Latin America had originated in Washington.[101] Another important result of the OIAA's information activities was that Nelson Rockefeller managed to learn a great deal about gauging and managing both mass and elite opinion. The knowledge he acquired was to be used to advantage for the remainder of his career.

Serving Presidents—Achievement Marred by Frustration

Between his service as coordinator of Inter-American Affairs and his service as Governor of New York State, Nelson Rockefeller served in a variety of roles, most directly involving government service of one kind or another. In those roles he displayed all the elements of executive style that he had developed in OIAA. In addition, he took advantage of every possible opportunity to pursue his life strategy as an offerer and seller of solutions to problems he had identified as significant to the survival and well-being of the United States.

The various positions that Rockefeller filled after leaving OIAA were: assistant secretary of state for South American Affairs (1944-1945); head of IBEC (International Basic Economy Corporation), a corporation he had founded to make capital investments in South America in hopes of raising living standards and also making a profit (1945-1953); adviser to President Truman's Point Four program (1949-1950); chairman of President Eisenhower's Advisory Committee on Government Organization (1952-1953); undersecretary of the newly created Department of Health, Education, and Welfare (1953-1954); special assistant to the president for foreign affairs (Cold War strategy) (1954-1955); chairman of the Special Studies Project of the Rockefeller Brothers Fund (1955-1958); and chairman of the Temporary State Commission on the New York State Constitutional Convention (1956-1958).

Rockefeller's tenure as assistant secretary of state was a brief one marked by great controversy. His resignation was requested by President Truman's secretary of state, James Byrnes, after about a year.[102] Convinced that Western Hemisphere solidarity would be essential in what he saw as the coming struggle between the Communist and non-Communist spheres, and motivated by his special affection for, and paternalistic view toward, South America, Rockefeller played the lead role in bringing about a mutual defense agreement among the American nations. He also won inclusion of a provision (Article 51) in the United Nations Charter allowing regional security alliances and helped gain admission to the U.N. for previously pro-Nazi Argentina. Consistent with the anti-Communist views he had developed in the 1930s, Rockefeller quickly developed a reputation as a cold warrior. Ever the pragmatist, he offended many top State Department officials as well as most of the liberal press by his view that the United States should accommodate itself to Argentinian leader Peron and other South American leaders who had displayed pro-Nazi sentiments. His view was that "Everybody is useful and we're going to convert these people to friendliness to the United States."[103]

The height of Rockefeller's triumph came at the United Nations Conference in San Francisco. Having been invited to attend by Secretary of State Stettinius because of his influence over the Latin American nations, Rockefeller conducted a skillful, if ruthless, campaign to insure the admission of Argentina to the U.N. and sanction for the mutual defense agreement he had earlier engineered.[104] Using his charm and persuasiveness, his contacts with South American diplomats, and his great tenacity,

Rockefeller succeeded in overturning the official State Department position on both the admission of Argentina and the matter of regional defense agreements. Victory on the latter was assured only when he outraged both Democrats and Republicans by personally winning to his side the leading Republican foreign policy spokesman, Senator Arthur Vandenberg. After a private dinner in Rockefeller's suite, Vandenberg let it be known that he would resign from the United States delegation unless the delegation supported Article 51 of the charter, the legal basis for regional defense alliances.[105]

Although Rockefeller succeeded in achieving his immediate goals at San Francisco, the price he paid was high. In addition to earning the enmity of Dean Acheson, soon to be secretary of state, he made enemies of numerous others in the foreign policy establishment including former Secretary of State Hull and future Secretary of State John Foster Dulles. But uncowed when informed that he was to be fired, he forced Secretary of State Byrnes to delay acceptance of his resignation until he had made a major speech on policy toward Argentina. He won this battle by warning that as a private citizen he would otherwise deliver a blistering critique of State Department policy toward South America.

Although Rockefeller made enemies, his experience as assistant secretary of state could only have added to the confidence in his abilities that he had developed at OIAA. As one veteran observer put it, "On the basic issues Rockefeller had his way, as a young and comparatively junior official, against the combined opposition of some of the most powerful men in Washington, including, on some issues, all three of the Secretaries of State under whom he served. . . ."[106] For a confirmed optimist like Rockefeller, the lesson must have been that anything is possible if one works hard enough, is persistent, and uses every possible weapon in bucking powerful opponents. The pattern was one he was to use throughout his career.

Out of government service, Rockefeller's first move was to reassemble his original South American group to determine what to do next with regard to the continent and, not incidentally, to advance his own political future. The result was the creation of two corporations, one a nonprofit foundation with the goal of promoting economic development through technical assistance projects and the other a profit-making corporation that, nevertheless, stated its primary purpose as that of economic development. The creation of both, the American International Association for Economic and Social Development and the International Basic Economy Corporation, was based on Rockefeller's unique blending of a commitment to the lofty goals of human betterment along with the traditional capitalist goal of making a profit.

Always uncomfortable with the idea that capitalism might sometimes be at odds with human welfare and even more uncomfortable with the idea that people in foreign countries might identify the capitalist system and the

United States as an enemy, he expressed himself as follows in inviting his father to become chairman of the board of AIA:

> You more than anyone have become a symbol to people throughout the world that democracy and the capitalistic system are interested in their well-being. The people must increasingly have reason to feel that their best interest and opportunity for the future are identified with our country and our way of life. Now more than ever before it is important that we as a family carry on with the courage and vision that led you and Grandfather to pioneer new fields and blaze new trails.[107]

Ultimately, however, IBEC was able to become profitable only after it acquired a number of successful domestic companies and began to concentrate more on making profits than on developing Latin American economies.[108]

Rockefeller's remaining federal experience prior to his entry into New York State politics was marked by further pursuit of his life strategy as well as the continuing appearance of elements of executive style that had characterized his performance as coordinator of Inter-American Affairs. Among the solutions he tried to sell to presidents were the centralization of all U.S. foreign economic programs in a new Overseas Economic Administration whose director would report directly to the president, creation of the Department of Health, Education, and Welfare, and the so-called "Open Skies" proposal.

The first of these proposals came while Rockefeller was serving as chairman of the International Development Advisory Board, a group responsible for carrying out technical assistance to underdeveloped countries, the famous Point Four of the four-part foreign policy that President Truman proposed in his second inaugural address. In spite of his success in garnering the support of a key congressional figure, Senator Robert Taft, Rockefeller resigned his post when it became clear that the Truman administration would not accept his plan.[109]

Rockefeller's second proposal, to create a Department of Health, Education, and Welfare came out of his work as chairman of President Eisenhower's Committee on Government Organization. Congress' acceptance of the proposal represented a considerable achievement for Rockefeller given the fact that HEW was to represent a consolidation of many preexisting agencies, some of which were chary of risking their identities within the new department.

The third of Rockefeller's proposals, made to Eisenhower in 1955 while the former was a special assistant, was the Open Skies proposal which Eisenhower presented at the Geneva summit with the Soviet Union. A great propaganda success, the plan would have allowed the United States and the USSR to engage in aerial survey of each other's territories in order to guard against surprise attack. Designed as a way to counter a Russian "peace offensive," including tentative acceptance of previous U.S. disarmament proposals, Open Skies bought great praise to Eisenhower.

There were other proposals that Rockefeller made while in federal service. However, the three discussed here reflect two of his greatest concerns. The proposals regarding technical assistance for developing countries and the Open Skies proposal both stemmed from what had been perhaps the concern closest to his heart, that of national security. As he stated before the House Committee on Foreign Affairs, "Seventy-three percent of our needs for strategic and critical materials come from the underdeveloped areas. We face the blunt fact that the United States no longer finds the base of its own security within its own borders."[110] His answer to these problems and similiar ones was to promote a foreign policy aggressive in its military, propaganda, and foreign aid aspects. His proposal for creation of the Department of Health, Education, and Welfare stemmed from his interest in human programs and the progressive Republicanism that he had come to represent. Like Eisenhower, he was not one who was likely to object to New Deal programs such as social security on the basis of any conservative political principles.

In typical Rockefeller fashion, the solutions that Rockefeller proposed during his years in the Eisenhower administration were developed with the use of both in-house and outside assistance including trusted personal friends and advisers. For example, the Open Skies proposal and a plan to take advantage of its propaganda impact were put together at seminars of staff, technical experts, and idea men which were held at the Marine base at Quantico, Virginia.[111] True to past practice, the Open Skies plan was then presented to the president in a one-page memo.

Other aspects of Rockefeller's executive style that reappeared during the Eisenhower administration included his addiction to visual aids and public opinion polls. For example, he used a poll of European countries (one showing that the United States was seen as a threat to peace in about the same degree as the USSR was) to help convince the president that he should offer the Open Skies proposal as a way of showing the U.S. to be peace-minded.[112]

One might well characterize Rockefeller's performance in the Eisenhower administration, and indeed all his federal service after OIAA, as being one in which he "lost the war" even though sometimes "won battles." Often he was able to succeed against substantial opposition in having his solutions adopted. The creation of HEW, the admission of Argentina to the U.N., and the Open Skies plans are good examples. His victories were the result of tenacity, hard work, cultivation of alliances based on personal charm and persuasiveness, and a willingness to enlarge the level and scope of conflict in order to have his way. In many cases he took on powerful men such as Acheson and Dulles and fought a virtual guerrilla action against the official position of an agency with key responsibility for the area in which he was interested. Because he had such a proprietary attitude toward his solutions he remained dissatisfied if he could not achieve a position in which he would have the authority and autonomy to implement those solutions. It is difficult to imagine that he could have achieved sufficient autonomy and authority to satisfy himself short of being made secretary of state, some equivalent of that position in the domestic arena, or president. The result of his mode of operation, combined with his great ambition, was that he would eventually accumulate many powerful enemies as well as many personal frustrations.[113] Then he would either resign, as in the case of his job as undersecretary of HEW and assistant to Presidents Truman and Eisenhower, or be fired, as in the case of his role as assistant secretary of state in the Truman administration.

Rockefeller's departure from the Eisenhower administration in December of 1955 was especially noteworthy as it capped a period of increasing personal frustration and was a portent of the great difficulty he would have in capturing the Republican presidential nomination. Both his mode of operation and his tendency to propose policies requiring large sums of money had earned him enemies in the Eisenhower administration, most of whom resented him as a "liberal do-gooder." When Secretary of Defense Charles Wilson offered Rockefeller a coveted role as his deputy, one of Rockefeller's most powerful enemies, Treasury Secretary George Humphrey, convinced Eisenhower to veto the appointment on the grounds that Rockefeller was a "spender."[114]

After leaving federal service Rockefeller was faced with a major decision. The possibility of advancement in the Eisenhower administration having been blocked, he could seek elective office or turn back to a more private role, concentrating on Rockefeller family interests. By the spring of 1958 he had decided to seek the Republican nomination for governor of New York. However, between leaving the White House and making that decision in 1958, he was involved in two of the more significant projects of his career. The first was his chairmanship of the Special Studies Project, funded by the Rockefeller Brothers Fund at Nelson's initiative.[115] Heavily funded, well-staffed, and enlisting the participation of numerous prominent leaders representative of major national interests as well as some of his long-time personal advisers, the project is the perfect symbol of Nelson Rockefeller as the nation's problem solver. For its lofty goal was to "define the major problems and opportunities that will challenge the United States over the next ten to fifteen years."[116] In terms of practical significance, the project provided him with a reservoir of ideas and proposals that he could use in later attempts to capture the Republican nomination for president. It also marked a continuation of his association with Henry Kissinger, then a young academic who had been a participant in the Quantico seminars. Kissinger was made staff director of the Rockefeller Brothers study and later became Nelson Rockefeller's major foreign policy adviser.

Just as the Special Studies Project provided Rockefeller with information and proposals relating to national affairs, his chairmanship of the New York State Temporary Commission on the Constitutional Convention provided him with knowledge of state problems and proposals to solve those problems. Created by the state legislature, the commission was to study and report upon possible changes in the state's constitution.[117] Just as important, Rockefeller's role as chairman allowed him to recruit staff who would later play a key role in his campaign for governor as well as in his administration itself. Staff director William Ronan, a dean at N.Y.U., was eventually to become his closest adviser.[118]

At the same time that he was serving as chairman of the commission, Rockefeller began to consider seriously the possibility of running for governor. Armed with poll results showing him with a better chance than other potential candidates of defeating incumbent Governor Harriman, and urged on by Republican State Chairman Judson Morhouse, who was staking his job on support of Rockefeller, he announced on June 30, 1958, that he would seek nomination.[119]

Nelson Rockefeller's career prior to his campaign for governor in 1958 reveals that he possessed a well-tested life strategy and executive style by that date. As many examples show, he had focused on identifying and offering solutions to problems he deemed significant for the survival and well-being of the United States. Furthermore, his executive style seemed well-suited to furthering his life strategy. In particular, Rockefeller's executive style seems to have contributed to the many successes that he did achieve as a relatively young political executive. Moreover, his executive style enabled him to do a good job of coping with some of the classic problems faced by all political executives, such as the problem of acquiring the information necessary to provide an accurate view of reality both inside and outside one's organization. That executive style can be characterized as displaying a high level of personal involvement, a high level of collegiality, and a relatively high level of structure and regularity, the latter tempered by a substantial degree of informality. The essential features of his life strategy and executive style were to remain unchanged for the remainder of his career.

Rockefeller's "failures" in Washington seem to have stemmed primarily from certain of his personal qualities such as his strong determination to achieve his own goals through aggressive means and his unwillingness to accommodate himself to powerful political figures by deferring to them and abandoning his commitment to elements of his own political beliefs, including his belief in activist government and costly programs. However, in acknowledging that certain of his personal qualities and certain of his beliefs led him into difficulties, one must not lose sight of the fact that these same factors helped him achieve some of his successes. For example, he would never have been able to achieve his victories in protecting OIAA's autonomy and winning support for its programs had he not been energetic, persistent, tough, and willing to make enemies. Likewise, he would likely never have caught the attention of presidents had he not had an eye for the grandiose proposal. As is the case with many dynamic and ambitious political executives, the task of analyzing the performance of Nelson Rockefeller is a very complex one. The way in which Rockefeller's executive style, personal qualities, and political beliefs contributed to his successes and failures as Governor of New York State is one theme of the remainder of this book.

3 Elections and Campaigns: Gubernatorial Successes and Presidential Failures

Political campaigns for elective offices are essentially organized appeals to various groups for support of one's candidacy. The political process indicates the order of principal events: the initial campaign involves an effort to secure nomination from the party's leaders or its members and the campaign for the office itself is launched to win votes from the broader electorate. An essential ingredient in these efforts is communication. The candidate attempts to communicate, in a political sense, who he is and what he stands for. Other important elements are organization and funding.[1] Nelson Rockefeller was an inveterate campaigner. The chronicle of his campaign efforts can best be described as a series of successes in his bids to become, and remain, governor of New York and failures in his attempts to secure the Republican party's nomination for the presidency. And all his campaigns offered him the opportunity to pursue his life strategy by identifying significant problems and offering solutions to those problems.

The seven statewide and national campaigns Rockefeller conducted between 1958 and 1970 were invariably efforts to market his leadership qualities: leadership potential and/or a record of demonstrated leadership. In gubernatorial campaigns the marketing of Rockefeller's leadership qualities was combined with charging that the New York State Democratic party was controlled by the New York City "bosses." His futile campaigns to become the Republican presidential nominee found the personal leadership issue joined by attacks on the leadership of the Republican party itself.

Each campaign is different if only because it involves a new battle at another point in time. However, Rockefeller's style of campaigning was modified only in degree in his four successful efforts at the state level. As the "art of campaigning" became more refined, Rockefeller was at the forefront in incorporating changes into his approach, especially the application of sophisticated polling techniques, extensive and inspired use of television,[2] and financing on a massive scale.

New York State Successes: The First Nomination

As chairman of the Temporary State Commission on the Constitutional Convention, Rockefeller was provided an opportunity to inform himself on specific problems of New York State. The commission was initially an executive and legislative approved body, but when Averell Harriman refused to approve its continuation, the legislature reestablished it solely as a legislative commission.[3] It held hearings, received testimony in several localities of the state, and reviewed studies it had commissioned from academics and other experts. Its primary focus was to study the background of, and current problems related to, the state's constitution, and to determine what changes could be made. Publicity related to this exhaustive examination made it possible for potential voters to perceive Nelson Rockefeller as a responsible and nonpartisan leader working toward solutions for state problems.

Participation in the commission permitted Nelson Rockefeller to review and digest considerable information about New York State. Equally as significant, he was able recruit a staff of experts, many of whom would ultimately become close advisers or staff members. Two good examples were prominent Binghamton Attorney George Hinman, counsel for the commission, and Dr. William J. Ronan, the commission's staff director.

In 1956, L. Judson Morhouse, chairman of the New York State Republican Committee, discussed with Rockefeller the possibility that the latter might run for the United States Senate seat being vacated by Irving Ives. Rockefeller declined this suggestion to seek legislative office by noting that his temperament was more suited to administrative duties.[4] Morhouse then discussed the gubernatorial race with Rockefeller, but his initial efforts did not arouse much response.[5] Later in the year Rockefeller was to discuss state elective politics with Assemblyman Malcolm Wilson, the popular Republican legislator from Westchester County. In September 1957 Nelson and Mrs. Rockefeller were invited to the home of George Hinman for dinner; the publisher of the Binghamton *Star*, William H. Hill, was also asked to come.[6] Eighty years old, Hill was a former member of Congress and the Republican leader of Broome County. They discussed in general terms how a statewide campaign might be approached, but Rockefeller did not give any indication of his attitude. Thus Hinman left the meeting believing that Rockefeller was not receptive to running.[7] However, Rockefeller had not entirely rejected the idea of running, and he would again visit Hill in November of 1957. He would also conduct his personal surveys of public sentiment within the state.

There were numerous indications that the political climate of 1958 did not appear favorable for a Rockefeller candidacy. Party leaders had warned Rockefeller that 1958 would be a "Democratic year."[8] Harriman was thought to be unbeatable, and there were several strong Republican hopefuls, including State Senate Leader Walter J. Mahoney of Buffalo,

Assembly Leader Oswald D. Heck of Schenectady, and former Congressman and retired Republican National Chairman Leonard Hall of Oyster Bay. Even the result of Rockefeller's extensive private surveys showed his chances at approximately "two-in-five of making it the whole way."[9]

Because Judson Morhouse believed that Rockefeller would be the strongest candidate the Republicans could nominate, he took it upon himself to urge party leaders not to declare themselves in favor of other possibilities until they had a chance to become acquainted with this potential candidate. Following a Republican party fundraiser in early June of 1958, Morhouse was to issue an ultimatum to about fifteen party leaders from around the state who had gathered in New York City. His message to the party leaders was that Rockefeller was the best man to provide the new leadership the party needed. Noting that Rockefeller would most likely be the most popular candidate that the party could nominate, he stated that unless the party did in fact nominate him, he, Morhouse, would resign his position as chairman.[10] William Hill had also been active with a newspaper "draft Rockefeller" campaign. He produced results from his private polls that purportedly agreed with the Morhouse results showing Rockefeller running better than other contenders in the field for the Republican nomination.

On June 30 Rockefeller called a press conference to announce "officially" the decision he had reached. The themes articulated in his brief remarks would become a mainstay of his political rhetoric for years to come:

> I have reached this decision because of my deep conviction that a new approach to government must be taken in New York State. Government must be given a new energy and efficiency to make it capable of solving the emerging and complicated social and economic problems of our times.... What we need is a transfusion of political courage to grasp the opportunities and the ideas of men who have convictions and creative talent and faith in the future. The challenge is to match the aspirations of the sixteen million people of this great state. Any man who accepts it must be mindful of the obligation it imposes.[11]

Prior to the convention, Assemblyman Malcom Wilson, Rockefeller, and the latter's son Steven canvassed the state in Wilson's automobile to give the leaders of the party a chance to meet the candidate for nomination. During the prenomination period, Rockefeller visited forty-nine of the state's sixty-two counties in his solicitation for delegate votes. Wilson knew the county leaders, those men who had control over the party machinery and selection process, on a first-name basis. Rockefeller was well received during these visits; his dynamic style of personal campaigning, one incorporating a broad smile, warmth, charm, and knowledge of the issues, and the support provided by Wilson served him well. Nomination by the Republican Convention on August 25, 1958, ensued with no significant dissent.[12]

The platform of the Republican party consisted of thirty-five planks that covered a broad spectrum of issues of concern to various constituencies within the state. Among the issues were promoting economic development, improving commuter transportation, providing vigorous law enforcement, combating juvenile delinquency, increasing aid to education, expanding educational opportunities, enforcing civil rights, providing additional benefits for civil servants, eliminating inequities in the tax structure, extending community health programs, expanding housing, and improving the state's road system.[13] In accepting the nomination, Rockefeller bemoaned the fiscal policies of the Harriman administration, especially tax increases, depletion of the reserves of the state, a "doubling" of the state's budget, and increases in state debt.[14] Many features of his campaign to win the nomination were utilized in the campaign immediately to follow and would continually be refined in successive campaigns.

The Prize: The Empire State

Rockefeller had won the Republican nomination and the right to campaign for governor of the Empire State that in 1958 was the premier state in the union in many important respects. Aside from having the largest population of any state, itself an important political asset, New York boasted numerous other qualities that gave it political preeminence.

Rockefeller sought to follow into the statehouse an assemblage of personalities of such renown that political analyst Neal Peirce would write that New York State had produced "a record that no other American state could begin to match."[15] A listing of past prominent governors would include the two George Clintons, John Jay, Dewitt Clinton, Grover Cleveland, Theodore Roosevelt, Charles Evans Hughes, Alfred E. Smith, Franklin D. Roosevelt, Herbert Lehman, Thomas E. Dewey, and Averell Harriman. Furthermore, since the Civil War, several former New York State chief executives had received their party's nomination for the presidency, including Horatio Seymore, Samuel Tilden, Grover Cleveland, Theodore Roosevelt, Charles Evans Hughes, Al Smith, Franklin D. Roosevelt, and Thomas Dewey. To be elected governor of New York was to provoke immediate speculation that one would attempt to use the position as a springboard to seek a presidential nomination.

Additionally, the office of governor in New York was recognized widely as a strong governmental institution "in terms of the formal powers conferred upon it by the State Constitution."[16] An analysis of constitutional and statuatory provisions as a source of power, based on data collected prior to and shortly after Rockefeller was first selected governor, found that the "index of power" of the office of governor in New York was exceeded by that of the governor's office in no other state.[17] And few would have argued with the conclusion that the governor of New York had "dominated the political life of the state in recent decades."[18]

The emergence of executive powers in New York extends back to colonial times when the office had a popular base, as only New York and Massachusetts provided for election of their chief executives.[19] In 1824 the New York governor was granted the power of the item veto with respect to appropriation bills. During this century the formal powers of the governor were strengthened even more. For example, a 1927 amendment to the constitution established an executive budget, and a 1925 amendment consolidated the state's departments and provided for the gubernatorial appointment of commissioners to head most departments and serve at the pleasure of the governor. In 1937 an amendment providing for four-year terms for the governor and lieutenant governor was passed.[20]

In addition to being regarded as the state with "financial power and cultural distinction beyond all others,"[21] New York is a state of diverse peoples. At mid-century the population of New York included substantial numbers of immigrants from Austria, Germany, Ireland, Italy, Poland, and Russia. In fact, almost one in four of all foreign-born people in the United States resided in New York State.[22] Migration of blacks and Puerto Ricans to New York State has also been significant. In 1972 Neal Peirce noted that "no other city or state in America approaches the totals of blacks as New York City or New York State."[23] Adding to the heterogeneity of the state were the substantial populations of both Catholics and Jews. In a nation in which the claims of minorities of one kind or another have often helped shape political debate, the state's diversity helped thrust it into the forefront of national politics.

Given the leading role played by the governor in proposing most of the state's major policy innovations during the past fifty-five years, political scientist Joseph Zimmerman suggests that the governor has indeed earned the title of "Chief Legislator."[24] The state's record of innovative legislation is impressive: curbing the excesses of utilities, regulating public service corporations, improving the civil service system, extending basic rights to industrial workers, and creating the first workmen's compensation law in the nation, to list but a few.[25]

Also notable is that many of the public policies embodied in New York State statutes are congruent with the policy preferences of a majority of its extremely diverse population. More than one study measuring the responsiveness of policymakers to the wishes of the citizens of the states in the enactment of statutes found that New York State consistently ranked highest of the fifty states in congruence of policy with public opinion.[26] Moreover, studies have shown that New York is one of those few highly esteemed American states from which most other states seek information and "take cues" respecting policy innovations.[27] Not only does the state serve as a bellwether for other states with respect to policy adoption, several of its departments and agencies are viewed by administrators in other states as the best in the nation in the administration of policy.[28]

Opponents, Issues, and Organization

In the gubernatorial elections held during a period of thirteen years, Rockefeller was to confront and defeat Democratic opponents in four statewide campaigns. His first opponent was Averell Harriman, diplomat, former administrator of the Marshall Plan and the incumbent governor in 1958; and his last, in 1970, was Arthur Goldberg, former secretary of labor and justice of the United States Supreme Court. Along the way he effectively fought off challenges by Robert Morgenthau, a United States attorney in New York (in 1962), and by Frank O'Connor, former district attorney for Queens and president of the New York City Council (1966).

Rockefeller's campaign messages were conveyed in a variety of formats. The annual messages to the legislature early in January during gubernatorial election years were viewed as the first salvos of upcoming campaigns,[29] but addresses at numerous locations around the state during the preconvention period and during the campaign were the primary vehicles through which Rockefeller tried to get across his message. The platforms produced by and for the several nominating conventions, speeches accepting nominations, personal contact with voters, and the use of mass media were other means through which he sought to reach the people.

It is important that the rhetoric and style of campaigns be tailored to particular audiences in order to achieve one's predetermined purposes and avoid undesirable consequences.[30] Doris Graber notes that political candidates may assume one of three postures in their political campaign rhetoric: the "statesman" employs reasoned argument on a high intellectual plane rather than an emotional plane; the "charismatic" leader appeals to emotional attachments and advances himself as a savior or superman; and the "rabble-rouser" attempts to arouse uncontrollable emotionalism and irrationality.[31]

By and large, Nelson Rockefeller assumed the posture of the statesman, a capable and concerned person who advanced and executed programs to meet pressing social needs. His rhetoric was not typical of the rabble-rouser or of the charismatic leader, but he regularly made appeals to the electorate to view him as a highly experienced and effective leader and did not hesitate to indicate the shortcomings of the opposition. To suggest that one's opponents have weaknesses is standard fare in most political campaigns. However, Rockefeller's methods and zeal in this respect would be called into question by many. For example, as a discussion later in this chapter shows, the Governor's campaign against Frank O'Connor in 1966 included some attacks clearly aimed at playing on the emotions of fear and outrage. In addition, charges that the "big-city bosses" would go to any length to gain power in New York State were calculated to arouse and capitalize on negative feelings of upstate voters toward the machinations of political leaders in New York City. Nevertheless, most observers would probably agree that the dominant campaign posture assumed by Rockefeller was that of the statesman.

In his four general election campaigns, Rockefeller touted his executive and administrative abilities and experience and his personal record as proof of his leadership. This issue along with bossism and the fiscal condition of the state (see Chapter 6 for a discussion of this issue) formed the core of his efforts to advance his position and repel the attacks of his opponents.

The emergence of the issue of bossism in 1958 was fortuitous. Governor Harriman had been humiliated by Carmine DeSapio, "boss" of New York City's Tammany Hall, at the 1958 Democratic State Convention in Buffalo. Harriman's choice as candidate for the United States Senate was Thomas K. Finletter, who was also supported by former Governor Herbert Lehman and Mrs. Eleanor Roosevelt. DeSapio used his political muscle to overcome Harriman's resistance and secure the nomination for his candidate, Manhattan District Attorney Frank Hogan. This gave Rockefeller the opportunity to stress the issue of bossism in his upstate campaign tour in the fall.[32] Again in 1962 and 1966 Rockefeller relied on this issue, one that had apparently served him well in his initial campaign.[33] For example, on one occasion in 1962 he acused the " big-city bosses" of handpicking "their candidate" at the state convention and handing him a platform "promising everything to everybody—with no thought of the fact that to pay for those promises would mean either a 50 percent state income tax increase or a deficit of more than $2 billion."[34] Rockefeller opened his attack on "the bosses" early in 1966 with a general admonition to the Republican delegates to "save New York State from this arrogant onslaught of the bosses."[35] The charges of bossism in 1966 related to the struggle in the Democratic party between the "old bosses," Charles Buckley of the Bronx and Stanley Steingut of Brooklyn, versus the "new boss," United States Senator Robert Kennedy.[36]

As noted above, the Governor's annual message to the legislature was viewed as a means of advancing basic issues to be addressed in an election-year campaign. A review of the goals stated in these messages and the speeches given on the campaign trail in support on these goals reveals a consistency in the nature and variety of issues addressed by Rockefeller in his several campaigns for reelection.

The 1962 message outlined three basic goals: New York will be made "a good place to work," natural resources will be protected, and educational opportunities will be increased. For 1966, four general goals were cited: New York was to be made safe, was to be made environmentally clean, was to offer the greatest economic and educational opportunities, and was to protect citizens against ill health. And finally, in 1970, the campaign issues were encompassed within a framework of five goals: eliminate poverty, make communities healthy and safe, restore and protect the qualify of the environment, improve the economic climate, and assure that the government remains responsive to the needs of people.

The emphasis candidate Rockefeller gave to issues varied from campaign to campaign, but some basic issues were present in each: eliminating poverty, expanding the state's economy, increasing educational opportunities, cleaning up the environment, making the streets safe, providing recreational facilities, and improving health services. As the incumbent, Rockefeller's one basic strategy in response to challengers was to strongly defend his record by denoting the achievements of his administration and promising to do more. The programs that he offered were designed with the intent of providing advantages to each of the numerous political and geographical elements within the state: farm, labor, business, minorities, and ethnic groups, the poor and the aged, professional groups, and residents of urban areas, suburban areas, and rural areas. There is every indication that Rockefeller firmly believed that success at meeting the needs of his diverse constituency was the key to reelection success.

As a campaigner running in a populous and highly diverse state, one faced with the same complex and seemingly intractable problems that faced the larger national society, Rockefeller was in an ideal position from which he could pursue his life strategy. In identifying the problems faced by New York and in offering his solutions to those problems, he was in many cases "naturally" addressing problems that were national in scope. Table 3.1 denotes the five "most important issues" tabulated from national opinion surveys conducted by the Gallup organization during the years Nelson Rockefeller ran for governor. An inspection of campaign speeches given by the Governor, as found in his *Public Papers*, shows that he spoke directly to many of these "most important" national issues, or to close variants of them, in his bids for election or reelection.[37]

A central element in the electoral successes of Nelson Rockefeller was his deftness in creating and molding campaign organizations that were sensitive and responsive to his personal objectives, the needs of the state, prevailing national trends in campaign strategies, and the essentials of effective campaigns.[38] Of major significance was his ability to build a loyal and effective campaign team. (In the initial campaign his business staff at Rockefeller Center would serve in an ancilliary capacity.) The persons forming the nucleus of the 1958 campaign staff were: L. Judson Morhouse, campaign manager; George Hinman, personal adviser; William Ronan, in charge of issue development and speech writting; Frank Jamieson, chief of staff; Roswell Perkins, director of research (Perkins having resigned from his position in HEW to join the campaign team); R. Burdell Bixby, in charge of speaking schedules (Bixby being a law partner of Thomas Dewey); Harry O'Donnell, in charge of state committee publicity; and Charles Metzner, director of financial affairs (Metzner being a former Dewey campaign

Table 3.1
Gallup Poll Results on "Most Important Issue" During New York Statewide Election Years: 1958-1970

1958	1962	1966	1970
Keeping the Peace (30%)*	Keeping the Peace (63%)	Vietnam (51%)	Campus Unrest (17%)*
Economic Problems (29%)*	Economic Problems (10%)*	Civil Rights (17%)*	Vietnam (22%)
Space Race with Russia (6%)	Unemployment (8%)*	High Cost of Living (16%)*	International Problems (14%)*
Integration (6%)*	Racial Problems (6%)*	Threat of War (4%)	Racial Strife (13%)*
National Defense (4%)	Juvenile Delinquency (3%)*	Spread of Communism (3%)	High Cost of Living (10%)*

SOURCE: George H. Gallup, *The Gallup Poll: Public Opinion, 1935-1971* (New York: Random House, 1972). Data for 1958 compiled from Volume II. Data for other years compiled from Volume III.

NOTE: The issues listed for each year are the five which were mentioned by the most respondents in the various polls. The percentages for 1958 are the averages of three surveys conducted on January 2, March 6, and September 10, 1958. The survey for 1962 was conducted on April 16, 1962. The percentages for 1966 are the averages of two surveys conducted on May 5, and August 18, 1966. The survey for 1970 was conducted on May 21, 1970.

*This issue or a closely related topic was one of Nelson Rockefeller's campaign issues.

worker). In addition, Oren Root, Jr., and Mrs. Russell Davenport were cochairmen of a Citizens for Rockefeller Committee and Roswell Gilpatrick, a former undersecretary of the Air Force, headed the Democrats for Rockefeller Committee. In the 1958 campaign and in later campaigns, Rockefeller's election team was generally viewed as a highly skilled and effective unit.[39]

Although the composition of the Governor's campaign team changed over the years, there were important elements of continuity. For example, William Ronan played a key role in every campaign, primarily because he became Rockefeller's closest personal adviser. Reinforcing Ronan's role in campaigns was the fact that he was appointed secretary to the Governor at the beginning of the administration. In this capacity he headed the Governor's "program staff," a group of staffers who were at the center of idea development and program production and who thus helped provide Rockefeller with a record on which to run for reelection. Among other members of the 1958 campaign team who played active roles as advisers in later campaigns were George Hinman and Burdell Bixby. The Governor's ability to place campaign advisers, Ronan, for example, and campaign staffers into positions in his administration helped provide an important measure of continuity to his campaign efforts.[40]

As he did in earlier stages of his career, Rockefeller turned to those he considered experts for advice in areas in which he himself was not an expert. As one member of his campaign team put it, "He was too good to be true. He listened and he would do anything you told him to do in campaigning."[41] However, this is not to say that the Governor removed himself from basic decisions regarding campaign strategy and tactics. Ever the activist, he enjoyed the electoral challenge and threw himself into the task of meeting that challenge. Resourceful and willing to consider any new idea for solving a problem, he occasionally came into conflict with members of his campaign team. A story related by close adviser and former campaign manager William Pfeiffer provides a good example of one such dispute.

Prior to the Republican nominating convention in 1966, the Governor asked Pfeiffer to arrange for the convention to give the Republican party endorsement for state comptroller to Athur Levitt, the incumbent comptroller and a Democrat. Stung by Levitt's continuing criticism of his spending and borrowing and expensive projects such as the giant project for construction of a state office and cultural complex then known as the "South Mall,"Rockefeller hoped to stifle that criticism by giving Levitt the Republican endorsement. Stating that he opposed the idea, Pfeiffer, nevertheless, agreed to talk to Levitt. After Levitt told Pfeiffer that he had no interest in dual endorsement and that his party would certainly be opposed, the Governor persisted in the idea. When Pfeiffer opposed the idea in the strongest terms, saying that the Republican party would be admitting to bankruptcy by nominating Levitt, Rockefeller insisted on personally bringing the issue to a meeting of campaign advisers and staff. When he came to the meeting, Pfeiffer explained what the Governor wanted and why he, Pfeiffer, was opposed. Then the campaign manager delivered an ultimatum. "If the Governor insists [on endorsing Levitt], I will call a press conference and resign and state my reasons."[42] After Pfeiffer left the room, Rockefeller polled all nine advisers who were present and all supported Pfeiffer against the Governor. "Really hot," Rockefeller left the room, but never again raised the idea of endorsing Levitt.[43]

Campaigns are normally of short duration, but one of Nelson Rockefeller hallmarks was to extend the length of his campaigns by beginning them early.[44] For his first campaign, his prenomination activities allowed him to begin his strategy sessions immediately following the nominating convention on August 28, 1958. The following campaign was kicked off two months before the 1964 nominating convention with the formation of a Platform Advisory Committee in July of 1962. The longest of Rockefeller's four campaigns was for the 1966 election. It was started by William Ronan in December of 1964 because of the fact that the Governor's popularity at that time was quite low. However, these early campaign efforts did not actively involve Rockefeller himself. Instead, they sought to sell his accomplishments.[45] The final state campaign was commenced in February of 1970, in part due to the early April 7 date for the nominating convention that year.[46]

The political diversity of the state and Rockefeller's status as an activist incumbent led to the creation of campaign organizations that would reach out to the state's various constituencies in an effort to sell his accomplishments. During his tenure, the Republican party was outnumbered by the Democratic party, which had an advantage in statewide registrations that increased from 59,559 in 1958 to 411,147 in 1962 and 876,440 in 1966. (The advantage dropped to 608,349 in 1970).[47] Moreover, the "conservatism" of upstate versus the "liberalism" of New York City was a factor that Rockefeller had to contend with. In the face of these difficult political realities, the Governor needed campaigns that were highly organized and sensitive to the need to build a winning coalition.

For example, committees to enlist the support of groups representing physicians, lawyers, the foreign-born, the elderly, and others were readied prior to the renomination of the Governor in 1962.[48] Thirty-one such committees existed in the 1966 campaign, among them Young Republicans for Rockefeller, the Columbian Republican League (Italian-Americans), Show Business for Rockefeller, Taxpayers for Rockefeller (conservative Republicans), Labor for Rockefeller, and Democrats for Rockefeller.[49] Similar committees were organized for the 1970 campaign, but special attention was given to securing the support on New York City "ethnic group" Democrats and independents. Arthur Massolo was placed in charge of thirty-one nationalities organizations, including even Syrians and Croations for Rockefeller,[50] and Fioravante Perrotta headed an operation aimed at converting conservative Irish, Polish, and Italian (the largest ethnic group in New York City) voters to the Rockefeller team.[51]

In deference to the political environment of New York State, Rockefeller appointed a Republican, a Democrat, and an Independent as cochairmen of the Citizens for Rockefeller and Javits Committee in 1962 and selected Dale Wright, the editor of *Ebony* and *Jet* magazines, as director of the Republican state campaign. In an effort to draw support from the Democrats in his third campaign, Jackie Robinson, the Governor's Negro Affairs Advisor, and Edward Cavanaugh, deputy mayor of New York City under Mayor Wagner, were named to head a citizens group to work for the reelection of Nelson Rockefeller. The upstate-New York City dichotomy was reflected in the 1970 campaign with Joseph Boyd being assigned as head of the upstate and suburban campaign and the New York City portion of the campaign being assigned to Hubert Hallberg and Fioravante Perrotta. In a tribute to the Governor's effectiveness at organizing and mobilizing numerous groups during campaign years, the man who served as his campaign manager in 1962 and 1966, William Pfeiffer, proudly remarked, "We had everyone organized except the prostitutes on Times Square."[52]

Getting and Using Information

Rockefeller returned to New York State in 1957 with a proclivity for being well-informed on issues of interest to him. (His experiences at the national level and association with the Rockefeller Brothers Fund studies are recounted in Chapter 2.) But even as the challenger against Harriman in 1958, Rockefeller had access to an impressive stockpile of information on issues pertinent to New York State. This was so because some members of the staff of the Commission on the Constitutional Convention joined his campaign staff. Rockefeller's habit of relying heavily on staff and other experts to gather and process information for campaining and for formulating policies continued throughout his entire tenure as Governor. For his initial campaign, he commissioned no less than 134 distinct studies related to his gubernatorial prospects and ambitions.[53] In late July of 1962, he established a Platform Advisory Committee to hold public hearings for the purpose of soliciting issues to be included in the Republican platform.[54] Following these hearings, Rockefeller selected thirty-one issues he could confront in his next administration, if reelected.[55] By his third campaign he was effectively utilizing members of his staff to supply him with needed information and ideas for his campaigns. The practice was for selected staff persons to take leaves of absence from their jobs with the state and then receive compensation from Rockefeller's campaign funds. However, in 1966, when William Ronan organized a substantive issues group to select and publicize campaign issues, the *New York Times* reported that "at least four key aides were still on the state's payroll although working virtually full-time on the campaign.''[56]

Another Rockefeller device for gathering and using information was to canvas the bureaucracy for details of his administration's accomplishments and to organize this information into ''county data books.'' Examples of items included were ''how many miles of highway had been built, and where; the number of new bridges; the number of state scholarships awarded to county students; even specific examples showing what property taxes would have been had it not been for the expanded state aid.''[57] Table 3.2 presents a synthesis of information found in six data books prepared for the 1966 election campaign.[58] The data books average forty-seven pages in length and each begins with a ''confidential section'' of political information the Governor was to keep foremost in his mind when campaigning in a particular area. For example, the following observation was noted in the Tioga book:

> This county is the birthplace of the governor's grandfather. The [county] chairman is giving some thought to asking the governor to pose at the academy his grandfather attended.... The people are eager to develop a County Mental Health program and money has been appropriated this year... [and] medicaid is not a major issue among the voters although criticism by doctors tends to make it somewhat touchy.[59]

The data contained in these books enabled the Governor to speak intelligently on issues that affected voters in every part of the state.[60] Moreover, a series of brochures was prepared, one aimed at each region of the state. Each detailed what the governor had done for that part of the state. These brochures were distributed to all campaign workers, Republican candidates, and voters. In all, thirty million pieces of printed matter were distributed in 1970.[61]

Rockefeller made extensive use of public opinion polls to secure a variety of information: to identify potential candidates, to ascertain his potential strength, to solicit views on issues, and to evaluate advertising themes. According to Lloyd Free, a private pollster who served the Governor from 1963 to 1973, Rockefeller ''would poll the state five or six times a year, more in election years. He is terribly interested in public opinion, terribly fascinated with it.''[62] His efforts at polling were labeled as quiet, smooth, and skilled.[63] In 1958, the results of private polls contributed to Rockefeller's decision to run and to informing him that it would be less desirable to conduct a ''party versus party'' campaign than a Rockefeller versus Harriman campaign.[64] As noted before, Rockefeller then conducted a campaign that featured his personality rather than his partisan affiliation.[65] Joseph Bachelder, President Eisenhower's pollster in 1952 and 1956, was Rockefeller's polling expert in 1962. He has indicated that Rockefeller used his polls to set up a line of communication between himself

Table 3.2
Synthesized Table of Contents from Six County Data Books for the 1966 Campaign

I. SUPPLEMENTAL DATA: CONFIDENTIAL

State involvement in local area conflicts: nature of issues; position governor might assume
Pending searches in county for appointments: status
How county has fared under recently publicized projects
Status of third parties in the county
Recent discussions with county party leaders
Fundraisings: past and contemplated

II. POLITICAL DATA

Public officials in the county
Republican organization
Vote totals in past elections
Appointments of county residents to positions: names and positions listed

III. PROGRAM DATA

Economy
- Industrial information
- Public works
- New employers and expansions
- Closings and contractions
- Largest communities in county and changes since the last census
- Agricultural information
- Employment covered by unemployment insurance
- Workforce data
- Unemployment insurance benefit claimants
- Personal income data
- Principal industrial and commercial employers
- Construction projects planned: commercial, educational, cultural, apartments, houses, other

Local Assistance
- By categories and amounts: last year's actual, this year's estimated, and percent changed

School Aid

Higher Education
- State aid to schools
- Scholar Incentive Awards: number of awards received, value of awards

SOURCE: County Data Books for 1966.

Table 3.2—*Continued*

Scholarships: Regents college, child of deceased or disabled veteran, basic nurse, war service, medicine, dentistry, and osteopathy
Number of students with outstanding loans and amounts
Capital Construction
- Contracts let during year: projects itemized with total amounts
- Major projects being planned

Highways
- Contracts let and contemplated

Recreation
- Projects

Pollution
- Projects

Youth
- Projects

Mental Health
- Projects

Rehabilitation
- Projects

Housing
- Projects

Arts
- Projects

---

and the voting public.[66] In 1966, early polls revealed that Rockefeller was rated favorably by only 25 percent of the voters.[67] His campaign organization then used polls to pinpoint six issue areas where the administration had achieved successes. These six issues were used in soft-sell, precampaign commercials in order to focus on the administration's accomplishments.[68]

Rockefeller's utilization of polling was perhaps most extensive in his final bid for reelection in 1970. Polls were used prior to the campaign to ascertain the mood of the electorate, to determine what issues were bothering the voters, to measure reaction to TV spots, to identify characteristics of voters favorably disposed toward, and critical of, Rockefeller, to identify the "pivotals" (those who had not made up their minds), and to inform a decision on a general strategy for the campaign.[69]

Nelson Rockefeller used his massive stockpile of data in communicating with voters in both personal and electronic modes. The 1958 campaign was essentially a get-acquainted effort by the candidate. Embarking upon handshaking tours to 103 communities, including stops in each of the sixty-two counties of the state, challenger Rockefeller made promises in his formal and impromptu speeches, promises that focused on the issues uncovered in the earlier research studies.[70] A key member of his campaign team remarked that Rockefeller "could not give a speech worth a goddamn, but let him

Table 3.3
Addresses of Nelson A. Rockefeller during Gubernatorial Election Years: 1962-1970

YEAR	PRECONVENTION PERIOD		CAMPAIGN PERIOD		POST-ELECTION PERIOD		TOTAL
	In State	Out of State	In State	Out of State	In State	Out of State	
1962	39	12	87	1	1	1	141
1966	125	0	109	0	3	0	237
1970	29	0	181	0	6	1	217
Total:	193	12	377	1	10	2	595

SOURCE: Compiled from State of New York, *Public Papers of Nelson A. Rockefeller, Fifty-Third Governor of the State of New York.*

ramble and he could get his message across."[71] The Governor spoke extensively as shown by the figures in Table 3.3. (This table is tabulated from the speeches reproduced in his *Public Papers* and thus tends to understate his total effort because many impromptu speeches are not included.)[72]

Rockefeller's special greeting was to call out "hiya fella" while campaigning personally during walking and handshaking tours, but each of his campaigns also included the use of the media. In successive campaigns, his utilization of the media would become extensive and sophisticated.[73]

Newspapers and television have been reported to be equal sources of political campaign advertising by Rockefeller in 1958.[74] When engaging in handshaking tours and interviews, Rockefeller took along cameras and tape recorders; the resulting products were reported on television ads that began on September 29, on radio spots, and in photographs appearing in newspapers.[75] For example, appearing in New York City newspapers were photographs showing Rockefeller eating blintzes on the Lower East Side, pizza in Little Italy, and hot dogs at Coney Island.[76] Extensive use was made of foreign language radio stations, in part to cover his tours in Spanish Harlem where he campaigned in Spanish, and in part in an attempt to reach non-English-speaking voters who had not been approached previously. For example, messages aired over the foreign language radio stations reminded potential voters of the extent to which philanthropic institutions related to the Rockefeller family had helped the "old countries."[77] During the final week of the campaign sixty-five telephone operators were hired in an attempt to reach 100,000 enrolled Republicans in the state.[78] Indicative of the extent of Rockefeller's efforts is the fact that his television campaign was two and one-half times larger than Harriman's.[79]

The basic pattern of media advertising established in 1958 was maintained in the 1962 campaign. For example, according to the *New York Times*, Rockefeller himself appeared on television on four separate occasions during 1962.[80] However, his approach toward television changed drastically in the campaign effort in 1966. In that year defeat seemed inevitable for the Governor, for early Democratic party polls revealed that three-quarters of the electorate said that they would vote for anyone except Nelson Rockefeller.[81] Opposition to the 1965 sales tax was paramount as an issue among those polled. (The Governor's campaign manager reported that private polls conducted by Rockefeller indicated that the primary concern of the electorate was not the tax itself, but what the Governor had done with the revenue produced by the sales tax.)[82] Thus, Jack Tinker and Partners, the nontraditional and creative advertising firm that had achieved success with Alka Seltzer and Gillette razor commercials, was hired to prepare television ads. Consistent with the discouraging findings of private polls, a mammoth campaign that included three phases was planned.[83] The first phase was designed to convey images and not ideas. The intent was to encourage voters to form new opinions about the Governor, rather than to seek to change existing opinions.[84] Beginning in July, the ads during the first phase were intended to be soft-sell in tone. They were not shown during prime time, the Governor did not appear, and his voice was not used. The idea in these preconvention ads was to stress the administration's accomplishments, and each ad was devoted to a single issue.[85]

The second phase began in September after the nominating convention and after the soft-sell commercials had been shown 700 times.[86] These ads featured *Governor* Rockefeller, but in voice-over simulations. The last three weeks of the campaign were devoted to third-phase commercials that featured weaknesses in the opposition. The magnitude of this television effort was staggering; James Perry's count is that "3,027 Rockefeller ads were shown on New York's 22 commercial television stations."[87]

Although even more lavish and costly, the media campaign of 1970 represented an extension of previous efforts. Jack Tinker and Partners were the producers of the media materials and the campaign was again divided into three phases. The television and radio campaign started in August with thirty separate television ads and fifteen radio messages. These phase-one ads were designed to show Rockefeller as a "combination governor and candidate" and to feature his record.[88] In phase two, Nelson Rockefeller was all candidate. In early September he was shown doing great things; later the same month and early in October he was shown making pledges for the future. Finally, in late October, as was the case in 1966, the media campaign began to focus on the opposition. The effort to reach the voters through the media was supplemented with telegrams and telephone calls to potential voters. Simulated telegrams asking for support were sent to 400,000 Republicans and independents in upstate New York on the Thursday before the election, and telephone calls were made to 932,470 households representing an estimated two million voters.[89]

The Rockefeller campaigns were all cast in terms of themes. The theme in 1958, "New Leadership," reflected the fact that he was a challenger; the object being to plant the idea that new leadership was needed for New York State and that Rockefeller possessed the qualifications to exert this "new leadership." However, the remaining three campaigns found Rockefeller as the focus of attacks that required him to defend his record and behavior. For example, contrary to his promises, he had increased taxes in 1959; he had been separated from his wife and then, in 1961, divorced; and he had spent considerable time during his first two years in office seeking the presidential nomination of his party. In addition, he had to deal with the fledgling Conservative party, a party that ran its own candidate for governor in 1962.

Variants of several of the "negative" issues in 1962 confronted the incumbent in 1966: remarriage in 1963, imposition of a sales tax in 1965, contrary to another promise not to raise taxes, and defeat in a second attempt for the presidential nomination. In addition, crime and drug abuse had emerged as prominent issues by 1966, and the state's medicaid program was incurring greater costs than anticipated.

The high cost of running the state government was the principal issue that the Governor was forced to confront in 1970, especially the escalating costs of the South Mall project. Moreover, there had been unpopular decreases in spending for welfare and municipal hospitals and a rising rate of unemployment on Long Island.

The impact of these and other problems was successfully blunted by Rockefeller the candidate. He did so by emphasizing his record of achievement, by evading as many issues as possible, and by aggressively pinning "specific and unpopular positions on his opponents."[90] In fact, the themes of his first two reelection campaigns were aimed at his opponents: the Morgenthau "Mistake Series" in 1962 and the O'Connor "Big Lie Technique" in 1966.

Robert Morgenthau challenged Rockefeller's record of effective leadership of the state by citing statistics that amounted to an indictment of that record. For example, he argued that business growth was slow or slower than what had been claimed to be the case, "progress" in education was misleading, wages for workers were lower than the Governor claimed, and unemployment was higher. As the incumbent, Rockefeller utilized "official" state statistics to argue that Morgenthau was in error on each of the above and other charges and thus claimed that Morgenthau had made nothing but a series of mistakes.[91]

The emergence of the Conservative party was also a factor that candidate Rockefeller chose to meet aggressively during his 1962 campaign. In order to get on the state ballot in its maiden effort in a statewide election, it was necessary for the party to obtain 12,000 signatures on nominating petitions with a minimum of fifty from each of the state's sixty-two counties. Given the potential threat posed by the Conservatives, Conservative party leader Daniel Mahoney alleged that Rockefeller attempted to organize a denunciation of the party by the New York delegation to the House of Representatives. According to Mahoney, this plan was dropped only when Rockefeller was rebuffed by several members of Congress.[92] Despite opposition by the Governor, the Conservative party succeeded in getting on the ballot. (Several other activities designed to thwart the Conservative challenge are discussed below in the context of Rockefeller's strategies for coping with the existence of "third parties" in the state.)

It is generally accepted that Frank O'Connor led an inept campaign against Rockefeller in 1966. Typical of O'Connor's misfortunes was an episode in a tenement area in New York City. After the time and expense of filming an entire day in the area, O'Connor could not use the commercial produced because the taping occurred in front of a door covered by graffiti. More directly, the Governor used official state statistics to demonstrate that the challenger's attacks on his programs for taxing, housing, narcotics, pollution, and waterways were in error. In doing so, Rockefeller dubbed the attacks made by O'Connor as the "Big Lie Techniques."[93] Ruthless is what James Perry called the third phase of Rockefeller's media campaign.[94] The commercials produced were so labeled not because they were oversimplified, but because of the "extraordinary vehemence" of the attacks on the Governor's "humbling and gentle opponent."[95] In seeking to pin unpopular stands on O'Connor, Rockefeller's ads stretched the truth somewhat. For example, several claimed that as a state legislator O'Connor had opposed the state thruway, wanted to eliminate subway fares in New York City, and, by opposing Rockefeller's narcotics program, was in favor of crime in the streets. These counterattacks badly garbled O'Connor's stand on these issues, but he was not able to effectively explain the subtleties involved. The facts were that O'Connor had been opposed to the thruway as a toll road, that he had mused on the possibilities of no fares on subways anywhere, and that he had said the Rockefeller narcotics program was bad because of its provision for ascertaining the identities of drug pushers and then subjecting them to *mandatory* treatment.[96]

One third-phase television spot clearly illustrates the extreme methods that the Governor was willing to employ. Focusing on O'Connor's opposition to the Rockefeller narcotics program, it showed

> an empty table on which a hand laid down one by one the implements used by drug addicts... the powder, spoon, hypodermic... and then in the same row... a gun, a knife, and brass knuckles. Then, as a voice explained the Rockefeller program to reduce crime by getting addicts of the streets, the hand picked up the implements until the table was again bare.
>
> Finally... the Governor himself appeared in short commercials, saying "If you want to keep crime rates high, O'Connor is your man."[97]

The theme for the media campaign in 1970 was "Rockefeller: He's Done a Lot, He'll Do More." Following through on this political slogan, the Governor sought to make his opponent, Arthur Goldberg, into the perfect foil by painting Goldberg as a man who did not measure up to the job of running New York State. During the early stages of the campaign, several "lack of stature" messages were advanced by Rockefeller surrogates. However, during the last month of the campaign, the Governor himself launched direct personal attacks against Goldberg.[98] In addition to derogating his personal qualifications, he accused Goldberg of being a "dupe" of the Democrats.[99] Moreover, a "Democrats for Rockefeller" television ad, in essence, accused Arthur Goldberg of not being a true Democrat by charging that he had opposed President Franklin D. Roosevelt's decision to seek a fourth term in 1944.[100] Within the last week of the campaign, a date that left Goldberg little time to reply, Rockefeller maintained that his Democratic opponent had offered New York City Comptroller Mario Procaccino a $70,000 position as chairman of the Metropolitan Transit Authority as a quid pro quo for his endorsement. When Goldberg demanded an apology from Rockefeller, the Governor said he merely "raised the question" of Procaccino and the MTA chairmanship.[101]

A highly derogatory "campaign biography," *Arthur Goldberg, the Old and the New*, had been written by Victor Lasky in six weeks and distributed during the campaign.[102] Among other things, Lasky wrote,

> The fact is that Mr. Goldberg does not have the background and experience to be a successful Governor at this critical time. Mr. Goldberg is always pounding his chest and emphasizing his concern for the people. The fact is, of course, that concern for others is not characteristic of a person who, like Mr. Goldberg, has kicked, scratched and thrust his way up the ladder to the position of prominence which he has held.
>
> Such progress is the result of a... drive, and is the result of continued thought about oneself, one's record-24 hours a day plus a lot of overtime.[103]

Four years later during the confirmation hearings attendant to Rockefeller's nomination to be vice-president, it was revealed that the Federal Bureau of Investigation had discovered that Rockefeller had known about, and actually approved, an expenditure of $60,000 by his brother Laurance to finance the Lasky book. But only a month before the hearings, Rockefeller had denied any knowledge of or any involvement in, this book.[104] In the face of substantial evidence to the contrary, Nelson Rockefeller capitulated and said that he had known about the plans to publish the derogatory book, but had "passed it off" as being of minor consequence.[105] A telegram of apology subsequently was written by "Nelson" to "Arthur" on October 12, 1974. In his testimony to members of the House Judiciary Committee, Rockefeller would explain his involvement with the following statement:

> Now, it puts me in a very embarrassing position. I have apologized to Mr. Goldberg. I have apologized to my brother. It was my own memory which, because of a 15-minute span in a hectic campaign in relation to something I thought really was not of any great significance, and in my judgement that was the only good thing about my judgement, it wasn't, but I should have stopped them. I should have killed

it. It was out of character of the family's operation before or since. We have never done anything like it and we should not have done it then.[106]

Kramer and Roberts conclude that the Lasky book "was a sad commentary on either the Governor's business sense, political savvy, or both."[107] Other observers have evaluated Rockefeller's role in the matter as involving issues much more significant than those of "business sense" and "political savvy." At the least, the matter would seem to involve the issues of undermining the integrity of the electoral process. This same issue is raised by Rockefeller's unbridled spending and sometimes deceptive campaign advertising. One Rockefeller "victim," Goldberg's running mate, expressed his frustration as follows:

I say the desired product is the thing we look at, and the purpose sought is to get a vote which is not exercised on the basis of the volition of voters-be it by economic threats, be it by the gun, or be it by psychological techniques used to deprive the voter of the free choice.

I say it comes down to the same thing. And that it will very quickly undermine the free election system. Nelson Rockefeller is not a menace in and of himself, but his techniques are a grave threat.[108]

The Governor spent $2.3 million in producing and airing his extensive television ads in 1970, but television was only one component of a media package that included radio, newspaper, and billboard advertisements and cost $3.2 million.[109] This media budget was four times greater than that of 1958,[110] and it exceeded the Democratic party's expenditures for all activities of the 1970 gubernatorial campaign. (See Table 3.4.)

It is clear that Rockefeller's aggregate campaign spending was enormous both in absolute terms and relative to spending by his opponents. Except for the 1958 campaign, he outspent his opponents by wide margins. For example, Perry describes Rockefeller's 1966 campaign as the "most expensive nonpresidential campaign ever put together in America. Not only the most expensive, but one of the most professional, one of the most astute, one of the most ruthless."[111] In reporting that the size of Rockefeller's 1966 campaign was staggering, Perry provides the following statistics: 3,000 to 4,000 television commercials; twenty-seven million buttons and brochures distributed, or about 4½ items for every person who voted; a personal staff of 307 persons; and headquarters of eighty-four rooms at the Hilton Hotel in New York City.[112] Rockefeller not only outspent his opponents, it is reasonable to assert that he "out-campaigned" them as well.[113]

Rockefeller's personal wealth and that of his family figured prominently in raising campaign funds. State laws requiring limitations and the reporting of campaign expenditures were not strictly enforced during his tenure as Governor,[114] but one report that Rockefeller filed during his 1970 campaign showed that $4.2 million of the $4.8 million spent had been raised from members of his family.[115] Another major source of campaign funds

Table 3.4
Campaign Spending in New York Gubernatorial Races by Party: 1958-1970

YEAR	REPUBLICAN EXPENDITURES	DEMOCRATIC EXPENDITURES	DEMOCRATIC EXPENDITURES AS PERCENTAGE OF REPUBLICAN EXPENDITURES
1958	$1,786,000	$1,138,000	63.7
1962	2,184,000	420,000	19.7
1966	5,230,982	576,000	11.0
1970	6,900,000	1,330,000	19.3

SOURCE: Robert H. Connery and Gerald Benjamin, *Rockefeller of New York: Executive Power in the Statehouse* (Ithaca: Cornell University Press, 1979), p. 58. Connery and Benjamin note that the data are from the *New York Times*, November 26, 1958; November 29, 1962; November 30, 1966; and November 28, 1970.

was the "Governor's Club" which he sponsored.[116] Formed in 1965, this club consisted of approximately 1,000 state officials, lobbyists, bankers, and businessmen who paid "dues" of $500 annually. In 1970, the group raised $386,000, most of which was contributed to Rockefeller's campaign.[117] In years with no gubernatorial election, monies collected by the Governor's Club was turned over to the Republican State Committee.[118] In addition, the state committee benefited from the attachment of the Rockefeller name to its $150-a-plate dinner, a dinner that produced another $750,000 annually.[119] The political and financial dominance of Rockefeller in New York State politics prompted the *Empire State Report* to write the following after his departure:

> [Although] Republicans may have mixed feelings about some of the buildings and disclaim credit for the State's bills, they'll miss Rockefeller's contribution to the party's coffers...for most Republicans, it is as hard to imagine the Republican party without Nelson Rockefeller as it is Christmas without Santa Claus.[120]

Electoral Success

Each time Nelson Rockefeller faced an election in New York there were signs of a potential victory for the candidate of the Democratic party. In 1958 he was an outsider against an incumbent, and there was a strong national trend in favor of the Democratic party. In 1962, 1966, and 1970 respectively, the polls showed that the Governor could be beaten by Mayor Robert Wagner or a strong Jewish candidate, that he could be beaten by virtually any candidate, and that he would probably lose to any potential Democratic opponent.[121]

Thus far in this chapter, we have discussed the Governor's campaigns primarily in terms of standard categories such as themes, issues, and financing. However, such an approach tends to lose sight of larger questions of political strategy and/or Rockefeller's skill at coping with important external "givens." Political strategies are executed within a framework of circumstances only some of which are subject to manipulation. Here we wish to focus upon the givens represented by four factors in the state's political environment. Such a focus enables one to gain an appreciation of Rockefeller's ability to cope with potential obstacles to his electoral success, obstacles that could not be surmounted by merely resorting to greater spending or minor tactical measures. The four givens are: first, the status of the Republican party as a minority party in New York State; second, the existence of significant third parties; third, changes over time in the proportions of the total vote contributed by different geographical areas and various types of communities, for example, central cities and suburban towns; and fourth, a heterogeneous electorate that is the product of a combination of factors including ethnic diversity and a conservative-liberal division that manifests itself in conflicts between conservative upstate and liberal downstate (New York City.) Certainly, the Governor's long tenure as chief executive of the Empire State, with its social and economic diversity and competitive politics, is an exception to the general rule that long tenures for governors tend to occur in less diverse, less competitive, states.[122]

As Connery and Benjamin point out, the Democratic party had a substantial enrollment advantage over the Republican party during the 1950s and 1960s. More specifically, the Democratic margin ranged from an atypically low 59,559 in 1958 to a high of 876,440 in 1966.[123] However, it is clear that the Democratic party, especially in New York City, was beset with factional strife that tended to decrease its ability to provide a united front against Rockefeller. The Governor was able to promote stability within the Republican party and to capitalize on, and on occasion contribute to, the strife within the Democratic party. It is fair to conclude that Rockefeller dominated the party by means of his personality, the efficacy of his political style, and his wealth. However, as noted before, he had little use for the party label, or its structure, in his electoral campaigns. Even in the first campaign, one in which he did utilize the party organization, his campaign literature was devoid of any indication that Rockefeller was a Republican. (However, although he conducted highly personal campaigns, with minimum reliance on the Republican label and organization, he never lost personal contact with local Republican leadership in the state. For example, materials contained in his County Data Books support this interpretation.)

It can be argued that contributing to Rockefeller's dominance of the Republican party was his ability to transcend whatever limitations that the label "Republican" normally confers. In this regard, Richard Rubin has pointed out that a few Republican party elites are adept a changing the "cluster or constellation of meaning that the voter attaches to the very political symbol 'Republican' itself."[124] One effect of this manipulation, notes Rubin, is that "working class people do not perceive Republican candidates as their opposition."[125]

Consistent with the above observation was Rockefeller's effectiveness at undercutting labor leadership support for the Democratic party as he personally altered "labor's perception of the meaning of the symbol 'Republican' and thus weakened...the relative pulling power of the symbol 'Democrat'" to members of the organized labor.[126] Rockefeller was able to secure strong labor union support in his election campaigns by adroitly deploying the power vested in his office. His strategems included using his power of appointment to flatter labor leaders, proposing and securing passage of bills and programs consistent with the interests of organized labor, for example, massive state-sponsored construction programs, and even, it has been claimed, stealing endorsements.[127] For example, Harry Van Arsdale, president of the New York City Central Labor Council, was appointed in 1959 to the Task Force to Study the State's Power Needs and Resources. Kramer and Roberts assert that a pattern was established whereby Rockefeller regularly appointed leaders of labor unions to honorific positions especially created in the state's Labor Department for providing posts for union representation.[128] The Governor was successful in his efforts to liberalize the state's minimum wage (which was always the highest in the country), enlarge workmen's compensation benefits, augment pension plans for firemen and patrolmen in New York City, and increase unemployment benefits.[129] Peter Brennan, a construction union leader in New York City and later Richard Nixon's secretary of labor, praised Rockefeller's building programs. "He got us jobs.... We had a pretty good feast when Rockefeller was around."[130]

If any Democratic challenger had a meaningful chance at the endorsement of organized labor in a gubernatorial election against Rockefeller it was Arthur Goldberg in the 1970 contest. Goldberg had been a union lawyer for two decades prior to his appointment as John Kennedy's secretary of labor. But, in spite of having been a friend of labor all his life, Goldberg failed to get the endorsement of organized labor in his bid to unseat the Governor. An explanation offered by Kramer and Roberts for this apparent unseemly occurrence is that the annual convention of New York State's Federation of Labor in September of 1970 was "rigged" by Rockefeller supporters Harry Van Arsdale and the state's AFL-CIO President Ray Corbett.[131] Although the executive committee of the AFL-CIO had voted 16-8 (with 11 of the votes coming from men representing the building and construction trades) to recommend an endorsement of Rockefeller, supporters of Goldberg believed they had a chance when the entire convention would vote. However, a list of delegates accredited to the convention was not provided for the Goldberg supporters, and the convention hall was packed with at least 2,500 persons when only 1,303 delegates were registered, Goldberg partisans demanded a roll-call vote, but Corbett adjourned the convention without taking a vote. The next morning the executive committee declared an unprecedented recess of one month. Subsequently, the convention was reconvened, and Rockefeller received the endorsement. These events prompted Victor Gotbaum of the Municipal Workers Union, and a Goldberg partisan, to confront Van Arsdale and declare: "You stole it from us, Harry."[132]

In addition to wooing support from labor, Rockefeller made direct and aggressive appeals to various ethnic groups, many of whom were normally loyal to the Democratic party. That his efforts met with some success is illustrated by the fact that he was consistently able to win from 20 to 30 percent of the votes of New York blacks, Jews, and Spanish-speaking voters, groups who usually give only about 5 percent, 12 percent, and 15 percent of their votes respectively to Republican presidential candidates.[133]

The second given of Rockefeller's political environment was the existence of strong third parties. New York has a multi-party system that includes two smaller parties, the Liberal party and the Conservative party. the Liberal party predates the Rockefeller administration and had its genesis on the national level in the American Labor party (ALP) and the Social Demcratic Federation of the 1930s. Evolving from a break with the socialists in 1936, and composed of many New York City unions, the ALP was formed for the purpose of pressuring President Franklin D. Roosevelt to live up to his New Deal policies.[134] After deciding that the ALP was being infiltrated by Communists and their sympathizers, union leaders David Dubinsky and Alex Rose decided to leave the ALP in 1944 and form the Liberal party.[135] The Liberals were able to carry the state for Harry Truman in 1948 but have not had such striking success since.

The Conservative party is of more recent vintage. With Richard Nixon's defeat at the hands of John Kennedy in 1960 and the election of liberal Republicans Rockefeller and Javits in New York, a group of New York City businessmen came to the conclusion that the country was headed in an unacceptable liberal direction and that Governor Rockefeller and Senator Javits did not represent the true interests of conservative Republicans.[136] Consequently, by 1962, in time to challenge the Governor in his first reelection attempt, the Conservative party was formed to protest the "liberal establishment" and the policies of the Rockefeller administration.[137] According to Kevin Phillips, party membership consisted largely of blue-collar and lower-middle-class Catholics who were "dedicated to the notion that the Governor was no good for the Republican party or the state of New York."[138] It is clear that the defeat of Governor Rockefeller was a central goal of the Conservatives.[139]

Given the aims of its leaders and the composition of its membership, the Conservative party provided a direct challenge to Rockefeller and therefore drew ample attention from him. Faced with the fact that the party had managed to achieve a place on the statewide ballot and the fact that some Republican candidates for the state legislature and local offices wanted Conservative endorsement, he, nevertheless, refused to cooperate with the Conservatives. For example, he did not agree to a joint slate of presidential electors until 1972.[140] However, he did seek to show that he was personally acceptable to moderate and conservative Republicans. For example, following a speech in 1962 by Conservative gubernatorial candidate David B. Jacquith in Syracuse, the Governor prevailed upon former President Dwight David Eisenhower to endorse his own candidacy in the same location.[141] In upstate areas he emphasized that he had administrated the state along sound conservative lines.[142] He had Judson Morhouse prepare and distribute to Republican leaders throughout the state a list of twenty-eight "conservative" fiscal measures and measures related to business that his administration had taken during his first term.[143] To show that he was not opposed to Conservative candidates, he endorsed William E. Miller for a seat in the House of Representatives. Miller was a leading member of the conservative wing of the Republican party and was later to become the vice-presidential running mate to Senator Barry Goldwater in 1964.[144] The Governor also included in his legislative programs items that he believed Conservatives could support, for example, a 10 percent rebate in the state income tax in 1961.[145] And in the 1966 and 1970 campaigns he included issues such as "law and order." Moreover, he refrained from directly attacking Conservative candidates for legislative seats. For example, in 1970, Arthur Goldberg challenged him to repudiate James Buckley, who was endorsed by the Conservatives for the U.S. Senate.[146] Instead, Rockefeller merely said he was supporting Republican nominee Charles Goodell. Indeed, Kramer and Roberts have pointed out that "Rockefeller seemed to be running with both men; the state was flooded with two sets of campaign buttons, one saying 'Rockefeller-Goodell,' the other 'Rockefeller-Buckley.'"[147] Although the conservative party became an important force in the politics of New York State, Rockefeller's tactics for dealing with the challenge it represented are generally regarded as having minimized the damage to his own electoral career.

Tabulations of votes for third parties in statewide elections during the period 1958-1972 are shown in Table 3.5, a table that also shows endorsements of Democratic and Republican candidates by the Conservative and Liberal parties respectively. With the exception of the election of 1966, one in which the Liberal party nominated its own candidate, Franklin D. Roosevelt Jr., it was unable to deliver more than 300,000 votes, approximately 4 percent of the total votes cast. Unlike the Liberal party, the Conservative party was able to make dramatic gains in the number of votes it could deliver to the candidates it nominated for governor. (The Conser-

Table 3.5
The Third Party Vote in New York State Elections: 1958-1972*

	CONSERVATIVES			LIBERALS		
	Candidate Endorsement			Candidate Endorsement		
	Republican	Conservative	Democratic	Republican	Liberal	Democratic
1958						
Governor						283,926
Senator						175,051
1960						
President						406,176
Associate Justice-Court of Appeals				423,035		
1962						
Governor		141,877				242,675
Attorney General						214,069
1964						
President						342,432
Senator		212,216				284,646

SOURCE: *Empire State Report* (April 1977), p. 169.

*This table shows how many votes candidates endorsed by the Conservative and Liberal parties received in statewide elections during the Rockefeller years. Some candidates receiving third party votes also were endorsed by one of the major parties. The "candidate endorsement" columns indicate the party lines on which the candidates receiving third party votes were running.

Table 3.5—*Continued*

1965					
Court of Appeals		207,387			207,942
1966					
Governor		510,023		507,234	
Chief Judge-Court of Appeals		365,575		326,377	
1968					
President					311,622
Senator		1,139,402		458,936	
1970					
Governor		422,514			263,071
Senator		2,179,640	255,793		
Attorney General		409,169	321,865		
1972					
President	368,136				183,128
Associate Justice		365,575		326,377	

vative party ran its own candidates for governor in every gubernatorial election in which it participated. The Liberal party usually endorsed the Democratic nominee.)

The combined vote of the two third parties was greatest in the 1966 election, 16.5 percent of the total cast, when both ran their own candidates against the Governor. Conservative Paul Adams received 8.3 percent of the total votes in that year and Liberal Roosevelt received 8.2 percent. It is a tribute to Rockefeller as a campaigner that he was able to win reelection by a margin of almost 400,000 votes. Both third parties had given him their "best shots" and yet he had prevailed.

A third distinguishing aspect of the political environment in New York is the changing nature of its political geography. Table 3.6 shows eight categories defined by geographic location and type of community and lists their respective contributions to the total vote in four gubernatorial elections from 1958 through 1970. In each election, New York City is the largest contributor, the category "New York City Suburban Towns" is second, and the category "Remainder of Upstate" is third.

When the categories are rank ordered, the upstate central city suburbs can be seen to have contributed a smaller share of the total votes than the upstate central cities for the 1958 and 1962 elections. However, the opposite was the case for the 1966 and 1970 contests. Furthermore, the suburban towns around New York City contributed a larger share to the total votes with each successive election, whereas the percentage of the total vote cast in New York City decreased. Less significant changes occurred in other categories.

An examination of vote patterns by John Gargan revealed that aggregate votes cast in the suburbs of upstate central cities increased by 32.6 percent over the four elections and that total votes cast in the suburbs around New York City increased by 32.0 percent.[148] Gargan noted that, over the four elections, the "natural constituencies of the Republican Party" in the state increased their contribution to the total vote from 43 percent to 50 percent, while the areas of traditional Democratic party strength declined in contribution to the total vote in the state from 53 percent to 46 percent.[149]

It can be argued that shifts in where the votes were during the Rockefeller years can be seen as working to the Governor's advantage since the shifts were in the direction of traditionally Republican strongholds. However, at least, this development could be viewed as only a partial explanation for Rockefeller's electoral successes. Because the Republican party remained a minority party in New York, it was essential for Rockefeller to maintain control of the Republican party vote and thus appeal to voters with conservative tendencies and at the same time appeal to Democratic voters, traditionally a more liberal group.

The fourth given with which Rockefeller had to cope was the diverse population of the state and the potentially conflicting demands that such diversity can bring upon the chief political executive of the state.

Table 3.6
Percentage of Major Party Vote Cast in Gubernatorial Elections in New York State by Geographical Location and Type of Community: 1958, 1962, 1966, 1970*

	1958	1962	1966	1970
New York City	41.1	41.7	40.8	38.1
New York City Satellite Cities	3.3	3.2	3.2	3.2
Upstate Central Cities	11.6	10.5	9.3	8.5
Upstate Satellite Cities	.8	.7	.7	.7
Upstate Independent Cities	4.8	4.4	4.1	4.1
New York City Suburban Towns	15.1	16.0	17.5	18.8
Upstate Central City Suburban Towns	8.5	8.9	9.6	10.7
Reminder of Upstate	14.9	14.6	14.8	16.0
Total	100.1	100.0	100.0	100.1

SOURCE: John J. Gargan, "Nelson Rockefeller and New York Election Politics: 1958-1970," *Center for Urban Regionalism* (Kent State University, 1972).

*The major party vote is defined as the vote for Democratic, Liberal, and Republican candidates for 1958. For the other three elections, the major party vote also includes votes cast for Conservative candidates.

Rockefeller's victories in four gubernatorial elections indicate that he was able to organize and execute campaigns responsive to the diversity of the state's population. His ability to fashion appeals that were effective in diverse constituencies is amply reflected by the data in the last column of Table 3.7. This statistical measure, known as the coefficient of variability, provides a way of comparing the degree to which the percentages of Republican votes in the sixty-two counties of the state vary. (Smaller coefficients indicate a greater clustering of scores about the mean and thus less variability "across counties.") The coefficients for the four gubernatorial elections support the view that by 1970 Rockefeller had become a candidate who was able to elicit "roughly similar aggregate responses" in all areas and types of places in New York.[150] (Although the coefficients of variability in Table 3.7 reflect only voting by county, the fact is that county boundaries in New York State often reflect various types of diversity, for example, type of community. Thus the five counties making up New York City are highly urbanized compared to the vast majority of upstate counties.)

Perhaps even more impressive than his apparent success in fashioning appeals that were effective in attracting the support of diverse constituencies was the ability of Nelson Rockefeller to maintain strong electoral appeal over the span of four elections. As Table 3.7 shows, his margin of victory over Democratic opponents reached a peak in his fourth and last election (1970), both in terms of absolute numbers of votes and the proportion of total votes represented by his margin.

Table 3.7
Selected Statistics for New York State Gubernatorial Elections: 1958-1970

YEAR	TOTAL VOTES IN GUBERNATORIAL ELECTIONS	ROCKEFELLER MARGIN OF VOTES OVER DEMOCRATIC OPPONENT	ROCKEFELLER MARGIN AS A PERCENTAGE OF TOTAL VOTES CAST	ROCKEFELLER PERCENTAGE OF MAJOR PARTY VOTE**	MEAN ROCKEFELLER PERCENTAGE OF MAJOR PARTY VOTE FOR SIXTY-TWO COUNTIES	COEFFICIENT OF VARIABILITY*
1958	5,795,481	557,062	9.6	55.0	65.0	.131
1962	5,921,503	518,218	8.9	53.4	62.0	.122
1966	6,159,568	392,263	5.2	44.8	50.1	.125
1970	6,150,477	714,859	11.6	52.4	57.7	.118

*The coefficient of variability is a standardized measure that allows for the comparison of the dispersion of scores in several distributions with different means. The smaller the coefficient, the greater the clustering around the mean. See John J. Gargan, "Nelson Rockefeller and New York State Election Politics: 1958-1970," *Center for Urban Regionalism* (Kent State University, 1972).

**For 1958 the major party vote is defined as the vote for Democratic, Liberal, and Republican candidates. For the other three elections, the major party vote also includes votes cast for Conservative party candidates.

In sum, the recipe for Rockefeller's success in his campaigns for Governor would include numerous elements: abundant amounts of money to finance campaigns; introduction and implementation of programs that had appeal to the respective elements constituting the state's diverse population; an ability to build an expert and loyal staff and to allow that staff to advise in the planning, management, and execution of his campaign; extensive use of highly refined information gathering and processing techniques; heavy reliance on sophisticated mass media efforts to inform voters what the Governor had done for them and to attack opponents; an ability to exploit personal qualities such as warmth, charm, vigor, and leadership; use of a personal style campaigning while downplaying partisan affiliation; and an astuteness at tailoring campaign promises to "fit" various groupings within the state's population.[151] During his time in office, Rockefeller was able to seize control of, and dominate, the Republican party, contribute to and capitalize upon factionalism within the Democratic party, and respond effectively to challenges posed by the Conservative and Liberal parties in the state.

Campaign Failures: Pursuing the Nomination for President

Various observers have concluded that Nelson Rockefeller had wanted to be president since his childhood. Whether they are correct is open to some doubt. However, it seems difficult to reject Frank Gervasi's conclusion that Rockefeller's "campaign in 1958 was a calculated first overt step up the ladder of a dream that led to the White House."[152]

Rockefeller's first inaugural address left little doubt that his political perspective was indeed quite broad. Speaking to a joint session of the New York Legislature, he intoned, "we are nearing...what could be a fatal testing time for free men—and freedom itself—everywhere.... Our neighborhood is the world [and]...I speak to you today...as a citizen of America and of the free world."[153] The Governor's focus on the nation and the world, and his theme of world survival, which occupied one half of the address, is one especially common to presidential addresses. He expressed his vision for New York in this way: "We cannot hope to spur economic progress and prosperity in the world unless...New York can itself help to lead America herself toward new horizons of well-being and equal opportunities for all our citizens."[154] This statement suggests that the Governor viewed the state of New York as a laboratory in which he would provide an indication of what a Rockefeller presidency would resemble. After fifteen years as Governor, he resigned with a reiteration of his concern with the nation and its problems.

I have great faith in our country, and I am optimistic about the future, but we can't take that future for granted. Therefore, after long and careful consideration, I have concluded that I can render a greater public service to the people of New York and the nation by devoting myself to the work of two bipartisan national commissions."[155]

Beginning in 1960, Rockefeller attempted to secure the nomination of the Republican party for the presidency on three successive occasions. Each effort met with failure. In the face of his electoral successes in New York, numerous postmortems were conducted on Rockefeller's unsuccessful quests to secure the nomination for the presidency. A typical, but perhaps, superficial, explanation for his failures is represented by the judgement of Kramer and Roberts: "The New York Nelson was bold, innovative, crafty, combative; the national Nelson...was indecisive, erratic, and inept."[156] Elaborating on the view of Kramer and Roberts, the *Empire State Report* noted that "Rockefeller never really ran for the Republican *nomination* for President. He admits that he ran primarily for the *general election* [emphasis added]. Rockefeller never adjusted to the necessities of preconvention organizing, relying too much on the media blitz and not enough on precinct organization."[157] With respect to the initial campaign, Theodore White has written that the Governor "stumbled through an amateurish effort to wrest the Presidential nomination in 1960 from Richard Nixon."[158]

It is commonly supposed that a large, industrial state such as New York provides an ideal base from which to seek a presidential nomination. As noted above, a succession of the state's governors had, in fact, won nomination. However, what might be ideal for a Democrat is not necessarily ideal for a Republican. Furthermore, conditions that support successful attempts by Republicans can change with the passage of time. On this score, Connery and Benjamin note that the imperatives of New York State politics which Rockefeller mastered mitigated against his attempts to secure the nomination of the Republican party nationally.[159] For example, they maintain that the Governor was required to be more liberal than Tom Dewey and that his activist approach and commitment to big government and massive spending did not appeal to the midwestern and far-western states and local GOP leaders who were in control of the party at the time he sought the presidential nomination.[160] Garry Wills agrees that the Governor might have met with greater success had he been more of a party man.[161]

A cluster of explanations for Rockefeller's abortive attempts to win the nomination relate to aspects of his personal life and political beliefs. For example, Wills concluded that "no matter what his other qualifications, Rockefeller was eliminated from consideration in 1964 by his divorce and precipitate remarriage...(Ronald Reagan, of course, hopes that divorce and less precipitate remarriage will be no obstacle in the future)."[162] "Branded a wife-stealer by the old moralists in his campaign against Barry Goldwater," writes Theodore H. White, "he and his new wife were openly mocked in public...."[163] White notes that:

The frank and open acceptance of a new marriage was a breach with the general indulgence of the hypocrisy of politics, and in Rockefeller's case was particularly hazardous. Rockefeller occupied few hearts as a politican; he had earned his strength by winning respect for his talents as a governor, his ability to solve problems and administer affairs. As a politician, he appealed to the mind-not the emotions. No counter reserve of emotion was available to him now that the emotions of millions of women across America were engaged against him.[164]

There were early and ominous signs that Nelson Rockefeller's political beliefs and values would meet resistance from the conservative wing of the Republican party and that, as a consequence, his leadership would face repudiation. A statement appearing in the *National Review* on the occasion of Rockefeller's attempt to secure the Republican gubernatorial nomination in 1958 chided, "Nowhere does Rockefeller speak up for Republican principles of free, non-statist society. His position seems to be that Republicans can do a superior job of implementing a Democratic philosophy of government."[165] Casting Rockefeller against the background of the Republican party, Theodore White offers the following silhouette:

Rockefeller is a man who believes in aggressive innovative managerial government in a Republican Party which distrusts government. What he shares with fellow Republicans is basically the old belief that the ethical engines of work, study, thrift, perseverance and striving flourish best in the American system of free, private enterprise. Rockefeller, however, also believes that government must act, at whatever cost, positively, to service this free-enterprise system, and that the roots of the system lie in individual opportunity which government must enlarge. The rank and file of the Republican Party believe that less action the government takes and the less interference it imposes on private enterprise, the better government is.[166]

During the 1960s Rockefeller's acceptance of big government may have become an increasing liability with respect to winning the Republican nomination. By 1968, maintains Wills, Republican delegates at Miami were not receptive to Rockefeller's views; such views were losing currency even in the Democratic party.

His whole effort was to shift the Republican Party's psychology back to the "starting" moment. That would be difficult in any circumstances. In 1968, it was impossible. He meant to compete with the Democrats in terms of New Deal rhetoric, just when the most vital elements of the Democratic Party were ready to stress, once more, the free motion of runners on their imaginary track. The glamour boys were trying to imitate John Kennedy, the new Roosevelt. But the Kennedy era had passed; no one knew that better than the Kennedy's shrewder heirs. Rockefeller's attempt to become a Republicanized version of the Kennedyized version of FDR was an exercise in irrelevance.[167]

Contrary to the Governor's confident and assertive behavior in campaigns conducted in New York were national efforts in which he appeared to lack confidence and a sure touch. A practice of entering and withdrawing from races gives the impression that he was merely *reacting* to events in a somewhat erratic manner. An outline of significant events pertaining to the politics of the Republican party and presidential contests from 1960-1976, including major decisions by the Governor, is provided in Table 3.8. In none of the campaigns did the Governor get into the race and stay in. In 1960, after his preliminary explorations indicated that Richard Nixons's forces had placed seemingly insurmountable obstacles in the path of a successful candidacy, Rockefeller announced a "definite and final" decision that he would not be a candidate for the presidential nomination.[168] Five months later, however, after the U-2 crisis and failure of the U.S./USSR Summit Conference, the Governor indicated he would accept the nomination if drafted by the convention. In November of 1963, the Governor was the first candidate of either party to announce for the 1964 presidential nomination. However, he withdrew a month prior to the Republican National Convention in mid-June. The pattern of announcements for 1968 was similar to that of 1960; in late March Rockefeller declared that he was not a candidate only to rescind his declaration and actively enter the contest five weeks later.

As Arnold Steinberg notes, the nominating process can be viewed as a marketing enterprise with the candidates as products and the convention delegates as consumers.[169] Of course, each national convention produces a nominee who consequently can be judged to have sold himself as an acceptable product. One element each of the successful Republican nominees in the 1960s had in common was an "extended campaign." For example, as vice-president, Richard Nixon had served his party well for eight years prior to his election in 1960 as his party's designee for the presidency. He had built up credits as he traveled throughout the country on speaking tours, helping local Republican organizations raise money. Following Barry Goldwater's defeat in 1964, Nixon again worked the circuit for his party for four years prior to securing the 1968 nomination.[170] Theodore White suggests that Nixon received the nomination in 1960 partly because the Republican party owed its loyalty to one who had worked hard for the party as opposed to one who was viewed as a sudden interloper, namely, Nelson Rockefeller.[171] The argument that the 1968 nomination also represented remuneration to Nixon for services rendered has also been made.

Goldwater, too, had made his move early. On Goldwater's behalf, Clifford White had begun in 1961 to plan and organize a campaign. White had "marked out each state with its dates, its procedures and its delegate count."[172] He and his volunteers had produced a "masterpiece of politics" for "their planning was more careful, more debated, and earlier begun than that of any previous Presidential campaign."[173]

The examples discussed would suggest that it is important for a candidate to begin a concerted effort well in advance of a convention and to enter the

Table 3.8
Significant Dates and Events Relating to Governor Rockefeller's Quest for the Republican Nomination: 1959-1975

DATE	EVENT
	1960 Nomination
January 1, 1959	Rockefeller takes oath as Governor of New York
June 1959	Rockefeller begins presidential exploration privately
December 12, 1959	Rockefeller begins Midwest and Southwest tour before finally deciding to challenge Nixon
December 26, 1959	Rockefeller withdraws from competition for the 1960 Republican presidential nomination
May 1-5, 1960	U.S. U-2 spyplane downed in USSR
May 16, 1960	Khrushchev cancels Eisenhower visit to USSR
Mid-May 1960	Morhouse-Rockefeller might conceivably be available for presidential draft
Late May 1960	Rockefeller acknowledges he is open to draft to meet the national crisis
June 8, 1960	Rockefeller statement repudiating policies of the Eisenhower administration: Republican party must articulate what it proposes to meet national crisis
July 22, 1960	Rockefeller/Nixon "Compact of Fifth Avenue"
July 27, 1960	Richard M. Nixon nominated on first ballot in Chicago (Nixon, 1321 votes; Goldwater, 10)
November 8, 1960	Nixon loses New York to Kennedy (52.5% to 47.3%) and loses presidential election
	1964 Nomination
May 4, 1963	Rockefeller marriage to Margaretta "Happy" Fitler Murphy
July 14, 1963	"A Matter of Principle Manifesto" by Rockefeller against "ultra-conservative fringe groups"
November 7, 1963	Rockefeller announces candidacy for Republican presidential nomination
November 22, 1963	President John F. Kennedy assassinated
January 3, 1964	Barry Goldwater announces candidacy for presidential nomination
March 10, 1964	Henry Cabot Lodge wins New Hampshire primary
May 15, 1964	Rockefeller wins Oregon primary
May 30, 1964	Nelson Rockefeller, Jr., born

Table 3.8—*Continued*
Significant Dates and Events Relating to Governor Rockefeller's Quest for the Republican Nomination: 1959-1975

DATE	EVENT
	1964 Nomination (continued)
June 2, 1964	Goldwater wins California primary
June 15, 1964	Rockefeller withdraws from race; urges unity behind Scranton
July 14, 1964	Rockefeller moves adoption of amendment against extremism at Republican National Convention
July 15, 1964	Barry Goldwater nominated on first ballot at Cow Palace (Goldwater 883, Scranton 213, Rockefeller 144)
November 3, 1964	Goldwater loses New York to Johnson (68.6% to 31.3%) and loses presidential election
	1968 Nomination
May, 1966	Rockefeller endorses George Romney
November 21, 1966	Rockefeller and Romney agree that governors must seek "consensus" not "ideology"
January 7, 1967	Richard Nixon has first planning session
February 1, 1968	Nixon announces candidacy for Republican nomination
March 21, 1968	Rockefeller announces that he is not a presidential candidate
March 31, 1968	President Johnson announces he will not seek reelection
April 11, 1968	Rockefeller becomes available for the nomination
April 30, 1968	Rockefeller announces active candidacy for the Republican nomination
May 20, 1968	Rockefeller meets privately with Reagan in New Orleans (no ideological gulf between them)
July 4, 1968	Reagan meets with Emmet Hughes (Rockefeller surrogate) and notes he is in the race to stay
August 5, 1968	Ronald Reagan formally announces candidacy for nomination
August 8, 1968	Richard Nixon nominated on first ballot in Miami (Nixon 692; Rockefeller 277; Reagan 182)
November 5, 1968	Nixon loses New York to Humphrey (49.8% to 44.3%) but wins presidential election

Table 3.8—*Continued*
Significant Dates and Events Relating to Governor Rockefeller's Quest for the Republican Nomination: 1959-1975

DATE	EVENT
	Afterward
December 11, 1973	Rockefeller resigns as Governor
August 20, 1974	President Ford nominates Rockefeller as vice president
December 19, 1974	Rockefeller takes oath as vice president
November 3, 1975	Rockefeller withdraws from consideration as President Ford's running mate in 1976

fray in a decisive fashion. On the other hand, vacillation would appear to carry the seeds of defeat. However, it is possible that the "delegates as consumers" were not in the market for the Rockefeller product, qua product, however steadfast and decisive the sales campaign might have been. In fact, it is our contention that the delegates did not wish to "purchase" what Nelson Rockefeller offered to them.

According to Steinberg, the candidate as product offers to the consumers "his physical appearance, image, rhetoric, issue positions, background experience, education, party affiliation, [and] family."[174] Given these components of the product, it would seem that the delegates might find a Rockefeller very attractive. Each time he had come to the convention, he came as a demonstrated winner. In addition to being vigorous and physically attractive, he was a proven and enthusiastic campaigner in a state with a diverse population and pressing problems, many of which were also national problems. Furthermore, he had established in New York "a record of activism unparalleled in the state's history."[175] He was both imaginative problem solver and experienced leader. The Governor told the delegates thrice assembled that he was a real Republican and that "his brand of Republicanism was best for the Party and the country."[176] He could win a national election was the Governor's claim; all the delegates had to do was to nominate him and let him try.

But any fight for the nomination is at once a fight to establish leadership and party unity. The candidate offers leadership in stressing issues with which he is personally identified, but also attempts to generate party unity by stressing issues of importance to the consumers. The simple truth is that Rockefeller failed at unifying the Republican party behind his leadership. In each attempt to win the nomination, he offered a challenge rather than accommodation and, as he saw it, capitulation. In 1960 he condemned the party's leadership and doubted its future vigor; in 1964 he attacked the supporters of his major rival as fanatical, ultraconservative, extremist fringe groups. In 1968, as in his first campaign to secure the nomination, he argued that without his leadership the party did not have a candidate who was aggressive and innovative or a competent manager.[177]

Perhaps as trouble-producing as any aspect of the Rockefeller candidacy were his efforts to remake the party in his own image. Examples from 1960 and 1964 illustrate the point. Prior to reentering the 1960 race, Rockefeller adopted the Churchillian posture of "the leader who raises alarm" by releasing this statement.

> I am deeply convinced and deeply concerned that those now assuming control of the Republican Party have failed to make clear where this party is heading and where it proposes to lead the nation. Now is the time to face and weigh these facts....[178]

At the 1964 convention Rockefeller made a vigorous attack on the course the party was taking as it united behind Barry Goldwater. The thoughts he uttered on that occasion were developed in "A Matter of Principle Manifesto" issued a year before the convention. The substance of his concerns are indicated by the following excerpts.

> While as a party and as a people we have been keenly aware of the grave threat to [our] principles posed by international Communism, I have now come to the conclusion that many of us have been taking too lightly the growing danger to these very same principles from the radical right. I am now convinced that, unless the vast majority of Republicans who subscribe to these principles are aroused from their present inaction—whether this inaction stems from complacency, from fear or from a fantastically short-sighted opportunism—the Republican Party is in real danger of subversion by a radical, well financed and highly disciplined minority.
>
> For it has become crystal clear that the vociferous and well-drilled extremist elements boring within the party utterly reject these fundamental principles of our heritage. They are, in fact, embarked on a determined and ruthless effort to take over the party, its platform and its candidates on their own terms—terms that are wholly alien to the sound and honest conservatism that has based the party in the best of a century's traditions, to the sound and honest liberalism that has kept the party abreast of human needs in a changing world, and to the broad middle course that accommodates the mainstream of Republican principles.
>
> This cannot be allowed to happen. The continuing commitment of the Republican Party to its historic principles, including the fundamental dedication to equality of opportunity for all men, cannot and must not be betrayed. No temptation of political gain through cynical expediency can be permitted to becloud our commitment to principle and purpose.
>
> The issue that confronts the Republican Party today is the gravest in its history. The party stands today at the crossroads of its destiny. Its destiny is to save the nation by first saving itself.[179]

Even in 1973, a few days before he resigned as Governor, Rockefeller was still trying to convince Republican leaders that their party must change its outlook so that it would become, in effect, the sort of party that he had created in New York State. As he said,

> I believe in the Republican Party; I believe in its purposes, I believe in the ideals that gave it birth in Lincoln's time and that sustain it today....In considering the challenge and responsibility which comfort us as Republicans—first we...are a minority party...[and] cannot win elections unless we understand the economic and social problems faced by people of all walks of life. We have got to be sure that they know we are aware of and concerned about their problems. We have got to be creative and imaginative in dealing with these problems.
>
> Secondly...we cannot afford the luxury of a monolithic point of view. We have got to be a party that has the wisdom, the understanding, and the courage to be confronted with honest differences in its ranks; that can argue and debate and then come to sound, conservative solutions.
>
> Third, with this approach and an 'Open Door' policy we can truly be the party of the people—the party Lincoln—and once again become the Majority Party in America.
>
> Fourth, if we are to be an effective instrument of political leadership and action for this country during these critical times, we have to concentrate on the objective of unity within diversity....
>
> Fifth, at a moment in history when people feel over-whelmed by the pace of change with less and less power to control their own destiny, this kind of strength was even more needed. It is essential to provide effective leadership that will command the confidence to the people—leadeship with a vision of the future—leadership with faith in America and our unique heritage![180]

Electoral Successes and Failures and Rockefeller's Life Strategy

It is true that being elected Governor of New York presented Nelson Rockefeller with an excellent opportunity to pursue his life strategy of identifying problems significant for the well-being and survival of the United States and offering solutions to those problems. However, although many of the problems he addressed as Governor of New York were also national problems, there were some national problems, national security for example, that his role of Governor allowed him to address only to a limited extent. Furthermore, the capacity to directly apply his solutions on a national scale was denied to him as Governor. Of course, Rockefeller was well aware that only the presidency offered him the opportunity to genuinely fulfill his life strategy. And thus he never really ceased to seek the presidency until he succumbed to pressure and withdrew himself from consideration as Gerald Ford's running mate for the 1976 election.[181]

The strength of Rockefeller's desire to be president is demonstrated not only by the fact that he gave up his ambition only after almost two decades of effort involving the expenditure of tremendous amounts of money and personal energy, but by the fact that he was deeply affected by his failures. As William Kennedy observed. Rockefeller candidly admitted one of the biggest causes of his "72 blues": "You know, it was the first time in 12 years I wasn't running for President."[182]

When confronted in 1977 with the question why he did not succeed in capturing the nomination for president, Rockefeller replied with a somewhat defensive argument, one that conveniently ignored the tremendous exertion that he had, in fact, made in the years he was Governor.

> I have got to be honest with you. I really didn't organize for it. I have watched in the last few years McGovern and Carter and these people who have spent three and four years working, planning and working the system to get the nomination.
>
> Of course, Nixon, too, took four years off. He was in a law firm, but he spent his time supporting Senators, making speeches. I was governor and that was a very interesting job, exciting job, and so I never really made a full-time occupation out of trying to get the nomination, because I was interested in government rather than politics....
>
> You know, I'm not basically a politician. A lot of people think I am. But politics is not my metier. My real interest is in solving people's problems.[183]

Nevertheless, there is some degree of truth in the explanation that Rockefeller offered for his failure. Despite the fact that he made his share of "campaign speeches," poured money into preconvention politics, and sometimes tailored his views to "fit the times," especially in the 1970s, we believe that in some important respects it can be said that he wanted the nomination only *on his own terms*.

One explanation for the Governor's refusal to accommodate himself to the views of those who controlled access to the Republican nomination is that it was primarily a product of simple willfulness. For example, Theodore White assessed the Governor's willfulness in this manner; "He was the one of the most stubborn men in the world; he was also one of the most high-principled....But what in other men would be simple arrogance was in Rockefeller the direct and abrupt expression of motives which since he knew them to be good he expected all other men to accept as good also."[184] However, the fact that the Governor divorced his first wife in 1962 and proceeded to marry again, this time to the former Mrs. Margaretta Murphy, less than a year prior to the first presidential primaries in 1964 is an indication that something more than mere willfulness motivated his reluctance to accommodate himself to the realities of presidential nominating politics. It is a fact that divorce and marriage to a recently divorced woman constituted serious political handicaps in the early 1960s. As one dispassionate observer noted, "the marriage can only be read historically as triumph of love over political ambition."[185]

Aside from "willfulness" and "love," we would argue that a more fundamental reason why Nelson Rockefeller would not make the accommodations necessary to woo the often-conservative leaders of the Republican party involves his life strategy and his conception of the role of the president. Seeing the proper role of the president as the activist problem solver, a role that should only be filled by an activist leader such as himself, and being committed to the ultimate exercise of his life strategy as president, he could not, and would not, abandon the rhetoric or behavior approporiate to this conception and commitment. Furthermore, he seems to have found it extremely difficult to believe that his performance as an activist problem solver would not bring him the presidency.

4 Executive Style: Structuring the Decision Process and Relating to Advisers

A superficial examination of the structure within which Nelson Rockefeller functioned as Governor might produce an impression of organizational chaos. However, a closer look would change that impression. Furthermore, it would reveal that the organizational arrangements that the Governor utilized were grounded not only in intuition and past experience but in a set of ideas about the needs of an executive, a set of ideas some of which he articulated from time to time and others which he did not. The substance of these ideas will be revealed in the course of this chapter and the next. However, a description of the way in which the Governor structured his administration and related to advisers and other officials should be prefaced by comments on some of the key aspects of his "executive philosophy."

One very important element in his executive philosophy was Rockefeller's belief that an executive must not allow himself to become excessively dependent upon any one adviser or set of advisers. A second was that an executive must utilize his own staff aggressively in order to give direction to, and maintain control over, the larger bureaucracy lying within his jurisdiction. Relevant to the organizational arrangements Rockefeller employed are the three principles he set forth in response to a direct question asking him to identify what he thought were the key aspects of his "style as an executive." To some degree the two ideas just identified are implicit in his response.

> First, and foremost, in my opinion is getting really top-flight people associated with you both in the staff work, which includes planning, and in the administration. Without that you are absolutely handicapped because of the size and complexity of government. Second, is to have a good organizational structure that is clear, and everybody knows what the policy is.... Then they know what their responsibilities are in carrying that out and that they have a clear delegation of authority for the car-

rying out of policy within a framework and that they are going to be backed up by the chief executive so that they are not uncertain.... [They] also [know] that they are not going to be cut in on by somebody else where there is rivalry and confusion and overlapping of functions. And the third is the development of policy by the use of task forces comprising outstanding people from different experiences who have abilities, knowledge, and integrity and who come together to study a problem facing the State to make recommendations.[1]

As a careful reading of the quotation will show, the Governor makes reference to three of the six elements which we see as constituting the total constellation of entities that he utilized for advice and other assistance as Governor. These three are staff officials, agency heads (those in "administration," as he put it), and "task forces," the latter often consisting partly or wholly of personnel drawn from the private sector. Other elements that occupied an important position in the decision process as it was structured by the Governor include: (1) agency heads *not* subject to the Governor's appointment or removal who were, nevertheless, drawn into the decision process as advisers (including the lieutenant governor and the attorney general); (2) personal friends or advisers (including Republican party officials) and members of his family; and (3) legislative leaders, both Republican and Democratic, depending upon political circumstances. One purpose of this chapter is to discuss the roles of those who occupied all but the last one of the categories.[2]

Any consideration of those aspects of Nelson Rockefeller's executive style that involve dealing with people must begin with the recognition that he was a gregarious person who had little need for solitude. His love of being with people emerged in widely varying contexts, from the hustle and bustle of campaigning to the small meetings at which important decisions were made on policies and programs. There are those in public life for whom meetings are anathema, but Nelson Rockefeller was definitely not one of them. He was clearly invigorated by interaction with others.[3]

As was the case in his earliest governmental experience, it was difficult to draw a line between Nelson Rockefeller's business as Governor and pleasure as private individual. Those who worked with him invariably comment on the fact that the Governor drew no clear line between business and pleasure. Working meals, idea sessions on Sundays and holidays, discussions running late into the evenings; all were typical of his routine. Indeed, for Rockefeller, business *was* pleasure. As one former commissioner pointed out, the Governor did few things that were strictly recreational. He almost never traveled for pleasure nor did he usually attend concerts or the theater.[4]

Observations attesting to the Governor's merging of pleasure and work are entirely consistent with his own characterization of himself as being primarily concerned with solving problems. It is doubtful that any public official could have worked harder at his job than did Nelson Rockefeller.[5] Very few of his personal advisers and staff failed to comment on his monumental capacity for work. What Nelson Rockefeller demanded of himself, he demanded of others. And his advisers and staff complied, for it was difficult to decline to take leave of their families on holidays, work late into the night, and be constantly on call. If the Governor was willing to drive himself constantly, then others would be expected to do the same. Commenting on his experiences with the Governor, including a role as the major architect for the South Mall Complex in Albany, long time associate and friend Wallace Harrison half-lamented, "we have worked together for fifty years. He is pleasant but I had to work hard. There was no give in him on that side. He demands his full money's worth."[6]

Being relatively uninterested in the details of state government, whether they involved drafting legislation, preparing budgets, or administering programs, the Governor wanted top staff aides and agency heads who had the experience and competence to "take care of the details."[7] As one former senior staff aide put it, "He valued ready expertise, persons who knew the process and how to use it to free him to initiate and sell his ideas without worrying about day-to-day matters."[8]

Clearly, Rockefeller seems to have beem more comfortable with the outgoing, practical doers than with those who inclined toward contemplation. He admired the man who could "get things done." Recounting his successful efforts to get Edward Logue to become head of the Urban Development Corporation, he recalled, "I was very impressed with the guy—tough, realistic guy."[9] Likewise, in praising the man who was his closest aide, William Ronan, for "taking on" the Port Authority of New York, Rockefeller admiringly pointed out that Dr. Ronan was "the only one who had the guts and the 'balls'..."to challenge that organization.[10]

The nature of the Governor's relationships to his top staff and agency heads varied considerably. Generally speaking, however, he drew a clear line between those who were "staff" and those who were friends. As one former staff member observed, Rockefeller was "a very private person. There was a public, political animal, the Governor, and a Rockefeller. The staff saw the Governor, not the Rockefeller."[11] This view is confirmed by the observation of a former department head. As he pointed out, the Governor would take staff and agency officials out to meals, introduce them to his family, and have them stay over at his apartment in New York City. However, in most cases there were certain "unspoken boundaries" to the relationships between Rockefeller and state officials. For example, he noted that one would not address the Governor as "Nelson," nor would one invite him to one's home. As he put it, "You never had the feeling that he was your pal."[12]

There were important exceptions to the general rule that the Governor kept a careful distance between himself and top aides. A few staff members crossed the unspoken boundary and became friends of the Governor. The most notable example was William Ronan who served as secretary to the Governor and later as head of the Metropolitan Transportation Authority. The Governor described Ronan as "a long time personal friend and associate."[13]

Staff Aides and Staff Units

Among his own appointees, the Governor's key staff consisted of the occupants of five positions. Although other officials had access to him, the bulk of his day-to-day interaction with those in state service was with those persons occupying those five positions. This was in line with his view that "I don't think anybody, any executive whether he is Governor or business, can deal with too many people very effectively."[14]

The five positions were secretary to the Governor, counsel to the Governor, director of the Division of the Budget, director of communications, and appointments secretary.[15] The key to understanding the Governor's staffing arrangements is to recognize that the person serving as secretary to the Governor functioned as a chief of staff, one who had the broadest possible responsibilties relating to both administration and policy.[16] Of the five key staff members all but one, the appointments secretary, had a major role in policy determination and the development and launching of new programs. With the exception of the director of communications, an official primarily concerned with the presentation, packaging, and selling of new programs, the remainding three staff members were likely to become involved at almost any stage in the development of policies and programs. Given Rockefeller's focus on developing and selling new programs, it is not surprising that these three, along with the lieutenant governor and the attorney general, were the most common attendees at the Governor's staff meetings.[17]

Rockefeller's decision to enlarge the traditional responsibilities of the secretary to the Governor was intimately related to his activist bent, his "executive philosophy," his life strategy, and his past experiences in the federal government. Both he and the secretary, William Ronan, were eager to organize the Governor's office in such a way so as to insure that the many proposals made in the 1958 campaign would be carried out. As Ronan put it, he saw his responsibility as chief of staff as "overseeing departmental functions from a policy point of view in an effort to have departments implement the Governor's campaign promises."[18]

Both Rockefeller and Ronan doubted the capacity and willingness of state agencies to translate ideas into programs on the scale that the Governor envisaged. One reason for their view was that agencies were heavily burdened with administrative tasks. Another reason, as cited by another secretary to the Governor, was Ronan's belief that "until an idea was nurtured, you would not dare turn it over to an agency because any new idea which cuts against the grain is squashed at birth."[19]

The Governor and Ronan also doubted the ability of other key staff units, the Office of the Counsel and Division of the Budget, to play the key role in program development. In addition to the fact that each had other major responsibilities, the preparation and execution of the state's budget in the case of the latter and the preparation of legislation in the case of the former, there were other more specific objections concerning the Budget Division. Traditionally a respected, powerful, and professional unit, it was viewed as ill-equipped to encourage program innovation and a potential obstacle to proposals for change, especially those that would cost substantial money.[20] One of Rockefeller's top aides characterized the division as follows: "The Budget Division had become very bureaucratic; there were many Dewey-oriented people there and they had to be circumvented."[21]

The Governor himself was known to have a generally skeptical view of budget offices as a result of his experiences in the federal government, especially his experience in the Eisenhower administration. Believing that a budget unit would necessarily emphasize fiscal constraints when considering new programs, Rockefeller gave expression to those views in 1960 when he appeared before a Senate subcommittee to propose the creation of the position of executive assistant to the president and a Bureau of Program and Planning. This bureau was to be part of a recommended Office of Executive Management and to contain units similar to the existing Bureau of the Budget. The executive assistant to the president was to be the director of the new office.[22] Rockefeller supported his recommendations with observations of his federal government experience, but by 1960 he had already implemented in New York a pattern resembling his recommendations for the federal government.

In response to a question from Subcommittee member Edward Muskie as to whether the Bureau and the Treasury Department had "overstepped their proper bounds in exercising undue influence on policy," Rockefeller articulated his philosophy concerning the role of a budget unit and shed some light on his motives for choosing the organizational format he had put into operation in New York.

> Let us say you are a Cabinet officer and you want to come over and talk about new plans and meeting problems. If you go solely to the Bureau as the only instrument in the White House to which you can present your case, there is a natural aversion to entering into some new program which is going to involve a pretty big commitment over the years. However, if you can discuss that with the man who is above both the

Bureau of the Budget and the Planning and Programming Division, you can get a more balanced decision. He can balance these things out as seen from the total national interest. You not only have to do this within a department but between departments.[23]

The Governor's comments strongly suggest that he viewed the post of executive assistant to the president as a chief of staff for domestic affairs.[24]

In the position of secretary to the Governor, Rockefeller established a position very similar to what he had recommended for the federal government, and although he had not created an "Office of Executive Management," he had created a small staff of "programs associates." With the creation of this group, the Governor now had at his disposal units that could carry out all the functions that the president's Advisory Committee had recommended be placed within a federal Office of Executive Management.[25] More significantly, the program staff was to provide him with a reliable means for developing ideas into proposals that could be advanced as part of his annual legislative program. The initial "theory," one that was never altered, was to staff the unit with generalists who, unencumbered by administrative, budget, or other responsibilities, could focus their attention upon providing assistance to the Governor in developing and launching programs. Directly responsible to the secretary to the Governor, the program associates were to play a key role in overcoming the inertia and resistance to change that typically characterize bureaucracies.[26] It was the kind of unit that an activist like Nelson Rockefeller could have been expected to create, and it represented a major innovation in New York State government.[27]

With the possible exception of his fourth term, it is clear that Rockefeller's major thrust was the creation and launching of new programs. It is also clear that the secretary and the program staff, consisting of about five or six persons at any given time, became the key elements in coordinating and giving focus to the activities that made this thrust possible. As chief of staff to a governor whose central interest was the development and launching of new programs, it was almost inevitable that the secretary to the Governor would play a key role in coordinating the program innovation process. In addition, the two individuals who filled the position during the first twelve years of the administration, William Ronan and Alton Marshall, were themselves oriented toward questions of policy and programs as being their key functions.[28]

Program associates served the secretary and the Governor as the main link to two important sources of ideas for new programs: state agencies and the study groups or so-called "task forces" that were frequently utilized by Rockefeller, especially during his first term. As William Ronan put it, "The primary importance of the program staff was to give focus to substantive issues and provide incentive and pressure to come up with a solution or solutions to problems."[29]

As a consequence of Rockefeller's orientation and his utilization of the secretary to the Governor as a chief of staff, the program associates superseded budget examiners as the main communications link between state agencies and the Governor. This resulted in the program associates playing roles as "trouble-shooters" on day-to-day questions relating in any way to policy questions.

Aside from identifying issues and problems and recommending solutions in the form of new programs, program associates played a role in other tasks related to developing and launching programs. The bulk of these tasks can be grouped under the heading of what was commonly referred to as "staffing-out" an idea. Staffing-out involved more than merely describing the elements of an idea for a program, a step that in itself sometimes formed the basis for a decision to include a proposal in the Governor's annual message to the legislature, an address that contained most of the items constituting his legislative program. Specifically, staffing-out involved analyzing "what it would take to put a program into operation" as well as identifying the ramifications of a program.[30]

In order to do a thorough staffing-out of any proposed program, an associate would have to determine questions such as: what new legislative authority might be needed; how much money would be required and how might it be provided; what administrative actions, for example, new regulations, administrative guidelines or organizational changes, might be necessary; and how many new positions might be required.

Generally speaking, a program associate did not develop legislation in the course of conducting a thorough analysis for a proposed program. Rather, he would develop ideas for legislation and specify what types of legal authority would have to be included in whatever bills might ultimately be drafted. During much of the Rockefeller administration, "costing-out" proposals for new programs was handled in a very informal way. As William Ronan put it, "Budget involvement was not a formal process. Usually everything was costed-out as ballpark estimates. The program staff had informal relationships with budget people, and it was this informal relationship that was utilized."[31] The role of the program associates in costing-out programs is further emphasized by the admission of one high-level official in the Budget Division: "In some cases [prior to 1971] the Budget Division didn't even get to cost out proposed programs."[32]

Program associates often obtained assistance from agency officials in estimating program costs, and they usually did so in determining requirements for administrative resources. The degree of reliance on agencies varied according to the nature of the policy area. For example, one former program associate noted that he and his colleagues were dependent on the Department of Environmental Conservation for detailed work on program proposals in its policy area: "DEC is full of scientific and biological expertise. The program associates often implemented ideas, but DEC usually drew up the details."[33]

In addition to staffing-out ideas for programs, program associates occasionally became involved in some activities that were performed *after* a proposal for a program had been advanced by the Governor, for example, drafting legislation, rules, regulations, and other administrative directives necessary for launching a program. Such involvement usually occurred with respect to programs of high priority, for example, those in which the Governor had a special interest or those that involved more than one department such as major reorganizations. The Pure Waters Program (1965) is a good example of a pet program of the Governor that also happened to involve the interests of two departments, namely the departments of Health and Conservation. The program staff was involved in the development of this program from the inception of the idea to the time that the program was ready to be put into operation. Specifically, two program associates worked closely with a high-level Health Department official and a staff member of the Office of Local Government as a team in the development of the program.

The creation of the Department of Environmental Conservation (1970) is a good example of another high priority program that involved taking both programs and administrative units from one department and transferring them to another. Specifically, creation of DEC involved transferring to it the Pure Waters Program and other pollution control programs and personnel from the Environmental Health Services unit of the Health Department. The core of the new department was to be the old Department of Conservation. In cases such as this, it should be obvious that a "losing" department could not be relied upon to develop and prepare for implementation a program that it might view as harmful to its interests. An official of one of the departments affected by the creation of the Pure Waters Program and the creation of DEC noted that the development of these two programs was done by the program staff and the "winning" department to the substantial exclusion of the "losing" department.

The "cases" described represent good examples of situations in which a program associate became the "resident expert" on a program and thus played a central role at every stage in the process of developing and launching that program.[34] However, except for routine "trouble-shooting" tasks, the activities of program associates tended to end once a new program had been successfully launched. Relatively little attention was given to monitoring the continuing administration of programs.[35]

The Office of the Counsel to the Governor was a second key staff unit. Among its routine responsibilities were assisting in legislative liaison and advising the Governor on legal and technical questions concerning bills sent by the legislature for his approval.[36] Another was carrying out the "legislative clearance" function with respect to proposals that state agencies wanted to have introduced in the legislature.

The most important functions performed by the counsel's office were two. The first was the preparation of required legislation after a decision had been made to incorporate a program in the legislative program.[37] The second was to assist the Governor by working with legislative leaders and their staffs in order to take legislative positions into account in drafting legislation and working for its passage. The key role that the office played in the legislative process put the counsel in a position to render essential service to the Governor.

Possessed of a long and proud history as custodian of the state's executive budget process, the Division of the Budget carried out many crucial functions during the Rockefeller administration, including preparation of the details of the executive budget that the Governor presented each year for the legislature's approval, and routine functions related to budget execution. However, the role of the Budget Division in the Rockefeller administration was less important than it had been in some preceding administrations, including those of Governors Harriman and Dewey. As previously noted, it is widely recognized that prior to the Governor's last term, the Budget Division was often asked for its views only *after* decisions had been made to advance a proposal. This was so despite the fact that the Budget Director was considered a member of the Governor's top staff and had good access to Rockefeller. Because of the Governor's own preferences and the conceptions of their role held by those who served as director, it is generally accepted that the director did not consistantly provide the Governor with critical analyses of program ideas based on fiscal or programmatic considerations. Acknowledging that the Division of the Budget was "not the strongest voice in big program decisions," a former director noted two reasons for this fact. The first was that "the Governor didn't want to hear about obstacles" and the second was that he depended on the director of the budget "to find a way."[38]

As noted earlier, the philosophy underlying the creation of the program staff was that the capacity to find and develop ideas for programs would be inhibited by institutional concerns for fiscal and legal limitations.[39] Understandably, the emphasis among program associates was on initiating new programs and not on identifying reasons why there should be no new programs. This was especially true prior to 1971 during the tenure of the first two secretaries to the Governor. The role of the Budget Division in the program innovation process remained fundamentally the same until about 1971, the time at which Rockefeller began to emphasize the necessity for cutting state spending.[40] The official who noted that the Budget Division sometimes had not been given the opportunity to cost-out proposed programs prior to 1971 stated that "budget now [1972] sees all proposed legislation."[41]

The Budget Division had a substantial role in activities necessary to put a program into operation. Just as the counsel's office was responsible for drafting legislation after the Governor made a decision to propose a program, the Budget Division was responsible for finding ways to finance programs and for preparing requests for necessary appropriations. Because it was responsible for executing the State's budget, the division was more deeply involved in the day-to-day administration of state programs than was the program staff and the Office of the Counsel.

Having always been convinced of the importance of public relations, it is not surprising that Nelson Rockefeller considered those responsible for his public relations as Governor to constitute one of the five key components of his staff. The positions that were concerned with public relations were the director of communications (a position created in 1969 to give formal status to the role played by the Governor's long-time public relations adviser Hugh Morrow), the press secretary, and several assistant press secretaries and speech writers. (Total staff size was in the range of fourteen to eighteen persons.)[42] The core responsibilities of these staff members related to gaining the support necessary to achieve legislative and/or electoral sanction for programs proposed by the Governor. Whether a vote of the legislature or a referendum was necessary, selling the program through the media could be of crucial importance. This is one reason that the director of communications was present at most of the meetings at which decisions were made as to which programs the Governor would propose. As the Governor explained, the director would be alert to the public relations implications of a proposal. "Communications will say 'look, I think this is very dangerous from this point of view or could be misunderstood or you ought to have a press conference tomorrow and explain what you are doing.'"[43]

The work of the Office of Communications as it related to program proposals culminated in the preparation of the annual message to the legislature and the several special messages to the legislature that together contained the Governor's legislative package for a given year. Routine functions of the Office of Communications included the preparation of press releases as well as speeches, the conduct of day-to-day relations with the media, and the operation of a clearance mechanism for all press releases prepared by state agencies.

The last of the key staff units that the Governor cited was that operated by the appointments secretary. The smallest of the staff units, this office's responsibility primarily involved the filling of relatively high-level positions, both paid and unpaid, that had sufficient status to be of importance to Rockefeller and of interest to Republican party officials as rewards for party faithful. Because of the existence of an extensive civil service system, it is generally agreed that New York does not have available the huge quantities of patronage positions that the size of its bureaucracy might suggest. (Connery and Benjamin estimate that the Governor's office exercised positive control over only about 8,000 positions, 2,000 of which might be "available" in any given year. However, they note the existence of a "large number'' of other patronage jobs available to be filled by ''lower levels in the administrative and political processes.'')[44] The job of the appointments secretary was primarily one of representing the interests of the Governor in the process of working with the Republican state chairman and county leaders in making recommendations for appointments. This meant taking into account Rockefeller's mandate that professional competence not be sacrificed to ''political'' considerations in filling top administrative positions and his insistence on personally choosing appointees to positions that he considered crucial to his own policy goals.[45]

In addition to the five staff units which existed throughout his administration, the Governor was served by a ''planning'' unit created in 1966. This unit, the Office of Planning Coordination (OPC), was the successor to the Office for Regional Development. The latter was the product of a mixture of motives. For example, the Governor was interested in developing a ''chart room'' as part of some sort of planning unit. Under ORD's first director, an architect who had been deeply involved in Rockefeller projects since before the war, the agency's focus broadened to include land-use planning in general. Eventually the agency produced a preliminary master plan for the state.

The office also helped develop the concept of regional meetings, meetings for which Rockefeller would occasionally travel to different areas of the state, accompanied by top staff and selected agency heads. Serving political as well as ''educational'' purposes, the meetings focused on the content of state programs and activities and their impact on a region. Utilizing extensive data contained in so-called ''black books'' prepared by the program staff, the Office for Regional Development would prepare charts, graphs, and slides that the Governor would use in his presentation. Beginning as meetings attended primarily by groups of local officials and community leaders, in later years they evolved into ''town meetings'' also attended by as many as several hundred local citizens. Although the Governor occasionally was confronted by hostile questioners, the meetings provided him with an important source of public exposure and a chance to test the depth of public opinion on issues, especially those related to local concerns.[46]

In 1966 the Office for Regional Development was moved out of the Executive Chamber and given a statuatory basis as the state's central planning agency. Growing rapidly to a staff of about 200 persons by 1971, the agency had a number of key responsibilities including joint responsibility (with the Division of the Budget) for the planning-programming-budgeting system the state introduced in 1965, providing a data base of all planning efforts by state agencies, and producing a full-fledged master plan to consist of physical, economic, and social components.

Always viewed with some hostility by the legislature as well as by the Budget Division and the program staff, OPC was severely trimmed in size in 1971. It became the Office of Planning Services and was stripped of most of its larger planning functions.[47]

State Agencies and "Independent" Authorities

Although the Governor had relative freedom to structure the duties and responsibilities of the staff units discussed above, both he and those units faced the necessity of operating within the environment constituted by the existence of twenty line departments, numerous "miscellaneous" boards and commissions, and a large number of semi-independent authorities.[48] As noted earlier in this chapter, the Rockefeller administration was one in which power and influence were centralized to a substantial degree in the Governor's office. This fact is symbolized by the prominent role given to the secretary to the Governor and his program staff and by the fact that Rockefeller's attention was generally fixed on the generation of massive, expensive, and innovative programs as opposed to the routine, but often important, concerns arising from the everyday operation of state agencies. However, a number of facts must be kept in mind with respect to the importance of the roles of traditional state agencies.

The first of these facts is that every chief executive is dependent on the bureaucracy no matter how large and skilled his own staff. If nothing else, agencies have some capacity to "drag their feet" with respect to programs generated at the top. In addition, those agencies that are the repository of highly specialized expertise are able to offer invaluable assistance in supplying, and developing, ideas for new programs. Second, Rockefeller sometimes took action to make state agencies vigorous forces for change. In most cases such action involved creation of "independent" authorities standing outside the normal structure of state government or reorganization of existing state agencies.[49] Creation of authorities gave him a virtual "second bureaucracy," one responsible to him but free of normal legislative constraints including those inherent in the appropriations powers exercised with respect to state agencies standing within the normal structure of government.[50] When determined to make an agency a force for change, the Governor would often appoint as its head a person of established reputation who had a strong personal commitment to him.[51] Thus by a combination of steps beyond the creation of a strong central staff, Rockefeller was able to transcend many of the obstacles inherent in dealing with an established bureaucracy.

As is probably inevitable in any administration in which a chief executive makes aggressive use of strong central staff units in attempts to energize a bureaucracy, tensions between staff and agencies arose under Rockefeller. Acknowledging that relationships between the program staff and the departments were sometimes poor, William Ronan noted that "the problem was a feeling that new people were looking at them and telling them to get their jobs done."[52] And Alton Marshall placed the blame for tensions on staff efforts to have departments put the Governor's programs into operation. As he said, "The whip cracking for implementation caused the departments goddamn headaches. The program associates did not always have a feel for administrative problems."[53]

Even highly professionalized departments with substantial political support were usually unsuccessful in opposing program ideas that emanated from the Governor's office. For example, the Health Department unsuccessfully resisted some aspects of the reorganization proposal that created the new Department of Environmental Conservation and the Governor's proposal that the state license chiropractors.[54] However, departments generally confined opposition to elements in the Governor's legislative program to in-house efforts. To attempt a public battle would have risked the wrath of a powerful chief executive.[55]

In general, the Governor viewed agency heads as representing resources to be harnessed to his purposes. He expected them to do everything they could to achive his goals as Governor. Thus, when he "went on the road" for "town meetings," he regularly took along a number of commissioners, including sometimes the commissioner of education, even though the latter was not his appointee. Consistent with his view of agency heads as part of his team and his expectation that established agencies are not usually sources of innovative ideas, Rockefeller tended to view agencies primarily as implementors of his programs.

The Governor's "Personal Team:" A Modern Day Court

As students of organizations have occasionally observed, a chief executive often discovers a need to build a team of advisers and aides who can be counted on to give first priority to assisting him in carrying out his goals. Without intending any negative connotation, Lewis Dexter has referred to such a collection of persons as the "court" of a modern executive. As Dexter puts it, the members of such a court "operate ideally to carry out the purposes and wishes of the top man—they are responsible to the man, not to their own careers or the professionally defined task."[56]

Like most other executives, Rockefeller did have a personal team or court that he used to help solve the problems all executives share, for example, energizing and controlling the established bureaucracy. However, because of the tremendous personal resources to which he had access, resources of wealth, contacts, experience, and prestige, he had a personal team that was not confined by the boundaries of state government. One way to conceptualize the relative position of the personal team vis-à-vis the Governor is a series of concentric rings such as is depicted in Figure 1. Ring Number Four (the outer ring) consists of all those state officials, bureaucrats, and legislators who had some ability to influence policy that might be of interest to a governor. (All those in government who are regarded as members of the remaining, more exclusive rings, are, by definition, regarded as members of this, the most exclusive, ring.)

Ring Number Three consists of all those in the fourth ring who were oriented primarily toward serving the Governor and his purposes. In addi-

Figure 1
Governor Rockefeller's Personal Team in the Context of State Officialdom

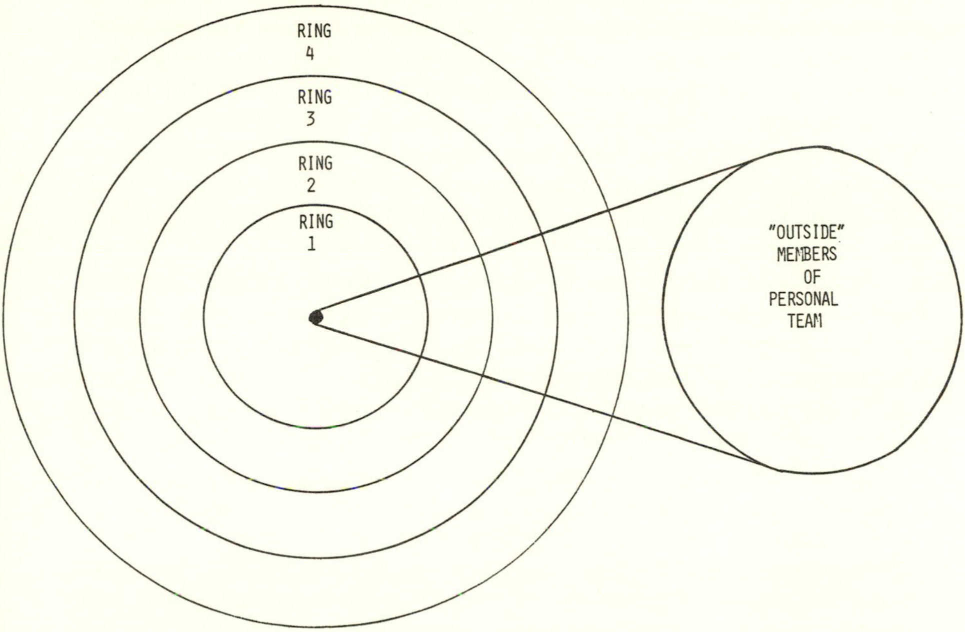

Ring 4

The most inclusive grouping; includes all those state officials, bureaucrats, and legislators who might have had some ability to influence policy and decisions of interest to Governor Rockefeller.

Ring 3

Includes all those in Ring 4 who were oriented primarily toward serving Governor Rockefeller and his purposes. In addition to those in staff units in the Executive Chamber and top-level officials in staff agencies such as the Division of the Budget, this ring includes agency heads and other top-level officials who were loyal to the Governor if for no other reason than the fact that they owed their appointment to him.

Ring 2

Includes all those in Ring 3 who had a special tie to Governor Rockefeller other than the fact that he had appointed them or could dismiss them.

Ring 1

Includes all members of Governor Rockefeller's personal team, including those from both inside and outside state government who were his personal friends or his "professional friends" (political/policy/technical confidants).

tion to most of the persons serving on the staff within the executive chamber, this ring includes those agency heads and other top level agency personnel who were loyal to the Governor, if for no other reason than the fact that they owed their appointments to him.[57] While those who occupy this second ring are assumed to have been generally loyal to Rockefeller and his interests, some of them did have competing loyalties and orientations. For example, the head of a very professionally oriented department such as the Department of Health would necessarily have to respond to the interests of the medical profession, a very powerful interest to which departments of health in every state must accommodate themselves.

Ring Number Two consists of all those in the third ring who had some special tie to the Governor other than the mere fact that he had appointed them and could dismiss them. Such reasons would include significant dependence on Rockefeller for future career advancement or an absence of potential competing role orientations (this latter condition would apply to most members of the program staff, for example).

Ring Number One consists of Nelson Rockefeller's "personal team," a personal team made up of all those members of the other three rings who were also either his personal friends or his "professional friends" and those persons from outside state government who as personal friends, professional friends, or relatives, assisted him in one way or another in carrying out his official role. The distinction between the categories of "personal friend" and "professional friend" (political/policy/technical confidant) is that the latter category includes those whose relationship to the Governor, which, while close, related primarily to "business." (Business is defined as involving matters which might be termed political, policy related, or "technical.") The Governor used those in the category of professional friend for various purposes, for example, as providers of technical expertise, ideas for programs or political advice, and as extensions of himself or his "eyes and ears." As one former agency head put it, Rockefeller viewed certain people as "dispensers of useful information."[58]

Rockefeller turned also to personal friends as sources of information and other forms of assistance. However, he also seems to have turned to personal friends for what only they could provide, the very human benefits of friendship. All those who were members of the Governor's personal team, whether personal friends or professional friends, were recipients of the prestige and other benefits implicit in their special access to Rockefeller. Needless to say, all had a high degree of loyalty to him.

As noted in Chapter 2's discussion of Rockefeller's needs, we take the position that his need to "achieve" by solving problems was more central to his personality than other needs such as affection, respect, or adulation. Nevertheless, it is clear that he derived pleasure as well as stimulation from being in the company of those he considered his friends. The fact that he also seems to have regarded his personal friends as persons who could help him achieve his goals as a problem solver is consistent with the attention he gave to his central need to "solve problems."[59]

There is good reason to believe that the Governor had a strong need to rely on a personal friend as his chief adviser. This view is supported by the fact that William Ronan continued to serve as the Governor's most important adviser even after he left his post as secretary to become head of the Metropolitan Transportation Authority. And although the Governor replaced Ronan with a man who was not a personal friend, Alton Marshal, he later replaced Marshall with another personal friend, Robert Douglass. Marshall himself felt that the Governor's choice of Douglass as secretary was motivated by a desire to achieve the sort of intimate relationship which Rockefeller had with Ronan. (As Marshall explained, Douglass was in some ways like a son to the Governor.)[60]

A long-time veteran of state government, Marshall was regarded by others as a man who was "really interested in making state government work." There are some indications that Marshall allowed this orientation toward "making things work" take precedence over his role as a member of the Governor's personal team. For example, Marshall himself noted that he saw as one of his major jobs that of keeping "bad ideas" away from Rockefeller.[61]

Only three of the Governor's key staff members, William Ronan, Hugh Morrow, and Robert Douglass, became his personal friends. However, several others who occupied key staff positions were professional friends, and thus by definition, part of Rockefeller's personal team.[62] The more prominent of these were Alton Marshall, Norman Hurd, and Richard Dunham. Although the Governor's personal team included several professional friends who were heads of operating agencies, only two agency heads, Joseph Murphy, commissioner of taxation and finance for the first ten years of the administration, and Keith McHugh, commissioner of commerce for much of the administration, were Rockefeller's personal friends. Among agency heads who were professional friends were Louis Lefkowitz (attorney general), James Gaynor (commissioner of housing and community renewal), General A. C. O'Hara (commissioner of the office of general services), Herman Hilleboe (commissioner of health), Alan Miller (commissioner of mental hygiene), and Henry Diamond (commissioner of environmental conservation). In addition to Lt. Governor Malcolm Wilson, Rockefeller could be expected to turn to the above state officials for advice and assistance. Some individuals, Ronan for example, were consulted on a broad range of matters while others, Miller, for example, were consulted primarily on matters relating to their areas of technical competence.

Consistent with his practice while in the federal service, the Governor utilized as part of his personal team several persons outside New York State government. Most were personal friends, a few were professional friends, but all were important members of his team. Included among such persons were some of those who had been part of his original group on Latin America, most notably Wallace K. Harrison, George Dudley, and Oscar Reubhausen. Others to whom the Governor turned for counsel included former Republican State Chairman William Pfeiffer; nuclear scientist Edward Teller; Detlev Bronk, president of Rockefeller University; Henry Kissinger; speech writer Emmet John Hughes; pollster Lloyd Free; the Governor's personal physician, osteopath Kenneth Riland; Republican State Chairman George Hinman; Labor adviser Victor Borella; and former baseball star Jackie Robinson.[63] Two of Rockefeller's brothers, David and Laurance, were also part of the Governor's personal team.[64]

Although a few of these "outside" members of Rockefeller's personal team advised him primarily concerning matters relating to national policy or politics, for example, Kissinger, Hughes, and Hinman, many assisted him in some way with state problems. For example, Riland is credited with selling the Governor on the idea for state licensing of chiropractors, and Teller is credited with some of the ideas relating to the Governor's proposals for protection against nuclear fallout. David and Laurance Rockefeller gave advice in their respective areas of expertise, finance and conservation, while Borella and Robinson served as important links to labor and the black community respectively.

Motivating Advisers, Aides, and Officials

One of the strengths of Nelson Rockefeller as a chief executive was his ability to motivate people, both insiders and outsiders. This capacity to evoke personal loyalty enabled him to reach beyond personal friends for people who would see their roles primarily as one of service to him and his goals. Acutely aware of the need to maintain loyalty among his staff and top-level agency officials, Rockefeller listed loyalty as one of the four qualities he most valued. As he stated,

> [I wanted] loyalty to me so that I knew that if they accepted the job they would carry out the policies of the administration. As long as they would do that then I would back them on their actions in administration. I insisted that they operate within the framework of policy as established.[65]

We see Rockefeller's capacity to maintain loyalty among others as based on three distinct resources. The first was his position as a member of one of the world's wealthiest and most powerful families. This enabled him to confer both material benefits and prestige upon those he wanted to bring into his service. One might legitimately ask whether any monarch has ever exceeded Nelson Rockefeller in his capacity to distribute a combination of material rewards and prestige. Three good examples of his uses of material rewards to retain and/or reward those who served in state government with him are represented by the cases of William Ronan, Edward Logue, and Alton Marshall. All three received gifts and/or loans. Not only did Ronan receive more than $500,000 in gifts and forgiven loans, he was named to a $100,000 position as senior adviser to the Rockefeller family in 1973.[66]

Edward Logue described in very practical terms the reasons for the Governor's gift and loan to him. According to Logue, he would have been financially unable to accept appointment as head of the Urban Development Corporation in the absence of the Governor's assistance. A gift of $31,389 was used to pay off debts he owed from his campaign for the Boston mayoralty and a loan of $145,000 was used to purchase a cooperative apartment in New York City.[67] Rockefeller's financial assistance to Logue was typical of his "can-do" approach and his willingness to use personal financial resources for his direct benefit as a chief executive and for what he regarded as the benefit of the state.

The case of Alton Marshall differs from that of Ronan and Logue in that gifts to Marshall were not given primarily out of close personal friendship or with the motive of attracting someone to state service. Rather it appears to have been the case of "taking care of" a very senior staff member who gave enormous quantities of time and energy to a demanding role. In addition to receiving gifts in the form of forgiven loans amounting to $306,867, Marshall was made president of Rockefeller Center upon his resignation.[68]

As is apparent from the listing in Table 4.1 of those members of his personal team who received loans and gifts, the Governor also rendered financial assistance to members of his personal team whose involvement in state government was only secondary to their primary careers. For example, Wallace Harrison, Kenneth Riland, and George Dudley all received interest-bearing loans, loans that they paid back in full.[69] Henry Kissinger received a gift of $50,000 in 1969, prior to his beginning service as secretary of state under President Nixon. According to Rockefeller, he gave the gift to help Kissinger in a time of financial stress resulting from a divorce settlement.[70] And while he received no loans, Oscar Ruebhausen is reported to have been the recipient of a $130,000 trust established on his behalf.[71]

At House and Senate hearings on his confirmation as vice-president, Rockefeller came under heavy criticism for his gifts and loans to those who were, had been, or were about to become, state employees. Although he was forced to state that he would not engage in such a practice as vice-president, the Governor vigorously defended his gifts and loans as having been appropriate expressions of friendship and compassion. The legal argument he submitted to rebut charges that the gifts might have violated a state statute prohibiting rewards for official conduct emphasized such a position.[72] In

Table 4.1
Governor Rockefeller's Gifts and Loans to Members of His Personal Team*

RECIPIENT	GIFTS**	LOANS	TOTAL
Victor Borella	$100,000		$100,000
Henry L. Diamond	100,006		100,006
George A. Dudley		$ 6,000	6,000
James W. Gaynor	107,000		107,000
Wallace K. Harrison		60,000	60,000
Henry A. Kissinger	50,000		50,000
Edward J. Logue	31,389	145,000	176,389
Alton G. Marshall	306,867		306,867
Hugh Morrow	135,000	30,000	165,000
Joseph H. Murphy	200,000		200,000
W. Kenneth Riland		6,000	6,000
William J. Ronan	550,000		550,000
Total	$1,580,262	$247,000	$1,827,262

SOURCE: U.S., Congress, House, Committee on the Judiciary, *Hearings on Nomination of Nelson A. Rockefeller to be Vice President of the United States*, 93rd Cong., 2d sess., 1974, pp. 36-38.

*Includes gifts and loans made while Rockefeller was Governor and loans made before he was Governor but not repaid in full until some date during his term in office.

**Includes loans that were later forgiven.

his oral defense, Rockefeller gave support to our argument that he did indeed view staff members as part of a personal team devoted primarily to his career goals.

> My sole intent [in giving gifts and forgiving loans] was to respond to cases of personal hardship, family need, or out of pure friendship.
>
> Whatever success I may have had, in both public and private life, has been due to the character, brilliance and continuing sense of common purpose of those with whom I have been associated.[73]

His official position as Governor gave Rockefeller the usual sorts of prerogatives that he could use to motivate and reward staff members as well as outside members of his personal team. Of primary importance was his ability to make appointments that represented career advancement. In addition to the many full-time, policy-level positions available in "normal" state agencies, he had available the "second bureaucracy" of authorities, many of which he had created, and a multitude of boards and commissions requiring only part-time service. Appointments to the latter often conferred substantial benefits to appointees in terms of both publicity and prestige. In addition, appointment to such bodies could serve to increase the retirement benefits of persons who had otherwise retired from state service. For example, by being appointed a member of the Board of Directors of the Power Authority of the State of New York after his resignation as head of the Metropolitan Transportation Authority, William Ronan would continue to accumulate years of state service that would have the effect of increasing the retirement benefits he would eventually receive.[74]

Aside from the possibility that the Governor might appoint them to some choice position, members of his staff enjoyed the kind of visibility within state government and elsewhere that could lead to a career advancement for many of them. This in itself constituted a valuable resource to the Governor in that it contributed to staff morale.

The third resource that Rockefeller was able to utilize in motivating those who served him stands apart from the material rewards and rewards of prestige that he was able to offer because of his position as Governor and his position as one of the Rockefellers. That resource consisted of a personal style and personal characteristics that many people found emotionally satisfying. It is impossible to know the exact degree to which Rockefeller's use of his personality was calculated to inspire people or win their support and the degree to which he attracted people merely by being himself. But there is little doubt that both phenomena were at work.

Rockefeller's ability to project warmth to large groups of people, for example, large groups at campaign gatherings, is well-known. But many of those who worked with him also comment upon the degree of warmth that he projected in small meetings, including individual meetings. For example, former Commissioner of Corrections Russell Oswald said "he was warm, not just friendly the way he was with everyone when out campaigning."[75] A veteran state bureaucrat who took on important operating responsibilities as a Rockefeller appointee late in the administration also testified to this aspect of the Governor's appeal. "He had a great ability to communicate warmth to an individual. He would put his arm around you and this *made you feel good!*"[76]

As was noted in Chapter 2 in a discussion of Rockefeller's childhood, he tended to be in the center of things. Just as his young brothers were drawn to him, just as those who were part of his Latin American group were drawn to him, so were those who worked closest with him when he was Governor as well as a national figure. It is undoubtedly true that many men are strongly drawn toward leaders who wield great power. However, it seems clear that men were also drawn to Rockefeller because of the qualities of personality that he was able to project, his warmth, his energy, his self-confidence, and the excitement that he radiated. Perhaps there is no better testimony to the emotional rewards that he could provide than remarks Henry Kissinger made when delivering a eulogy in Riverside Church. "That Nelson Rockefeller is dead is both shattering and inconceivable. One thought him indestructible, so overpowering was he in his energy, warmth and capacity of love."[77] Kissinger went on to give a specific example of what Rockefeller's presence meant to him when the former returned from foreign missions. "He would give me a bearhug—saying little—and drive off. By these gestures he infused strength and hope and inspiration."[78] One of Rockefeller's oldest and closest associates, Oscar Ruebhausen, made comments that suggest feelings similar to those of Kissinger. "He [Rockefeller] has a superb sense of confidence and he instills this sense of confidence in others.... Really, inside he is not that optimistic, but the outward optimism has a tremendous influence on others."[79]

As natural as his personal appeal may have been, Rockefeller worked at motivating members of his staff and agency heads, trying to make them feel that they were part of the team. As a former counsel testified, "he would let them [staff members] know that he respected, recognized, and appreciated what they were doing. He would go out of his way to thank them. This was his way of securing support and encouraging openness and frankness."[80]

Taking into account all three of the resources discussed here, the Governor's status as a Rockefeller, his official prerogatives as Governor, and his possession and exploitation of valuable personal qualities, it can justifiably be concluded that his capacity to maintain a loyal and hard-working personal team was almost unique in the history of American politics.

Meetings and More Meetings

Viewed from one perspective, Nelson Rockefeller's career as Governor was an endless round of meetings, ranging all the way from formal, full-scale "cabinet meetings" with thirty or more persons present to individual conferences with top-level staff, agency heads, and members of his personal team. A brief sketch of the types of meetings and their various purposes is basic to a full understanding of their significance to the Governor and his style as an executive.[81]

Typically, cabinet meetings were the largest meetings that the Governor held, with attendance of about fifty. In addition to Rockefeller and his top staff, the heads of all twenty departments plus an equal number of other large state agencies were in attendance. Scheduled only a few times each year, the meetings were not working sessions at which decisions on programs and other matters were made. Rather, the Governor used the meetings primarily as a forum for explaining policies, programs, and decisions that had already been made. Consistent with his practice throughout his career in government, Rockefeller often made heavy use of slides to present graphs and charts at cabinet meetings and other large meetings. He did this not only because he felt it an effective method of communicating with others, but perhaps more important, because this method was the one that was most effective for him as a presenter. With the history of reading difficulties associated with his childhood dyslexia, he never felt comfortable with a conventional written text. As the man who served as his chart man put it,

> The Governor was a very visual person. He would use slide presentations as a script, in effect. Putting together the presentation would prepare him for making the presentation at a meeting or a TV appearance. He would have a lot of information in his head and a given slide would help him bring out that information. He would say 'May I have the next slide please,' and then he could add a lot to what the slide showed.[82]

As noted above, the Governor's meetings with his top staff, unlike cabinet meetings, were held on a frequent and regular basis.[83] Although the most frequent attendees of staff meetings were the secretary, the counsel, the budget director, the lieutenant governor, and the attorney general, attendance varied substantially depending on the nature of subjects under consideration. However, the people named here were almost always present when final discussions were held as to which programs were to be proposed in the Governor's annual legislative program. And once decisions had been made on what to propose, the director of communications as well as the chief speech writer would attend meetings at which the content of the annual message was planned and necessary legislation presented to the Governor.

In addition to group meetings, Rockefeller had numerous meetings with individuals. (The Governor's appointments calendar for 1966 lists 257 meetings between the Governor and individuals. The calendar does not include the normal day-to-day interchanges that he had with the secretary to the Governor.) Many of these appointments were with political figures, publishers and journalists, federal officials, or representatives of interest groups. However, forty of them involved state officials who were either agency heads or served on the governor's staff. To be more specific, during the year 1966 the Governor had sixteen meetings with individuals who headed state agencies, fifteen meetings with individual members of his top staff (including the lieutenant governor), and nineteen meetings with individual members of his personal team who were not in state service.[84] Perhaps the most notable fact about meetings with individuals in the latter three categories is that there were relatively few of them. In the context of his daily contact with his chief of staff, a very large number of individual meetings with persons who were neither state officials nor part of his personal team (about 200 in 1966) and the many group meetings with top staff (136 in 1966), a total of forty meetings seems rather small. That there should be so few is a reflection of three factors: a heavy reliance on group staff meetings, a practice of dealing with agency heads through a chief of staff, and a heavy reliance on informal contacts with top staff, agency heads, and outside members of his personal team.

The informal settings in which the Governor interacted with state officials and friends were many. They included campaign trips, regional town meetings, trips to foreign countries, routine trips in his private plane, social gatherings in a variety of locations including his apartment in New York City and the executive mansion in Albany, and the everyday working setting in which he operated, whether in New York City or Albany.[85] Reflecting Rockefeller's penchant for mixing business and pleasure, social gatherings were often not purely social. As one former commissioner explained, the Governor made very effective use of social gatherings. "He used his various homes extensively, and going to one of his affairs had a profound impact on people. He would bring in state and local politicians and, through his social gatherings, oil the machinery of government."[86]

The Governor's heavy reliance on meetings undoubtedly reflects what we see as the satisfactions that he derived from being around people. However, it also reflects an element in his belief system, an element that he articulated in an interview.

> I believe in meetings. I believe in group therapy. I believe in, as Dr. Carrel told me many years ago, that people working together can achieve far greater penetration and conceptual insights than any one individual alone. . . . You say something, Hugh Morrow says something, I react to both of you, I say something. That gives Hugh more insight into what you are thinking and that gives you a different point of view and a broader one, and we have different backgrounds and cumulatively and collectively we then achieve far greater understanding and perception.[87]

One should not conclude from this quotation that the Governor preferred meetings that were unstructured. Staff meetings, cabinet meetings, and meetings with legislative leaders were generally run in a well-organized, "down-to-business" manner. For example, the attorney general said, "Meetings with him always had an agenda. He prepared it himself, sometimes it was in his hand, sometimes it was typed. He was a great man for preparation."[88] The Governor gave emphasis to his own philosophy regarding meetings when he explicitly disclaimed a preference for an ad hoc, "brainstorming" approach. "I am a much more structured guy. I want to come to a meeting with an agenda, and I want to plan ahead of time myself. I want to have read the memos, and I want to be prepared."[89]

Rockefeller's approach to meetings was also characterized by a substantial degree of regularity. At least one staff meeting was held each week, and meetings with legislative leaders were normally held on the same day each week during the legislative session. Norman Hurd tells a story that illustrates the Governor's reluctance to let anything interfere with staff meetings. As he tells the story, Rockefeller "missed" only one day of work in his entire term because of illness. Agreeing to stay in bed for the day on the advice of his physician, he summoned his top staff to his bedside where they spent a full day working.[90]

Although a key feature of his executive style, the regularity and structured nature of the Governor's formal group meetings should not be overemphasized. Attendees testify that he never allowed himself to become a "captive" of his agenda. And the fact that attendees varied according to the purpose of particular meetings tended to enlarge the range of viewpoints expressed.

Finally, it should be remembered that formal meetings constituted only a portion of Rockefeller's personal contact with both insiders and outsiders. The substantial degree of structure and regularity that the formal meetings contributed to his style as an executive was complemented by a pattern of informal working relationships that encompassed his everyday dealings with top staff, especially the secretary, and his rather extensive interaction with outside advisers, relatives, and family contacts.

Structuring the Process for Generating and Offering New Programs

The way in which the Governor structured the process through which his legislative program was developed is interesting for at least three reasons. The first is that the process illustrates just how Rockefeller approached a task that he saw as central to his role as Governor and his larger life strategy. The second is that an examination of the process illustrates important aspects of the roles of key units and officials, including members of Rockefeller's personal team. Finally, the Governor's shaping of the process and his role in that process illustrate various aspects of his style as an executive.

The major actors involved in developing Rockefeller's legislative program were the Governor and a few close advisers including the lieutenant governor and the attorney general; a group referred to herein as the "annual message group" consisting of the Governor's secretary, his counsel, the director of the budget, and, beginning in 1966, the director of the Office of Planning Coordination; the Office of the Counsel; the program staff; the director of communications and speech writers; and, beginning in 1970, the Office of Program Analysis and Review in the Division of the Budget.

In one sense the process of putting together the annual message was a year-round activity. For example, Rockefeller's top staff aides, the men who constituted the annual message group, often consulted together and were the primary attendees at the Governor's regular staff meetings. Because Rockefeller used these meetings as a forum for discussing emerging problems and possible solutions, they had an important impact on the process of developing the annual message even when they were not specifically directed to the contents of the message as such. In addition, program ideas grew out of the normal responsibilities of the program associates, the annual budget process, and the continuous program analysis and review

(PAR) activities that began in 1970 as a substitute for the state's short-lived planning-programming-budgeting system.

The process of developing the message began in earnest during the summer preceding the year in which it was to be delivered. In July agencies submitted proposed legislative programs to the Governor's counsel, who had the legislative clearance responsibility.[91] (In later years the Program Analysis and Review unit would at the same time provide the Budget Director with its program ideas for inclusion in the annual message.) During August the secretary to the Governor would ask each program associate to submit program ideas covering the areas for which he had responsibility. In turn, the program associates would issue a call to departments for program ideas for possible inclusion in the message. (As one might expect, agencies varied greatly in their capacity to generate ideas for programs that would be appropriate for inclusion in the Governor's legislative package.)[92]

Initial screening of program ideas during September was the responsibility of the program staff with the secretary to the Governor acting as liaison to the Governor. At this time proposed ideas were written up in brief outline or "program sheet" form to include information such as problem definition, constraints on solving problems, program concept and component elements, and location of "proposed administrative responsibility." Especially during the earlier years of the administration, there were occasional meetings with the Governor at which program associates would present program proposals to him and a few members of his top staff.

During late October or early November a second screening was conducted by the annual message group. A final review was conducted in December by Rockefeller, members of that group, a few additional members of his personal team, including sometimes the state Republican chairman, the director of communications, and the speech writers who had the responsibility for drafting the message. This final review focused on the one-page program sheets that were contained in a loose-leaf notebook prepared for Rockefeller's use.[93] The flow of program ideas to the annual message group is presented graphically in Figure 2.

Because they were not the only channel through which program ideas reached the annual message group, program associates were not in a position to hold a monopoly in the screening process, even at its first stages. For example, program ideas from departments could also reach the annual message through the channel represented by the counsel's call for departments' legislative programs.[94] However, the program staff did play a key role as the major channel of contact between the agencies and the Governor's chief of staff and thus, indirectly, the Governor himself. It was also a key link between temporary study groups and the Governor's office.[95]

As noted before, Rockefeller considered his use of task forces or study groups made up wholly or partially of outsiders as one of the three key aspects of his style as an executive.[96] While noting that study groups often

Figure 2 Flow of Program Ideas and Materials Containing Program Proposals for the Governor's Annual Message

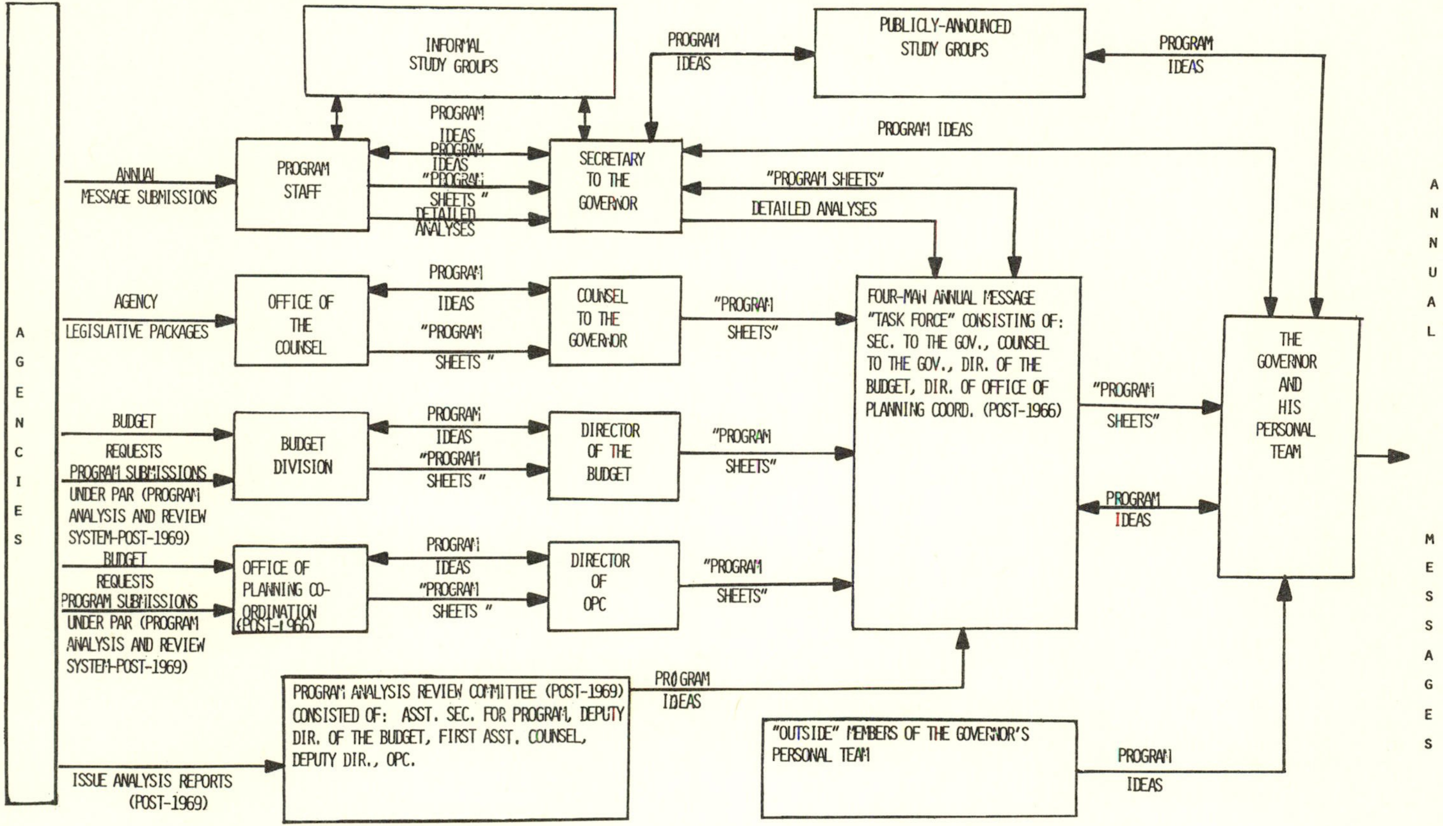

NOTE: This diagram is necessarily an oversimplification. It should be noted that program ideas could be introduced into the "flow" by any of the participants included here. However, the volume of the "flow" was greatest through the channel represented by the program staff and the Secretary to the Governor.

served "political purposes," such as "taking the heat off" when a difficult issue faced the Governor, staff members, including most program associates, acknowledged them as occasionally being valuable sources of ideas for programs.

The high point in the use of study groups came in the first year or two of the administration, a point at which Rockefeller and his staff had yet to accumulate substantial experience. William Ronan, the man responsible for overseeing the creation of the several dozens of task forces created in the first year of the administration, noted that he and the program staff were given responsibility to "follow-up and coordinate the activity of the task forces to facilitate their work."[97]

Any discussion of task forces as sources of problems and program ideas for the program staff must take into account the fact that it was sometimes difficult to distinguish between the efforts of the two. A comment by one of the early program associates indicates the extent to which the program associates involved themselves in study group operations.

> Proposals for major studies would be turned over to the program associates so they could develop a work plan, a recommendation whether the study should be done in-house or out. Program associates would critique reports produced and make recommendations to [Secretary] Ronan. The associates would sometimes throw a report out, force a new director on a group and themselves become deeply involved in a group's work. This would happen if a group produced little or a report that was completely unacceptable.[98]

Rockefeller's values, attitudes, and inclinations were well-known to program associates. In general, program associates tried to "think like the Governor" as they carried out their screening roles. Given the fact that they were not tied down by any responsibilities for administration or by any broader institutional loyalties, it seems quite understandable that the program associates were able to identify closely with Rockefeller's purposes. As one former associate put it, "I tried to act as the Governor would have acted. If the Governor was in a liberal mood, then I was in a liberal mood."[99]

Throughout the administration, campaigns had an impact on the role of the program staff. Not only were gubernatorial campaigns a source of ideas for the program staff, but Rockefeller's reelection goals as well as his attempts to capture the Republican nomination for president influenced his selection of proposals for the annual message. Furthermore, program associates became an integral part of campaigns. For example, in 1966 all but one of the program associates either resigned or took leaves from the state payroll and went to work in the reelection campaign.[100] In that campaign most of them served as researchers and idea men and helped to develop statements on problems and issues. Ideas that were included in campaign addresses as campaign promises often were included in the annual message.[101]

It is difficult to identify the sources of the ideas that eventually found their way into the annual message. Participants themselves give widely varying estimates of the proportions of ideas contributed by various parties. However, there is general agreement on three points. One is that the Governor and outsider members of his personal team (including those serving on task forces) were a major source of program ideas. A second is that with the exception of a few aggressive ones, state agencies were not major sources of program ideas. And a third is that the Governor's secretary and the program staff were a major source of program ideas, a more prominent source than other staff units.[102]

The Governor and Key Executive Tasks

How an executive handles the related problems of establishing jurisdictions, delegating authority and responsibility, controlling subordinates, and dealing with "dissenting views" is central to his role. Furthermore, the way in which Rockefeller handled these problems reflects three dimensions of executive style in which we are interested: the level of involvement in his job, the degree of structure and regularity in his activities and those of his associates, and the degree to which he works in the company of others.

Just as it is very hard to separate questions of delegation from questions of jurisdiction in the "real world," it is hard to separate Nelson Rockefeller's views on the two subjects. One of his comments regarding key aspects of his executive style gives some insight into his thinking on both subjects.

> [I like to] have a good organization structure that is clear, and everybody knows what the policy is. And then they know what their responsibilities are in carrying them out and that they have a clear delegation of authority for the carrying out of policy within a framework and that they are going to be backed up by the chief executive so that they are not uncertain and also that they are not going to be cut in on by somebody else where there is rivalry and confusion and overlapping of functions.[103]

An examination of Rockefeller's career as Governor reveals that his actions were in many ways consistent with the view described here. However, before noting some examples, it is worth pointing out that he did not always adhere to his own views regarding clear lines of jurisdiction. As a matter of fact, he often put two or more persons to work on the same problems. As will be noted, there is some indication that Rockefeller did this as a means of ensuring that he would not become too dependent on any one person. However, this practice may also be explained as a result of his enthusiasm for getting things done. In some instances, one of the persons working on a problem would be an outsider and one would be an insider. In addition to sometimes causing resentment among his staff, this had the effect of "keeping people on their toes." One outsider member of his personal team who also served in various official state capacities offered an observation that is shared by some who worked with Rockefeller. "Nelson didn't do it intentionally as F.D.R. did, but he went away from people letting them think that they had the major role. Another person may have thought so also. Nelson called it a team effort and may have thought it was clear delegation, but it was not." He added, "He thought he was following the organization chart but he would work in other ways. He would keep revising it."[104]

Both the Governor and agency heads tend to agree on one important aspect of his style, namely, that he did indeed delegate abundant authority and responsibility to heads of operating agencies. His philosophy was to give agency heads relatively free rein as long as they were willing to operate within the bounds of approved policy. Examples of leading instances in which the Governor gave especially broad authority to agency heads include Joseph Swidler, head of the Public Service Commission, Edward Logue, head of the Urban Development Corporation, William Ronan, head of the Metropolitan Transportation Authority, and Henry Diamond, head of the Department of Environmental Conservation. The first two were nationally recognized experts in their fields, and Diamond was a protege of Laurance Rockefeller. Ronan, of course, was the Governor's closest adviser even after he departed his post as secretary to become head of MTA. Although these four were granted exceptional freedom of operation, other agency heads testify that they could operate freely without undue interference from the Governor as far as departmental operations were concerned.[105]

Just as he delegated substantial authority to agency heads, Rockefeller did the same with key members of his top staff. He did this on the basis of an explicit philosophy of management, one that relates to the old idea of span of control. As he put it, "I don't think anybody, any executive whether he is Governor or business, can deal with too many people effectively."[106] Perhaps the leading consequence of this conviction was his delegation of substantial authority to the secretary to the Governor as his chief of staff. Not only was the secretary "the chief administrative officer of the staff," he had the main responsibility for day-to-day supervision of operating agencies. The Governor's views on this arrangement were clearly set forth in testimony given before a Senate subcommittee early in his administration, a time when William Ronan was the secretary.

> The Secretary to the Governor . . . works on policy and operating problems and the department heads see him and he will come to me. I can get from him in a matter of 5 or 10 minutes the essence of the problem. I know him. I trust his judgment. I know his background. We have worked together, I get the feel of the thing and I can make that decision very fast if he feels that he should ask me about it. Or he will inform me of decisions he has made. I just have not the time to hear these people. If a department feels very strongly that they have been shortchanged on a decision and it was wrong they will come to me and I will listen to them. But he is a fair minded

man and they have confidence in him. That, I think, is the kind of relationship which is true in big operation. There needs to be a delegation of responsibility.[107]

There is every indication that Rockefeller succeeded in insulating himself from heads of operating agencies to a degree sufficient to allow him to concentrate on those kinds of matters in which he was most interested, namely, initiating and selling new programs. Although he is reputed to have had an excellent memory for certain details, such as budget figures, he did not relish dealing with budgetary and administrative details. Thus he delegated most of these details to others. For example, in addition to relying on the secretary to keep the wheels of government turning, he relied heavily on the lieutenant governor and the director of the budget for dealing with the details of budget preparation.[108]

As noted, Rockefeller spent relatively little time in formal, individual meetings with agency heads. However, depending on the closeness of their personal relationship to Rockefeller, almost all agency heads had some informal contacts with him, and all saw him occasionally at larger social functions. Because the Governor was always willing to "talk business," such informal meetings and social gatherings provided important access for agency heads. For example, at a social gathering at the executive mansion, the chairman of the state's Parole Board told Rockefeller that the department would like to set up a program for gifted parolees but that it lacked the money. When the Governor asked how much money, the commissioner said he would call with an exact figure the next day. It is a measure of the responsiveness of the Governor to new ideas from agency heads that his office was in touch with the commssioner the next day before the latter could himself get around to the matter.[109]

The fact that the Governor was a religious reader of memos and reports also gave agency heads an opportunity to get his attention. Because he returned memos quickly with his written comments, they served an important means by which two-way communication could take place. The fact that the secretary was accessible to agency heads and was empowered to speak for the Governor also helped to compensate for the relatively small number of formal meetings between the Governor and agency heads.

Access to the secretary was easily available to agency heads, and they took advantage of the opportunity when they wanted the ear of the Governor or they had special problems in their agencies, including major crises. Thus, one former agency head said that weeks might go by without contact, and then there might be two or three contacts in a single day.[110] Another explained that it was sometimes preferable to deal directly with the secretary rather than Rockefeller. "The problem with meetings with the Governor was that he was in such a hurry that it was difficult to get adequate time with him. Sometimes it was better to meet just with the secretary to the Governor. They had more time."[111]

Despite the fact that Rockefeller relied heavily on his chief of staff and other top staff aides, there is little support for the notion that he thereby "lost touch" with the operations of state government. Generally, he followed a prescription that he put forth for presidents. "Members of the President's personal staff . . . must be his eyes, his ears, and often an extension of his mind—but never his crutch. He must not shrink from immersing himself, when necessary, in the details and issues of a particular problem before his administration. It is this kind of absorption that usually creates a genuine 'feel' for a problem."[112] Because the Governor had little intrinsic interest in the details of administration, he was most likely to intervene in agency affairs when the matter at issue related to launching a new program. In so intervening, he was not always sensitive to the niceties of bureaucratic relations. His sometimes cavalier attitude toward agencies and their perogatives is nicely illustrated by the way in which he arranged to launch a drug program that was to emphasize prevention through education. On February 25, without any advance consultation, the secretary to the governor called the commissioner of education and asked him to come to a press conference that same day, a conference at which the Governor would announce a proposal to train 10,000 teachers in drug education.[113] Following the press conference, Rockefeller left the preparation of the details of a program to the Education Department. He also enlisted the commissioner of education to assist him in explaining the program at meetings around the state.[114]

Rockefeller was well aware of the need for an executive to exercise control over subordinates, whether staff or operating officials. Previous experience in the federal government, especially as undersecretary of the Department of Health, Education, and Welfare, had given him an understanding of how to try to exercise control over constituent units of a large organization. Compared to his experience in the federal government, he felt that maintaining control over operating agencies in New York State was a relatively easy one. As he pointed out, he appointed agency heads with the understanding that he would relieve them if they did not adhere to his policies.[115] And because he made a practice of appointing members of his personal team as heads of line agencies and authorities in which he had a special interest, his ability to control those entities was greatly enhanced. In addition, we have already noted that he used his own staff to maintain control over agencies by a variety of means including budgetary powers, the exercise of legislative clearance, and the use of program associates as everyday links to agencies.[116]

Early in his career as coordinator of Inter-American Affairs, Rockefeller had resolved never to put himself into a position in which he was totally dependent on one staff aide. And although as Governor he relied very heavily on the secretary as chief of staff, there is no evidence that any of the four persons who occupied the position or any other top aide ever succeeded in making himself into a force independent of the Governor. One reason for this is that most of those who served in top staff positions identified so closely with Rockefeller's goals and purposes that the question of them turning their positions into separate power bases would never arise. The second reason is that in the words of a former director of the budget, Rockefeller "delegated with accountability." As he put it,

> His most common criticism of me was that I had done something without checking with him. He was even more critical of Marshall on this count. Sometimes the Governor would say to Marshall, "Al, sometimes you think you are the Governor."[117]

The third factor that relates to the Governor's ability to control his staff is perhaps best illustrated with his own explanation of how his "system" worked to prevent staff from acting contrary to his intentions. To illustrate how this system worked, the Governor related an instance in which his counsel at the time, Robert McCrate, was "dragging his feet" on drafting legislation to implement the Governor's plans to finance expansion of the state university through a quasi-governmental authority that would finance construction by selling bonds to be redeemed with the use of newly-imposed tuition charges.[118] Finally growing impatient, Rockefeller confronted McCrate at a staff meeting, saying, "All right, Bob, I am not asking for your advice any more. I am telling you now I want this legislation drafted along these lines."[119]

The Governor's belief was that his "system" for controlling staff, utilizing face-to-face meetings, and involving three different officials in the development of an important program ensured that he could discover and cope with the "opposition" of a key staff member. His explanation was as follows:

> Now this sytem gave him a chance to express himself and oppose it [the Governor's plan for expanding the state university] and his ability to drag his feet emphasized his opposition, but I could tell what was going on because we discussed it every week and I could find out where we were and why wasn't the legislation being drafted and why wasn't I seeing it. And through the budget people and the program people I was informed his people were opposed to it. So . . . the system actually brought out where my opposition was whereas if I hadn't had a system and it had been in his hands alone . . . I probably would never have gotten it going. I wouldn't have known what was wrong. It is very hard to get around a single person with whom you are working on a thing if that person is your only source of knowledge about the subject. He could have given me enough arguments why this couldn't be done, if it hadn't been for Norm Hurd and Bill Ronan who were also involved in it, and they said, "Look, Bob is just dragging his feet on this thing. He doesn't believe in it because Jim Allen doesn't believe in it and he is a close friend of Jim Allen."[120]

As this incident illustrates, Rockefeller did not want staff to continue to oppose an idea once he had made a decision to go ahead with that idea. One must remember that his whole emphasis was on "doing things" and finding ways to do those things, not on finding reasons why something could not be done. As the Governor put it, "I am not keen about people who are trying to save me from myself by maneuvering around."[121]

Rockefeller's motives for controlling his staff went beyond the simple desire that top staff accept his decisions as final. Committed to a high level of personal involvement in the program innovation process, he did not want top staff to develop independent empires that were cut off from him in any way. Generally speaking, the Governor managed to work in harmony with his top staff members, including the four men who served in the key post of secretary. One of the few indications that any of the four ever overstepped the bounds of the role as perceived by the Governor involves the latter part of Alton Marshall's tenure. More than one former senior staff member has related a story that was "making the rounds" regarding the Governor being annoyed because he felt that Marshall was "competing" with him and that the program staff was serving Marshall more than the Governor himself.[122]

There are those, some who served on the Governor's staff, some who observed his administration closely from positions in the legislature or executive agencies, and some journalists, who believe that none of Nelson Rockefeller's staff were willing to tell him that he was wrong or that his ideas were bad ones. According to his view, the Governor was served by men who were mere sycophants. Representative of this view is Lewis H. Lapham. Writing in *Harpers* at the time Rockefeller was testifying at the hearings on his nomination to be vice-president, Lapham argued that the former was victim of a self-delusion common to those who have inherited great wealth. In Lapham's view the Governor's aides were men of "questionable worth."[123]

Although it is true that some of those on Rockefeller's staff hesitated to criticize ideas that he seemed to be strongly committed to, our own conclusion is that the charge that this staff consisted largely of yes-men is exaggerated. The reality is much more complicated. First, it is true that the Governor was very impatient with staff members who consistently pointed out reasons why something should *not* be done. Furthermore, he wanted to consider "technical" objections, such as those based on cost, as part of the problem to be solved, not as reasons for rejecting a proposal. And there is no question that he strongly preferred people who had a "can-do" attitude.[124]

A second point is that senior staff members often found it more effective to argue their cases against the Governor's ideas in private rather than in staff meetings. Secretary Ronan is reputed to have employed this method with particular effectiveness. A third point is that Rockefeller would not tolerate criticism of his ideas or "footdragging" on developing them once he had made a decision to propose a program to the legislature. His dispute with Robert McCrate illustrates this point well. As a former senior member of his staff said, "One could say no in the development stage. After this stage if you said no, he considered you a pain in the ass."[125]

A fourth point is that some members of the Governor's staff did argue openly and forcefully against his ideas when they considered them flawed. (In contrast, some were characterized by a former senior staff member as "quivering masses of jelly.") Examples of ideas to which there was substantial opposition from various staff members include the state office building/cultural complex (the South Mall), the proposal for fallout shelters, and various proposals to deal with drug addiction, especially the harsh proposals of 1973. In the case of the drug proposals of 1973, both the Governor's counsel, Michael Whiteman, and the director of the Office of Planning Services, Richard Wiebe, were highly critical. Expressing himself bluntly in meetings, Wiebe is reported to have called the measure "bull shit."[126] In this case the Governor heard the criticism, but went ahead with his proposal. The fact that he did go ahead is a reflection of what was sometimes an almost compulsive conviction that he could solve any problem, no matter how dififcult, if he simply applied enough resources and energy.

William Ronan is generally credited by knowledgeable insiders as the staff person who did more to restrain the Governor's enthusiasms than any other staff member. Presumably, the fact that Ronan and the Governor had "compatible" personalities and were close friends made it easier for the former to argue against the latter's ideas than it was for other staff members. It is also likely that Ronan's style of low-key opposition expressed in private was the most effective style for dealing with Rockefeller. Although Alton Marshall was a tough-talking, forceful personality, the fact that he was primarily oriented toward producing new programs causes most observers to feel that he did not play the restraining role that is attributed to Ronan.[127] Although many noted that Lt. Gov. Malcolm Wilson, universally regarded as a conservative, was critical of some of the Governor's programs, the prevailing view is that he was "heard but not heeded."

A final point is that Rockefeller did, in fact, keep people on his staff who were willing to express strong opposition to his ideas. And although he could react heatedly to what he perceived as unwarranted opposition, he was willing to give a hearing to those staff members who felt aggrieved by his accusations.[128]

A good indication that Rockefeller was indeed keenly aware of the need to elicit the "best" advice from staff relates to his practice of requiring staff to "put themselves on the line" with their recommendations regarding new programs. As he put it,

> In Washington they go for option papers which will give three alternative courses of action. I know how those are developed. I have worked in Washington. You pick two extremes and the one you want. And the two extremes are so absurd; so it looks as though you are getting an option but you are really not. But you don't find out what is wrong with the one you are going to pick, whereas if they come up with a recommendation they have got to put themselves on the line.[129]

Although Rockefeller was able to tolerate some degree of criticism of his own ideas, he did not enjoy being opposed. Most of his staff regarded him as being stubborn and having a tendency to react strongly to what he perceived as opposition. And while some of those closest to him assert that one could cause him to reverse his position even on a pet project, few examples are offered.

It is quite possible that Rockefeller's emphasis on loyalty and teamwork and his rather paternalistic attitude toward his staff help explain his sometimes testy reaction to opposition "from within." It also seems that he was oblivious to the potential ill effects of his paternalistic solicitude toward staff members. For example, it seems never to have occurred to him that those who received loans and gifts might thereby become more reluctant to offer vigorous criticism of his ideas and pet projects. As he said before the Senate Committee considering his nomination to be vice-president, he could not imagine that the behavior of those to whom he gave loans and gifts would be affected in any way.

> If you knew Dr. Ronan and these other people for whom I have made the loans, I think you would understand. These are very independent people of the highest caliber and the highest integrity, they are my close, dearest friends. . . .
>
> Dr. Ronan and I have had, as I have had with other members of my staff, violent differences and disagreements over issues.
>
> I have never been one who sought to have, or to be surrounded by 'yes men'.[130]

This attitude of benevolent paternalism that he took toward staff members is illustrated by a portion of his statement before the same committee.

> My sole intent [in providing gifts and loans] was to respond to cases of personal hardship, family need, or out of pure friendship.
>
> Whatever success I may have had, in both public and private life, has been due to the character, brilliance and continuing sense of common purpose of those with whom I have been associated.
>
> What kind of a human being would I be if under the circumstances, I had not returned their confidence, affection and commitment, if I had not welcomed opportunities to be helpful to them in their needs and problems.[131]

Producing New Programs: The Focus of the Decision Process

One obvious conclusion that emerges from an examination of the organizational arrangements that Nelson Rockefeller used and the ways in which he related to staff and advisers is that they reflected his preoccupation with producing new programs and having them adopted. In accordance with his larger life strategy, organizational arrangements were designed to minimize obstacles to successful initiation of new programs, regardless of objections based on "practical" factors such as cost or bureaucratic resistance. Only in his last term, and then only after a fiscal crisis emerged, did he make some changes that tended to blunt the emphasis on producing new programs.

Nothing better symbolizes the Governor's commitment to producing large numbers of innovative, expensive programs than the secondary role assigned to the Division of the Budget and state agencies that were part of the established bureaucracy. Conversely, the dominant role assigned to the secretary and his program staff symbolize Rockefeller's commitment to his role as problem solver.[132] There is almost universal agreement among participants in, and close observers of, the administration that the mechanism of a program staff did, in fact, result in programs very different from those that could have been produced if the Governor had relied mainly on established state agencies for program ideas. Typifying this view was the comment of Norman Hurd. "Virtually all of the Governor's program legislation involved the program staff. As a consequence the programs were bolder, more expensive, more pioneering, more ambitious, spread over fewer years, more vigorous."[133] In short, the creation of a program staff unfettered by routine administrative responsibilities and producing ideas for a Governor who wanted to see the "best ideas" regardless of cost or other practical difficulties resulted in exactly what one might expect.

The importance we assign to the roles of the secretary to the Governor and the program staff should not be allowed to obscure the fact that other officials and units played important roles in producing and launching new programs. However, the reality is that Nelson Rockefeller managed to build a complex set of organizational arrangements almost ideally suited to the elimination of obstacles to producing and launching new programs. Setting aside questions regarding the quality of new programs, we believe his accomplishment to have been a considerable one.

As numerous points in our discussion indicate, Nelson Rockefeller was an activist executive not only in his commitment to positive government and executive leadership but in the sense that he worked full-time at his job.[134] In addition to his grueling schedule of formal meetings and informal contacts, he regularly spent portions of his evenings reading memos and reports. In managing his schedule, he seems to have used every available minute. For example, never without his briefcase, he utilized time spent traveling to read memos and other materials and make written comments on them. Those who traveled with him would inevitably be drafted for assistance. As Louis Lefkowitz said, "I had a briefcase too, but I never got mine open."[135]

An inveterate collector of information, Rockefeller himself linked the information-collecting role as important for an executive who is committed to problem solving. "As Governor I tried through . . . task forces and through reading and through contact with my own staff and the department heads and interested groups to keep a broad sensitivity to what was going on and often would come up with ideas myself which I would then turn over to the staff to staff out."[136]

Although it is unquestionable that the Governor liked collecting information, he wanted to do so in the most painless and efficient way possible. Thus he liked short presentations, short memos, and graphic displays.[137] Memos were preferably one-page "with a lot of white space." As one former program associate put it, "You could get away with two-page memos, but if you went to three pages you were in trouble."[138]

As deeply involved in his role as he was, the Governor did not try to monopolize all the tasks involved in creating new programs. When asked to describe his role in the context of the whole range of activities constituting the program innovation process, Rockefeller identified his chief roles as those of "catalyst and final decision-maker."[139] The Governor's own perception of his role in the program innovation process is matched by that of most senior staff who worked with him.[140]

Rockefeller's role as catalyst involved a number of dimensions related to "getting the process going" and keeping it going. They included designating problems for the attention of staff, supplying program ideas to be "looked into," and keeping abreast of the progress of staff work on new programs. Because he was such an active executive, keeping in touch by means of numerous meetings, informal contacts, and memos, and because he believed in "dipping in and out" of the program innovation process, staff were always aware of his presence and his interest. Examples of major program proposals that were developed in response to the Governor's personal initiative in choosing problems for attack were the Pure Waters Program (proposed and passed in 1965), the third drug-control program (proposed and passed in 1973), and the proposal for universal health insurance (proposed in a number of years beginning in the early 1960s, but never passed by the legislature.)

Rockefeller's personal involvement in defining problems and suggesting solutions often related to major issues of national import which had obvious implications for his stature as a potential candidate for the presidency. However, his fascination with problem solving and program initiation as such is illustrated by his involvement in "little" issues as well as "big" ones. For example, it was at his initiative that the state began to license chiropractors.[141]

One of the more interesting features of the Rockefeller administration is the kind of constant, but indirect, struggle that went on between the official staff and the Governor's outside advisers. The struggle manifested itself in Rockefeller's constantly bringing to his staff ideas that had originated in his interaction with the outsiders. Most staff recognized that a chief executive is wise not to rely wholly on his staff. Nevertheless, they often regarded particular ideas as impractical or simply wrong on the merits. The licensing of chiropractors, the fallout shelter program, and the third drug program are all good examples of outside ideas that were opposed in varying degrees by different staff members. For example, the Governor explained that his ideas for a hard-line approach to drug problems came from varied outside sources including the children of his second wife and a personal acquaintance whose son had undergone a bad experience with drugs.[142]

Describing his efforts to keep bad ideas from going anywhere as "a constant job," Alton Marshall expressed the view that outside advisers were often carried away by enthusiasms to which insiders would not fall victim because the latter had to face up to the tough responsibilities of actually making ideas work.[143] Marshall's view is consistent with a senior staff member's report that at one point the Governor felt he was not "getting into it" as much as he should be. "The Governor wanted to participate with his outsiders more. Al would cut them out."[144]

Devoted to "taking responsibility" and committed to offering and selling programs as a life strategy, Nelson Rockefeller as Governor wanted to be sure that *he* decided which programs would be proposed. Although he wanted to get a broad range of views in advance of his decisions, he had no commitment to "democratic" decision making. Many staff members noted his predilection for ending discussions on a potential program by simply saying "Well, I am the Governor and this is my decision." The Governor himself recognized this tendency and embraced it as appropriate for a chief executive. As he put it,

> Most people think I am, you know, sort of run-the-show and dominate the show. Well, in a sense I suppose that is true. . . . Now at the end it is like Lincoln is quoted as saying when everybody voted no on something and he voted yes. "The ayes have it!" Now, that is my tendency at the end of a meeting. But it is only after listening to all who are concerned.[145]

Although he tended to concentrate his energies at certain points in the policy-innovation process, Rockefeller was capable of immersing himself in some pet projects "from beginning to end." For example, because the state office building and cultural complex meant so much to him personally, he participated in every major decision involving it, including the architectural judgments such as which way the project's skyscraper would face.[146] And because he put his personal prestige on the line by promising to make the Long Island Railroad the best commuter railroad in the nation, he worked on that task on a day-to-day basis.[147]

Conclusion

The way in which Nelson Rockefeller structured the decision process and related to advisers and subordinates reveals a style as an executive that is generally consistent with the style he displayed during his federal service.

Furthermore, it reflects his continuing commitment to the life strategy that he chose at the beginning of his public career, that of the problem solver. It is clear that Rockefeller manifested a high level of involvement in his role as Governor. Indeed, it is difficult to imagine an executive who would give more time, energy, and emotional commitment to his job. In addition, he spent the major portion of his time working in the company of others. Although he did spend a certain amount of time alone reading memos and reports, he was almost the antithesis of the solitary decision maker who retreats to the quiet of his study to make the "tough" decisions. Although he liked to take responsibility for decisions, he worked in a group context. Finally, he imposed a substantial degree of structure and regularity on his activities and those of his subordinates. However, there were also aspects of flexibility and informality in his style, most notably his willingness to turn to multiple sources, whether inside or outside his staff, for ideas and advice. Furthermore, his high level of involvement in his job and his practice of working with many different people helped to protect him from potential dangers in a style with a substantial degree of structure and regularity.

5 Executive Style: Gaining Approval for Programs

The aspects of his job that Nelson Rockefeller most enjoyed were identifying and proposing solutions to problems and selling those solutions to those whose approval was required, whether the legislature or the voters. It is not surprising that the executive style he employed in carrying out both tasks had the same basic elements. Our consideration of the Governor as a "seller of solutions" offers abundant illustrations that underscore this point.

In attempting to win approval for his programs, Rockefeller was required to deal with a large number of political actors, most of whom can be placed in one of several categories. The most prominent of these categories includes legislative leaders and rank-and-file legislators. The remaining categories include state and local party leaders, municipal officials, federal officials, interest groups, and the public. The basic approach that Rockefeller used in relating to the legislature and other political actors as well as the various tactics he employed in winning approval for particular proposals are examined in this chapter.

A Record of Legislative Success

The Governor is widely credited with having enjoyed remarkable success in winning legislative approval for his programs. Although he suffered some notable defeats in referenda on bond issues, he also scored some notable successes in that realm. Tables 5.1 and 5.2 respectively include summaries of information related to the record of the Governor in winning approval for legislation and state borrowing.[1]

As is apparent from Table 5.1, the Governor's success in gaining passage of his program bills varied rather significantly over the eleven years for which data is available. The percentage of bills approved for the period is 57 percent.[2] As one might expect, the Governor's success rate in the seven legislative sessions in which both houses were controlled by the Republican party was higher, 60 percent, than his success rate in the four legislative sessions in which the Democratic party controlled one or both

Table 5.1
Legislative Success of Governor's Program Bills: 1963-1973

YEAR	PARTY CONTROL OF LEGISLATURE	PROGRAM BILLS SUBMITTED*	PROGRAM BILLS PASSED	PERCENTAGE OF BILLS PASSED
1963	Republican	53	41	77%
1964	Republican	31	23	74%
1965	Democratic	60	35	58%
1966	Split	65	26	40%
1967	Split	81	37	46%
1968	Split	88	49	56%
1969	Republican	83	42	51%
1970	Republican	140	91	65%
1971	Republican	118	71	60%
1972	Republican	55	30	55%
1973	Republican	69	34	49%
Total		843	479	57%

SOURCE: Data compiled from records of action on program bills provided by the Office of the Minority Leader of the New York State Assembly, Perry B. Duryea.

*Excludes all bills appropriating funds or providing revenues and all bills passed in special sessions of the legislature.

houses, 50 percent. However, the difference in these rates of success is not as substantial as might be expected in a legislature in which there has traditionally been a high degree of partisanship. And although the Governor's lowest success rate (40 percent) came in a year in which there was divided control of the legislature, 1966, a success rate of only 49 percent occurred in 1973, a year in which Republicans controlled both houses. Furthermore, the Governor achieved a success rate of 58 percent, one percentage point above the 11-year rate, in the only year in which Democrats controlled both houses. All things considered, the data relating to party control of the legislature is not inconsistent with our view that other factors also influenced the Governor's success in having his programs adopted. For example, Rockefeller's relatively low rate of success in the 1972 and 1973 sessions may reflect what was widely regarded as a deterioration in his personal relationship with Assembly speaker Perry Duryea.

It should be obvious that the success rates shown in Table 5.1 do not constitute a complete assessment of the Governor as a legislative leader. Among other things, one must look at how the Governor fared in seeking approval for those programs that were highest on his list of priorities. Even a cursory examination of his administration reveals a very high rate of success for "pet programs." Indeed, a search of the record and questioning of both participants in, and observers of, the Rockefeller administration reveal only a few pet proposals that failed to win legislative approval. Those that did fail include proposals for mandatory nuclear fallout protection in new and existing structures, universal health insurance, construction of a bridge over Long Island Sound between the towns of Rye and Oyster Bay, and construction of a fourth commercial jetport at the site of Stewart Air Force base. (The defeat of two of these proposals is discussed later in the chapter.) In contrast, the Governor managed to win approval for numerous pet proposals, some of which were highly controversial. Included among these victories were the creation of an Adirondack Park Agency with wide-ranging powers over land use, creation of the Urban Development Corporation to spur construction of low- and middle-income housing and industrial development, passage of the nation's toughest drug control laws, a major expansion of the state university system, and the construction of a massive state office building/cultural complex initially known as the South Mall.

Table 5.2 shows that the Governor had a mixed record in gaining voter approval for proposed state borrowing designed to finance certain programs. Although he suffered some notable defeats on borrowing proposals, his record can be considered impressive given the size and number of the bond issues he proposed. (A discussion of his dependence on bond issues for "pet programs" is included in Chapter 7.)

Rockefeller and the Legislature: Basic Approach

Having offered some general assessment of the degree to which the Governor succeeded in gaining necessary legislative approval for his programs and necessary voter approval for state borrowing, we now turn to a description and analysis of the way in which Rockefeller went about the task of selling his proposals. The Governor involved himself deeply in the task of gaining legislative approval for his programs. True, he delegated substantial responsibility for legislative relations to top aides, including the secretary to the Governor and the counsel.[3] Nevertheless, he regularly involved himself personally in dealing with the legislature, especially its leadership. Furthermore, working with the legislature to achieve adoption of programs was clearly a job to which he brought great enthusiasm. For example, he reminisced fondly about an instance in which he had to assume an extraordinary role.

> I will never forget the night which was the last night of the session and Earl Brydges, the leader of the Senate, . . . had a heart attack. Now I had very close relations with these leaders personally, both sides of the aisle. So, I went up and I went into his office. This is not exactly traditional, and I ran the closing of that

Table 5.2
Success in Winning Voter Approval for State Borrowing: 1959-1973

YEAR	PROPOSITION	PASSED	FAILED	YES	NO	BLANK
1960	Authorizing State Debt in the Amount of $75 Million to Acquire More Open Lands.	X		32.4%	12.0%	55.6%
1962	Authorizing State Debt in the Amount of $25 Million to Purchase Open Lands for Parks.	X		30.1%	15.0%	54.8%
1964	Authorizing State Debt in the Amount of $165 Million for Slum Clearance and Low-Income Public Housing.		X	19.4%	28.8%	51.8%
1965	Authorizing State Debt in the Amount of $1 Billion to Combat Water Pollution.	X		49.8%	11.8%	38.4%
1965	Authorizing State Debt in the Amount of $200 Million for Slum Clearance and Low-Income Public Housing.		X	20.1%	34.7%	45.2%
1966	Authorizing State Debt in the Amount of $200 Million to Provide Monies for Outdoor Recreation.	X		39.0%	27.0%	34.0%
1967	Authorizing State Debt in the Amount of $2 Billion, 500 Million for Highways and Mass Transportation.	X		49.4%	35.4%	15.2%
1971	Authorizing State Debt in the Amount of $2 Billion, 500 Million for Highways and Mass Transportation.		X	31.7%	49.7%	18.5%
1971	Authorizing State Debt in the Amount of $1 Billion, 150 Million to Improve the State's Environment.	X		42.8%	21.1%	36.0%

SOURCE: New York State Board of Elections.

Table 5.2—*Continued*

YEAR	PROPOSITION	PASSED	FAILED	YES	NO	BLANK
1973	Authorizing State Debt in the Amount of $3 Billion, 500 Million to Facilitate Transportation Capital Facilities.		X	30.9%	42.8%	26.3%

session from his office with Bobby Douglass. And we still had some major pieces of legislation to pass. And I want to tell you that had to be one of the most interesting nights.

We got through about seven o'clock in the morning. But we were on the phone with county chairmen all night. I will never forget Bobby Douglass, who was a marvelous guy, talking to some county chairman to get his legislator lined up on something and he said, "By God, there is a highway coming in your district and that highway is going to go right through your house." He said, "You don't know it yet but that is the plan, as to where this road is going." I mean, really, it is amusing and interesting but you have got to be this strong.[4]

As this quotation indicates, the Governor not only enjoyed dealing with legislative matters, but he deeply involved himself in them. Furthermore, he saw no alternative to so involving himself if he were to accomplish his goals. Indeed, he was convinced that the legislative process would break down in the absence of strong executive leadership. His conviction stemmed not only from his recognition of the potential for stalemate in a system built on the concept of separation of powers but also on his perception that the New York legislature contained important divisions beyond those of party. In his view, these divisions heightened the difficulty of making the system work. Denying that he "dominated" the legislature, he, nevertheless, saw himself as Governor as playing an essential role.

Now I mentioned the *New York Times* being critical that I dominated the legislature. I didn't dominate them, I led them. They have got a very disparate group because they have upstate, suburbia, and the City. And they are three different points of view. And as they are today, suburbia has the balance of power. . . . This is a shift that took place while I was there. So they needed an outside catalyst who could help bring them together, see, and who could see these problems, and who could balance them out, but do it in conversation with them. . . .

But I helped pull these guys together, I had the staff. I had the technical people and we would come up with programs.[5]

It is interesting that the Governor described his role vis-à-vis the legislature as resembling in one important feature the role he sought to play vis-à-vis his staff. That is, he saw himself as a catalyst. And although he did not, and could not, see himself as the "final decision-maker" when it came to getting his programs through the legislature, his discussion of the issue of his dominance of the legislature makes it clear that he was determined to exercise the greatest possible influence over the decisions by that body.

Now Malcolm Wilson who was my dear friend, and Lt. Governor, and brilliant, and had been in the legislature 20 years, felt that I dominated the legislature too much. So, when he became Governor . . . he said to the legislators "Now it is up to you." Well, the thing just went to pieces. They didn't know what to do. They had no system to work it out, and the *New York Times* was then complaining that there was no leadership.[6]

Consistent with the fact that selling his programs was an integral portion of his life strategy as it revealed itself in his role as Governor, Rockefeller's involvement in legislative relations was extensive and personal. As one former speaker of the assembly said, "He was personally in touch with the leadership. There was nothing impersonal about him. Nothing was done by subordinates."[7] Although this view is overstated as to the limited role of subordinates, it does reflect the perceptions of legislative leaders that the Governor personally carried out the bulk of communication with them. Their perceptions are reflected in the fact that Rockefeller spent more time meeting with legislative leaders than he did with anyone else with the exception of his top staff and closest personal advisers. For example, he spent far more time with legislative leaders than with agency heads. Much of this time was represented by regular once-per-week meetings presided over by the Governor and attended by legislative leaders. Held at the executive mansion, these meetings took place on Monday mornings throughout the legislative session.[8] In addition to these regularly scheduled weekly meetings, Rockefeller would meet with legislative leaders on an "as-needed" basis throughout the session. Thus, the Governor's appointments calendar for 1966 lists 34 meetings with legislative leaders, all except one meeting coming during the five months that the legislature was in session.[9]

In years in which the Republican party controlled both houses of the legislature, the Governor would usually not invite the Democratic leaders to his weekly meetings. In years in which control of the legislature was divided, the leaders of both parties were usually present. In addition, the Governor almost always had his top staff present as well as Lieutenant Governor Wilson and Attorney General Lefkowitz. The Republican state chairman often attended those meetings that did not include Democratic leaders. Depending on the subject to be discussed, one legislative leader or more than one might well be accompanied by a staff member. In addition, the Governor often invited one or more agency heads to discuss particular problems. Thus, as many as fifteen or more persons might be present at one of the regularly scheduled sessions.[10]

Consistent with his preferences, the Governor prepared an agenda for most meetings with legislative leaders. However, the leaders could add items to the agenda, and the Governor was sufficiently flexible so that discussions were not strictly limited to items on the agenda. His approach was to try to involve the legislative leaders in his plans so that harmful deadlocks could be avoided. As he put it, "I took them into my confidence, and I went over with them on programs just as I was doing on my own staff so that they had a chance to get in on the thinking and have an input in the formation."[11]

Although the dominant strategy pursued by the Governor in dealing with legislative leaders was one that sought to co-opt them as members of his team, the specific tactics he used as regards the leaders and the legislature as a whole encompassed a wide range. They included persuasion and charm, patronage and other rewards, various forms of coercion, mobilizing support from the public, interest groups, and the media, and, as a last resort, circumventing the legislature in some way.

Although Rockefeller changed some elements in his approach to dealing with legislative leaders during the course of his administration, one feature remained the same; he generally respected the prerogatives of the leaders by refraining from dealing directly with the rank and file. As he pointed out, this was a deliberate policy chosen so as to help him maintain a good working relationship with the leaders. "I worked through the leaders. I didn't go around them. That way they got the prestige of being the ones who had the contact with me. . . ."[12]

Although the Governor sought advance consultation with the leaders on his proposals from the beginning of his administration, it must be understood that this consultation generally took place after, not before, he had made decisions on what he would propose in his annual message and subsequent special messages. His consultation was aimed primarily at producing consensus on the precise shape of the legislation necesssary to provide the statuatory authority for his programs. All agree that he was willing to compromise on the details of legislation and willing to work over a period of years to get exactly what he wanted. By nature an impatient man, he learned to practice patience for the sake of achieving difficult but highly valued goals.

There is some indication that Rockefeller's capacity to deal diplomatically and tactfully with legislative leaders increased after difficulties that he experienced early in his administration. One source of initial legislative dissatisfaction with the Governor was that the quantity of his proposals was many times greater than that of his predecessors.[13] Another was that many of the Governor's programs emerged full-blown from task forces with attendant fanfare and publicity. This tended to put legislators "on the spot" and thus produced resentment. Combined with the Governor's aggressiveness in trying to sell his ideas to the leaders, these factors caused him some difficulties. As former speaker of the assembly and ally of the Governor Republican Joseph Carlino explained, "If anything, Rockefeller was a little abrasive in the leaders' meetings. He would come in with a finished product that he would try to sell us on."[14] Although Carlino described the Governor as "personable and easy-going," he added that he was "strong-willed." According to Carlino, convincing the Governor that he was wrong was possible, but just as he did in staff meetings, Rockefeller sometimes ended a discussion by simply asserting "I am the Governor."[15]

But if Nelson Rockefeller could be headstrong in those early days, he discovered that the legislative leaders, especially Senate Majority Leader Walter Mahoney, could also be stubborn. Many observers, including Assemblyman and author Alan Hevesi, regarded Mahoney as having been one of the Governor's toughest foes. Specifically, Hevesi notes that "after giving the Governor a one-session honeymoon (1959), [Mahoney] felt free to organize the rural contingent in the Senate in opposition to Rockefeller on state-financed welfare programs, to demand unsuccessfully (due to Democratic support) of a token tax cut, and, earlier than anyone else of prominence in New York State, to endorse Richard Nixon publicly for the presidency, well before Rockefeller dropped out of contention."[16] Hevesi also notes that Senator Mahoney played a role in thwarting one of the Governor's proposals for encouraging the construction of nuclear fallout shelters.[17]

A Significant Defeat: Selling Protection from Nuclear Fallout

The story behind the failure of the Governor to win acceptance for some of the key elements in his plans for protection from nuclear fallout provides a good illustration of the tensions that resulted when he tried to overwhelm the legislature by presenting leaders with fully developed and well-publicized plans on the assumption that legislative approval would be forthcoming.

With considerable publicity the Governor had appointed two task forces that had studied the problems of providing protection from nuclear fallout.[18] He had also taken the lead in pushing the issue within the National Governor's Conference. Armed with the recommendations of his task forces, he submitted legislation at the 1960 session which would have required new construction to incorporate protection from nuclear fallout and modification of existing construction to provide such protection. Then he called a meeting of legislative leaders in which he made an elaborate presentation and a strong case for vigorous state action.[19] To add emphasis to his concern, the Governor brought a number of "big names" to the meeting including Edward Teller and a representative from the Joint Chiefs of Staff. But Senator Mahoney was unimpressed. He told the Governor flatly that he would not support his program because it was "politically impossible" and would be too hard to sell. He suggested only that the Governor might possibly be able to get a portion of his civil defense program passed if he waited another year.[20] The end result for 1960 was that the legislature passed an innocuous resolution calling on the Congress and president to adopt a national policy ensuring that every citizen would have protection from fallout.[21] Forced to drop his grandiose plans, the Governor was finally able to get some civil defense proposals passed in a special session held late in 1961. The most significant elements were appropriations to establish a program of financial aid for the construction of fallout shelters at schools and colleges and increased funds for the construction of shelters in state buildings.[22]

Although he had his differences with Senator Mahoney, Rockefeller generally managed to achieve passage of his program bills during the years 1959 through 1964, a period in which Republicans controlled both houses of the legislature. His success was due partly to the fact that Assembly Speaker Joseph Carlino, a skilled political operative, was an ally.[23] As Carlino noted, the Governor used legislative leaders to "persuade, cajole and convince."[24] Because Mahoney was not as cooperative as Carlino, the Governor had to invest more of his own time in winning senate support for his program bills. It is not that Mahoney made a common practice of opposing the Governor, it is simply that he was not always willing to "go all out" on behalf of programs that were not particularly popular.[25] In such cases he would shift the burden of winning votes to Rockefeller. As the senator put it, "I gave him carte blanche to go directly to members if I thought I would have difficulty selling one of his program bills."[26] Mahoney also noted that he would sometimes ask the Governor to line up his "own" senators, those from Westchester and Nassau counties, before he as the majority leader would ask upstate Republicans to support a politically unpopular program.

It is likely that Nelson Rockefeller's difficulties with Senator Mahoney helped to prepare him for two future situations that he would face in dealing with the legislature. One was the control of one or both houses of the legislature by the Democrats, a situation that prevailed from 1965 through 1968. The second was the accession to power of Republican leaders in the assembly who were determined to exercise a degree of independence from the Governor.[27] Both these situations presented serious potential difficulties for the Governor, and yet he managed to maintain a general mastery of the legislature. His ability to do so is at least partially a reflection of an approach that emphasized cooperation and co-optation through advance consultation as opposed to an approach emphasizing confrontation.

Dealing Successfully with Democratic Leaders

The Governor's ability to deal successfully with the Democratic leaders of the senate and assembly during the period from 1965 through 1968 was enhanced by his role in supporting their initial selection as majority leader and speaker respectively: Senator Joseph Zaretski and Assemblyman Anthony Travia. They were elected only after a protracted struggle that involved a number of leading Democrats including New York City Mayor Robert Wagner and Senator Robert Kennedy.[28] After weeks of deadlock during which time the Democratic legislators of each house could not agree on the question, the Republicans finally entered the fray. They cast sufficient votes for Zaretski and Travia so that those two were able to win majorities in their respective houses and defeat their opponents, Senator Jack Bronston and Assemblyman Stanley Steingut.[29] Governor Rockefeller was widely credited with bringing about the Republican intervention on behalf of Zaretski and Travia. While many motives have been suggested for his actions, the relevant point for our purposes is that his having supported the winning candidates established a good basis for the productive relationship he was to have with them. However, it also helped lay the basis for later difficulties that the Governor would have in his relationship with Assemblyman Steingut after the latter became minority leader in 1969.

The Governor's relationship with Zaretski was a good one which Rockefeller cleverly cultivated with the use of charm and personal attention. His success is reflected both in Zaretski's failure to mold the senate Democrats into an effective opposition force and later comments that he made regarding the Governor. He said, "He and I got along well. We were good personal friends." Zaretski added that the secret of the Governor's success was "his personality."[30]

In many ways Assembly Speaker Tony Travia presented a more formidable challenge to the Governor than did Senator Zaretski. Speaker for four years, Travia had many opportunities to frustrate the Governor's plans. Yet although he sometimes drove a hard bargain, Travia generally cooperated with Rockefeller. This was due partly to the fact that the Governor applied some of the same charm and flattery that he used with Senator Zaretski. For example, one observer related the following story.

> Rockefeller handled Travia in a masterful way. When Rockefeller and Travia met for the first time, in a leader's meeting, he gave up his own seat at the head of the table to Travia and moved to a seat at the middle of the table. You could see Travia in that chair just glowing and imagining himself as Governor, presiding over a meeting at which Rockefeller was at the middle of the table. Rockefeller used such techniques to play up to the vanities and weaknesses of the leaders of the state legislature.[31]

If part of Rockefeller's success with the Democratic leadership was due to personal charm, part of it was also due to the fact that the Democrats were generally sympathetic to many of the programs that the Governor favored. As Joseph Zaretski put it, "The Governor should have been a Democrat."[32] And no less a solid Republican than former Lt. Gov. and Governor

Malcolm Wilson has acknowledged that in some ways Mr. Rockefeller enjoyed the 1965 legislative session, the only one in which the Democrats controlled both houses, more than any other session. As Wilson pointed out, the Democrats had less reservations about big, new programs, especially social programs that were popular in New York City.[33]

The relationship between the Governor and Speaker Travia deserves special note inasmuch as it demonstrates not only the Governor's ability to use his personal warmth and charm as a tactic but, perhaps more important, his capacity for forging a mutually satisfying personal relationship with a "tough" and direct man who was jealous of his perogatives and eager to do battle with his opponents.[34] He and Rockefeller often fought hard over particular bills, but in most instances they compromised their differences so that both were satisfied.[35] Consistent with Malcolm Wilson's observations about the Governor's relationship with Democratic leaders, Rockefeller described his relationship with Travia as follows: "My relationship with Tony Travia was the best relation I ever had with anybody. I mean, this guy, he and I were fantastic friends and saw eye to eye even though we were different parties."[36]

Difficulties with a Republican Leader

In a number of ways the Governor's relationship with Perry Duryea, minority leader of the assembly from 1966 through 1968 and speaker for the remainder of Governor Rockefeller's term, was more difficult than his relationship with Tony Travia. Although his basic approach remained one of attempting to co-opt the majority leadership, the history of the Governor's relationship to Duryea reveals Rockefeller's acting as "the tough guy" in a number of instances. As Duryea freely admitted, "Sometimes when I opposed him in a meeting, the Governor was purple and jumping up and down."[37] However, Duryea denies that the Governor had a better relationship with Democrats than with Republicans, citing Rockefeller's well-known difficulties in getting along with Stanley Steingut, former minority leader and speaker of the assembly. As Duryea put it, the Governor and Steingut "were like oil and water."[38]

Regardless of Duryea's own view of Rockefeller's relationship with Democratic leaders, the fact is that Duryea pursued a more independent stance vis-à-vis the Governor than did any Democratic legislative leader with the possible exception of Stanely Steingut. (The only Republican leader who approached Duryea in independence was Walter Mahoney.) The motives for Duryea's independent stance are not all clear, but there is no doubt that one was his desire to succeed Rockefeller as Governor. Another is that Duryea did not have the same degree of enthusiasm for "big spending" as did the Governor. In addition, it has been speculated that Mr. Duryea somewhat resented Rockefeller's continuing efforts to work closely with Democratic leaders and to secure Democratic voters to overcome occasional Republican opposition. According to former Speaker Joseph Carlino, the Governor's dealings with the Democrats "made him [Duryea] cantankerous."[39]

Perry Duryea did, in fact, mold assembly Republicans into a force capable of standing up to the Governor. Essentially a middle-of-the-road Republican, Duryea sometimes had to walk a tight line between the demands of a big-spending Governor and the demands of a bloc of conservative upstate Republicans, many of whom won election by running with the endorsement of the state's young Conservative party as well as that of the Republican party.[40] Accustomed to working with cooperative leaders on both sides of the aisle, especially after Senator Mahoney's defeat in 1964 and expecting to make Republican legislative leaders part of his team, the Governor had difficulty appreciating increasing reluctance of assembly Republicans to accede to his wishes. And as Duryea grew more confident and skilled in his role as speaker, he became a more formidable obstacle to Rockefeller. As a former top aide to Duryea explained, the Governor was "incredulous" at opposition by assembly Republicans. With cooperative leaders in the senate, both Democratic and Republican, and demonstrated ability to win needed Democratic votes in the assembly, by 1970 the Governor faced a situation in which the assembly Republicans were his most important source of opposition on some proposals. The view of Duryea's aide was that aside from assembly Republicans, the Governor "owned the State, he owned the Democratic Party."[41]

Despite their differences, Rockefeller and Duryea cooperated to a considerable degree in achieving the former's goals. Although he worked closely with Anthony Travia as speaker, the Governor did not ignore the assembly minority leadership. And when minority leader Duryea became speaker in 1969, Rockefeller pursued his standard approach of trying to bring the speaker into his orbit and make him a member of the team. Because he was usually willing to alter his programs in their details if not in their essential thrust, the Governor's approach often succeeded. Duryea himself has suggested that "the secret of the Governor's legislative success" was that he informed the leaders of his plans at an early stage and thus bills could be tailored to take objections into account. According to Duryea, the Republican leaders had a virtual veto over proposals prior to the point at which they were put into the form of draft bills.[42]

There are numerous good examples of Duryea's playing the loyal lieutenant's role in working for the passage of Rockefeller proposals. One occurred in the 1972 session when the Governor was having great difficulty in obtaining legislative support sufficient to pass a tax package necessary to achieve the balanced budget required by state law. Although the speaker was not enthusiastic about the tax package, he did his best to deliver the largest number of votes possible.[43]

Making the Best of a Bad Situation: the "Budget Revolt" of 1971

The 1971 "budget revolt" by assembly Republicans, a revolt led in large part by Duryea, represented a somewhat atypical relationship between the Governor and the speaker. However, that event is instructive in many ways. Not only does it illustrate the new reality of Republican independence in the assembly, it provides a good illustration of Rockefeller in his role as chief legislator. More specifically, it shows how the Governor reacted in the face of unexpected, but almost certain defeat, how he coped with the loss of "normal" support from the Democratic minority that had saved him in previous times of difficulty, and how he tried to put the best face on what could only have been a very unpleasant, embarrassing, and politically damaging situation. Not least, it also shows the Governor at his most pragmatic.

Many Republican legislators had long been critical of what they saw as excessive spending by the state. Nevertheless, the Governor had usually succeeded in having his budget accepted with only minor cuts. In those instances in which sufficient Republican votes were not available, he had always been able to "cross the aisle" and pick up necessary votes from cooperative Democrats.[44] Nevertheless, most Republican legislators usually supported Rockefeller's budget after some largely cosmetic cuts had been made. However, when the Governor proposed his budget for fiscal year 1972, he asked for $1.1 billion in new taxes. As one knowledgeable reporter put it, "Republicans vowed not only to 'cut the hell' out of the budget proposal—but make up for a decade of what they concluded was overspending by reducing nearly every major state program."[45] Not long after the Governor had delivered his budget message, the speaker himself set in motion a carefully constructed effort to bring about substantial cuts in the budget as proposed. Among other elements, this effort included a series of presentations by fiscal staff outlining those areas of the budget that might be cut without violating existing legal mandates. These presentations took place at conferences of the assembly Republicans, conferences that revealed strong budget-cutting biases on the part of members, many of whom were particularly concerned about proposed increases in welfare spending, especially as such increases would require spending by local governments.[46]

When senate Republicans joined assembly Republicans in demanding that $700 million be cut from the proposed $8.4 billion, Rockefeller was faced with a full-scale revolt.[47] His first reaction was to launch a major counteroffensive. Denouncing "irresponsible" efforts to cut what he had originally termed his tight "stop-gap crisis" budget, he had two of his commissioners begin to issue statements of concern about the effects of cuts on their departments.[48] However, it was not long before Rockefeller realized that this situation was hopeless and that his efforts to persevere in opposition to legislative and public sentiment were fruitless. The fact that the Republican party in the assembly had only a 79 to 71 margin (with 76 votes required to pass the budget) meant that the Governor could afford very few Republican defections unless he were to win substantial Democratic support. By the middle of March it was clear that most Republicans were holding firm for substantial cuts and that the Democrats, led by Stanley Steingut, were not likely to cooperate. At this point Rockefeller made a strategic retreat by acknowledging that his budget proposals must be revised downward, largely because proposed tax increases threatened to drive businesses from the state. Stating at a press conference that "it is now plain that the tax program I presented February 1, in combination with local tax demands . . . could have a disastrous effect on the state's economy," the Governor said he was joining in the task of cutting his own budget proposals in order to prevent "meat-ax" cuts made on an across-the-board basis.[49] Uncharacteristically for him, Rockefeller began to make the kind of statements that conservatives rather than liberals are fond of making. For example, he said:

> Under the circumstances, it is clear to me as well as the legislative leaders that both state and local governments must lower their sights . . . we must face the fact that some esential needs simply cannot be met, that we must limit ourselves to the high priority programs that are within our severe financial limitations.[50]

Because some Republicans were insisting on deeper cuts than the approximately $700 million proposed by the Republican leadership in the assembly, reaching agreement on both spending and taxing measures was very difficult. It was not until April 2, a day after the constitutional deadline for budget approval, that a compromise which could gain majority approval in both houses was reached. Unable to make any deal with Democrats and faced with determined Republican legislators, the Governor had been forced to accept cuts of $760 million in spending and withdrawal of proposals for some of the tax increases he had initially sought.[51] Among the more notable cuts were a 10 percent decrease in welfare benefits in certain "high-cost" (urban) areas, benefits that Rockefeller had originally wanted to increase, more restrictive income limits for medicaid eligibility, and cuts in spending for mental health programs.

Perhaps the most notable aspect of Rockefeller's handling of the 1971 fiscal rebellion was that he reacted with sufficient nimbleness and flexibility so as to prevent a legislative defeat from blossoming into a full-scale disaster that might have destroyed his ability to exercise forceful leadership in the legislative process. By doing a fast turnabout and acknowledging that criticism of his spending and taxing proposals had merit, he managed to some degree to co-opt the very issue that was being used against him. That he could accomplish this feat without being seen as weak or indecisive is impressive. Although it is true that he was criticized as a political opportunist and as abandoning his liberal principles, those charges were probably less damaging to his reputation as an effective "chief legislator" than charges of indecisiveness and weakness could have been.

Rockefeller's new attitude on spending was accompanied by support for some ideas that most people would term "conservative." For example, he supported a welfare residency requirement that passed the 1971 session and also successfully pushed for the creation of a welfare inspector general to root out fraud.[52]

The larger issue of the extent to which the Governor made a deliberate "turn to the right" in 1971 will be considered in Chapter 7. Suffice it to say here that by June of 1971, he was praising Republican legislative leaders for having taken the initiative in cutting growth in state spending, growth for which he had been primarily responsible.[53]

Perry Duryea Is Indicted: Rockefeller Is Blamed

The Governor's battles with Speaker Duryea over the shape of his budget in the 1971 session carried over into a special session held at the end of the year to consider Rockefeller's proposals for tax increases for fiscal 1972-1973. The relationship between the Governor and the speaker continued to have difficult moments through the 1972 and 1973 sessions and reached a low point in 1973 when the speaker, his majority leader, another assemblyman, and some aides were indicted on charges of violating election laws related to the distribution of misleading campaign literature.[54] Such was the Governor's reputation for being tough, and even ruthless, that many legislators, including outraged Republican assemblymen and journalists, believed that the Governor had a hand in bringing about Duryea's indictment by a grand jury in Manhattan.[55] Even more believed that he was at least guilty of giving tacit approval to the attorney general's decision to turn over evidence of possible election law violations to prosecuting attorneys in Albany and New York City. And almost no one believed that Lefkowitz would have proceeded had he believed that the Governor was opposed to his course of action.

The motive most commonly attributed to Rockefeller was a desire to ensure that his chosen successor, Lt. Gov. Malcolm Wilson, would be spared a primary challenge by Speaker Duryea. Although Duryea refused to offer his own comment on the episode, he did indicate agreement with the view that one could look upon the Governor's role as involving "doing something nice for a loyal friend and servant, Malcolm Wilson."[56] Despite the fact that charges against Duryea were shortly dismissed on the grounds that the relevant section of the election law was unconstitutional, the rift between the two men never healed. In fact, as late as 1978, Rockefeller went out of his way to praise Duryea's opponent in the gubernatorial campaign, Governor Hugh Carey. Attending a ceremony at which Governor Carey was announcing an official change in the name of the South Mall complex from the Empire State Plaza to the Governor Nelson Rockefeller Empire State Plaza, Rockefeller heaped praise upon Carey. Rockefeller did refer to Duryea as a "very able and dedicated Republican leader," but he mainly praised the Governor. Among other remarks, he stated that "the people of this state have every right to be proud to have a Governor who has the vision and sensitivity to understand the aesthetic values of beauty and art in terms of influencing peoples' lives."[57]

Playing the Game of Legislative Politics: Using Carrot and Stick

As a number of instances demonstrate, the Governor's reputation for toughness was well-deserved. Speaker Duryea was not the only one with whom Rockefeller did battle. However, before discussing some instances that helped give the Governor this reputation, it should be pointed out that "being tough" and coercing legislators was only one in a whole range of tactics that he employed. We do not see this type of tactic as inconsistent with Rockefeller's basic approach of attempting to make legislative leaders part of his team and maintaining a generally cooperative relationship with them. However, when a cooperative approach with the leaders did not produce results, then the Governor would try whatever tactic he thought might succeed. In some cases this meant going directly to rank-and-file legislators with the knowledge and approval of the leaders. (As noted earlier, the Governor would occasionally bypass Democratic leaders totally when they were in the minority.) In other cases it meant trying to overwhelm the leaders through pressure from the public, interest groups, the media, or party leaders.[58]

Only on those rare occasions when he was being frustrated in attempts to gain approval for one of his pet projects or when he felt that one of the leaders had broken a commitment or treated him with deliberate disdain did the Governor "lose his cool" and let the combative part of his nature lead him into a personal confrontation. For example, Hevesi reports that Rockefeller replied to a request from aides to Walter Mahoney and Joseph Carlino with a tart "F--- Walter Mahoney." Mahoney had reportedly previously applied the same phrase to the Governor in the course of a disagreement over a bill on the floor of the Senate.[59] Another more publicized incident involved the Governor's admitted shoving of assembly minority leader Stanley Steingut when the latter informed the Governor that the Democrats would vote to override the Governor's veto of a bill blocking construction of the proposed bridge over Long Island Sound. Depending on whose version one believes, the Governor either pushed Mr. Steingut with his finger or punched him in the chest. In any event, an angered and stunned Steingut stalked out of the room, and the Governor later apologized, claiming to reporters that he reacted in the way he did because he felt that Steingut was going back on a previous understanding. The minority leader was not much mollified by the Governor's apology.[60]

Not only could the Governor be combative and tough in a spontaneous way, he clearly *believed* that a governor must be willing to be tough in order to succeed in selling his programs. But he appreciated the use of the carrot as well as the stick. And in some cases he used one in combination with the other with great skill in gaining approval for a favorite program. The strategy and tactics he used in gaining approval for creation of the Urban Development Corporation (1968) and adoption of his third drug program (1973) illustrate this aspect of his approach.

Reversing a Defeat on the UDC

Rockefeller had proposed creation of the Urban Development Corporation, a quasi-governmental corporation with bonding power, as a means of furthering slum clearance, the construction of low-income and middle-income housing, industrial development, and community facilities. At the suggestion of Edward Logue, the man the Governor was trying to persuade to become head of the corporation, Rockefeller had included in his legislative proposal a controversial provision that would have allowed the UDC to override restrictive zoning codes and building codes in local areas. Faced with difficulty in gaining legislative approval, the Governor seized upon the occasion of Martin Luther King's death and the resulting sympathy toward the needs of minorities as a means of overcoming legislative resistance. He proposed to leaders that the bill be passed as a memorial to Reverend King. Gaining a commitment that the bill would be passed on the day of the funeral, he left Albany accompanied by the eighteen blacks who were members of the state legislature. However, after passing the senate easily, the bill was defeated in the assembly early in the evening of April 9 by a vote of 85 to 48.[61] Speaker Travia and minority leader Perry Duryea managed to save the bill from a final defeat by a parliamentary manuever. For the next three hours, the speaker, the minority leader, and the Governor and his staff worked to change enough votes to pass the bill. Perhaps the Governor's own words best describe the nature of his role in that effort.

> I was absolutely furious and I got Tony Travia on the phone . . . and Tony said, "Look," he said, "I am not going to carry this alone." He said, "Your people . . . welched on their commitment, but I saved it by recommitting it." . . . So I said "I am going to get my people lined up and I am going to get this passed before midnight tonight."

I got my people on the phone, got the leaders. And I have got to tell you that this was the one time I really let loose politically and I said to this fellow, a Republican leader, "You have double crossed me on this. I had a commitment and I want you to get these people back." He said, "They are all gone." I said, "I don't care, I will send the state police after them. We will get them back on the floor tonight. I want this thing passed tonight." And I said, "I want a record of who votes how and if they don't show up I am going to send the police after them and I don't care who it is; anybody that doesn't fulfill that commitment that we had; their patronage, their total—all of the thing they got they just can forget it. If they have got some judge or something else that they have got, it is finished."

Well, Bobby Douglass, who was counsel, and our political people all got going and they got everybody out and, by God, it was a very rough occasion but they had it back before midnight. And it was passed eighty something to fifty something. . . .[62]

The fact that the Governor candidly explained to a press conference his use of political pressure to gain passage of the UDC bill suggests that he didn't feel the least bit defensive about using such a method.[63] Furthermore, the fact that his actions in the UDC affair is one of his favorite stories suggests that he took some pride in being tough when he felt the circumstances were appropriate.[64]

It should be noted that it is likely that both carrot and stick tactics were employed in the UDC battle. Legislators are dependent on a governor for many actions important to them, including his signature on "their bills." (As noted previously, a governor normally vetoes a large number of bills, and these vetoes are almost never overridden.)[65] One assembly Republican recalls an instance in which he was "punished" for refusing to provide his vote for a key tax package sought by Rockefeller and the leadership. The punishment consisted of the Governor's vetoing one of the assemblyman's bills. In what the assemblyman saw as an attempt to deliver a clear message to him and other legislators about the consequences of not "going along," the Governor's veto message was read aloud in the assembly chamber soon after the Governor acted on the bill.[66] Legislative leaders are also dependent on the Governor for the issuance of "messages of necessity," a device that allows them to consider bills they wish to rush through near the end of a session without having to wait the three days after introduction otherwise required by the constitution.[67]

Some journalists and other observers believed that the UDC vote was reversed partly because the Governor's approval was needed for a generous new legislative pension plan that the leaders badly wanted. Shortly after the UDC vote, Rockefeller issued a message of necessity allowing quick action on the pension bill. He later signed the bill into law.[68] Whether one considers his action on the pension bill as a reward or his threat to refrain from normal cooperation with the legislature as coercion is largely a question of semantics. When asked at the news conference at which the UDC bill was signed whether he promised any personal favors in exchange for votes,

Rockefeller merely said, "No, I put it the other way around, that I would be unable to continue to do the personal favors."[69]

An Antidrug Crusade: Overwhelming the Legislature

It is clear to us and most other observers that the Governor accepted as legitimate the sorts of transactions that have been taken for granted at both state and national levels as a normal part of legislative politics. Committed first to trying to do things on the basis of "the merits," he showed little hesitation in "playing the game" when that was required. Thus he doled out personal favors and engaged in bargaining, compromise, and logrolling as well as the use of "political muscle."

Rockefeller's approach in gaining legislative approval for his harsh drug proposals in 1973 illustrates his use of the carrot. More imporant, it also illustrates his forcing a program through a reluctant legislature by allying himself with public opinion and using that public opinion and the support of certain organized groups to virtually bludgeon the legislature into submission. The program was opposed by the bulk of the legal profession, including judges, court administrators, prosecutors and criminal lawyers, by some police officials, by influential groups such as the American Civil Liberties Union, and by political leaders such as Mayor Lindsay and assembly minority leader Stanley Steingut. Harsh elements included in the program as originally proposed included: (1) mandatory life sentences for selling or conspiring to sell any quantity of hard drugs, hard drugs being defined to include even hashish (with elimination of plea bargaining, suspended sentences, the possibility of parole for all persons, and elimination of treatment under "youthful offender" status for those between the ages of sixteen and nineteen, the only exception being that persons in that age group could still be considered for parole); (2) mandatory life sentences for those found to have committed serious crimes after taking drugs (with the same restrictions regarding plea bargaining and other options, as in No. 1); (3) mandatory life imprisonment for possessing or conspiring to possess more than an ounce of one of the "big four" drugs (heroin, cocaine, opium, and morphine); and (4) the payment of bounties of $1,000 to those informing on a pusher who is later convicted.[70]

Carrying out a vigorous public campaign in behalf of his proposals, Rockefeller had considerable success in appealing to public opinion. For example, a Gallup poll announced in February of 1973 showed that 60 percent of those surveyed agreed with "a Governor's [Rockefeller's] proposals" that all sellers of hard drugs be given life imprisonment without the possibility of parole. (Only 29 percent disagreed. Seventy percent supported the Governor's proposal for bounties.)[71]

Because polls had been showing that people regarded crime as the nation's number-one problem and because they also showed that people believed that drug-use was a major cause of crime, it is not surprising that Rockefeller's proposals found wide favor with the public. And knowing his heavy use of his own polls, the Governor was undoubtedly well-aware of public sentiment. In any event, he made masterful use of general public sentiment as well as antidrug and anticrime sentiment among particular groups, including organized labor. For example, early in March he told a meeting of the legislative conference of the state AFL-CIO that he was seriously considering proposing the death penalty for members of organized crime who were convicted of commerce in drugs. Receiving a huge ovation at his mention of the death penalty, the Governor responded by assuring the audience that "I'm going to stay with the people of the state on this."[72]

It would be wrong to think that Nelson Rockefeller was merely exploiting public sentiment about drugs and crime which arose primarily in response to peoples' personal experience with, or knowledge of, the use of narcotics and its effects. We assume that society's problems are in a very important sense social creations. And in the 1960s and 1970s drug-use and crime were viewed as problems not only because their incidence was rising but because those who shape opinion, the media, political leaders, and other institutions, chose to define them as problems. Rockefeller himself had been working for years to make the public conscious of "the drug problem." Thus, in one important sense he had helped to create the public mood that was to prove so hospitable to the harsh proposals he made in 1973.

Just as the issue of protection from nuclear fallout became a crusade for the Governor, so did the issue of drugs. One has only to read what he wrote about the drug problem in 1971 to appreciate this fact.

> How can we defeat drug abuse before it destroys America? I believe the answer lies in summoning the total commitment America has always summoned in times of national crisis. . . . Drug addiction represents a threat akin to war in its capacity to kill, enslave and imperil the nation's future; akin to cancer in spreading deadly disease among us, and equal to any other challenge we face and deserving all the brainpower, manpower, and resources necessary to overcome it. . . . Are the sons and daughters of a generation that survived the great depression and rebuilt a prosperous nation, that defeated Nazism and Fascism and preserved the free world, to be vanquished by a powder, needles, and pills?[73]

Taking his view of the seriousness of the drug problem as being sincerely held, as we do, it is not surprising that the Governor went all out in 1973 in his third major attempt to deal with the problem. Given his convictions about the drug problem, plus his normal determination to succeed in any challenge, it is not surprising that he engaged in a careless use of exaggerated statistics in building a case in favor of drastic action.[74]

Unlike numerous observers, including the sophisticated and knowledgeable Edward Jay Epstein, we doubt that Rockefeller's hard-line approach to drugs in 1973 and earlier was motivated primarily by a desire to woo conservatives in a last, desperate attempt to win his party's presidential nomination.[75] Indeed, the Governor's actions on drugs were perfectly consistent with his life strategy of identifying problems he saw as endangering society and then offering solutions to those problems. In large part, his public career was based on crying wolf, but there is no reason to doubt that he truly believed there were, in fact, dangerous wolves about. And we think that he feared drugs just as much as he feared a nuclear attack in the 1950s and early 1960s and a Nazi triumph in Latin America in the 1940s. The latter two fears sent him into crusades similar to the one he launched against drugs. All these crusades involved elaborate use of speeches, articles, and assorted public relations techniques to convince others of the dangers he saw and to sell his solutions to those dangers. And although some form of legislative action was required as an important component of all these crusades, the arena he operated in was much broader than the legislative arena itself.

Although we do not agree that the Governor's motive in the drug area was primarily one of short-term political advantage, we do agree with Epstein that the Governor was ingenious in his employing "hyperbole, statistical artifacts, and dreaded images" to win support for his drug proposals. As demonstrated by Epstein, the Governor's use of statistics to buttress his case was misleading to say the least. For example, Epstein notes that a statement by Rockefeller that crimes by addicts cost citizens of New York up to $5 billion per year was ludicrous. According to Epstein, less than $250,000,000 in property was reported stolen in New York City in 1972.[76]

The Governor's misuse of statistics with regard to drugs suggests that, like many politicians, he viewed data primarily in instrumental terms once he was personally convinced that there was, in fact, a problem that required action. In other words, gathering the "facts" became not an attempt to discover reality but an attempt to convince others of one's own view of reality.

In spite of his success in arousing public pressure on the drug issue, the Governor was eventually forced to compromise in order to gain passage of his program. Two of the more significant changes he agreed to were the elimination of hashish from the list of hard drugs and authorization for the appointment of up to one hundred judges to deal with the expected increase in drug cases.[77] The latter change was made in response to a barrage of criticism charging that the Governor's legislation would cause massive delays in the judicial system. In addition, the authorization of new judgeships represented a carrot that could be held out to legislators and local party leaders who were otherwise reluctant to support the Governor's plan. Judgeships in New York are considered plums, and many legislators aspire to move up to the bench. As has been noted by many observers, Rockefeller "was the master of the use of judgeships to achieve his political ends."[78] In any event, there is little doubt that inclusion of the provision for new judgeships contributed to the ultimate passage of the Governor's drug program, albeit in a somewhat softened version. Thus the passage of the 1973 drug program resulted not only from Rockefeller's skillful use of public opinion but from the liberal use of potential rewards for legislators and other political leaders.

Working through State and Local Party Leaders

The fact that he was both chief executive and party leader provided the Governor with considerable resources that he could either grant as reward or withhold as punishment. His personal wealth enabled him to be the major supporter of the state's Republican party. Between 1956, the year in which he began to involve himself actively in party affairs, and 1974, he gave over a million dollars to the state party and various local party committees and clubs.[79] In 1965 alone, he gave $303,120 to the Republican state committee.[80] Being chief executive carried with it all sorts of resources available for exerting leverage over legislators, including substantial patronage power in the form of appointments to the bench, to state agencies, and to a host of state commissions, boards, and so-called temporary state commissions. (The latter sometimes were used for investigative purposes and thus had substantial publicity value.)[81]

Although the Governor often dealt with legislative leaders himself and occasionally dealt directly with rank-and-file legislators, he also made heavy use of party leaders in seeking to win adoption of his programs. As noted in Chapter 4, the Republican state chairman was made an integral part of Rockefeller's team of top advisers. In some cases, that official was used to bring pressure upon recalcitrant legislators in the interest of passing programs. For example, when the Governor needed a vote for a tax package in a special session in December, 1971, upstate Republican Assemblyman Clark Wemple was called to see the state chairman after assembly Republican leaders failed in an attempt to convince him to vote yes. Only after he resisted a forty-five-minute plea for his vote by the chairman was he called to a meeting with the Governor himself.[82]

Although Republican county leaders sometimes resented the Governor's willingness to seek help from Democratic county leaders, usually those in New York City, they normally gave strong support to him. (One of the few exceptions occurred in 1973 when Brooklyn Republican leaders led a revolt of city leaders against the Governor's plan to give the Republican mayoral nomination to former Mayor Robert Wagner, a Democrat.) Because most legislators from the city were Democrats, and because Democrats were often more liberal, the Governor often found it necessary to "deal" with local Democratic leaders in order to pass programs. Perhaps the most notable example of his doing so in a critical situation involved his successful effort to win votes of Brooklyn Democrats sufficient to pass the controversial tax package he submitted to a special session in 1971. Having managed to join Republican-led budget cutting in the regular session and gain Republican support for additional taxes, Rockefeller was faced with the need for even more tax increases in order to achieve a balanced budget for fiscal year 1972-1973 (beginning April 1, 1972). But he could not gather sufficient Republican votes for a second round of tax increases. Eventually he succeeded in getting sufficient Democratic votes by agreeing not to make budget cuts in "social" areas including those of education, mental health, and welfare. The means by which the Governor maneuvered to get those votes reveals a lot about his willingness and ability to deal with local Democratic leaders.

The Governor described his efforts to win the support of Brooklyn Democrats in terms that illustrate the satisfaction he gained from direct personal involvement in the politics of selling his programs.

My leaders who were at that point Republicans said that they couldn't pass it [a $500 million tax increase]. And that is when I became a very good friend of Meade Esposito. I asked Meade up to my apartment. I had never met him. He was the Democratic boss of Brooklyn. Jerry Finklestein, . . . was the Democratic head of the City Committee who was a friend or acquaintance, and a very good friend of Bill Pfeiffer's, so I could develop through him [Pfeiffer] an intimate contact. And so he [Finklestein] brought Meade up to my apartment, whom I had never met. And I sat down and I told Meade, "We have two alternatives. One is to cut $500 million more from the budget, which had to be taken from social services. That is the only place we can take it." And I said, "This is what it is going to do in these areas to the people of the State." And I said, "I don't know you except by reputation and I have a feeling that you have the same concern that I do for people and that this is something that neither you nor I want to see happen."

But I had given him all the figures. I said that the only alternative is through taxes and I explained what those would be. And I said, "There is only one way I can pass them and that is with your help. There is no one else in this state that can do it. The Democratic leaders of the legislature, they can't do it. . . ." (The majority of the key legislators came from Brooklyn.)

So, after about 45 minutes or an hour during which an amusing incident took place which was that my kids who were then pretty small were chasing each other and came through the room unannounced. One of them was just in an undershirt, nothing else. And my wife was trying to stop them and she was barefoot and came through. And Meade felt sort of family warmth. He was a family man. This looked like a scene from little Italy.

So he said to me after about 45 minutes or an hour, "Okay, you have convinced me." He said, "Let's go out and get the whips and we will get the votes," figuratively speaking.

Well, that guy stuck with me and we got those votes. . . .[83]

Others have testified to the effectiveness of the Rockefeller charm in making Esposito his ally. Then Congressman Hugh Carey, present at the meeting recounted by the Governor, is quoted as saying that "Esposito thinks Rockefeller is 'a helluva guy,' " and "if he runs in 1976, I'd have a helluva time being against him—my wife loves the guy."[84] But as many observers have pointed out, the relationship between Rockefeller and the county leader was not a one-way street. Esposito has been credited with receiving many benefits, including choice appointments for friends and associates, through his alliance with the Governor.[85] The relationship between the two men was perceived as so close that it produced resentment on the part of George Clark, Jr., the man who took over as Republican leader of Kings County (Brooklyn) in 1972. As the story goes, Clark was first annoyed upon discovering that the Governor was negotiating with Esposito on state reappointment plans. Then he became outraged when he discovered that Rockefeller had given to Esposito a Picasso lithograph that the latter had admired when at the former's apartment.[86] (Clark later led the revolt of New York City Republican leaders against the Governor's plan to give the Republican endorsement for mayor to Democrat Robert Wagner.)

Being Patient, Persistent and Stubborn: Strategy and Personality

There is no question that persistence, indeed doggedness, combined with a considerable degree of patience, sometimes helped the Governor overcome legislative resistance. For example, his refusal to give up on drug proposals, even in the face of important opposition, ultimately brought success. A second example of persistence and patience in the face of significant opposition was his campaign to achieve state-supervised land-use planning for the Adirondack Mountain region of the state. As the former commissioner of Environmental Conservation pointed out, Rockefeller pursued a step-by-step strategy rather than a strategy of trying to win everything he wanted in one fell swoop. Given the substantial opposition from upstate legislators, local officials and developers, especially those from the Adirondack region and Adirondack citizens themselves, Diamond felt that the Governor's step-by-step strategy was the key to achieving his ultimate goal.[87]

Rockefeller's strategy for land-use control in the Adirondacks included at least three separate steps: the creation of one of his study groups, the temporary study commission on the Future of the Adirondacks (1968); legislative approval of his proposal to create the Adirondack Park Agency, an office with authority to promulgate a master plan for management of state lands and develop land-use controls for private lands (1971); and legislative approval of controls over private land-use as developed by the Park Agency (1973).[88] The legislature resisted Rockefeller's plans to the bitter end, even passing a bill early in the 1973 session which would have deferred legislative consideration of the agency's controls for private land until 1974. However, after the Governor vetoed the bill, the legislature reversed itself and passed a bill allowing the system of controls to take effect.[89]

At times, Rockefeller's persistence became stubbornness and led him into almost hopeless struggles in the face of overwhelming odds. Indeed, it sometimes seemed almost impossible for him to accept the idea that he could not prevail. Thus, even though the voters administered a sound defeat to his proposed transportation bond issue in 1971 ($2.5 billion), he tried again in 1973 ($3.5 billion) and failed.[90]

The Governor and other political figures had campaigned vigorously for passage of the 1971 bond issue. A group formed especially to promote passage conducted a hard-sell campaign featuring television and radio spots. (The group even took the position that it would not disclose details of its financing.)[91] In contrast, an environmental bond issue gained easy approval in 1972. That success was achieved after a soft-sell campaign featuring support by environmental groups and a bicycle tour of the state by the commissioner of Environmental Conservation, but no active role for Rockefeller. This led the Governor to decide upon a soft-sell campaign without his direct participation for the 1973 transportation referendum.[92] Although the bond issue had support from newspapers, labor leaders, and political leaders, including New York City Mayor John Lindsay, and although passage was said necessary to keep subway and bus fares from skyrocketing, voters soundly rejected the proposal.[93]

Rockefeller's attempts to bring about construction of a bridge to link Long Island with Westchester County illustrate the Governor at his most stubborn. Advocated by William Ronan, then head of the Metropolitan Transportation Authority and supported by legendary public works king Robert Moses, the proposal drew intense and well-organized opposition from residents and officials of the communities that the bridge would link, Rye and Oyster Bay.[94] Although the bridge proposal was strongly supported by business groups, some local officials, and some regional planning groups, opponents scored a key tactical victory in 1968 when the town of Oyster Bay transferred over 3,000 acres of wetlands to the Department of Interior as a wildlife refuge.[95] Because approach roads for one end of the bridge would have to traverse the wetlands, the Department of Interior now had an effective veto over the project. As the years passed, the Governor adhered to his plans for the bridge despite growing opposition from a variety of sources including the legislature. Refusing to capitulate, Rockefeller twice vetoed legislation prohibiting the Metropolitan Transportation Authority from proceeding with the bridge.[96] When in 1973 the Interior Department ruled against placing approach roads through the wildlife sanctuary, the prospect of federal funds for those roads was killed. Rockefeller reacted with defiance as he answered reporter's questions. According to William Buckley, an exchange with a reporter went something like this. Question: "Do you still intend to build the bridge?" Answer: "Yep." Question: "How will you build it without federal aid?" Answer: "That's up to me. You'll find out as the scenario unfolds."[97] An oftimes critic of the Governor, Buckley caustically wrote, "Who knows, perhaps the Governor has decided to pay for the bridge out of his own pocket."[98]

As the battle over the Rye-Oyster Bay Bridge illustrates, Rockefeller would abandon his pet ideas only with the greatest reluctance. This is evident not only from a perusal of the public record but from interviews with those who worked closely with him. Although most firmly believe that the Governor could change his mind on the basis of rational argument, they could supply few examples of his having done so. One example of the Governor's changing his position that was cited by two different persons was the Rye-Oyster Bay Bridge. Noting that although the Governor had the capacity to believe that he was right and everyone else was wrong, Henry Diamond cited the proposed Hudson River Expressway and the Rye-Oyster Bay Bridge as genuine "major turn-arounds" by the Governor.[99] But the Governor's "turn-around" on the bridge would seem to illustrate not a well-developed capacity to re-assess the correctness of a firmly-held position, but rather a capacity to recognize that in certain extreme cases, one simply would not be able to prevail. In short, there were limits even to Nelson Rockefeller's determination and stubbornness; he could recognize a lost cause for what it was, even when it involved one of his pet ideas. That his surrender on the Rye-Oyster Bay Bridge represents the exercise of this capacity is supported by the Governor's own testimony and that of one of those with him when he made the decision to give up. As T. Norman Hurd remarked, the Governor was a "realist" and based his decision on a belief that continuing to press for the bridge would require such great effort and provoke such great opposition that "it would not be worth it."[100] Rockefeller himself viewed his failure to win approval for the bridge as one of the few significant failures he had experienced in dealing with the legislature. Commenting on his basic approach of working closely with the legislative leaders and trying to make them part of his team, he made the following "confession of error."

> Well, I compromised one too much, to tell you the truth. That was on Long Island, that bridge I wanted to put across. This was a suburban problem and they just said this is a devastating thing for us in suburbia, and that suburban delegation was a key one in the legislature. So they said, could you wait a year, so I postponed it. Then they wanted to wait another year and then the ecologists got in. So I never built that bridge.[101]

The Governor's capitulation regarding the bridge is consistent with the observations of various observers as well as his behavior in a number of other instances. For example, former Speaker Joseph Carlino, a Rockefeller ally, noted that the Governor would back down "on occasion." He added, "he only appreciated strength. He'd give in if there was a martialing of strength from the other side."[102] When considering the Governor's reluctance to abandon one of his pet proposals, it should be remembered that he was quite capable of changing direction once he was convinced that a revised program or policy was necessary. (However, until that point he generally argued that past programs were, in reality, succeeding.) Thus, he was willing to label his earlier drug proposals as failures once he had committed himself to a new approach. Furthermore, he was adept at using his admission that a program had failed as a means of conveying his determination to propose, and sincerity in proposing, a new or revised program. Thus he prefaced his proposals to the 1972 legislature for a new harsh drug program with the following remarks:

> This is a time for brutal honesty regarding narcotics addiction.
>
> In this state, we have tried every possible approach to stop addiction and save the addict through education and treatment—hoping that we could rid society of this disease and drastically reduce mugging on the streets and robbing in the homes.
>
> We have allocated over $1 billion to every form of education against drugs and treatment of the addicted through commitment, therapy, and rehabilitation.
>
> But let's be frank—let's tell it like it is:
>
> We have achieved very little permanent rehabilitation—and have found no cure.[103]

Circumventing the Legislature and the Voters

One tactic of the Governor that remains to be considered is that of circumventing the legislature and/or the public when it was clear that neither was willing or able to provide support for, or approval of, his proposals. The two major options he pursued in such circumstances were the creation of quasi-governmental "public benefit corporations" or "authorities" with the power to finance their own operations through sale of bonds and to resort to the federal government for financial support.

There are numerous examples of the Governor's winning legislative authorization to create authorities with bonding power. Although the legislature was reluctant to appropriate money for expensive construction projects because increased taxes might thus be required, it was usually willing to create authorities that could finance construction through borrowing. Because the authorities were not part of state government in a technical sense, their debt was not considered a legal obligation of the state. Had such debt been so considered, it would have been subject to the state constitution's requirement of voter approval for all state borrowing. (In order to meet the investment community's concerns about the financial safety of the bonds, the Governor proposed, and the legislature approved, provisions that a reserve fund would be created, a fund to which the legislature could appropriate funds to be available should an authority find difficulty in paying bondholders. The details of this arrangement, its origins, and its eventual consequences, are discussed in Chapter 6. Rockefeller candidly explained his motivation and strategy for creation of the first authority with the power to issue so-called moral-obligation bonds.

> I first went . . . with a bond issue for low income housing and it was turned down by the voters. . . . So that I figured that on housing I wasn't going to be able to get through the voters because they did not want to put up money for low income housing and we had run out of money. . . .
> John Mitchell was our bond counsel and I think we have got to give him credit for the idea that if you had a bond issue that said that the legislature will have the right to contribute annually to the surplus account, and you build up an adequate surplus account and made provisions that if you got into trouble the legislature would come forward. . . . This would make it possible to sell the bonds which were not full-faith-and credit bonds.
> I liked the idea. We tried it and we set up a Housing Finance Agency. And the legislature passed it and I could then sell the bonds, and they could vote for housing in their districts and they didn't have to vote any money. I had to take the responsibility for selling the bonds.
> So this worked very well.[104]

As the Governor indicated, creation of the Housing Finance Agency was not the only instance in which he created an authority in order to overcome legislative or public resistence to regular state borrowing or increased spending. For example, after failing to gain legislative approval in the first step of an incremental strategy designed to achieve a major expansion of the state university, Rockefeller resorted to creation of the State University Construction Fund, an authority that was to manage and finance construction. Funds for the construction were to be raised through the sale of moral-obligation bonds by the Housing Finance Agency. Debt service was to be paid from revenue gained from the imposition of a tuition charge in the previously tuition-free system and from certain other fees and income.[105] The first step in the incremental strategy that failed was a budget proposal that the legislature appropriate $20 million for the construction of eleven gymnasiums at teachers' colleges scattered throughout the state, a step that Rockefeller thought would be very attractive to the legislature. But to the Governor's surprise and chagrin, "The legislature cut out all but one and that was the district of the Chairman of the Senate Finance Committee. He kept his."[106]

There are several good illustrations of the Governor turning to the federal government for resources necessary to finance his programs. He made relatively more attempts at this later in his administration as a result of a worsening fiscal situation in New York and increasing legislative and public resistence to state spending.[107]

One early example of the Governor's basing his programs on aggressive pursuit and utilization of federal dollars was his policy of "pre-financing" what his Pure Waters Program established as a 30 percent share to be contributed to projects by the federal government. Although by the end of 1973 the federal government had actually provided only about 13 percent of the costs for construction of treatment facilities in New York, Rockefeller's policy of prefinancing had enabled construction to proceed much faster than otherwise would have been possible. In addition, his aggressive efforts succeeded in causing the federal government to change its policies to allow some retroactive payments to New York.[108]

Perhaps the most spectacular success that the Governor achieved in winning federal resources was in leading the effort to have Congress pass a federal revenue-sharing program. A leading student of federal-state relations credits Rockefeller with a key role in convincing President Nixon to make revenue sharing his top domestic priority for 1972 and in leading the campaign to ensure congressional adoption of a revenue-sharing bill.[109]

According to Donald Haider, the Governor decided to make an all-out effort to bring about a federal revenue-sharing program when he was faced with the prospect of state deficits beginning in 1971.[110] In working to maintain White House commitment to revenue sharing and win congressional approval of the president's proposals, Rockefeller employed a wide range of tactics in building a coalition of supporters made up of governors, state legislators and New York congressmen, elements of the media, and state and local officials and their national organizations.[111] For example, he instigated the organization of two groups that served as rallying points for supporters, the New York State Citizens Committee in Support of Revenue Sharing and the National Citizens Committee for Revenue Sharing.[112] In addition, he carried out an endless round of speeches, press conferences, meetings, and testimony before congressional committees. Taking the ultimate step in his "selling" role, he even sat in on crucial deliberations and strategy sessions among committee and party leaders in the House of Representatives.[113] Furthermore, at crucial stages in the delicate process of working out a formula that would please both larger urban states and smaller rural states and thus maintain vital support of members of the Governor's conference and powerful congressional committee chairmen, most notably Wilbur Mills of House Ways and Means and Russell Long of Senate Finance, the Governor himself supplied the key features of needed compromises.[114]

Although Rockefeller's approach to selling Congress on revenue sharing involved a wide range of conventional tactics such as using "P.R." and applying personal charm to key congressional figures, there was considerable audacity in some elements of his approach. For example, the state budget he proposed for fiscal year 1971-72 was balanced only because of his assumption that Congress would indeed act later in the year to pass a revenue-sharing plan that would provide $400 million to the state.[115] In order to provide some credibility for his relying on a yet-to-be passed measure, Rockefeller managed to persuade Wilbur Mills to sign a letter early in January of 1972 stating that the Ways and Means Committee would make revenue sharing a top priority in the congressional session.[116] By boldly making a balanced state budget dependent on federal revenue sharing and pointing out to the public that the alternative to federal action would be increased state taxes, the Governor sought to increase pressure on those who were in opposition to support revenue sharing. As Connery and Benjamin point out, "this strategy placed the Nixon administration, the state's congressional delegation, and House Democratic leadership on notice that further tax increases in New York would be tied to their inactivity in an election year. . . ."[117]

To those familiar with Nelson Rockefeller's style in dealing with other political leaders and bureaucrats while serving in Washington in the forties and fifties, the virtuosity of his performance as an advocate for his state and the program it needed should come as no surprise. That the more aggressive aspects of his style did not cause him as many problems while Governor as they did earlier may simply be a reflection of the fact that as Governor he had no boss and no boss's advisers on whose toes he could step.

The Congress did, in fact, pass a revenue-sharing bill into law during 1972. The bill was to provide $30.2 billion in federal aid over a five-year period. Although the legislation as finally adopted fell substantially short of what Rockefeller advocated, it, nevertheless, constituted a landmark program that would provide substantial assistance to hard-pressed state and local governments, including New York State.[118]

Conclusion

An analysis of Nelson Rockefeller's efforts at gaining approval for his programs leads to conclusions relating to the nature of his executive style, the nature of his basic approach and the specific tactics that he utilized, the reflection of his life strategy in his selling efforts, and certain elements of his personality. One basic conclusion is that the Governor's performance in selling programs is consistent with our characterization of his executive style as it was revealed in his decision making about programs to propose. His level of personal involvement was high, and although he carried much of the load of selling programs on his own shoulders, his style remained highly collegial in nature. And as was the case with his approach to making decisions on programs, the substantial degree of structure and regularity he imposed on his activities was tempered by flexibility and a willingness to improvise and employ ad hoc arrangements.

Rockefeller's approach to selling programs was to try to organize those whose support he needed as part of a collective effort. This was true whether he was operating in the legislative arena, the public arena, or the Washington arena. At the same time, the Governor was quite willing to play the game of legislative politics as it was normally practiced in the United States in mid-century. Not only did he accept the idea of "wheeling and dealing" with its associated compromises, rewards, and punishments, but he was very adept at it. Never seeming to seek conflict for its own sake, he nevertheless was willing to go all out in battle when the normal give-and-take of legislative politics did not produce results. Beyond this, he seemed to genuinely enjoy playing the tough-guy role. Finally, when all tactics failed to produce success and the legislature or public balked, Rockefeller proved adept at shifting the conflict to a new arena or finding a novel way to circumvent those who opposed his proposals.

That the Governor's efforts to win approval for his programs was an integral part of his life strategy should be self-evident. His efforts to sell his programs also underscore certain of his important personal characteristics; tremendous energy, combativeness, determination and persistence, and inability to admit defeat except under the most hopeless conditions.

6 Financing and Spending: Substance and Method

A fundamental maxim relating to governmental decisions on taxes and expenditures is expressed in this statement by Ira Sharkansky: "Because money appears to be common to all government programs, decisions about taxing and spending appear to play a central role in much of what the government does."[1] This observation certainly applies to the Rockefeller administration, an administration that compiled a record of taxing and spending unparalleled in the state's history. Any consideration of the taxing decisions of the Rockefeller administration must take notice of the dynamic political environment in which taxes are imposed and collected, including the availability and use of a wide variety of taxing devices, and the burdens and liabilities imposed in the creation of new taxing instrumentalities. Other elements associated with taxing and spending decisions came into play as well. Taxing policies had to be explained and sold, each major form of taxation imposed a different burden on different types of taxpayers, and each object of expenditure offered a distinct set of rewards for social and economic groups within the state.[2]

A review of taxing and spending during the Rockefeller administration ultimately involves an examination of the patterns of values, beliefs, and behavior of Nelson Rockefeller, architect of taxing and spending policies. An essential element of his belief system was that all obstacles could be overcome, including constitutional limitations on borrowing by the state. Convinced of the efficacy of big government and fearful of voter reaction to proposals for tax increases and borrowing, and committed to his particular life strategy, the Governor was compelled to advise innovative revenue producing mechanisms to permit an effective attack on what he saw as mounting public needs.

Fiscal Policy: A Review of Rhetoric

The 1958 platform for the Republican party, the platform on which Nelson Rockefeller ran, did not approve of increased taxes, increased debt, or the depletion of reserves attributed to the Harriman administration.[3] The issue of fiscal crisis was central to the campaign which followed Rockefeller's nomination at the Republican State Convention in Rochester on August 25, 1958. Following his election, the Governor repeated this "fiscal crisis" theme in his inaugural address by stating that "we must put the state's fiscal house in order."[4] He also remarked that "We must be conservative—for we know the measureless value that is our heritage, to save and to cherish and to enrich."[5] However, he followed with a statement embodying a conflicting sentiment.

> We shall be liberal—for we are vastly more interested in the opportunities of tomorrow than the problems of today, and we shall be progressive—for the opportunities and the challenges are of such size and scope that we can never halt and say: our labor is done.[6]

Although they were not necessarily consistent with one another, the themes articulated in the inaugural address were clear: to be frugal and yet be active. They would be repeated as themes for the budget message and the annual message to the legislature which quickly followed. In the 1959 budget message Rockefeller stated two fiscal objectives, namely "reestablishment of sound fiscal policies based on pay-as-you-go," and the "minimum use of bond financing."[7] In his annual message he was more explicit about alleged faults of the previous administration: "Deficits during the last four years have been avoided only by the use of bond funds and by drawing on the reserves of the Capital Construction Fund of the State. . . . Clearly the State cannot continue on this course without fiscal disaster."[8] And later, returning to the "liberal" and "progressive" remarks of his inaugural address, the Governor pointed out that there were no new major programs for his administration this year, but "we must face that fact that our steadily rising population will . . . result in constantly increasing State expenditures."[9] To deal with the needs of the growing population, the Governor asserted: "It is imperative that sufficient revenues be collected to meet the expenditures of state government."[10]

Thus in three addresses early in his first term, Rockefeller articulated views that contained the seeds of a "tension" he would ultimately resolve during his tenure. On the one hand, he saw the state's fiscal situation as requiring a conservative pay-as-you-go approach. And on the other, he noted that opportunities, challenges, and increased population would demand increased expenditures. Initially, he would attempt to follow a pay-as-you-go approach to finance needed social services. He would do so by pursuing policies aimed at stimulating economic growth and thereby increasing state revenues with only moderate increases in taxes on the individual taxpayer. Later in his tenure the Governor would abandon the conservative approaches of "limited tax increases" and "pay-as-you go" financing. He was to initiate more tax measures than any other governor in this century, he was to utilize moral-obligation bonds, and he was to vastly expand the role of the public benefit corporation, setting precedents for other states. At the close of his administration, New York would lead the nation in state taxes as a percentage of personal income. By then, the Governor would have obligated future generations of New York State taxpayers by unprecedented borrowing.

An examination of Rockefeller's rhetoric shows the continuing tension that occurred between the goal of meeting "pressing social needs" and the restraints encountered in generating necessary revenue. In his 1960 budget he stated that "It is fiscal folly to borrow during periods of rising income,"[11] because "it is less expensive to pay for construction out of current revenues than to issue bonds."[12] According to the Governor, this approach was desirable because during favorable economic periods current revenues would be sufficient and during bad times revenues for capital construction could be diverted to cover operating expenditures to compensate for the short fall in revenues. Capital construction would continue, Rockefeller argued, "although financed in other ways."[13] However, he emphasized that in the last analysis "all money for capital construction must . . . come from current revenues."[14]

In both the annual messages and budget messages for the next two years, the Governor noted that the fiscal integrity of the state had been restored with a policy of pay-as-you-go, and that this policy had not been "accomplished at the expense of progress toward meeting other urgent problems."[15] In the 1963 budget message he recommended, and the legislature adopted, two expenditure provisions for which he later would be severely criticized by Arthur Levitt, the state comptroller. The two provisions were: the use of "first instance" appropriations and the payment of debt service, in part, from the proceeds of previously issued state bonds.[16] The first-instance appropriations, he maintained, represented temporary loans of "revolving funds" that would be repaid and, therefore, could be properly chargeable against capital reserves until repaid. The payment of debt service with excess funds from bonds for specific capital construction projects need not be reinvested, according to Rockefeller, but could be used constitutionally to retire outstanding debt. This latter device was a practice he apparently did not support when he criticized the fiscal practices of the Harriman administration in his annual message to the legislature in 1959.[17] The Governor concluded his 1963 budget message by stating: "We have not waited for the Federal Government to take action in areas of public need. Instead we have led the way in seeking new paths toward economic growth and fuller employment of both our people and our resources."[18]

By 1964 Nelson Rockefeller no longer emphasized pay-as-you-go quite so strongly in his speeches. The budget message of 1964 spoke of a balance between financial expenditures and human needs. The Governor pointed out that his budget was balanced *financially* "because recommended expenditures have been kept within income estimated to be available for the year ahead."[19] It was balanced in terms of meeting human needs because it meets "our *needs* within our ability to pay for them."[20] In the following year's budget message he presented to the legislature another kind of balance, a balance between "increases in taxes and fees and use of borrowed funds." Prior to his 1965 budget message, Rockefeller had made his first formal declaration that he had indeed abandoned his commitment to pay-as-you-go. As he explained,

> For the six years of my administration, the state's credit has been scrupulously maintained, with pay-as-you-go financing and substantial reductions in the State's tax-supported debt. Our capacity to borrow for emergency purposes has been enhanced through this policy. In my judgment, the criticial task of achieving pure waters for ourselves and our children is just such an emergency purpose.[21]

Thus the Governor had made a major step toward resolving the tension between his commitment to conservative fiscal policies for New York State and his long-time desire to attack big problems with the instrument of big government.

In the years 1966-1968, the emphasis in the Governor's messages was on the escalating social needs of the state and the difficulty of meeting these needs within the existing revenue structure. For example, he characterized the 1966 budget as being within the bounds of "sound financing, efficient management, and prudent choice."[22] That is, explained the Governor, my budget is "financially sound and socially responsible. It meets the pressing needs of New York's residents for essential social services, while preserving fiscal integrity and doing so within our present revenue structure."[23] In the annual message for the same year, he noted, "Realistically, however, we face significant mandated increases in the cost of ongoing programs. . . ."[24]

The 1967 messages contained several observations pertaining to Rockefeller's beliefs concerning the responsibilities of governmental leaders. Although he did not recommend an increase in taxes that year, he did state that through "the judicious use of bonds to finance necessary capital investments vital to our future"[25] the state would be able to maintain the momentum of its progressive leadership. He thus stipulated that it would be necessary to draw on already authorized bond funds to finance mandated increases in state programs because anticipated growth in current revenues would not be sufficient.

In a more general sense the Governor wrote the following:

> Leaders of government do not have the right to evade the responsibility for meeting the vital problems facing the people whom they represent . . . A lack of positive action on our part would lead only to stagnation and deterioration in our State and present an open invitation to intervention by the Federal Government to take over the administration of basic programs which are primarily the responsibility of State and Local governments.[26]

But being a responsible leader was not without fiscal consequences. The language found in the annual message of 1968 reflects the Governor's growing concerns and frustrations:

> We may well be reaching a point where the level of expectations of the American people is rising at a rate which is out-running our capacity to raise the revenue on a sound basis. . . . We are already close to being dangerously over-committed at all levels of government. We must exercise a determination to strike the balance between what is do-able and what is desirable.[27]

The following year Rockefeller reported to the legislature that the fiscal situation in the state was New York's single greatest problem.[28] "The challenge before us is to continue our progress in meeting human needs while exercising the foresight and prudence . . . to take steps within our power to eliminate the escalation of future fiscal crises."[29] The steps he had in mind involved looking beyond the resources commanded by the state. "It is clear that we have reached a point where the Federal Government . . . must share a larger percentage of its tax revenue with state and local governments."[30] According to Rockefeller, the state had borne its responsibility and had not retreated from its mission. As he pointed out, "New York State and local taxes combined now [in 1970] represent the highest tax effort of any competitive state."[31]

In his last inaugural address, in 1971, the Governor stated that New York had reached a critical point. The mission of the state and the responsibility of its leadership were unchanged but only additional revenues from the federal government could permit New York to live up to that historic mission.[32] He concluded his inaugural address as follows: "There is truly nothing America [and by implication New York State] can't achieve—if we will only believe in ourselves again."[33] But in the following week in his annual message he cited another component of the state's fiscal difficulties. "Our fiscal outlook is further complicated by the fact that we are rapidly running out of bond authorizations to meet the capital needs of our people for such services as transportation and housing."[34] Rockefeller reiterated that the federal government had an obligation to share tax revenues with the state. The current crisis presented a time of testing, not only for New York

State, "but for our entire system of Federalism."[35] The budget recommended for fiscal 1972, he bemoaned, had been "shaped largely by forces over which we have little control."[36]

The budget messages of 1972 and 1973 reflected the need to curtail state expenditures, a need made obvious by the fiscal crisis of 1971. Rockefeller characterized those budgets as "economy budgets" which, nonetheless, preserved "essential services." His annual messages for these two years could be classified as philosophical in nature, messages in which the Governor expressed both "justifiable optimism" and "realistic caution."[37] In 1972 Rockefeller acknowledged the assurances of congressional leaders and the president that the federal government would increase aid to New York State to assist the state with its $12.5 billion deficit. But the dominant theme in this message was the declining status of public confidence and a perceived deterioration in public services, a situation the Governor found ironic.

> People's hopes have been lifted by lofty rhetoric, only to be dashed by faltering performance and evidence of corruption. Not surprisingly, there has been a steep decline of public confidence in government at all levels. . . . This situation is ironic, for in actual fact, coincidentally, there has never been a period of greater progress for the individual and for minority groups within our society. This progress was overshadowed, however, by the fact that people's expectations were raised to unattainable heights.[38]

He went on to say that perhaps we could learn from this experience because "adversity can be a stern but useful teacher. Perhaps the difficulties of the times we are passing through will bring us closer to reality in matching our aspirations to our capabilities."[39]

In his final annual message, delivered eleven months prior to his departure as Governor, Nelson Rockefeller's words reflected a considerable degree of resignation, tempered only by vague optimism about the future. He reported to the legislature that "there is no longer any new source of money, no longer any level of government to which we can turn."[40] State governments faced great obstacles, he continued, "No state alone—not even a pioneering resourceful state—can meet the needs of its people and determine its destiny from within its own borders alone."[41] But a challenge was still there to be confronted, especially by the Empire State. "New York State," he observed, "has been the innovator, the leader, the pace setter for the nation. In this moment of both challenge and opportunity, we must not default on that great heritage."[42] The Governor insisted that the experience of confronting human needs and the challenge of raising sufficient revenues to meet those needs had not been in vain. He concluded his final annual message: "We have learned what the State can and cannot do within the means available . . . the lessons will serve us well as we look toward the future . . . which can open the brightest chapter in our lives."[43]

The substance of Rockefeller's fifteen annual messages and fifteen budget messages reflects an evolution in fiscal policy which culminated in a crisis: from pay-as-you-go to nowhere-else-to-go for additional revenues. Bold as it sometimes was, his rhetoric did not match the audacity of his fiscal policies and practices. Perhaps this is a reflection of the fact that the Governor was more a doer than a sayer.

Fiscal Policies: Taxing

Nelson Rockefeller introduced an unprecedented number of taxing measures during his tenure as Governor. Table 6.1 shows sixteen different tax sources and the year in which measures either instituting or increasing a tax were passed by the legislature. The year with the highest number of tax measures is 1968, the second year of Rockefeller's third term, a year in which nine separate tax measures were initiated. There were only three years in which there were no new taxes or increases: 1960, 1963, and 1967.

It should be obvious that all tax increases do not have the same political impact. Perhaps the most unpopular tax increase was the sales tax introduced in 1965 at 2 percent, increased to 3 percent in 1969 and 4 percent in 1971. A controversial measure in 1971 extended the sales tax to receipts from sales of prepared food and drink of less than one dollar, and it was dubbed the "hot dog" tax. A device the Governor utilized to increase revenues in a given year was to change due dates and thus accelerate the schedule of payments for taxes. This device was employed with respect to the bank tax and corporate franchise tax in 1962, the insurance premium tax in 1961, and employer payment of personal income tax withholdings in 1959.

Annual total income from five major sources for the years 1959 through 1973 is shown in Table 6.2. Income from the sources included in this table increased by 350 percent during the Rockefeller administration, an average of 11.35 percent compounded annually. However, not all of the sources contributed equally to the increases. For example, the relative contributions over time of the personal income tax and business taxes to aggregate state revenues varied greatly. As time passed, Governor Rockefeller relied less upon business tax increases and more upon revenues generated by personal income taxes. During his fifteen-year tenure, personal income taxes produced nearly two-fifths (38.4 percent) of the total income for New York State. Business taxes, however, consistently contributed less than one-half as much as personal income taxes to the state's total income. In fact, the contribution of business taxes to the aggregate income for the state decreased in relative terms for the first three terms and leveled out only during the fourth term.[44] The ratio of personal income tax revenues to total New York State income was 2.1 times that of business taxes assessed and collected during the Rockefeller years. A second striking feature of state

Table 6.1
Source of Tax Increases, 1959-1973

YEAR	ALCOHOL CONTROL FEES	ALCOHOL BEVERAGE TAX	BANK TAX	CIGARETTE TAX	CORP. & UTIL. TAXES	CORP. FRANCHISE TAX	ESTATE TAX	HIGHWAY USE TAX	INS. PREMIUM TAX	MOTOR FUEL TAX	MOTOR VEHICLE TAX	PARI-MUTUEL TAX	PERSONAL INCOME TAX	SALES AND USE TAX	STOCK TRANSFER TAX	UNINCORP. BUSINESS TAX	TOTALS
1959				X						X			X				3
1960																	0
1961									X								1
1962			X			X	X										3
1963																	0
1964	X						X										2
1965				X							X	X		X			4
1966															X		1
1967																	0
1968			X	X	X	X			X	X		X	X			X	9
1969			X		X	X		X						X			5
1970												X					1
1971			X		XX	X								X			5
1972		X	X	X						X			X				5
1973												X					1
Totals	1	1	5	4	4	4	2	1	2	3	1	4	3	3	1	1	40

Table 6.2
Income of New York State Government 1959-1973 (in millions)

YEAR	TOTAL INCOME	PERSONAL INCOME TAX	USER TAXES AND FEES	CURRENT REVENUE BUSINESS TAXES	OTHER TAXES AND RECEIPTS	BOND FUNDS
1959	$1,734.2	$ 565.8	$ 427.1	$ 386.9	$ 236.1	$ 118.3
1960	1,998.8	756.6	554.0	399.1	289.1	—
1961	2,117.5	803.7	573.9	425.3	314.6	—
1962	2,366.3	988.6	591.2	453.0	333.5	—
1963	2,597.3	1,018.7	613.1	579.8	385.7	—
1964	2,785.3	1,136.3	640.2	581.1	417.7	—
1965	2,903.8	1,131.7	666.6	695.6	409.9	—
1966	3,463.9	1,270.9	1,126.9	569.4	378.1	118.6
1967	4,025.6	1,527.1	1,425.4	632.0	319.5	121.6
1968	4,629.2	1,787.9	1,499.9	609.9	341.8	389.7
1969	5,523.8	2,151.6	1,658.3	858.4	419.2	436.3
1970	6,211.2	2,506.4	2,025.6	962.2	413.0	304.0
1971	6,724.3	2,550.2	2,216.1	869.6	480.4	608.0
1972	6,939.2	2,516.3	2,613.4	1,148.9	502.3	158.3
1973	7,812.6	3,065.2	2,974.2	1,282.6	947.5	56.4

SOURCE: State of New York, Division of the Budget.

revenues as revealed in Table 6.2 is the heavy reliance on the use of bond funds in the third and fourth terms. That feature illustrates the Governor's departure from his allegiance to the pay-as-you-go philosophy. Data in Table 6.3 makes very clear the extent to which revenue from both taxes and borrowing outpaced the growth of personal income in the state during the years Rockefeller was Governor.

Expanding Public Authorities: Building Without Increasing Taxes

Public authorities have existed in New York State since 1921 when the Port of New York Authority was created, but Nelson Rockefeller employed the device of the "public benefit corporation" or public authority more than any other state chief executive. As a leading student of public corporations said of Rockefeller, "He knew what he wanted for the State, and he had learned during his wartime experience in the federal government that an important quality of the corporation is its adaptability to the needs of different situations."[45]

The construction projects financed by New York State public authorities have been of three varieties. Historically, authorities financed, constructed, and operated facilities that were revenue producing and self-sustaining facilities, such as bridges and roads. Later projects such as state university and mental hygiene facilities, projects traditionally financed by the state itself, were also undertaken with the assistance of public authorities. And finally, during the later Rockefeller years, public authorities assumed responsibility for projects that were once provided by private enterprise, such as the operation of public transportation systems.[46] These projects were not intended to be self-supporting and thus were to be heavily subsidized by the government and taxpayers. As one author notes, most of the authority bonds were exempt from dollar ceilings, the requirement of voter approval, limits on interest rates, and other constitutional restraints on general obligation debt.[47]

Arguments commonly cited in support of public authorities are that they overcome unrealistic debt limits, provide needed services and facilities without increasing taxes, shift cost burdens to the user, facilitate intergovernmental cooperation, are divorced from politics and thus provide for independent, efficient, and businesslike operations, promote citizen participation, are convenient and flexible, and raise capital more easily and at no more cost than other methods.[48] However, Rockefeller's extensive use of authorities for massive borrowing ultimately drew heavy criticism and demonstrated that disadvantages are also associated with their use.

The Governor used the system of authorities to achieve his goals for the state by avoiding a key political problem. Specifically, he was able to avoid securing the required approval of the voters for borrowing backed by the

Table 6.3
New York State Economic Data: 1959-1973

FISCAL YEAR	STATE POPULATION (IN MILLIONS)	STATE PERSONAL INCOME (IN BILLIONS)	PER CAPITA STATE PERSONAL INCOME	PER CAPITA ADJUSTED STATE TAX COLLECTIONS	RATIO, ADJUSTED STATE TAX COLLECTIONS PERSONAL INCOME	PER CAPITA STATE DEBT
1959	16.6	$ 41.8	$ 2,518	$ 94	3.7%	$ 54
1960	16.7	44.4	2,661	119	4.5	59
1961	16.8	46.3	2,746	129	4.7	62
1962	17.1	48.0	2,796	125	4.5	61
1963	17.2	50.7	2,948	138	4.7	62
1964	17.4	52.7	3,029	142	4.7	62
1965	17.5	56.0	3,200	151	4.7	62
1966	17.7	59.5	3,362	186	5.5	70
1967	19.9	63.7	3,559	215	6.0	74
1968	18.0	68.7	3,817	228	6.0	98
1969	18.2	75.0	4,121	275	6.7	124
1970	18.3	80.9	4,421	316	7.2	138
1971	18.3	86.4	4,721	324	6.9	171
1972	18.4	91.7	4,984	360	7.2	183
1973	18.5	97.7	5,281	422	8.0	187

SOURCE: State of New York, Annual Reports of the Comptroller.

"full-faith-and-credit of the state."[49] Prior to his assuming office, the voters had rejected a limited-profit housing bond proposal for the third time (1956) and had rejected for the second time (1958) a highway bond issue. Also rejected (for the fourth time) was a 1961 proposal to guarantee bonds for higher education and a number of proposals in the early 1960s to increase state subsidies for housing and slum clearance.[50]

Through the use of authorities, Rockefeller could bypass a key unit in the established bureaucracy, the Department of Public Works, and thus build faster without the necessity for annual legislative appropriations. He could also avoid reliance on state architects known for a lack of creativity. Another compelling reason for his relying heavily on authorities is cited by Annmarie A. Walsh, namely:

> . . . his pay-as-you-go political slogans and the normal difficulties of balancing a budget. . . . In 1962, state law governing accounting methods was changed to eliminate the requirement that advances to authorities appear in the budget. The fiscal profile of the Rockefeller administration would have looked significantly less pay-as-you-go if it were not for this change and other innovations of authority finance.[51]

Rockefeller was personally able to exercise effective control over authorities in New York State due to a combination of factors. He appointed loyalists to positions as authority executives or directors, he had direct and immediate access to members of the financial community, and he secured advisers who knew the bond markets.[52] Many of the officials appointed as heads of authorities or to authority boards owed their public careers to the Governor, and some were the recipients of loans or gifts from him. Among the latter were William J. Ronan (Metropolitan Transportation Authority, Port Authority, Power Authority) and Alton G. Marshall (Urban Development Corporation, Sports Authority), both former secretaries to the Governor, and Edward J. Logue (Urban Development Corporation and its subsidiaries). Included among other persons appointed to high level authority positions who had close ties with Rockefeller were former program associates William A. Sharkey (Dormitory Authority), and Richard Wiebe and Edward Kreske (Metropolitan Transportation Authority).

As of 1973 the number of public authorities operating on a statewide or regional basis had increased to forty-two from the twenty-six which existed in 1960.[53] The forty-two authorities, the nature of their activity, and the date of their creation are listed in Table 6.4. During the Rockefeller administration, twenty-three authorities were created, more than half (55 percent) of the authorities active in 1973. In only two categories had there been no authority created during Rockefeller's tenure: port development and market centers. Nine were created in the category of transportation and transit, four in commerce and development, eight in finance and housing, and two in sports and recreation.

Table 6.4
Statewide Public Authorities: 1973

CLASSIFICATION Authority	Year Created
TRANSPORTATION AND TRANSIT:	
Buffalo and Fort Erie Public Bridge	1933
Capital District Transportation	1970*
Central New York Regional Transportation	1970*
East Hudson Parkway	1960*
Jones Beach State Parkway	1933
Lake Champlain Bridge	1927
Long Island Rail Road	1966*
Manhattan and Bronx Surface Transit Operating	1962*
Metropolitan Transportation	1965*
New York City Transit	1953
New York State Bridge	1932
New York State Thruway	1950
Niagara Frontier Transportation	1967*
Ogdensburg Bridge and Port	1950
Rochester-Genesee Regional Transportation	1969*
Staten Island Rapid Transit Operating	1971*
Thousand Islands Bridge	1933
Triborough Bridge and Tunnel	1933
PORT DEVELOPMENT:	
Albany Port District	1925
Port Authority of New York and New Jersey	1921
Port of Oswego	1955
COMMERCE AND DEVELOPMENT:	
Atomic and Space Development	1962*
Environmental Facilities Corporation	1970*
Industrial Exhibit	1933
New York Job Development	1961*
Power Authority of the State of New York	1931
United Nations Development	1968*

SOURCE: Compiled from various reports of the comptroller of the state of New York.

*Authority created during Rockefeller administration.

Table 6.4—*Continued*

CLASSIFICATION Authority	Year Created
FINANCE AND HOUSING:	
Battery Park City	1968*
Dormitory	1944
Facilities Development Corporation	1968*
Higher Education Assistance	1957
Housing Finance Agency	1960*
Medical Care Facilities Finance Agency	1972*
Municipal Bond Bank	1972*
State of New York Mortgage Agency	1970*
State University Construction Fund	1962*
Urban Development Corporation	1968*
SPORTS AND RECREATION:	
Bethpage Park	1933
New York State Sports Authority	1972*
New York State Thoroughbred Breeding and Development Fund Corporation	1973*
MARKET CENTERS:	
Central New York Regional Market	1933
Genesee Valley Regional Market	1951

Table 6.5, a composite balance sheet for public authorities showing assets (investment in fixed assets and other assets), liabilities (bonds and notes outstanding, outstanding government advances, and other liabilities and reserves), and gross revenues, shows a consistent pattern of growth from 1960 to 1973. Total assets had grown by 300 percent in these 14 years, liabilities by 306 percent, and revenues by 243 percent.

Borrowing: Full-Faith-and-Credit Debt

During the Rockefeller administration the amount of debt increased and the manner in which the state incurred its debt changed. A discussion of state debt prior to 1960 would have focused almost completely on full-faith-and-credit debt, but in the decade to follow it would become necessary to include two additional types of capital financing through borrowing: lease-purchase agreements and moral obligation bonding, both forms of indirect

Table 6.5
New York State Public Authorities Assets, Liabilities, and Revenues: 1960-1973 (in millions)

	ASSETS		LIABILITIES		REVENUES	
Fiscal Year	Total	Percentage Annual Increase	Total	Percentage Annual Increase	Total	Percentage Annual Increase
1960	4,378	—	3,395	—	528	—
1961	4,723	7.9	3,604	6.2	552	4.5
1962	4,968	5.2	3,719	3.2	575	4.2
1963	5,568	12.1	4,239	14.0	727	26.4
1964	6,227	11.8	4,756	12.2	763	5.0
1965	6,762	8.6	5,142	8.1	836	9.6
1966	7,202	6.5	5,431	5.6	925	10.6
1967	7,959	10.5	5,915	8.9	1,059	14.5
1968	9,274	16.5	6,935	17.2	1,137	7.4
1969	9,921	7.0	7,433	7.2	1,187	4.4
1970	11,265	13.5	8,539	14.9	1,404	18.3
1971	13,342	18.4	10,248	20.0	1,545	10.0
1972	15,485	16.1	12,113	18.2	1,611	4.3
1973	17,535	13.2	13,808	14.0	1,814	12.6

SOURCE: State of New York, Annual Reports of the Comptroller.

debt. Each type of debt involves a special kind of liability for the state. New York State and seventeen other states require special elections or referenda for the approval of general obligation borrowing proposals.[54] When voters give their approval, the bonds or notes then issued are backed by the full-faith-and-credit of the state and thus its power to tax. This means that the state cannot choose to default on repayment to investors. Should the legislature fail to appropriate monies to pay principal and interest on full-faith-and-credit bonds, the constitution requires the comptroller to set aside the first tax monies available and pay the amortization costs. In the event the comptroller refuses, bondholders may go to court and force payment. Thus, the pledge of full-faith-and-credit makes these bonds attractive securities; in order to default the state would have to stop collecting taxes. Humphrey S. Tyler was to note in 1975: "with the exception of $750 million in authority bonding power approved by the voters, none of the obligations issued by New York authorities carry the state's full-faith-and-credit pledge of redemptions."[55]

Table 6.6 shows New York State's full-faith-and-credit net debt for the years 1959 to 1973. The net debt issued and outstanding includes term and serial debt, temporary debt incurred in anticipation of the sale of bonds payable from state revenues, and short-term tax anticipation notes.[56] (Since full-faith-and-credit backed debt is only one form of public purpose capital financing, the net total debt as shown in Table 6.6 does not include all the outstanding debt for the state.) As Table 6.6 also shows, total net full-faith-and-credit debt for New York State was $897.0 million in 1959 and had increased to an all-time high of $3,451.3 million by March 31, 1973. The average annual increase in such debt was 10.6 percent, and the growth from 1959 to 1973 was 284 percent. Expenditures for debt service had grown an astonishing 1,633 percent during the Rockefeller years.

Table 6.7 shows the various types of activities that were financed through full-faith-and-credit debt from the years 1963 through 1973. Especially notable are the great increases in two areas, transportation and "pure waters." Both reflect voter approval of massive bond issues in the mid-1960s.

Borrowing: Lease-Purchase Agreements and Moral-Obligation Bonding

There are two varieties of lease-purchase agreements: lease-purchase agreements between the state and public authorities or municipalities and lease-purchase agreements supported by programs of state aid. These forms of lease-purchase agreements and other "debt-like" commitments in the form of moral-obligation bonds constitute the "indirect" financing devices employed during the Rockefeller administration. Unlike full-faith-and-credit borrowing, these devices do not require voter approval. Out-

Table 6.6
New York State Full-Faith-and-Credit Debt: 1959-1973

FISCAL YEAR	EXPENDITURES FOR DEBT SERVICE (IN MILLIONS)	PERCENTAGE INCREASE	DEBT INCURRED (TERM BONDS, SERIAL BONDS, TEMPORARY DEBT) (IN MILLIONS)	PERCENTAGE INCREASE	NET TOTAL DEBT (IN MILLIONS)	PERCENTAGE INCREASE
1959	$ 250.3	—	$ 508.7	—	$ 897.0	—
1960	428.6	71.2	523.8	3.0	998.1	11.3
1961	299.4	−30.1	282.0	−46.2	1,034.5	3.6
1962	318.1	6.2	276.3	− 2.0	1,052.2	1.7
1963	449.9	41.4	437.8	65.7	1,072.0	1.9
1964	899.5	100.0	815.9	88.4	1,081.6	.9
1965	800.3	−11.0	742.6	− 9.0	1,088.7	.7
1966	938.7	17.3	1,017.8	37.1	1,236.1	13.5
1967	1,024.1	9.1	1,028.6	1.1	1,323.2	7.0
1968	1,492.7	45.8	1,874.1	82.2	1,769.1	33.7
1969	1,883.7	26.2	2,148.1	14.6	2,258.3	27.7
1970	1,186.0	−37.0	1,330.6	−38.1	2,552.6	13.0
1971	1,590.0	34.1	2,052.5	54.3	3,129.6	22.6
1972	2,622.2	64.9	3,141.5	53.1	3,362.2	7.4
1973	4,337.3	65.4	3,102.6	− 1.2	3,451.3	2.7

SOURCE: State of New York, Annual Reports of the Comptroller.

Table 6.7
New York State Full-Faith-and-Credit Debt by Activity: 1963-1973 (in millions)

FISCAL YEAR	TRANSPORTATION CAPITAL FACILITIES	HOUSING	MENTAL HEALTH	PURE WATERS	PARK AND RECREATION	OTHERS	TOTAL
1963	$ 188.1	$ 670.0	$ 115.9	—	$ 49.0	$ 49.0	$ 1,072.0
1964	174.4	713.1	105.1	—	46.5	42.5	1,081.6
1965	161.1	722.7	94.3	—	74.0	36.6	1,088.7
1966	295.1	756.2	83.5	—	69.5	31.8	1,236.1
1967	350.0	784.1	92.7	$ 3.4	65.0	28.0	1,323.2
1968	663.7	815.1	126.9	50.0	71.5	41.9	1,769.1
1969	1,056.2	849.1	157.1	55.0	83.0	57.9	2,258.3
1970	1,290.7	838.2	159.7	85.6	78.5	69.9	2,522.6
1971	1,760.0	820.3	174.7	153.9	100.4	120.3	3,129.6
1972	1,914.3	802.2	168.3	192.0	129.0	156.4	3,362.2
1973	1,931.5	784.3	161.3	274.1	141.3	158.8	3,451.3

SOURCE: State of New York, Office of the Comptroller, *1974 Annual Report*.

standing indirect debt commitments for the state of New York based on one or more of these devices totaled nearly $6 billion dollars as of June 30, 1972. Table 6.8 contains summary statistics on indirect debt for a ten-year period beginning with fiscal year 1962. The figures show a substantial increase in debt commitments without voter approval from $129 million in fiscal 1962 to $5,620 million in 1972, an increase of 4,256 percent. Moreover, the $5,620 million represents only 54 percent of the potential debt that had been authorized ($10,347.0 million) but not yet issued in the case of those programs with statutory spending limits. Comptroller Arthur Levitt consistently criticized indirect devices for financing new facilities for the state on grounds that a potential state liability is created and that indirect financing schemes circumvent Article VII of the state constitution. This consitutional provision stipulates that long-term debt of the state may be contracted "if the Legislature authorizes it by law for some single work or purpose and only if the law is subsequently approved by vote of the people at a general election."[57]

The lease-purchase device initiated during the nineteenth century is not as complicated as the formation of an authority. Utilizing this financing device, a state or local government contracts with another level of government or an authority to issue revenue bonds and invest the proceeds in the construction of a project that is desired and designed by the sponsoring (tenant) government. The tenant government then signs a long-term lease to pay rent to the borrowing agency until the outstanding bonds are paid off. Title to the facility is transferred to the tenant government when the bonds are repaid and the lease expires. The rents for the lease-purchase agreements "result in annual charges against the state's tax revenues or against earmarked revenues used to augment the tax revenues."[58]

Of the total indirect debt outstanding in 1972, the amount attributable to the first category of lease-purchase agreements was $2,389.6 million. The various lease-purchase rental debt commitments and the specific dollar amounts associated with these activities were: mental hygiene facilities financed by the Housing Finance Agency (HFA), $473.9 million (19.8 percent); state office buildings financed by Albany County (state office building/cultural complex-South Mall), $438.1 million (18.4 percent); state office buildings financed by other municipalities, $54.9 million (2.2 percent); state office buildings financed by retirement systems, $40.3 million (1.6 percent); and State University of New York academic-type facilities, $1,382.4 million (58 percent).

A second category of lease-purchase agreement, municipal lease-purchase agreements supported by programs of state aid, contributed $497.6 million to the total indirect debt for the state as of June 30, 1972, as follows: city university facilities financed by the Dormitory Authority, $183.2 million (36.8 percent); municipal health facilities financed by HFA, $298.1 million (59.9 percent); mental health and retardation facilities financed by HFA, $4.8 million (1 percent); and youth facilities, $11.5 million (2.3 percent).

Table 6.8
New York State Commitments in Debt Without Voter Approval: 1962-1972 (in millions)

FISCAL YEAR	BONDS	DEBT OUTSTANDING AT CLOSE OF AGENCY FISCAL YEAR NOTES	TOTAL	DEBT AUTHORIZED BUT UNISSUED ON PROGRAMS WITH BORROWING LIMITS
1962	$ 114	$ 91	$ 129*	$ 554.6
1963	384	185	569	1,298.8
1964	620	150	770	1,210.3
1965	784	246	1,030	1,600.0
1966	998	239	1,237	1,756.9
1967	1,297	363	1,661	2,215.4
1968	1,696	498	2,207*	4,336.6
1969	1,966	616	2,582	4,654.3
1970	2,460	741	3,200	6,793.9
1971	3,316	1,086	4,401	8,083.9
1972	3,795	1,372	5,067*	10,790.4
June 30, 1972**	4,193	1,427	5,620	10,347.0

SOURCE: State of New York, Office of the Comptroller, *Debt-Like Commitments of the State of New York*, January 1973.

*The Office of the Comptroller is unable to offer a satisfactory explanation of the fact that there is an apparent error in calculating this total.

**The fiscal year ends on March 31.

One of the most controversial lease-back projects for New York State was the construction of the state office/cultural complex originally known as the South Mall project and later as the Governor Nelson A. Rockefeller Empire State Plaza. The state contracted with Albany County, which does not require voter approval to sell its bonds, to construct the complex adjacent to the existing capitol in Albany. Started in 1964, it was not yet completed when the Governor resigned in December, 1973. The preliminary estimated cost of the project was approximately $250 million, and the original financing agreement authorized $480 million in bonds. The lease with Albany County was drawn for forty years, running through 2004 when the state is to assume title. The ninety-acre complex has been criticized primarily because of its alleged opulence and excessive cost overruns. By 1981 the estimated final cost was $1.7 billion, nearly four times the original bond authorization.[59] Under the terms of the arrangement with Albany County, additional costs are automatically passed along to the state in the form of higher rents required to cover debt service.

The remainder of the state's indirect debt outstanding as of June 30, 1972, was $2,732.6 million, and it has been classified by the state Comptroller Arthur Levitt in the category of "other commitments." This latter category consists primarily of programs financed by so-called moral-obligation debt.

Discouraged by the defeat of spending and borrowing proposals at the polls during his first term, the Governor had looked for a way to involve private investment in public housing and other state construction programs, ways of funding that would not need the approval of a reluctant electorate. A series of discussions with future United States Attorney General John N. Mitchell, then a leading New York City bond attorney, and James W. Gaynor, state housing commissioner, produced a novel idea to create a new type of authority whose bonds would be secured not only by income from revenue-producing projects but by the "moral obligation" of the state to make contributions to an authority reserve fund in any circumstances in which such a fund had insufficient resources to cover the payment of principle and interest costs in a given year. The type of statutory language utilized is illustrated by the language contained in the statute creating the Housing Finance Agency.

> To assure the continued operation and solvency of the agency for the carrying out of the public purposes of this article, provision is made . . . for the accumulation in the equity reserve fund of an amount equal to the maximum amount of principal and interest maturing and becoming due in any succeeding calendar year on all equity bonds of the agency then outstanding. In order further to assure such maintenance of the equity reserve fund, there shall be annually apportioned and paid to the agency for deposit in the equity reserve fund such sum, if any, as shall be certified by the chairman of the agency to the governor and director of the budget as necessary to restore the equity reserve fund to an amount equal to the maximum amount of principal and interest maturing and becoming due in any succeeding calendar year on the equity bonds of the agency then outstanding. The chairman of the agency shall annually, on or before December first, make and deliver to the governor and director of the budget his certificate stating the amount, if any, required to restore the equity reserve fund to the amount aforesaid and the amount so stated, if any, shall be apportioned and paid to the agency during the then current state fiscal year.[60]

Although the statute does not specifically mention the legislature, the ultimate source of funds to be "apportioned" by the Governor and director of the budget would, of course, be the legislature itself in its exercise of the power of appropriation.

Bonds secured with this guarantee were called "moral-obligation" bonds because they did not satisfy the "legal" full-faith-and-credit provisions of the state constitution. The prospectuses for the bonds of the State Housing Finance Agency (HFA), the first agency created (in 1960) to sell moral-obligation bonds, contain this caveat: "The Bonds of the Agency are not a debt of the State and the State is not liable on such bonds." This caveat was necessary because, technically, "one legislature cannot dictate actions to future legislatures."[61]

By the Governor's fourth term, mechanisms of indirect financing, lease-purchase and moral-obligation bonding, were being used to finance thirty-four different programs. Table 6.9 shows that, in 1972, the largest number of capital programs authorized without voter approval (eight) were financed by the Housing Finance Agency. The Dormitory Authority, regional transportation districts, and municipalities each financed five programs. By 1972 the Housing Finance Agency had more debt outstanding, $3,812.1, than the total amount of full-faith-and-credit debt of New York State.

Housing Finance Agency: An Indirect Funding Conglomerate with Subsidiaries

The Housing Finance Agency became the prototype of the corporation that would serve as the state's "financial intermediary," substitute private investments for direct governmental expenditures, and secure these investments with the state's "moral obligation." (Thirty states had created seventy-nine authorities of this type by 1975.)[62] Rockefeller closely monitored the HFA and its operations, state government departmental heads dominated its board, and its activities were executed partly through the existing staffs of the state government. With the aid of the state's "moral guarantee," the HFA borrowed money and invested the proceeds in the projects of other public agencies and limited-profit private firms.[63]

By 1974, the HFA could be described by one scholar as a conglomerate with subsidiaries.[64] It had developed a multipurpose banking business and had financed a variety of public and private projects as shown in Table 6.10, including middle-income housing, hospitals and nursing homes, community mental health services, youth facilities, community senior citizens' centers, state university academic facilities, mental hygiene facilities and health facilities. Included in Table 6.10 is information which shows that HFA's programs, excluding state university construction, had a combined authorized borrowing capacity of $6,183,228,240, involved thirteen discrete transactions with agencies of the state (some agencies were involved with more than one program), and relied on a wide variety of revenue sources for financing debt service costs.

The Governor used the HFA and another semiautonomous government corporations to secure funds to expand the state university system without going through the legislature for appropriations. The mammoth construction costs associated with converting the state's system of teachers colleges into a major university system was accomplished by creating the State

Table 6.9
New York State Commitments in Debt Without Voter Approval: Financing Entities in 1972

FINANCING ENTITY	NUMBER OF PROGRAMS	AMOUNT OF DEBT OUTSTANDING 1972 (IN MILLIONS)
Atomic and Space Development Corporation	1	$ 10.0
Battery Park City Authority	1	200.0
Dormitory Authority	5	637.2
Environmental Facilities Corporation	1	57.5
Housing Finance Agency	8	3,812.1
Job Development Corporation (General Revenue Bonds)	1	0
Municipal Bond Bank	1	0
N.Y.S. Mortgage Agency	1	49.7
Regional Transportation Districts	5	1.1
Thruway Authority (State Highway)	1	0
United Nations Development Corporation	1	0
Urban Development Corporation	1	318.9
Municipalities	5	493.0
Retirement Systems	2	40.3
Total	34	$5,619.8

SOURCE: State of New York, Office of the Comptroller, *Debt-Like Commitments of the State of New York*, January 1973.

University Construction Fund (SUCF) in 1962. The indirect funding mechanism employed was the lease-purchase agreement. SUCF contracts with HFA to float bonds to construct new and expanded academic facilities. SUCF receives its rent revenues from the State University of New York (SUNY), which is responsible for the maintenance of the facilities once completed. SUNY obtains its revenues in the form of tuition and fees from student funds, which are then deposited in the SUNY Income Fund. The funds from the Income Fund are transferred to the SUCF, and the latter then pays rent to HFA to retire the bonds that provided the initial revenue for the construction.

Table 6.10
New York State Housing Finance Programs: 1974

PROGRAM	STATUTORY AUTHORIZATION	STATUTORY BORROWING LIMITS	STATE AGENCIES ACTING WITH HFA	ELIGIBLE BORROWERS	FINANCIAL BASIS	PRIMARY SOURCE OF REVENUE
1. Middle-income housing			Division of Housing and Community Renewal	Regulated housing companies	Mortgage loan	
General housing loan Nonprofit housing Urban rental housing equity loan	Article II, Private Housing Finance Law	$2,100,000,000 (includes $50,000,000 Equity Loan Program authorization)			General obligation	Project
Capital grant low-rent assistance	Article III, Private Housing Finance Law	Total state appropriation $33,228,240			Lease and sublease	State appropriations
2. Hospitals and nursing homes	Articles 28-A, 28-B and 44, Public Health Law	$1,950,000,000	Department of Health	Regulated nursing home companies, nonprofit hospital and medical corporations	Mortgage loan	Project and borrower
3. Community mental health services and mental retardation services	Article 75, Mental Hygiene Law	$100,000,000	Department of Mental Hygiene	Regulated mental health or mental retardation services companies	Mortgage loan	Project

SOURCE: Annmarie Walsh, *The Public's Business: The Politics and Practices of Government Corporations* (Cambridge: MIT Press, 1978).

Table 6.10—*Continued*

PROGRAM	STATUTORY AUTHORIZATION	STATUTORY BORROWING LIMITS	STATE AGENCIES ACTING WITH HFA	ELIGIBLE BORROWERS	FINANCIAL BASIS	PRIMARY SOURCE OF REVENUE
4. Youth facilities	Title 5-A of Article 6, Social Services Law	$100,000,000	Department of Social Services; Community Facilities Project Guarantee Fund	Regulated agencies authorized to provide care for children	Mortgage loan	Project
5. Community Senior citizens' centers	Article VII-A, Private Housing Finance Law	$50,000,000	Department of Social Services; Community Facilities Project Guarantee Fund	Regulated community senior citizens' centers and services companies	Mortgage loan	Project
6. State university construction	Article 8-A, Education Law	Controlled by the Master Plan of the State University	State University of NY; State University Construction Fund	State University of NY and State University Construction Fund	Sale and lease-back	Tuition and other fees paid by state university students deposited in Income Fund of State University

Table 6.10—*Continued*

7. Mental hygiene improvement	Facilities Development Corp. Act (McK. Unconsol. § 4401-4417)	$1,050,000,000	Facilities Development Corp.; Department of Mental Hygiene	Facilities Development Corp. and Department of Mental	Sale and lease-back	Fees paid by patients in state mental institutions deposited in Income Account of Facilities Development Corp.
8. Health facilities	Facilities Development Corp Act (McK. Unconsol. § 4401-4417)	$800,000,000	Facilities Development Corp.; Department of Health	Municipalities	Sale and lease-back or lease and lease-back	Rentals paid by municipalities

Once the semiautonomous corporations, HFA and SUCF, were in place, the legislature had little involvement in financial transactions. By 1974 more than 1,300 projects on thirty-four SUNY campuses had been constructed through lease-purchase financing at a cost of $1.8 billion.[65] It was estimated that by 1980, HFA would have financed another $500 million to $1 billion worth of projects for SUCF.[66]

The year that Rockefeller resigned from office, HFA's executive director became chairman of the New York State Mortgage Agency, popularly known as "Sonny Mae." Sonny Mae was considered as the

> step brother to the federally sponsored Fannie Mae and federally owned Ginny Mae (Federal and Government National Mortgage Agencies). The Sonny Mae overlap was particularly useful for HFA's relationship with institutional investors. Sonny Mae was authorized to borrow $750 million to buy up old mortgages with low interest rates that banks were stuck with, on the condition that the banks use the proceeds to purchase new residential mortgages paying higher interest rates.[67]

HFA had financial strength because it could accumulate an enormous reservoir of short-term money to finance projects with notes during construction. Long-term bonds were issued only when the projects were ready to produce revenues. This latitude enabled HFA to avoid the risk of project noncompletion from being a factor in long-term financing. The Urban Development Corporation (UDC), created in 1968 for the purpose of community development, including housing and industrial projects, had to pay higher rates because it issued long-term financing for projects as yet unconstructed. However, it was short-term borrowing that would ultimately lead to difficulties for both HFA and UDC.[68]

The Urban Development Corporation and Financial Crisis

The HFA had balanced books on its mortgage operations, but the projects supported by HFA were subsidized as its operating revenues benefitted from a variety of state and public aid for medical facilities, housing, and higher education. The Urban Development Corporation did initially finance its middle-income housing projects through HFA, but in order to be free of the restrictive mortgage policies of HFA, it began to use its own bond funds. UDC was able to achieve an unprecedented building rate throughout the state because, unlike HFA, which was a banking enterprise, UDC had operating authority. However, 90 percent of the units built by UDC were dependent on federal subsidies, and cutbacks in housing subsidies by the Nixon administration hurt it severely as did rising interest rates, delays in construction caused by local opposition to some projects, cost overruns, and rental problems.[69]

The last year Rockefeller was in office the financial standing of UDC became shaky. Institutional investors demanded the appointment of a new financial officer, its bond rating was dropped from A to Baa-1 by Moody's, and auditing accountants cited "material uncertainties relating to receipts of required amounts of subsidies"[70] as sufficient reason not to express an opinion on UDC's 1973 financial statement. This situation would have ruled out the issuance of new bonds for a firm in the private sector, but UDC managed to sell $200 million in bonds in May of 1973. Twenty-two months later UDC was in default, and the credit of the state was in jeopardy. UDC was unable to pay bond anticipation notes due banks from late February to the end of April in 1975. In the midst of a great uproar, the legislature brought UDC out of default by authorizing a money package to bring its reserves to the level of its annual debt service in 1975 and again in 1976. The report of the New York State Moreland Act Commission on the financial collapse of the Urban Development Corporation highlighted the painful truth about moral-obligation borrowing. "UDC's failure to meet the maturing obligation of its bond anticipation notes made it clear that the debts of moral obligation agencies were debts of the State, thus exposing a large burden on the State's credit for which no provision has been made."[71]

The situation was not much better for HFA. For fifteen years it had "rolled over" its enormous short-term borrowings into long-term bonds without difficulty, but after the collapse of UDC, private investors began avoiding New York State bonds. Thus HFA could no longer engage in this practice, and heroic month-by-month efforts were necessary to stave off default on HFA bonds until the corporation finally regained access to the market late in 1976. However, the state found it necessary to initiate a "Build Out Plan" of refinancing all bond anticipation notes as a means of enabling all partially completed projects to be finished. In addition, ceilings were placed on all future authority bonds that were to be backed by the state's moral obligation.

By the time UDC and HFA were rescued, Nelson Rockefeller was no longer governor and his "indirect" mechanism of financing capital construction "without voting money" had been saved only when the "moral obligation" was, in effect, converted into a guarantee of direct access to the state's tax revenues.

Borrowing: Lending First-Instance Appropriations to Authorities

In order to facilitate some activities of public authorities, Governor Rockefeller engaged in the practice of appropriating advance monies, chargeable against capital reserves, to finance federal shares of a program which were repayable under long-term agreements. As noted in his executive budget for 1963, the Governor considered these first-instance appropriations as revolving funds rather than true state expenditures because they would be "fully reimbursed."[72] State Comptroller Arthur Levitt opposed the first-instance appropriations primarily on two grounds. First, he argued that charging the advances to the public authorities against capital reserves rather than the general fund tended to obscure the state's pattern of expenditures. Levitt was to point out that the 1969 executive budget covered only two-thirds of the expenditures for the state. In addition to advances to public authorities, the executive budget excluded some of the expenditures financed from bond and note proceeds, federal funds, and "earmarked funds." Among Levitt's recommendations was curtailing first-instance appropriations and making appropriations to the public authorities through the general fund.[73]

The comptroller also criticized the first-instance appropriations as too extensive and, eventually, as bad debts. Contrary to Rockefeller's expectations, first-instance appropriations were not always repaid. In 1970, a Democratic minority member of the Senate Committee on Finance, Samuel Greenberg, called the first-instance appropriation "fiscal foolery" because of the alleged financial manipulations it permitted. For example, Greenberg noted that the Metropolitan Transit Authority had been provided first-instance appropriations as seed money to purchase the Long Island Railroad. He criticized the fact that some of the funds were used "to cover payments on cars that were being leased to the Long Island Railroad by the Port Authority which had purchased them with its own bonds issued with a special New York State Guarantee."[74]

In 1970 Comptroller Levitt reported that first-instance advances had been made at the rate of $35 million a year from 1965 to 1969. At the end of calendar year 1969, the amount due from authorities as a result of these advances totaled $156.3 million. By March 31, 1971, the amount due stood at $190 million. Levitt also reported that substantial amounts of the advances had to be liquidated by regular state appropriations rather than by authority repayments. In fact, between April 1964, and December 31, 1969, $87.7 million of these advances had been written off as "bad debts," and much of the remaining advances were of "doubtful collectability."[75] The effect of the legislature's voting to "forgive" these advances, a common practice, was to turn the first-instance loans into permanent appropriations, another means of providing "back-door financing" for the public authorities.[76]

The General Fund: Expenditures By Departments and Payments to Local Governments

The fund structure of New York State consists of funds that derive from sources both within and outside the state's treasury. The pattern of state spending previously discussed underscores this point. However, the state's most significant fund, the general fund and related accounts, provides for expenditures approved by the legislature and is the basis of the executive budget the Governor submits annually for consideration. Table 6.11 lists annual expenditures from the general fund for fifteen years beginning in

Table 6.11
Expenditures from the General Fund of New York State Government: 1959-1973

YEAR	TOTAL EXPENDITURES (IN MILLIONS)	PERCENTAGE ANNUAL INCREASES	PERCENTAGE OF TOTAL EXPENDITURE FOR 15 YEARS
1959	$1,797.5	—	
			Term I
1960	1,992.6	10.9	
			13.2
1961	2,087.4	4.8	
1962	2,324.2	11.3	
1963	2,594.5	11.6	
			Term II
1964	2,780.8	7.2	
			18.8
1965	2,893.5	4.1	
1966	3,460.0	19.6	
1967	4,021.5	16.2	
			Term III
1968	4,629.2	15.1	
			32.7
1969	5,518.9	19.2	
1970	6,206.6	12.5	
1971	6,747.5	8.7	
			Term IV
1972	7,422.3	10.0	
			35.3
1973	7,785.0	4.9	
Total	$62,261.5		100.0

SOURCE: State of New York, Division of the Budget.

1959. This fund accounts for major state spending in three subareas, each of which has its own separate fund account: state purposes (which includes the bulk of expenditures for the twenty departments of the executive branch), capital construction, and aid to localities. Expenditures such as debt service and first-instance appropriations also created obligations against the three subfunds that constitute the general fund. (In addition to the general fund, the state has a variety of special funds, among the more notable being funds for various forms of federal aid and employee pension programs).

There was a surge in expenditures from the general fund during the years 1966 through 1970 when the average annual increase was 16.5 percent, nearly double the rate of 8.3 percent for the preceeding years, 1959-1965. It is notable that total expenditures for the three-year fourth term were $21,954.8 million, or 35.3 percent of total general fund expenditures of $62,261.5 million, and thus exceeded total expenditures for any other term.

Although general fund expenditures increased each year, expenditures from the fund decreased as a percentage of total state expenditures during the Rockefeller years. In 1958 expenditures from the general fund encompassed 79 percent of state expenditures, but by 1973 only 62 percent of total state expenditures were from the general fund.[77]

The major portion of spending by most departments and agencies of state government is included within the general fund. However, expenditures by the departments involve some funds from other sources, for example, special revenue funds and federal funds. Not included in the category of departmental expenditures are funds for local assistance (e.g., per-capita assistance and grants) and funds for capital construction (e.g., state highway construction and improvements). As shown in Table 6.12, "departmental expenditures" by the three branches of government (plus expenditures for employee fringe benefits) for the years 1959 through 1973 totaled $26,324.6 million. Well over half this total (56.8 percent) was accounted for by expenditures in only three categories: education (23.6 percent), mental hygiene (22.2 percent), and employee fringe benefits (11 percent). In terms of substantial increases over the fourteen-year period, two areas are prominent: education, with a 1,062 percent increase, and fringe benefits for employees with an increase of 718 percent. The increases in expenditures for employee fringe benefits reflects, in part, the substantial growth in the total number of governmental employees for New York State as shown by the figures in Table 6.13.

State expenditures for local assistance were financed in part from funds other than the state's general fund. In fiscal 1973-1974, approximately 35 percent of the local assistance expenditures were financed outside the general fund, primarily from federal funds.[78] As Table 6.14 shows, local assistance in 1973 totaled $5,252,930,000, a figure that represents a 452 percent increase over total assistance in 1959. Social services was the area with the highest growth rate; local assistance for social services had increased by 694 percent from 1959 to 1973. The two areas with the highest aggregate expenditures for the four terms were education and social services, which, when combined, totaled more than three-quarters of state payments to local governments from all funds. In 1967 New York State was the leader among the states in per-capita assistance provided to its local

Table 6.12
New York State Expenditures by Executive Branch Departments, Judiciary, and Legislature: 1959-1973 (in millions)

YEAR	EDUCATION	HYGIENE	EXECUTIVE	TRANSPORTATION*	CORRECTIONAL SERVICES	TAXATION AND FINANCE	DRUG ABUSE CONTROL COMMISSION
1959	77.3	206.5	35.5	56.9	40.8	31.2	—
1960	81.3	213.9	38.9	50.2	41.0	31.9	—
1961	95.5	229.3	49.9	55.6	48.9	28.7	—
1962	132.4	244.7	60.6	61.7	49.8	30.2	—
1963	195.9	255.6	71.3	96.8	53.2	30.6	—
1964	228.5	263.6	77.9	97.6	54.3	31.5	—
1965	279.1	288.9	83.2	103.7	55.9	34.6	—
1966	348.4	333.9	95.4	114.4	59.0	41.7	—
1967	445.5	376.2	114.0	140.1	60.2	44.8	—
1968	503.2	457.3	127.0	157.6	67.1	51.9	—
1969	601.0	483.0	143.1	167.5	70.7	55.2	38.4
1970	708.8	562.8	194.5	185.0	84.1	67.2	63.0
1971	795.5	595.2	205.7	199.0	101.3	72.0	89.7
1972	833.7	630.2	232.2	184.9	110.2	68.7	54.8
1973	898.6	711.2	284.0	213.6	146.4	72.3	62.4
Totals	6,224.7	5,852.3	1,813.2	1,884.6	1,042.9	692.5	308.3

SOURCE: Compiled from various reports of the Comptroller of the State of New York.

*Transportation figures for 1959-1962 are for the Department of Public Works, the predecessor of the Department of Transportation.

Table 6.12—*Continued*

YEAR	HEALTH	ENVIRONMENTAL CONSERVATION	MOTOR VEHICLES	SOCIAL SERVICES	AUDIT AND CONTROL	LAW	LABOR	INSURANCE
1959	23.0	15.6	—	10.9	5.4	4.0	—	—
1960	22.0	16.6	3.2	11.1	5.5	3.8	—	—
1961	23.9	18.6	13.1	12.6	6.3	4.4	—	—
1962	25.2	20.4	12.8	14.0	6.7	5.1	—	—
1963	26.7	32.0	16.7	18.5	7.6	7.9	85.2	6.4
1964	27.4	33.2	17.2	18.8	7.9	8.4	90.2	7.0
1965	28.8	34.0	21.0	21.1	8.2	8.6	93.0	7.0
1966	35.1	42.4	22.3	24.1	10.1	9.4	104.8	7.6
1967	40.6	47.4	24.0	36.4	10.9	10.0	105.8	6.9
1968	46.6	58.3	28.4	33.7	13.2	11.3	118.1	8.8
1969	60.1	60.0	29.3	41.0	14.1	12.8	144.6	9.6
1970	63.5	45.4	35.8	45.1	17.7	15.2	173.3	9.8
1971	63.2	39.2	37.8	24.7	18.1	16.3	187.0	10.7
1972	63.5	33.5	39.2	18.7	19.1	17.9	221.0	12.8
1973	71.2	48.5	46.9	27.8	21.5	21.1	216.3	13.3
Total	620.8	545.1	347.7	358.5	172.3	156.2	1,539.3	99.9

Table 6.12—*Continued*

YEAR	BANKING	ALL OTHER** DEPARTMENTS AND AGENCIES	JUDICIARY	LEGISLATURE	EMPLOYEE FRINGE BENEFITS	OTHER CHARGES	TOTAL	PERCENTAGE INCREASES IN TOTAL EX-PENDITURES
1959	—	32.6	12.3	8.0	57.4	7.3	624.7	—
1960	—	33.1	6.6	8.6	61.8	6.5	636.0	1.8
1961	—	36.8	7.2	10.0	69.9	7.7	718.4	11.5
1962	—	43.3	8.3	10.7	73.1	8.5	807.5	11.0
1963	4.7	45.7	15.5	11.6	87.8	12.4	1,082.1	25.4
1964	5.0	48.9	17.2	9.2	109.0	11.1	1,163.9	7.0
1965	5.1	54.4	18.5	13.0	106.7	12.5	1,277.3	8.9
1966	5.7	63.2	21.2	17.5	147.1	8.9	1,512.1	15.2
1967	5.2	77.0	23.2	13.0	172.1	12.2	1,755.5	13.9
1968	6.6	77.6	27.0	18.0	206.9	13.3	2,030.9	13.6
1969	7.1	57.4	30.4	20.4	238.0	14.5	2,298.2	13.2
1970	7.3	77.5	32.6	21.8	255.0	13.3	2,678.7	16.6
1971	7.9	110.8	37.0	25.4	392.5	17.9	3,010.9	12.4
1972	9.2	120.0	41.7	26.5	432.8	19.6	3,190.2	6.0
1973	10.4	105.2	46.2	29.3	470.0	21.9	3,538.2	11.0
Total	74.2	983.5	344.9	243.0	2,880.1	187.6	26,324.6	

**This column includes, for example, departments of State, Commerce, Public Service, and Civil Service.

Table 6.13
New York State Government Employment

YEAR	CLASSIFIED SERVICE	OTHER THAN CLASSIFIED SERVICE	STATE UNIVERSITY SYSTEM	TOTAL STATE EMPLOYMENT	ANNUAL PERCENTAGE INCREASES
1959	93,250	8,459	7,482	109,191	—
1960	94,735	8,206	7,411	110,352	1
1961	100,934	9,109	8,565	118,608	7
1962	105,737	11,107	10,903	127,747	7.7
1963	108,187	11,722	12,310	132,219	3.5
1964	110,917	12,724	13,909	137,550	4
1965	114,719	13,605	17,767	146,091	6.2
1966	120,680	12,681	16,619	149,980	2.7
1967	129,680	13,973	18,965	162,322	8.2
1968	137,914	15,301	21,212	174,454	7.5
1969	138,767	15,504	21,838	176,109	.9
1970	151,053	15,559	23,963	190,575	8.2
1971	169,920	19,045	31,245	220,210	15.5
1972	172,453	21,428	31,407	225,288	2.3
1973	156,633	24,886	34,342	215,861	− 4.2

SOURCE: State of New York, Department of Civil Service.

governments, and four years later New York was providing 25 percent more to its local governments than was California, which was ranked second in the nation in aid to local governments.[79]

Funds from the Federal Government

Federal aid payments to state agencies under programs not requiring appropriation action by the legislature increased nearly nine times to $3.54 billion during Rockefeller's tenure.[80] Although one can make a strong argument that New York and other large industrial states should receive higher amounts of federal aid than they do, the fact is that New York improved its share of federal aid during the Rockefeller years. Pointing out that the state "experienced formidable increases in federal assistance during the 1958-1973 period," Connery and Benjamin provide data showing that such increases caused federal aid as a percentage of state and local revenue to rise faster in New York than in most of the nine other largest states. Nevertheless, by 1972, the Governor was not satisfied with the rate of increase in federal aid.[81] According to him, the allocation to New York did not take sufficiently into account the effort the state was making to meet its own needs.

Table 6.14
New York State Government Payments to Local Governments from All Funds: 1959-1973 (in thousands)

FISCAL YEAR	TOTAL	EDUCATION	GENERAL PURPOSES	HEALTH AND MENTAL HEALTH	HIGHWAYS AND TRANSPOR-TATION	HOUSING AND COMMUNITY RENEWAL	NATURAL RESOURCES	PUBLIC SAFETY	SOCIAL SERVICES
1959	951,053	564,476	115,388	42,089	58,077	15,108	58	355	155,502
1960	1,049,546	635,123	118,351	43,319	65,751	17,520	58	428	168,996
1961	1,141,141	721,700	116,753	43,577	68,625	17,168	80	584	172,654
1962	1,274,928	813,699	128,796	49,549	73,907	21,120	1,452	1,128	185,277
1963	1,398,481	908,476	134,775	54,354	70,506	25,324	8,013	1,600	195,433
1964	1,552,159	1,027,443	135,557	57,728	76,271	28,676	2,265	5,764	218,455
1965	1,677,909	1,102,251	136,719	56,836	74,677	32,659	3,094	6,493	265,180
1966	2,204,500	1,291,528	318,431	76,764	93,296	37,316	2,171	8,741	376,253
1967	2,524,090	1,472,520	384,360	88,538	116,890	44,540	1,605	13,373	402,264
1968	2,972,770	1,642,200	465,161	108,215	117,175	51,510	2,490	14,357	571,662
1969	3,587,623	1,831,957	537,032	141,540	130,342	46,201	18,455	16,345	865,751
1970	4,146,193	2,195,160	591,175	151,886	266,857	40,277	2,849	17,339	880,650
1971	4,236,352	2,250,237	627,656	161,031	211,691	65,304	28,543	19,134	872,756
1972	4,777,680	2,269,711	807,283	240,553	217,369	52,676	35,767	22,523	1,131,798
1973	5,252,930	2,649,742	802,063	250,574	206,174	66,139	21,353	22,692	1,234,193
Total	38,747,355 (100%)	21,376,223 (55.2)	5,419,500 (14.0)	1,566,553 (4.0)	1,847,608 (4.8)	496,234 (1.4)	128,253 (.3)	150,856 (.4)	7,696,824 (19.9)

SOURCE: State of New York, Department of Audit and Control.

One of the last times that Rockefeller chose systematically to set forth his position on the issue of federal assistance to New York State was his Annual Message to the Legislature of January 18, 1972.[82] The content of that message can be viewed as a response to the deteriorating fiscal situation in the state, a situation brought to a head by the revolt of the assembly Republicans against the budget the Governor submitted in the spring of 1971.

Rockefeller argued that national, state, and local governments had been slow in adapting their structures, fiscal practices, and patterns of operation to the changes taking place in the world. Stating that the consequences of the slow process of adjustments were severe in their financial dimensions, he indicated a continued commitment to liberal goals by asserting that the consequences were worse because "they affect our ability to respond to fundamental human needs." President Nixon had in 1971 recognized the need for change when he made his goal of a "New Federalism" the keystone of his domestic policy. Rockefeller acknowledged this proposed change, but asserted that the times called for even more changes, fundamental in nature, to enable the federal system to deal with the plight of the overburdened taxpayer.

Asserting that the crisis in the federal system had evolved over a forty-year period, Rockefeller noted that the states had slipped from their once-dominant position, a position in which they collected two-thirds of the nation's tax revenues, even though the problems they faced were fewer then. He observed that the federal government was now collecting 90 percent of all income taxes and benefits. The irony he saw was that urban areas for which states were responsible had incurred additional responsibilities stemming from factors such as increased welfare rolls, increased migration, and industrial pollution. Furthermore, he argued, the structure of federal aid programs imposed additional burdens on states. For example, categorical grant programs required additional funds to be expended by the state and local governments to expand existing specified programs and to add others. In addition, states were not permitted to use categorical grant monies to reduce expenditures even when they were already meeting needs designated by the federal government. Finally, contended the Governor, after identifying needs and raising expectations, the federal government had failed to provide funds sufficient to solve those problems.

The crux of the problem, according to Rockefeller, was that state governments, caught between rising expectations and diminishing fiscal resources, were simply running out of money. For example, he noted that New York's combined state and local taxes were the highest per person in the nation in 1966 through 1970 and that the bulk of the tax revenues was provided for aid to schools and local governments. The painful consequence of limited funds for the state was a cut in welfare expenditures and a cut in the projected growth of the state university system. Rockefeller's exposition of the root causes of the fiscal crisis was followed by his plan for restructuring the federal system.

The Governor recommended that the national government take on the full financial responsibility for several additional programs it was uniquely qualified to perform, namely, a federally operated system of contributory universal health insurance, welfare and medicaid, and a program on the scale of the Manhattan Project to find answers to the problem of drug abuse. He also recommended a restructuring of the federal aid system to include a replacement of categorical grants with block grants in major areas such as education and crime control, and the development of a formula for revenue sharing which would recognize the amount of effort a state was making to meet its own needs.

If the federal government assumed the financial and structural responsibilities outlined, then the states, argued Rockefeller, would be able to meet the needs of its citizens in the areas of education, courts, community development, transportation, housing and urban development, health, and mental health, and cleaning up the environment. Under the Governor's plan it would be necessary for the states to assume greater financial obligations and make some major structural changes. For example, the financing of the costs of all major courts within states would be assumed by states, programs in housing and urban development would function on a metropolitan basis, and transportation and health programs would operate on a regional basis. But there would also remain some form of involvement by the federal government in some of these areas, for example, in cleaning up the environment. Pollution, asserted the Governor, knows no boundaries, and there would be a responsibility for the national government to set standards and share technology and funds with the states in attacking the problem. With the burden of welfare, financing of health care, and control of drug abuse in the hands of the federal government, and states sharing the responsibility for education and the court system, local governments would be freed administratively and financially to focus on the efficient management of basic local services.

The Governor believed that his recommendations, if implemented, would provide the basis of a "new federalism" and enable the federal system to better serve the needs of people. He maintained that the design for restructuring the government was essential in order to prevent "financial chaos" and the "collapse of government services." Clearly, Rockefeller viewed his Annual Message of 1972 as serving a purpose much larger than merely advancing a legislative program. Faced with a fiscal crisis which prevented him from offering the kinds of innovative and expensive state programs that had become his trademark, he turned instead to a bold plan for restructuring the role of all levels of government in the United States. Because of his status as a national figure and his long experience with state and national problems, the Governor saw himself as more than "another state politician." As his chief speech writer pointed out, Rockefeller believed, and expected, that "people would listen" when he spoke.[83]

Rockefeller was disappointed when the media did not give what he thought was proper emphasis to his plan. And although he managed to win his campaign for a federal revenue-sharing program, the broader proposals he made in the annual message never did win a serious hearing in Washington. Moreover, the price of winning Senator Russell Long's support for revenue sharing included limitations on federal aid for social services.[84]

The hard reality was that Nelson Rockefeller's spending policies had been such that by 1971 New York State was in a position in which its own resources were insufficient to allow for the maintenance and expansion of programs at the levels to which New Yorkers had become accustomed. Thus the state's fiscal health had become increasingly sensitive to, and dependent upon, levels of federal aid and fluctuations in those levels. The Governor's proposals for restructuring the federal system were in large part a response to the increasingly vulnerable position in which the state found itself. New York's taxing, borrowing, and spending capacity had been stretched and strained to the limit. There was truly no where else for the governor to turn for additional funds.

The Balance Sheet: Taxing, Borrowing, and Spending in New York State From 1959 to 1973.

During his tenure in office Nelson Rockefeller aggressively employed a wide range of strategies for obtaining the revenues necessary to meet what he regarded as problems that New York State must solve. Arthur Levitt, the state comptroller who preceded the Governor in office by four years, was one of the leading critics of the Governor's financial methods. Levitt often criticized borrowing and spending by public authorities as being so massive as to overshadow the fiscal operations of the state. Specifically, he criticized the authority device as circumventing legal debt regulations and other constitutional provisions, increasing public debt without limits, being uncontrolled by the electorate, being inherently less efficient than the regular structure of state government, and being more costly than regular financing methods.[85]

In 1972, Levitt noted that during the years 1967-1971, a period when the population and personal income of New York had grown at a slower rate than the national average, the "net long-term nonguaranteed debt was greater than that of any other state, . . . and grew faster than the 50-state total, constituting 16.3 percent of national total in 1967 and 18.2 percent in 1971."[86] Specifically, he noted that "Statewide public authorities had almost $8.9 billion of bonds and notes outstanding. By contrast, comparable New York State direct debt was about $3.1 billion. In other words, Statewide authorities debt was more than two-and-a-half times the level of debt of the State itself."[87] However, Levitt was not willing to sue the Governor to prove his financial devices unconstitutional, and few of Levitt's proposals to the legislature recommending limitations on public authority debt and tighter controls over public authority activities were ever enacted.[88]

When Rockefeller left New York at the end of 1973, he had been hamstrung in his efforts to deal with mounting problems, in part because of the state's inability to raise additional revenues through taxing and borrowing. The system of authorities that he had developed was also being overtaken by economic events. A little more than a year later the authority system was on the verge of disaster. In January 1975, the forty-three authorities had a combined debt of over $14 billion and a projection of expenditures that suggested outright appropriations from the state of $1.9 billion over the next five years. Estimates were that eleven public authorities would need support on a continuing basis for operating costs and that twenty would not be able to pay back their first-instance appropriations.[89]

When campaigning for the presidential nomination in 1964, the Governor had proclaimed his belief in fiscal integrity. "I believe in fiscal integrity in government, control of government spending—and not massive deficit spending and piling up of debt to be paid either through inflation or mortgaging the future of our children or our children's children."[90] Later, when some would chastise the Governor for deserting his liberal principles, he was to assert: "It doesn't make you liberal to spend money you don't have. It just makes you a damn fool."[91] But this expressed belief in controlling government spending had not prevailed over his desire to meet challenges and respond to human needs. In hindsight it seems clear that he responded overambitiously in a manner oblivious to economic realities. Pay-as-you-go was abandoned, every variety of state tax was increased, a variety of fiscal "gimmicks" were employed, and there was precious little restraint on moral-obligation borrowing by public authorities. In short, Nelson Rockefeller did mortgage the future. When fiscal crisis hit the state and the federal government proved unwilling to provide the amount of assistance that he demanded, the Governor called it quits. Lacking the resources to continue the aggressive pursuit of his life strategy in his role as Governor of New York, he abandoned that role. As he put it,

> The real reason I quit was because the ability to meet the needs of the people of the state of New York no longer was in primarily the hands of the state itself. It was in Washington.... So this is why I just figured, well, unless New York State could have a strong, vital economy it couldn't meet its own problems and it couldn't have a strong vital economy unless the federal government changed some of its policies.[92]

7 The Substance of Rockefeller Programs

Observers of the Rockefeller administration are often impressed by the new programs produced by that administration. The very number of new programs, the magnitude and great cost of many programs, and the innovative quality of some of the more notable programs are commonly cited.[1] Our goal in this chapter is to move beyond these commonly made generalizations to look at three aspects of the product of the administration. The first relates to the nature of the product taken as a whole. How many programs were adopted, in what terms were they adopted, what policy areas did they represent, and what changes were there over time in the emphasis accorded to different policy areas. The second relates to about two dozen programs and projects that we define as "pet programs" of the Governor. Specifically, we explore a number of aspects of these programs and projects which we regard as significant. Among the more prominent aspects are the innovative qualities of many programs and projects, the unusual methods by which many of them were financed, and the amount of construction which many involved. The third question we focus upon is the degree to which his programs and positions reflect the "turn to the right" late in his administration which is commonly attributed to Governor Rockefeller.

Program Output as a Whole

It should be evident to any observer that the output of programs in the Rockefeller administration is in itself a strong indicator of activist government. As Table 7.1 shows, more than 700 pieces of program legislation advanced by the Governor during his fifteen years in office were signed into law.[2]

Although program bills differed greatly in their significance, size, and cost, the number itself is indicative of Rockefeller's eagerness to confront problems facing the state. Thus even when the state entered a period of

Table 7.1
Governor Rockefeller's Legislative Output by Policy Area: 1959-1973*

	BUSINESS AND INDUSTRY	GOVERN-MENTAL AFFAIRS	SOCIAL DEVEL-OPMENT	HEALTH	PERSONAL SAFETY	TRANS-PORTATION	EDUCATION	HOUSING AND COMMUNITY DEVELOP-MENT	RE-CREATION AND CULTURAL ENRICHMENT	NATURAL RESOURCES	TOTAL
Term I (1959-62)	21 (7.8%)	101 (37.5%)	46 (17.1%)	10 (3.7%)	27 (10%)	18 (6.7%)	21 (7.8%)	15 (5.6%)	9 (3.3%)	1 (.49%)	269 (100%)
Term II (1963-66)	13 (10.6%)	35 (28.5%)	9 (7.3%)	16 (13%)	6 (4.9%)	13 (10.6%)	7 (5.7%)	11 (8.9%)	11 (8.9%)	2 (1.6%)	123 (100%)
Term III (1967-70)	24 (11%)	57 (26%)	32 (14.6%)	25 (11.4%)	19 (8.6%)	21 (9.6%)	7 (3.2%)	21 (9.6%)	3 (1.4%)	10 (4.6%)	219 (100%)
Term IV (1971-73)**	16 (11.9%)	23 (17%)	23 (17%)	12 (8.8%)	13 (9.6%)	13 (9.6%)	5 (3.7%)	11 (8.1%)	6 (4.4%)	13 (9.6%)	135 (100%)
Total	74 (9.9%)	216 (29%)	110 (14.7%)	63 (8.5%)	65 (8.7%)	65 (8.7%)	40 (5.4%)	58 (7.8%)	29 (3.9%)	26 (3.5%)	746 (100%)

SOURCE: Data for the years 1963 through 1973 compiled from records of program bills provided by the Office of the Minority Leader of the New York State Assembly, Perry B. Duryea. Data for the years 1959 through 1962 compiled from State of New York, *Public Papers of Nelson A. Rockefeller, Fifty-Third Governor of the State of New York*. The Governor's legislative proposals were drawn from his Annual Message to the legislature for each year, special messages to the legislature, and memoranda of approval which the Governor submitted for most items in his legislative program subsequent to their being passed. Because the method employed for compiling data for the years 1959 through 1962 is less precise than use of the Minority Leader's records used for the years 1963 through 1973, the data in this table very likely understate legislative output for the Governor's first term. Utilizing this method for later terms generally resulted in lower figures than are contained in the records of the Office of the Minority Leader. The total number of passed bills discovered by using the "Public Papers method" for all fifteen years of the administration is 635.

*Includes bills signed into law which were advanced by the Governor as part of his legislative program except for appropriations and revenue measures, and legislation passed in special sessions of the legislature. The ten policy area categories are those used in the Executive Budget. For a description of the categories see State of New York, Division of the Budget, *Executive Budget 1969-70*, p. A 106. Because we have classified all legislation which creates a new governmental unit in the category Governmental Affairs, that policy area is to some degree "artificially" over populated. That category is also the most diverse, including legislation relating to most "staff-type" departments, e.g. Audit and Control, the judiciary, government employees, the legislature, miscellaneous commissions and numerous other units and subjects.

**Includes only three years because the Governor resigned before the beginning of the fourth year of his term.

financial stress in which costly new programs were all but impossible to propose, the Governor's fourth term, the total amount of program bills signed into law stayed at a relatively constant level, as indicated in Table 7.1.[3] As one might expect, the first term of his administration stands as Rockefeller's most productive in the sheer number of programs that were approved. This accords with the impression of a number of insiders who point out that it is natural that there were more problems to solve at the beginning of the administration than there were later.

A few general comments on the distribution of programs among policy areas would seem appropriate before moving to a discussion of changes in distribution over time. The first is that although the area of "governmental affairs" contains by far the largest numbers of programs, the total for the second of these categories is somewhat inflated as a result of the classification scheme we employ. Specifically, we place all programs involving the creation of a new governmental unit into the policy area of governmental affairs rather than the policy area in which the new unit is to operate. The effect of this method is to increase the total number of programs in the governmental affairs category and decrease the number in all other categories.

The second comment relates to two of the three policy areas that contain the smallest numbers of program bills: natural resources, education, and recreation and cultural enrichment. Although the Governor gave some degree of emphasis to education, the fact that the Education Department was not under his jurisdiction made that department an additional source of significant proposals in that field. The natural effect was probably to reduce the number of proposals made by Rockefeller in this policy area. It is not surprising that the policy area of recreation and cultural enrichment contains a relatively small amount of legislation. The fact is that it is simply a smaller area than any of the others, one that would likely receive less attention from almost anyone else who might have been Governor.

Without at this point raising the issue of the Governor's alleged turn to the right in the 1970s, seeming changes in emphasis from policy area to policy area as revealed in Table 7.1 deserve comment. The fact that almost half of all the programs in the policy area of governmental affairs were adopted during Rockefeller's first term in office seems readily understandable. In trying to structure state government to his liking, any first-term Governor is likely to propose certain changes in organization. Many of the programs in the category of governmental affairs during Rockefeller's first term did involve changes in government organization, including numerous changes recommended in the Ronan report, the administration's one effort to undertake a comprehensive program of reorganization measures.[4] As Table 7.1 shows, the proportion of legislation in the category of governmental affairs declines steadily over the course of the administration.

Perhaps the most dramatic increases in emphasis on a particular policy area are represented by the steady increase in numbers of programs in the policy area of natural resources. It is likely that this increase is due not just to factors peculiar to the Rockefeller administration but to factors operating in the larger environment of national politics. As is common knowledge, concern with the environment reached a peak in the late 1960s and early 1970s with numerous pieces of landmark legislation being passed, including the National Environmental Policy Act and tougher versions of legislation governing control of air and water pollution.

Perhaps the most notable fact about changes in the relative proportions of program legislation in different policy areas over the course of the administration is that there are, in fact, relatively few dramatic changes. One plausible interpretation of this finding is that the institutionalization of the program innovation process in the Rockefeller administration made such a result all but inevitable. The program staff was, of course, organized in such a way so as to ensure that legislative proposals were generated in all policy areas.

Governor Rockefeller's Pet Programs

An examination of the sum total of the program output of the administration of any governor or president is undoubtedly important in trying to capture the essence of an administration. However, it is most likely that an examination of the leading programs of an administration would be even more revealing. Thus we have selected twenty-two programs or projects that we designate as "pet programs" of Governor Rockefeller, programs to which he had a very strong personal commitment. Table 7.2 presents information on those programs. Doubtless, other observers would compile lists that differ from ours. Indeed, for certain purposes other lists may be better than ours. For example, our list does not necessarily represent the most successful, the most expensive, the most controversial, or the most innovative programs. Rather, we have attempted to compile a list of significant and well-known programs to whose proposal and adoption the Governor was willing to invest large amounts of personal and political resources. In short, there is every evidence that Rockefeller was personally convinced of the merits of these programs. Such evidence exists not only in the public record and in observations made by state officials in personal interviews but in the Governor's own response to our inquiry as to which programs he regarded as the most significant of his administration.[5]

A quick glance at Table 7.2 reveals that at least one of the pet programs falls into each of the ten policy areas utilized as a category in this chapter. Although the policy area of transportation contains more programs than any other area, six, it also is the area in which the Govenror had the most difficulty. Specifically, he was forced to give up his plans for the Rye-Oyster Bay Bridge and a new jetport, and voters twice defeated proposals for bond issues to fund transportation projects.

Aside from transportation, no policy area includes more than three pet

Table 7.2
Governor Rockefeller's Pet Programs

PET PROGRAM	PROGRAM OBJECTIVE	POLICY AREA	NATIONAL ISSUE	INNOVATIVE	PRIMARY METHODS OF STATE FINANCING	NEW STRUCTURE OR UNUSUAL POWERS	CONSTRUCTION COMPONENT
Creation of MTA Passed 1967	Improve Mass Transit in N.Y.C. Area	Transportation	Yes	Yes	Voter-approved Bonds (1967)	Independent Authority - MTA	Yes
Transportation Bond Issue Passed 1967	Finance Transportation Capital Facilities	Transportation	Yes	Yes	Voter-Approved Bonds-$2.5 Billion	No	Yes
Transportation Bond Issue Defeated 1971	Finance Transportation Capital Facilities	Transportation	Yes	Yes	Voter-Approved Bonds - $2.5 Billion	No	Yes
Transportation Bond Issue Defeated 1973	Finance Transportation Capital Facilities	Transportation	Yes	Yes	Voter-Approved Bonds - $3.5 Billion	No	Yes
Stewart Jet Port Passed 1971 (allowed to die)	Develop a Fourth Jet Port in the N.Y.C. Area (Newburgh)	Transportation	No	No	Voter-Approved Bonds (1967)	Independent Authority - SALA	Yes

Legend: MTA - Metropolitan Transportation Authority; SALA - Stewart Airport Land Authority; HFA - Housing Finance Authority; UDC - Urban Development Corporation; ADA - Atomic Development Authority; PWA - Pure Waters Authority; APA - Adirondack Park Agency; SUCF - State University Construction Fund; COA - Council on the ARTS; NACC - Narcotic Addiction Control Commission; HMHFIC - Health and Mental Hygiene Facilities Improvement Corporation.

Table 7.2—*Continued*

Long Island Sound Bridge Passed 1967 Rescinded 1973	Construct a Bridge Linking the Towns of Rye & Oyster Bay	Transportation	No	No	Voter-Approved Bonds (1971 Proposal)	No	Yes
Creation of HFA Passed 1960	Subsidize Private Housing Construction	Housing and Community Development	Yes	Yes	Moral-Obligation Bonds	Independent Authority-HFA	Yes
Creation of UDC Passed 1968	Plan, Finance & Construct Housing, Community Facilities, Business Facilities	Housing and Community Development	Yes	Yes	Moral-Obligation Bonds	Independent Authority-UDC, Power to Override Building Codes	Yes
Nuclear Attack Protection Proposed 1960	Plan & Finance Construction of Shelters, etc.	Personal Safety	Yes	Yes	Legislative Appropriations	No	Yes
South Mall Complex Passed 1963	Construct State Office/Cultural Complex	Governmental Affairs	No	Yes	Lease Purchase Device (with Albany Co. Bonds)	No	Yes
Creation of ADA Passed 1962	Develop a Nuclear Industry	Business and Industry	Yes	Yes	Moral-Obligation Bonds	Independent Authority - ADA	Yes

Table 7.2—*Continued*

PET PROGRAM	PROGRAM OBJECTIVE	POLICY AREA	NATIONAL ISSUE	INNOVATIVE	PRIMARY METHODS OF STATE FINANCING	NEW STRUCTURE OR UNUSUAL POWERS	CONSTRUCTION COMPONENT
Electric Power Program Passed 1968	Provide for Adequate Electric-Power Supply	Business and Industry	Yes	No	Moral Obligation Bonds and Revenue Bonds	No	Yes
Pure Waters Program Passed 1965	Reduce Pollution in State Waters	Natural Resources	Yes	Yes	Voter-Approved Bonds $1 Billion (1967)	Independent Authority - PWA (a secondary element)	Yes
Creation of APA Passed 1971	Preserve Character of Adirondack Area	Natural Resources	Yes	Yes	Legislative Appropriations	Board in the Executive Dept.-APA, State Land Use Controls	No
Expansion of State University Academic Facilities Through SUCF Passed 1962	Provide Higher Education for State Residents	Education	Yes	Yes	Lease Purchase Device (with SUCF, using HFA Bonds)	Independent Authority-SUCF	Yes

Table 7.2—*Continued*

Office of Education Performance Review Established 1973	Improve Operation of Education Dept. & Performance of Schools	Education	Yes	No	Legislative Appropriations	Staff Unit in Executive Department-Office of Education Performance Review	No
Aid to the Arts Passed 1960	Encourage Development of the Arts	Recreation and Cultural Enrichment	Yes	Yes	Legislative Appropriations	Temporary State Commission - COA (Made a unit in the Executive Dept. in 1965)	No
Universal Health Insurance Proposed 1967 thru 1971	Provide Basic Coverage for the Employed	Health	Yes	Yes	Legislative Appropriations	No	No
Construction of Hospitals and Nursing Homes Passed 1968	Provide Additional Beds for the Sick & the Aged	Health and Social Development	Yes	No	Moral Obligation Bonds (of HFA)	No	Yes

Table 7.2—*Continued*

PET PROGRAM	PROGRAM OBJECTIVE	POLICY AREA	NATIONAL ISSUE	INNOVATIVE	PRIMARY METHODS OF STATE FINANCING	NEW STRUCTURE OR UNUSUAL POWERS	CONSTRUCTION COMPONENT
Creation of Welfare Inspector General Passed 1971	Investigate Alleged Abuses in Welfare System	Social Development	Yes	No	Legislative Appropriations	Staff Unit in Executive Dept.-Office of Welfare Inspector General	No
Narcotic Control Program Passed 1966	Reduce Narcotic Addiction by Commitment and Rehabilitation	Personal Safety	Yes	No	Legislative Appropriations and Lease Purchase Device (with HMHFIC, using HFA Bonds)	Independent Commission within Dept. of Mental Hygiene-NACC, Compulsory Treatment	Yes
Narcotic Control Program Passed 1973	Reduce Narcotic Addiction by Criminal Penalties Commitment, and Rehabilitation	Personal Safety	Yes	Yes	Legislative Appropriations and Lease Purchase Device (with HMHFIC, using HFA Bonds)	No	Yes

programs. However, it is inevitable that there would be disagreements over the appropriateness of our assigning programs to categories. In general we have tried to classify programs consistent with the way in which they were thought of within the Rockefeller administration. However, some programs could legitimately be viewed as falling within either one of two categories. Thus the Governor himself tended to justify his transportation proposals and even the expansion of the state university partly on the grounds of their likely contribution to economic development.

Inevitably, any assessment of the wisdom of Rockefeller's choices of problems to which he was willing to make a major commitment of time and energy is colored by the biases of the observer. Nevertheless, one can conclude with substantial confidence that many of Rockefeller's pet programs and projects were aimed at conditions that were widely perceived to represent genuine problems. For example, at some time in Rockefeller's administration, New York faced great needs in the fields of mass transportation, water quality, narcotic use, education, care of the elderly, and housing. To give just one example, Neal Peirce noted that by 1970, 1.4 million citizens of New York "lived in dilapidated or deteriorated housing that needed replacement."[6] As he also noted, housing starts had declined almost in half from 1959 to 1969.

Even some programs and projects for which Rockefeller was most heavily criticized, for example, his proposals to protect citizens from the consequences of nuclear attack, were directed at conditions that other leading public figures regarded as demanding answers. President John Kennedy's advocacy of fallout protection shelters is a case in point.

Aside from being aimed at conditions that were widely perceived as constituting significant problems for New York State and its citizens, most of Rockefeller's pet programs or projects involved issues that were either existing or potential national issues. With the exception of the South Mall project, the Rye-Oyster Bay Bridge proposal, and the proposal for a fourth jetport for the New York metropolitan area, every item in Table 7.2 seems to have had national relevance of some sort. True, an item such as aid to the arts was proposed before it had become a national issue, yet potential for a national issue was clearly present.[7]

The Governor and those who worked closely with him regarded his administration's spawning of innovative programs as the most notable feature of that administration. As noted above, other observers have also commented on the innovative nature of many of the Rockefeller programs. Among the twenty-two pet programs almost all qualify as innovative by virtue of either their departure from past practices by states or the magnitude of the effort they encompassed. For example, creating a state council on the arts and authorizing it to promote the various arts and provide financial assistance to "cultural organizations" was in itself a genuine innovation in a field in which the private sector had dominated. As Dick

Netzer has pointed out, the "creation of state councils on the arts marked the emergence of systematic public support [for the arts] at the nonfederal level. The first of the grant-making councils—even antedating the National Endowment for the Arts [NEA]—was the New York State Council on the Arts."[8] In addition, the magnitude of New York's effort in support of the arts is indicated by the fact that by 1971 New York's appropriations for the arts (over $20 million) constituted 80 percent of total appropriations by all forty-six states supporting the arts.[9] Unlike the situations in the field of aid to the arts, New York and some other states traditionally had provided minor financial assistance to municipalities for construction of sewage treatment facilities. However, Rockefeller's Pure Waters Program was a pathbreaking innovation in that it provided $1 billion with which to pay 30 percent of the costs of local projects and, when necessary, to "pre-finance" the federal share of local projects. Thus the truly massive scope of this program of state aid constituted its primary innovative quality.[10]

In some instances the method of financing a program was the primary, or a secondary, element of innovation. Although the device of so-called moral-obligation bonding apparently had been utilized before, the extent of its use in New York, and in particular its use to finance a number of the Governor's most significant programs, makes it especially notable. As Table 7.2 shows, pet programs financed by moral-obligation bonds include housing programs of the Housing Finance Agency; activities in community development, industrial development, and housing carried out by the Urban Development Corporation; Atomic Development Authority (later the Atomic and Space Development Authority) programs involving efforts to develop a nuclear industry in New York and to assist in carrying out the state's electric-power program; and the program of HFA loans for the construction of nonprofit hospitals and nursing homes.[11] (The electric-power program also contained a role for the Power Authority of the State of New York, an authority that utilized conventional borrowing backed neither by the full-faith-and-credit of the state or its moral obligation.)

Of the remaining programs which were, in fact, put into operation, only six were financed wholly or substantially through the normal means of annual appropriations by the legislature. As Table 7.2 shows, the other four were financed by voter-approved borrowing or the so-called lease-purchase arrangements discussed in Chapter 6. (Notably, of the three projects presented to the voters for authorization of full-faith-and-credit borrowing, two, the transportation bond proposals of 1971 and 1973, met defeat at the polls.) Just as the device of moral-obligation bonding constitutes a way to borrow to achieve public purposes without the necessity of gaining voter approval, so does the lease-purchase arrangement. Three of the programs included in Table 7.2, the expansion of state university academic facilities, the construction of the South Mall complex, and the construction of drug addiction treatment facilities, were based primarily on the lease-purchase device. By June 1972, the expansion of academic facilities through lease-purchase arrangements between the Housing Finance Agency and the State University Construction Fund (the authority to which tuition and fees were channeled as the source of revenue to meet rental payments) had been financed by the issuance of HFA debt of close to $1.5 billion.[12]

At the end of his tenure as Governor, Rockefeller cited his use of moral-obligation bonding in the housing area as one of the major achievements of his administration. Referring to the key clause in the statue creating the HFA, a clause that provided for, but did not legally mandate, a state contribution to that agency's reserve fund if adequate funds were not available to cover anticipated costs of principle and interest on agency bonds, Rockefeller characterized the clause as, "shall we say, rather imaginative, somewhat ingenious."[13]

As our discussion of the financial arrangements for pet programs reveals, reliance on the device of the authority or "public benefit corporation" was a key element. In addition to providing a way of avoiding the requirement of voter approval for state borrowing, the device of the authority provides administrative flexibility and autonomy. As noted in Chapter 6, Rockefeller managed to avoid losing control over the authorities by ingenious use of a variety of measures, including appointing members of his personal team to head certain authorities.

The success of the devices of moral-obligation bonding and lease-purchase agreements rested partly on conditions special to New York State. For example, after presenting a convincing argument that both arrangements were patently illegal in light of provisions in the state constitution that prohibit the state's contracting a debt without voter approval or giving or lending its credit to any public or private corporation, one legal scholar notes that New York's doctrine that a citizen-taxpayer had no standing to sue prevented any legal test of the devices of moral-obligation bonding and lease-purchase.[14]

As noted in Chapter 6, creation of the Housing Financing Agency was motivated by Rockefeller's concern over difficulties in achieving voter approval for full-faith-and-credit borrowing for middle-income housing. This body eventually came to play a key role not only in the financing of middle-income housing but in the financing of many other state programs including several pet programs other than middle-income housing. Among the latter were the expansion of state university academic facilities, loans for construction of hospitals and nursing homes, and construction of drug addiction treatment facilities.[15]

The creation or use of authorities with bonding power or access to the bonding power of other authorities through lease-purchase arrangements is a feature of eight of the programs discussed in this chapter.[16] But there are several other interesting structural features involved in some of the programs. Perhaps most notable are certain features inherent in the structure and powers of the Urban Development Corporation (UDC), the Metropolitan Transportation Authority (MTA), and the Adirondack Park Agency (APA).

Both the UDC and the APA were noteworthy because they represented devices extraordinary in their capacity to assume prerogatives normally reserved to local governments. In the case of UDC, this meant the power to override local zoning ordinances and substitute the state construction code for local construction codes in locating and building its projects. Although the power to override local zoning codes was seldom used by UDC, its importance in defusing opposition to a project was significant. As the authority itself acknowledged, "the ultimate availability to UDC of the opportunity to go forward with a documented plan after public review has frequently produced a climate of reasonable compromise instead of endless obstruction by a vocal minority."[17] In other words, the legal power provided to UDC gave it a very strong bargaining chip in dealing with local governments. In the case of APA, the agency was given the power to devise land-use regulations for private as well as public lands within the extensive boundaries of the area defined as the Adirondack Park. Although the regulations for private land needed, and received, legislative approval, the role of the agency was unprecedented in state government.[18]

Although the Metropolitan Transportation Authority was authorized to issue moral-obligation bonds, it did not, in fact, finance its program through this means. Among other means it utilized its unique position as a kind of holding company for several subsidiary authorities as a way of financing its operations. The MTA also financed its activities from federal funds and proceeds of the 1967 transportation capital facilities bond issue. In particular, one of the MTA's subsidiary authorities, the Triborough Bridge and Tunnel Authority, was required by legislation passed in 1972 to distribute to the MTA a major portion of its annual surplus.[19] In addition to the Triborough Bridge and Tunnel Authority, a number of other authorities were converted into, or created as, subsidiary units of the MTA in furtherance of the goal of providing central direction to planning and operating public transportation in the New York City area. These bodies included the Triborough Bridge and Tunnel Authority (preexisting), the New York City Transit Authority (preexisting), the Manhattan and Bronx Surface Operating Authority (preexisting), the Staten Island Rapid Transit Operating Authority (created in 1971), the Stewart Airport Land Authority (created in 1971) and the Metropolitan Suburban Bus Authority (created in 1973).[20]

Including the four notable structural innovations represented by the HFA, UDC, the APA, and the MTA, ten pet proposals that achieved approval involved the creation of new organizational entities. As was the case with the UDC and HFA, the creation of three, the Narcotics Addiction Control Commission, the State University Construction Fund, and the

Atomic Development Authority, reflected a desire to utilize the device of moral-obligation bonding. The creation of two others, the Office of Welfare Inspector General and the Office of Education Performance Review, reflected the desire of the Governor to gain tighter control over two large departments that had been resistant to his attempts to gain more control over their operations.[21] Interestingly, the Office of Education Performance Review was the only structural innovation among the list of pet programs which was accomplished by executive order, this device being utilized by the Governor when the assembly failed to act on his legislation proposing creation of such an office.[22] The remaining new structure, the Council on the Arts, was created in 1960 as a so-called temporary state commission, but was given permanent status in 1965 by the legislature at the Governor's urging.[23] Beginning in 1970, the council was authorized to provide direct subsidies to nonprofit cultural organizations such as orchestras which were sustaining operating deficits.[24] Thus the council became a channel for the regular distribution of public money to private organizations promoting the arts.

An additional feature found as an important component of a number of pet programs is in some ways the most interesting. As one former program associate noted, "the Rockefeller administration was characterized by concepts and devices which permitted public money to flow to private areas and agencies."[25] The Governor himself is on the record as being opposed to the idea of public ownership of enterprises which have traditionally been operated by the private sector.[26] However, he had no ideological commitment to "pure" private enterprise and was always eager to experiment with joint efforts in attempts to marshall the largest possible pool of resources with which to attack what he thought were significant problems. Among the pet programs and projects that involved a partnership of one sort or another between the public and private sectors were the program of aid to the arts operated by the Council on the Arts, activities of the Atomic Development Authority, the electric-power program, the activities of the Housing Finance Agency and the Urban Development Corporation, and the expansion of the State University of New York through the device of the State University Construction Fund. Although the primary expression of the public-private partnership in the case of HFA, UDC, and SUCF consists of the financial arrangements for utilizing private capital through the device of moral-obligation bonding and/or lease-purchase arrangements, elements of partnership went beyond these arrangements in some cases, for example, those involving the activities of the Atomic and Space Development Authority and the Power Authority of the State of New York under the state's electric-power program and those involving the role of the UDC in community development.

As signed into law by the Governor in 1968, the power program authorized the Power Authority to enter into contractual arrangements with private utilities to construct pumped storage plants for the generation of electric power to be used to help satisfy peak load demand. The authority was also authorized to join with private utilities and the Atomic and Space Development Authority in constructing and operating advanced reactor facilities such as a fast breeder reactor.[27] The role of the Atomic and Space Development Authority under the 1968 power program provides other examples of the public-private partnership that the program made possible. The authority was empowered to: acquire and develop sites, "atomic energy reservations" as they were sometimes called, to be used by private utilities for the construction and operation of nuclear-power plants; contract with private utilities to provide features of nuclear-power plants essential to protecting the environment and human health from hazards associated with the operation of such plants; contract with private utilities to provide the nuclear fuel for nuclear-power plants; and participate in joint efforts with private utilities in the construction and operation of advanced reactor facilities such as the fast breeder reactor.[28]

The range of powers granted to the UDC by the statute creating it is truly impressive. Unlike the HFA, an agency limited primarily to a role as a *financer* of housing and other projects, UDC was given a wide variety of powers. In addition to the power to finance mortgages, UDC was authorized to construct and rehabilitate properties, to acquire land by purchase or condemnation, to hire architects and engineers to prepare and develop plans, specifications and designs, to let construction contracts to developers and builders, to manage projects and to enter into agreements with local governments or private parties to manage projects, to create subsidiary corporations, and to override local zoning and building codes.[29]

The range and mix of UDC's powers make it apparent that this public benefit corporation combined functions that have traditionally belonged either to governmental bodies or private organizations, but not to both. Armed with crucial governmental powers such as the power of eminent domain as well as many of the capacities that would belong to a bank or a construction firm, the UDC was well-equipped to become the nation's premier developer.

Many journalists and other observers have made reference to Nelson Rockefeller's alleged "edifice complex."[30] Because of persistent questioning on the topic of his edifice complex, Rockefeller was occasionally put in the position of having to defend the vast amounts of construction for which he had been responsible. As the following quotation demonstrates, he was capable of an aggressive defense. "Some people have said I'm more interested in buildings than people. Maybe that's because when they look at all the new construction I've sponsored, all they see is steel and concrete. When I see construction under way, I see jobs. Not only construction jobs, but clerical jobs, service jobs, all kinds of jobs for all kinds of people."[31]

The fact that Rockefeller's construction projects provided jobs was not lost on labor leaders in New York State. As construction union leader Peter Brennan noted, "There was always guys who didn't want to go for him, so I'd take them around and show them the buildings he was responsible for, the work he was responsible for. Hell, they could see the buildings, I didn't have to do any more persuading after that. In the construction industry it's either feast or famine. We had a pretty good feast when Rockefeller was around."[32]

A glance at Table 7.2 confirms that many of the Governor's pet programs and projects involved construction. Most notable in this respect were the South Mall office/cultural complex, the expansion of the state university, the Pure Waters Program, the housing projects of the Housing Finance Agency, the housing, industrial, and community development projects of the Urban Development Agency, the construction of municipal hospitals and nursing homes under state loan programs, and highway and mass transit projects carried out under the aegis of the Department of Transportation and the Metropolitan Transportation Authority, utilizing in part funds from the transportation capital facilities bond issue approved by voters in 1967. Although they did not approach the amount of construction that the above programs did, the narcotics program of 1966, the nuclear development program of the Atomic Development Authority, and the electric-power program also involved some amounts of construction.

Perhaps even more indicative of the Governor's willingness, indeed eagerness, to engage in great construction projects is the fact that five of the six pet programs that failed to gain approval also involved substantial amounts of construction. Only universal health insurance did not.[33] The proposals for construction of a bridge across Long Island Sound and development of a fourth jetport for the Metropolitan New York area, both to be accomplished by the Metropolitan Transportaiton Authority, represented major building projects. Finally, one purpose of the two proposed transportation bond issues that met defeat at the polls was to provide money for highway construction and mass transit projects.[34]

Although some are inclined to explain the Governor's penchant for building to primarily political motivations, such an interpretation ignores his lifelong interest in architecture and one other factor. That factor is what we see as a paternalistic view of New York as "his" state and New York City and Albany as "his" cities, his in the sense tht he felt a responsibility for their physical appearances and the visual impressions that they had for others. Nothing illustrates this better than Rockefeller's love affair with the so-called South Mall project, the state office-cultural complex that borders the capitol in Albany. Plagued by cost-overruns and dubbed Rockefeller's folly by critics, the project eventually became his monument, just as Rockefeller Center became his father's monument.

The Governor defended the South Mall project before the Senate committee considering his nomination to be vice-president.[35]

> We are ending up with what is going to be undoubtedly the most beautiful urban development in the United States. This is my prejudiced opinion. I think this is going to be a center of attraction for the city, for the State, that is commensurate with the dignity of the Empire State, and its tradition. . . .
>
> The same things are said about this as were said about Rockefeller Center when my father built it. It was Rockefeller's Folly and it was a disaster, and so forth and it turned out to have been the thing that saved the midtown of Manhattan. . . .[36]

Mayor Corning of Albany, a key figure in developing the scheme for financing the South Mall complex, later to be called the Empire State Plaza, provided some good insights into Rockefeller's concern for the appearance and status of the capital city. Commenting on the generally accepted story regarding the origin of the idea for the mall, Corning said,

> There's no question that the idea of the Empire State Plaza was a result of his [Rockefeller's] tour through downtown with Princess Beatrix of the Netherlands, when she came here in 1959 for the Hudson-Champlain Celebration. He felt that the buildings they saw were not as goodlooking or as appropriate for a capital city as he thought they should be. . . .
>
> His vision was that of an architect.[37]

As one former agency head remarked, Nelson Rockefeller "loved technology."[38] Perhaps it is not surprising then that a number of his pet programs depended heavily upon technology. They include his proposals for nuclear fallout protection, the electric-power program, the Pure Waters Program, and the nuclear development program of the Atomic Development Authority.[39] Perhaps the latter provides the best illustration of the Governor's faith that science and technology held the key to the solution of a wide range of problems facing New York State and the larger society.

Referring to the "hope and expectation the immense potential and use of atomic energy for peaceful and productive purposes," Rockefeller proudly cited the goals of the newly created Atomic Research and Development Authority:

1. development of a "Western New York Nuclear Service Center" that would encompass both a nuclear waste storage facility and a nuclear fuel reprocessing facility;
2. construction of a nuclear-powered plant for the desalinization of seawater;
3. establishment of a pulsed reactor facility as the first component of a "Space Technology and Radiation Center;"
4. promotion of the nuclear shipbuilding industry in the state.[40]

The Governor's commitment to nuclear technology predated creation of the authority by at least three years. In fact, by December 1959, an atomic development plan for the state had been produced by the Office of Atomic Development, a staff unit created by the legislature at the urging of Rockefeller.[41]

The Governor's goals in promoting the development of atomic energy in New York were not merely the product of a fascination with technology for technology's sake. Rather, he saw the development of a nuclear industry in the state as a key to economic development, just as he saw development of the state's transportation system, and even its system of higher education, as keys to such development. Thus his goal was to make New York State the leading state in nuclear industry, an industry which he saw as one with a bright future.[42]

(Other Rockefeller initiatives in the area of science and technology which were motivated in part by a concern for economic development were creation of the New York State Science and Technology Foundation, a public corporation that made grants to educational institutions to strengthen graduate programs in science and engineering and creation of the Advisory Council for the Advancement of Industrial Research and Development, an organization that sought to promote the expansion of industrial research and development in the state.)[43]

A Turn to the Right?

As noted in a discussion of changes that occurred over time in the numbers and proportions of programs that gained approval in the various policy areas, there remains to be considered the question of the extent to which those changes and related changes in emphases support the common perception that the Governor and his administration "turned to the right" beginning about 1970.[44] After his departure from the governorship, Rockefeller himself addressed the question of his alleged movement toward a more conservative stance. Consistent with the position he had taken throughout his public life, he was reluctant to classify himself as either a liberal or conservative. For example, during the Senate hearings on his nomination to be vice-president, Rockefeller was asked by Senator James Allen of Alabama to provide some examples that would support the view that as Governor he had "moved philosophically to the right."[45] The Governor prefaced his response by saying that "I think basically I have to say that I am a progressive or liberal in terms of trying to find ways of meeting human needs, and that I have been more conservative in terms of fiscal affairs."[46] That Rockefeller could seriously state that he had been conservative in fiscal affairs is truly astonishing given the record of financial management revealed in Chapter 6. That he was frustrated by his inability to spend at the end of his administration is perhaps best indicated by his comments in a 1977 interview. "That is what swung me over to the right . . . , the hard reality of the lack of money. I had no alternative and if you have ever faced a billion and-a-half deficit; I want to tell you that is an awful uncomfortable feeling."[47]

The two examples that Rockefeller cited to Senator Allen as examples others had used to argue that the former had turned to the right were those of welfare and drugs. Refusing to label as liberal or conservative his measures designed to reduce welfare rolls and expenditures, he portrayed them as being aimed as "mismanagement," a phenomenon to which he admitted making some contribution. At the same time, he asserted that he acted out of serious concerns for the well-being of society with respect to both welfare and drugs. Noting projections that the percentage of the population on welfare in New York City might rise from 18 percent in 1971 to 23 percent, he said "I did not see how a society could survive with 23 percent of the population nonproductive."[48] Referring to what he said were 135,000 addicts "robbing, mugging, murdering, day in and day out for their money to fix their habit" and bemoaning "the destruction of the security of individuals in our communities," he defended his tough drug proposals.[49] He concluded his discussion of his welfare and drug "reforms" by saying "that is why I got the reputation of having swung to the right—I tried to do an effective job in representing the peoples' interest through efficient management, sound fiscal management and human concern."[50]

The view that Nelson Rockefeller and his administration became more "conservative" during his last term is based on a number of programs, actions, and decisions in addition to the two examples cited above, those involving reforms in the areas of welfare and drugs. Especially prominent among them are the Governor's handling of the rebellion at Attica Prison in 1971 and his creation of an Office of Education Performance Review in 1973. (The question of the Governor's role in the Attica affair will be considered in Chapter 8). However, it would seem desirable to look at a wider range of Rockefeller's policies and actions in his fourth term in order to make a satisfactory assessment of the degree to which he did turn to the right. To this end, we will look at the substance of pet programs advanced in the fourth term; his positions on certain issues commonly viewed as involving a liberal-conservative dimension, for example, levels of welfare benefits, borrowing proposals, abortion reform, school busing, and universal health insurance; and the relative emphases placed on different policy areas over the course of the administration.

Of the eight programs in the fourth term which we identify as pet programs of the Governor, only three were in policy areas of special interest to liberals, namely, social development, education, and health. The three proposals were those to create a Welfare Inspector General and an Office of Education Performance Review and a proposal for universal health insurance, the latter also advanced in each year of Rockefeller's third term. (The Governor did not offer the latter after 1971). A quick look at the basic nature of the first two of these proposals reveals some preliminary basis for a claim that Rockefeller was moving to the right. This is so in the sense that his proposals involved questioning the conventional wisdom on how to deal with problems of education and welfare. More specifically they involved introducing management approaches based on the values of efficiency and economy as opposed to relying on the traditional liberal emphasis on delivering services through the expansion and maintenance of large bureaucracies dominated by professionals who believe that generous spending provides the major answers to the problems under their purview. It seems legitimate to us to conclude that the nature of these two programs constitutes some support for the view that the Governor moved away from liberal positions during his third term. Additional indications of movement in that same direction are provided by a number of other examples.

Although the problem at which Rockefeller's earlier drug programs were aimed was always perceived partly as one of crime and personal security, the problem was also viewed partly as a health problem. For example, although one of its major components was "forced" rehabilitation of addicts, the 1966 program did at least place a heavy emphasis on the concept of rehabilitation.[51] However, as noted in Chapter 5, the 1973 program involved a drastic increase in the use of punishment as deterrent as opposed to the traditional liberal preference for rehabilitation.

It is clear then that three of the eight pet programs advanced in the Governor's last term represent some degree of movement toward a more conservative stance. All of the remaining five pet programs are difficult to place on any liberal-conservative dimension and thus are not helpful in trying to detect any move to the right.

Aside from the three pet programs discussed above, perhaps the best indication of any turn to the right were various aspects of the Governor's 1971 welfare reforms beyond the creation of a welfare inspector general. Among these aspects were proposals for a residency requirement of one year designed to discourage poor persons from moving into the state, authority for the Health Department to declare a housing emergency in overcrowded areas from which persons without the means to acquire adequate housing would be excluded, federal authorization for a program to provide expenses to relocate welfare recipients from New York to other states, a requirement that employable welfare recipients be required to pick up checks in person, regulations denying welfare assistance to those who voluntarily quit jobs without "good cause" or refuse jobs they are able to perform, and establishment of an experimental program under which certain categories of welfare recipients would be able to "earn back" substantial reductions in their benefits.[52]

In addition to representing the normally restrictive approach to welfare advocated by modern American conservatives, some of the Governor's proposals deserve special comment. For example, residency requirements for welfare had been declared unconstitutional by the Supreme Court in

1969.[53] In striking down the 1971 statute implementing the Governor's proposal, the Court's opinion described the law as a transparent attempt to subvert its earlier decision.[54]

Rockefeller's proposal that certain categories of welfare recipients have their grants cut, but be given the "opportunity" to earn additional benefits to bring their total grants up to the "normal" level authorized by state law seems to us to represent one of the more offensive ideas in the history of social welfare in America. Contingent upon gaining the approval of the Department of Health, Education, and Welfare, the Governor's proposed program was designed to be compatible with the welfare reform plan sponsored by the Nixon administration in 1971. Under the latter plan, an eligible family of four would have received welfare benefits of $2,400 per year, a figure far below the $3756 paid in New York under then-existing state law.[55] Quickly dubbed the "brownie point plan" by the press, the Governor's experimental plan would have reduced benefits to $2,400 in anticipation of a federal program setting benefits at that level. However, as he put it, recipients of benefits under the welfare program known as aid-to-dependent-children "would have the opportunity to bring their payments to the full benefit level $3,756 through supplemental incentive benefits for regular school attendance and participation in work and work-training programs, as well as other programs designed to promote social responsibility."[56]

That the incentive point system was based on the kind of insensitivity to human worth that might be expected in a totalitarian system should be apparent to anyone seeing the list of activities eligible for incentive points under the plan that New York State submitted to the Secretary of Health, Education, and Welfare. For example, a family could gain one incentive point, worth twenty-five dollars of benefits per month, if its caseworker determined that a school-age child (ages five to fifteen) was "cooperating with the teacher." The same family could also earn an incentive point worth twenty-five dollars in benefits if a child participated in a "citizen building activity" such as the Boy Scouts or a 4-H Club.[57]

Elizabeth Wickenden's assessment of the incentive-point system seems fair, if harsh.

> In all respects a sub-class of impoverished families is to be created subject to the most detailed scrutiny of their private lives. Not even the Poor Law imposed such conditions...
>
> The Incentives Project assumes the most detailed monitoring of personal behavior by the casework staff and honest reporting of such behavior by the client on an extremely complex series of requirements. Of necessity it also leaves important questions of judgment to the individual worker because of the vagueness of some of these requirements.[58]

Among other issues on which there tend to be identifiable liberal and conservative positions are abortion and the death penalty. The Governor's actions with respect to the issues of abortion and the death penalty provide some evidence that any turn to the right in his last term was not clear and unambiguous. Having signed a bill in 1965 which permitted the death penalty for those convicted of murdering law officers and correctional officers and those who committed murder while serving a life sentence, the Governor never actually submitted any proposals calling for the death penalty for other categories of defendants.[59] After the New York death penalty statute was declared unconstitutional in 1973, the Governor occasionally stated that he might propose a bill to restore the death penalty.[60] However, he never did so, and in September of 1973 he said that while he would not veto such a bill if passed by the legislature, he preferred to deal with crime "without going to the death penalty."[61]

Following the report of a task force he appointed to study problems associated with illegal abortions, the Governor proposd liberalization of prohibitions against abortions.[62] In 1970 the legislature passed a bill that removed almost all restrictions against abortions within a period of twenty-four weeks from conception. Although the Governor preferred a more restrictive approach which would have allowed abortions only through eighteen weeks, an approach to liberalization that he himself had proposed, he nevertheless signed the bill into law.[63]

Under intense pressure from foes of abortion, including the growing "right-to-life" movement, the legislature passed a bill in 1972 repealing the liberalized abortion statute. Presented with a clear opportunity to please "conservative" forces, Rockefeller, nevertheless, vetoed the repeal bill as he had promised he would before its passage.[64] Inviting the wrath of anti-abortion forces, he stated that "I do not believe it right for one group to impose its vision of morality on an entire society," and went on to complain of the "extremes of personal villification and political coercion brought to bear on members of the legislature" by supporters of repeal.[65]

The Governor's positions on the death penalty and abortion are not the only indications supporting the view that any turn to the right in his fourth term was at best an ambiguous one. In spite of antispending rhetoric which he began to adopt after the legislature's assault on his budget in 1971, he continued to advocate massive state borrowing. In his Annual Message of 1971 he proposed as one of his two items of highest priority a "community development bond issue" whose proceeds would be used to rehabilitate urban slums.[66] A typical Rockefeller "big-spending" measure, the proposal was to include authorization for about $4 billion in state borrowing authority that would then be utilized primarily by the Urban Development Corporation in providing subsidies to the private sector for the construction and operation of housing, industrial installations, and community facilities.[67] The proposed bond issue would have had the advantage of easing the increasingly tight budget situation which the Governor faced in his last term. However, primarily because of opposition by the Republican leadership in the assembly, the Governor never submitted legislation to authorize the bond issue.[68]

Undaunted by his failure to overcome legislative objections to his community development bond issue in the 1971 session, Rockefeller proposed, and the legislature approved, a proposal for a $2.5 billion transportation bond issue in that same session.[69] In addition, the Governor gained approval for the Metropolitan Transportation Authority to issue $30 million in bonds from the transportation bond issue of 1967 to be used for development of one of his pet projects, a fourth major jetport to serve the metropolitan New York area.[70] Additional evidence of the Governor's commitment to "big spending," even in his last term, came near the very end of that term, a special session of the legislature in the summer of 1973. Unwilling to accept the voters' defeat of his 1971 bond proposal, the Governor gained legislative approval to submit a $3.5 billion transportation bond issue to the voters in November of 1973.[71] (As noted above, the voters defeated this proposal also.)

That the Governor's natural inclination to spend was not fundamentally altered by the difficult financial circumstances of his last term is supported not only by his spending proposals in the area of community development and transportation, but in his responses to other problems in 1973 after economic growth and consequent growth in tax revenues caused the state's financial situation to ease a bit. For example, stating that his welfare reforms had succeeded in slowing the rate of growth in welfare case loads, the Governor proposed in his budget message that the legislature restore a 10 percent cut in benefits to recipients in the categories of home relief and aid to dependent children.[72]

One must conclude that an examination of the substance of certain key Rockefeller programs and positions with reference to his alleged turn to the right produces no clear-cut evidence supporting the existence of such a move. Although it is true that a number of Rockefeller's proposals, those dealing with drugs, welfare reform, and education were conservative in the modern sense of that term, there were also proposals including, but not confined to, those involving huge amounts of proposed state debt, which would commonly be labeled liberal. Thus while one can legitimately conclude that the Governor proposed some notable conservative programs in his fourth term, more than in earlier terms, one must recognize that there were also liberal initiatives.[73] The record simply does not support any wholesale turn to the right in the last term.

The Substance of Rockefeller Programs: A Reflection of an Activist Problem Solver

Just as Nelson Rockefeller's management of state finances illustrates a commitment to confronting big problems in comprehensive and bold ways, so do the scope and substance of the programs and projects which he proposed and, in some cases, launched. In particular, the pet programs described in this chapter represent a truly notable collection, not just in terms of cost, but in terms of innovative qualities, relevance to national problems, and in what might be described as the audacity of the goals that most of them sought and the ingenuity of the means that many incorporated. There is no better reflection of Rockefeller's continuing commitment to his life strategy than these aspects of the product of his administration. Even the most mundane sorts of statistics used to describe the product of key programs leave a powerful impression of the man's accomplishments. For example, by the end of the administration, well over 300 academic buildings and other facilities had been constructed at various campuses of the State University of New York, over 10,000 new beds in nursing homes and hospitals had been provided and more than 90,000 units of housing had been provided through the combined efforts of HFA and UDC.[74]

8 Coping with and Creating Crisis and Controversy: Four Cases

A consideration of Governor Rockefeller's role in a wide variety of tasks, including campaigning, structuring the decision process, producing programs and winning their adoption, and managing fiscal policy, provides a significant but not complete picture of his performance. Although Rockefeller occasionally found himself in the midst of crises or controversy when involved in the tasks cited above, some of the more controversial and crisis-laden episodes of his administration involved activities that do not fit neatly into any of the above categories.[1] The four cases presented here involve such crises and controversies. For example, all four of the cases relate in some way to "following through" in the implementation of programs or decisions or maintaining oversight of the activities of other officials. And three of the cases involve questions that put the Governor in the position of making some difficult moral judgments.

In addition to providing one with a further opportunity to examine Nelson Rockefeller's personality, his style as an executive, and some aspects of his beliefs, the cases discussed in this chapter provide an opportunity to address another important question, namely, the ways in which the Governor rationalized his actions and defended himself against criticism, including criticism of both the widsom of his actions and their propriety.

Nursing Homes: Failures in Program Administration

Some of the more intriguing and more controversial questions relating to the Rockefeller administration involve the so-called nursing home scandals that gained their widest publicity after Nelson Rockefeller left office. This case raises a number of issues including possible impropriety involving "special treatment" for those who had provided political and financial support for elections and the quality of the Governor's performance and that of his staff as it relates to implementing programs.

Although there were numerous facets of the Rockefeller administration involvement with nursing homes, those discussed here would seem to be among the more significant. In 1966 the legislature approved the Governor's program for providing financial assistance for the construction of nonprofit nursing homes as a means of helping deal with the huge demand for facilities to provide care for the elderly.[2] State subsidies under this program were made available in the form of mortgage loans provided by the Housing Finance Agency.[3] As noted in the discussions of the Governor's pet programs, about $450 million of debt had been created for these programs by June 30, 1972.[4] The Department of Health, the Public Health Council, and the Hospital Review and Planning Council were given substantial regulatory powers over nursing homes. Included among these were the power to issue required "operating certificates," to set reimbursement rates under the medicaid program, to approve changes in the state hospital code relating to both physical structure and facilities as well as operation, and to inspect facilities to ensure compliance with the hospital code and with medicaid and medicare regulations. Most of these powers could also be used against proprietary nursing homes.[5]

Although the quality of patient care has been an issue with respect to both nonprofit and proprietary nursing homes, the issue of improper or illegal profits involves proprietary homes. One common source of such profits was excessive reimbursements from medicaid funds. Thus, one of the leading figures in the New York nursing home industry, Bernard Bergman, was convicted and sentenced in 1976 on charges of defrauding the federal and state governments of $1.2 million in medicaid payments.[6] Aside from activities that were clearly illegal, those in the nursing home industry had motivation to seek the most favorable decisions possible from state officials concerning applications for operating certificates, proposals for reimbursement rates, and requests regarding tolerance of structural and operating deficiencies including those relating to the care of patients.

The most notorious case involving alleged preferential treatment for a member of "the nursing home industry" revolved around Bernard Bergman, one of whose goals was to gain state approval to operate the Danube Nursing Facility on Staten Island as a nursing home or as a facility to house mentally retarded patients to be transferred from the overcrowded Willowbrook State School operated by the Department of Mental Hygiene.[7] Beginning in 1972, Bergman used his friendship with Samuel Hausman, a Rockefeller supporter and friend, in an attempt to gain approval for his Danube application.[8]

As the Moreland Act Commission investigating the state's nursing home problems pointed out, Samuel Hausman, "a wealthy Republican businessman" and fund raiser for various "good causes," was "Rockefeller's unofficial advisor on Jewish matters, in essence the governor's eyes and ears to the Jewish community." [9] In order to fully appreciate the role that

Hausman played vis-à-vis the Governor and the Jewish community, it should be noted that the Governor tended to follow a pattern of utilizing particular individuals as links with identifiable segments of the state's population. Just as Hausman was his main link to the Jewish community, so was Jackie Robinson his main link to the black community, at least to the middle-class black community. However, as noted in Chapter 4, Robinson served on the state payroll as a special assistant to the Governor. Unlike Robinson, Hausman did not serve on Rockefeller's staff.

The relationship between Hausman and Rockefeller was warm and mutually beneficial. On the basis of the testimony of the Governor's personal secretary, the commission investigating nursing home problems concluded that Hausman was "considered a 'top person' in the Rockefeller administration."[10] The commission also noted that Hausman had contributed from $500 to $1,500 to each Rockefeller campaign and had raised about $25,000 from other sources for each campaign. In 1973 the Governor appointed Hausman to two bodies that played roles in the state's involvement with nursing homes: the Hospital Review and Planning Council and the Medical Care Facilities Finance Agency.[11]

That the Jewish community in the state was important to the Governor's electoral efforts should be self-evident. Without questioning the sincerity of Rockefeller's commitment to good causes, one must, nevertheless, note that the massive contributions he made to the United Jewish Appeal of Greater New York represent a way of cementing good will that is unavailable to any but the very wealthiest of politicians. To be more specific, from January 1957 to June 1974, Rockefeller gave over half-a-million dollars to the United Jewish Appeal of Greater New York.[12]

Given Hausman's relationship to Rockefeller, it is not hard to believe that Bernard Bergman, Orthodox rabbi and well-regarded member of the Jewish community, would seek Hausman's assistance in getting favorable treatment on his applications for nursing homes. Indeed, Rockefeller testified before the commission on nursing homes that Hausman had come to him early in 1972 or late in 1973 with a report that the latter believed a friend of his was being discriminated against by the Department of Health regarding applications for nursing home approvals. The Governor told Hausman that he would ask his chief of staff T. Norman Hurd to look into the matter and also advised Hausman to get in touch with Dr. Hurd.[13]

The Governor's meeting with Samuel Hausman led to intensive involvement by Hurd with questions concerning Bernard Bergman's application for state approval for nursing homes and other health-related facilities. The Moreland Act summarized Hurd's involvement in one of those applications as follows:

> From 1972 through 1974, Hurd was extensively involved in the problems associated with Bernard Bergman's Danube Nursing Home applications. Most of this involvement occurred while Hurd was Rockefeller's and then [Governor] Wilson's

> Secretary of chief of staff. . . . There were some ten or eleven meetings in which Hurd met with Bergman or his associates; a substantial number of telephone calls and letters to heads of various state agencies; and frequent directions to his staff to inquire and report regarding these applications.[14]

There is no evidence that Rockefeller himself was involved in, or cognizant of, the details of Hurd's continuing efforts to assist Bergman. As the Governor testified before the commission on nursing homes, "My total relationship with this subject [Bernard Bergman] is about 10 minutes long, five minutes with Hausman and five minutes with Hurd."[15] Furthermore, the Governor noted that since no significant policy or financial question was at issue in the Bergman case, Hurd would not be expected to keep him informed of his activities in the case.[16] Nevertheless, knowing Hurd's deep loyalty to the Governor and his concern for the latter's wishes, it seems very unlikely that he would have pursued the Bergman matters as aggressively as he did if he had thought that the Governor might have disapproved of his actions.[17]

Although acknowledging that one reason for his having given attention to Bergman's problems was that Bergman had been referred to him by Hausman, "a special friend of the Governor's," Hurd defended his actions as being of the character of "inquiries" that one in his position might properly make in the capacity of an ombudsman.[18] Nevertheless, the commission was very critical of Hurd's activities.

> Hurd's involvement . . . continued in the face of his knowledge that the Department of Health was processing Bergman's application expeditiously and that it considered Bergman undesirable as a nursing home operator. . . .
>
> Moroever, the quality of Hurd's "interventions" or "inquiries" was such that it must be concluded that at best he was insensitive to their effect on state agency personnel or at worst he intended them to have the effect of influencing their decisions.[19]

Although there is no evidence that Rockefeller himself was directly involved in any impropriety relating to nursing homes, there is ample reason to question the quality of his performance with respect to monitoring the implementation of programs relating to nursing homes. The Moreland Act commission on nursing homes establishes clearly that the Governor and his staff were made aware of the existence of substantial waste and fraud involving medicaid reimbursements to nursing homes and of gross deficiences in patient care, but the Rockefeller administration organized no effective attacks on such problems. For example, despite repeated requests by the Health Department for additional funds and other authorizations required to provide additional auditors to root out waste and fraud, the Governor did not respond with the necessary budget recommendations.[20]

It is true that Rockefeller had created a broader structure, what amounted to a state franchising system for all health care facilities, under which effective regulation of nursing homes was in theory possible.[21] It is also true that one of his pet programs resulted in the provision of large numbers of additional beds for nursing care. But it is in the task of monitoring the implementation of programs related to nursing homes that Rockefeller and his aides failed. For example, failure to take the leadership in assuring funds for additional auditors was a case of inadequate program implementation. Furthermore, his defense of "tight budgets" is hardly credible given the nursing home commission's well-supported argument that additional auditors would have resulted in net savings to the state given the potential recovery of excess reimbursement and the availability of a federal subsidy of 75 percent of the cost of an auditing program for medicaid programs.[22]

Also indicative of ineffective program administration is the fact that the Rockefeller administration did not wage a vigorous effort to remedy deficient patient care in nursing homes. Given the many problems that needed attention, one might forgive such an omission. However, both the failure to provide additional auditors and the failure to work harder to insure good quality patient care tend to support a common observation by those familiar with the Rockefeller administration, namely that nitty-gritty problems of administration, those with little glamour attached, were consistently given low priority.

A poignant example of the Governor's treatment of such programs is illustrated by his response to a question asked by the chairman of the commission on nursing homes. The question concerned a program that Rockefeller had announced approximately three months before the 1970 gubernatorial election. The press release announcing the "unique citizen involvement program" proudly stated: "This first-in-the-nation program will give us a direct feeling for what the state's elderly and chronically ill patients personally feel about the quality of medical care they are receiving in the state's 636 nursing homes."[23] When told by the chairman that the program was given no budget and no personnel, the Governor merely acknowledged that he did not know what had happened to the plan.[24] It is doubtful that a better example could be found of what one former state official characterized as the "program planning by press release" which he alleged as typical of the Rockefeller administration.[25]

The Morhouse Case: Taking Care of One Who Had Served

As noted in Chapter 3, then Republican party chairman Judson Morhouse was instrumental in securing the gubernatorial nomination for Rockefeller in 1958. One of the more controversial events in the Governor's administration relates to a scandal during his second term, a scandal in which Morhouse was a central figure. Specifically, in 1966 Morhouse was convicted for his part in the bribing of the chairman of the state liquor authority by executives of the Playboy Club who were seeking a liquor license for a new club in New York City.[26] The official who was alleged to have received a bribe was Martin C. Epstein, chairman of the New York State Liquor Authority (the SLA). However, Epstein fled to Florida and was never brought to trial.[27] Morhouse had resigned his salaried position as chairman of the State Thruway Authority and his unsalaried position as party chairman shortly after Epstein was indicted and reports had begun to circulate about Morhouse's own possible involvement. However, Morhouse was not indicted until 1965 and was not convicted until May of 1966. Before Morhouse began serving his sentence, after exhausting all appeals, the Governor commuted his sentence on the grounds that Morhouse's ill-health would prevent him from surviving a prison term.[28]

The elements of controversy surrounding the Morhouse case and the Governor's involvement in it are: first, the question whether Rockefeller was derelict in not being aware that Morhouse might be likely to involve himself in unethical or illegal activities; second, the question of the propriety of the Governor's commuting Morhouse's sentence; and third, the question of the propriety of his providing financial assistance to Morhouse both before and after the latter's involvement in the scandal concerning the Playboy Club and the Liquor Authority.

Rockefeller testified in the course of hearings on his nomination to be vice-president that as early as 1959 he was concerned about the possibility that Morhouse was a man who lacked "independent means," and thus might yield to "temptation" because his job as Republican party chairman was unsalaried.[29] Although there is no evidence that Morhouse had been involved in clearly illegal activities before the SLA affair, he had been involved in an event in 1959 which led to a trial of several men for passing a $100,000 "political contribution" to him. It was alleged that the money was given as a means of expediting the granting of a racetrack license, Morhouse refused to testify in the case on the grounds of possible self-incrimination.[30]

At his confirmation hearings Rockefeller noted that during a Republican fund-raising dinner in June of 1959, Morhouse had told him about a $100,000 contribution he had been handed. According to the Governor's testimony, he had instructed Morhouse to have the money returned, but took no further action on the matter because he did not regard the contribution to the party chairman as illegal.[31] Given the concerns that Rockefeller noted he had about the possibility that Morhouse might yield to temptation and given his knowledge of Morhouse's role in the $100,000 political contribution, it seems difficult to disagree with Senator Harrison Williams' conclusion that there were all kinds of warning that Morhouse did not have his feet on solid and moral grounds. Indeed Rockefeller conceded that Williams' point was "well-taken."[32]

The Governor's method of dealing with the possibility that Morhouse might be tempted is typical of his method of taking care of the financial needs of his closest associates. In addition to appointing Morhouse as head of the New York State Thruway Authority in 1959, a position paying $17,000 per year, he took two other steps. The first was to lend him $100,000 to purchase some income-producing property, and the second was to arrange for his brother Laurance to lend Morhouse $49,000 to purchase growth stocks that presumably would yield sufficient profits to allow payment of the loan plus substantial profits.[33] As was the case with so many of his loans to close associates, Rockefeller forgave his loan after leaving office.

The Governor's decision to commute Morhouse's sentence was subjected to numerous questions in the hearings on his confirmation as vice-president. Rockefeller's defense of his action was based on the general grounds that Morhouse's life would be placed in jeopardy by his incarceration. More specifically, he noted that details of the case had been handled by the counsel to the Governor and that the counsel's recommendation for a commutation had been based upon evidence submitted by the applicant's physicians and an independent assessment by three other physicians.[34] At the time his sentence was commuted, Morhouse was suffering from Parkinson's disease. He had also undergone surgery for cancer of the colon and removal of the prostate. A newspaper story in November of 1974 described Mr. Morhouse at that time as "no longer able to maintain his law practice or attend to business."[35] According to Rockefeller, there were five other cases during his administration in which he commuted sentences on the grounds of ill health.

An examination of the Governor's behavior in incidents involving Morhouse suggests that he regarded considerations of propriety as being secondary to that of the personal obligation to take care of close associates.[36] The same elements of paternalism as are revealed in the pattern of dispensing jobs, loans, gifts, and other benefits to many of his close associates are present in the Morhouse case.

It must be granted that not all aspects of the Governor's conduct in the Morhouse case can easily be condemned on ethical grounds. For example, one could make a strong case for his commuting Morhouse's sentence on humanitarian grounds. However, some aspects of Rockefeller's conduct show an obvious insensitivity. In particular, few reasonable men would doubt that the Governor had ample reason to fear that Morhouse might be subject to temptation. Under these circumstances the prudent course for a chief executive would have been to see that a replacement was found before the worst fears were realized.

Attica: Managing a Crisis

In addition to being the most controversial single period of the entire Rockefeller administration, the rebellion at Attica state prison in 1971 is remarkable in that it provides an opportunity to examine numerous intriguing questions. Among them are: the nature of the Governor's executive style as it manifested itself in handling attempts to end the crisis by negotiation and, later, by an armed assault on the prison; the nature of certain elements in the Governor's belief system as they may have affected his conduct, especially as those elements are revealed in the way in which he later defended his conduct; and the impact that certain elements of the Governor's personality and his goals may have had on his handling of the Attica crisis.

Beginning on Thursday, September 9, 1971, the Attica prison uprising ended with an assault that left twenty-nine inmates and ten hostages dead or dying and many other prisoners and hostages injured. The state commission investigating the uprising, the McKay Commission, wrote, "With the exception of Indian massacres in the late 19th century, the State Police assault which ended the four-day prison uprising was the bloodiest one-day encounter between Americans since the Civil War."[37]

For most of Rockefeller's tenure, the area of corrections policy had not been one to which great attention had been given. As a former program associate who had responsibility for the area said, "Correction was not a politically attractive area, the public wants it out-of-sight, out-of-mind."[38] Rockefeller himself admitted after Attica that he had been derelict in not paying more attention to this area.

> If I could go back 14 years instead of six months . . . I would have to say that one of the things I regret most is my own lack of perception of the tremendous need which existed in this area . . . I say this is a big area that I did not fully understand and perceive.[39]

It is ironic that the Governor and other state officials had, in fact, begun to pay somewhat more attention to the area of corrections in the year preceding the Attica uprising. One indication of this was the creation early in 1971 of a new Department of Correctional Services, a product of a merger of the old Department of Corrections and the Division of Parole.[40] More significant was the appointment of Russell Oswald, a respected reform-minded professional committed to the standard liberal emphasis on rehabilitation as opposed to punishment. Bringing with him extensive professional experience in Wisconsin and Massachusetts and as chairman of the New York State Board of Parole, Oswald faced the herculean task of reforming a poorly staffed, underfinanced corrections system which had numerous additional problems.[41] Prisons were outmoded and tensions within them were high because their populations consisted disproportionately of urban blacks and Latins, and the guard population had disproportionately large numbers of whites from rural backgrounds.

Within a few months of his appointment, Oswald had begun a series of planned reforms in the corrections system.[42] However, his efforts were seriously handicapped by virtue of the fact that the state was in the midst of the tightest budget in the Rockefeller administration. (As noted in Chapter 5, 1971 was the year of the legislature's fiscal revolt.) The consequence of the fiscal crisis was that the Department of Corrections had to lay off more than 400 employees, including 160 at two of the state's five maximum security prisons, those at Green Haven and Great Meadows. Although no layoffs were made at Attica, staff vacancies were not filled during fiscal year 1971-1972.[43] Later Oswald was to express frustration with his situation.

> I came out of the budget squeeze with a per annum figure of $94,022,900, which we would live with, even though we were conscious of the fact this was less than 5 percent of total state expenditures. As Deputy Commissioner van Eckeren subsequently commented, "Prisons are not visible. There is no political gain in putting money into prisons when there are so many other more visible priorities."[44]

Beginning shortly after he took office, Oswald became more and more concerned that "radicals," "militants," and "revolutionaries" would spark more uprisings in New York prisons, uprisings similar to a riot at the prison at Auburn in 1970. In addition to mentioning his fears in speeches that he gave, Oswald made the Governor aware of these fears, both in monthly reports and in a face-to-face meeting. According to Rockefeller, the commissioner met with him just four weeks before the Attica uprising and asked that the Governor double the number of guards in state prisons.[45] Former Budget Director Richard Dunham has confirmed Rockefeller's assertion that he did, in fact, authorize some additional guards, but had additional guards been the "answer" for Attica, they would have come too late.[46]

By September of 1971, it was clear to anyone who looked that an uprising at some state prison was only a matter of time. And because he was viewed by prison personnel as a "do-gooder" who was too permissive in his approach, Commissioner Oswald was in a very difficult position.[47] Because Attica was regarded as the most secure of the state's prisons, prisoners who proved to be "difficult cases" were often transferred there. This practice and a number of other developments helped to raise tensions at Attica. Although Commissioner Oswald responded sympathetically to letters from prisoner groups asking for immediate changes such as more showers and cleaner conditions in the mess hall, few, if any, immediate changes took place. In fact, fearful of trouble and resentful of promised change, authorities at Attica made attempts to tighten discipline and curtail existing prerogatives of prisoners.[48]

Tensions reached a new peak after inmates became aware that George Jackson, a revolutionary black leader who had gained fame by protesting inhumane prison conditions, was killed in August 1971 by prison officials at

Soledad State Prison in California.[49] Another incident contributing to the tension at Attica was the fact that Oswald substituted a taped message for a message to the inmates that he was to have delivered in person. In the taped message he reiterated previously announced goals and noted that they could only be achieved over a period of time. The inmates concluded that Oswald really did not care about their conditions because he did not appear in person and because they felt his taped message lacked any sense of urgency and, therefore, was not responsive to their demands for immediate improvements.[50] The stage had thus been set for the Attica uprising.

Following a series of incidents including scuffles between guards and inmates on Wednesday, September 8, inmates took over most of the prison the next day, including all five cellblocks and six other buildings. (Later in the day prison authorities retook some areas that had been abandoned by inmates.) Although some prison personnel thought the uprising had been a well-planned effort, the McKay Commission rejected that conclusion.[51] By 10:30 A.M. on September 9, there were 1,281 inmates and forty-three hostages assembled in D yard, one of the four such "yards" within the prison. Following an initial period of confusion, order had been established by inmate "leaders." A system of inmate security guards had been set up to maintain order, and the hostages, moved to the center of the yard, were put under the protection of Black Muslim inmates.[52] After an inmate nurse answered a call from inmate leaders for medical volunteers, four wounded hostages and a few inmates with chronic conditions were released from the captured area. For the first three days of the takeover, inmate leaders permitted an area surgeon to enter the yard and care for hostages and inmates.[53]

Between the time of the prison takeover on Thursday morning, September 9, and the state's assault on the prison on Monday morning, September 13, there was an almost continuous process of negotiations and confrontations between inmates and a variety of state officials and outside "observers," some of the latter requested by the inmates. Although there was initial optimism that negotiations might succeed, the prospects of success declined steadily beginning early on Friday. Although he was not present at Attica, Rockefeller kept in close touch with the situation through some of his closest aides. Even though he later stated that he felt it was a mistake to have negotiated with the inmates, he did allow negotiations to take place. His reason was that others, most notably Russell Oswald, had preferred to try that option. The decision to retake the prison by force was Rockefeller's decision. Secretary to the Governor Robert Douglass, Director of State Operations T. Norman Hurd, and A. C. O'Hara, Commissioner of General Services, all played key roles. The latter two were sent to Attica on Friday evening to assist Oswald and serve as the main channels of communication to the Governor. Douglass arrived late on Saturday afternoon to perform a similar role. Although he later made it clear that he had serious reservations about Oswald's approach, Rockefeller testified that he refrained from overruling the commissioner because of his belief that a chief executive should support the decisions of his appointees.[54]

One consequence of the Governor's view on delegating authority to the heads of departments was that Douglass, Hurd, and O'Hara did not assume command of negotiations. Commissioner Oswald was allowed the freedom to make key decisions throughout the process of negotiations that began on Thursday afternoon. And as the McKay Commission points out, the commissioner explicitly rejected the advice of Douglass, the man closest to Rockefeller, on at least two occasions.[55] Furthermore, Oswald even ignored the Governor's view that the committee of observers should not be allowed one final visit inside D yard before an assault upon the prison became inevitable. When Douglass told Oswald of the Governor's opposition, the commissioner explained his reaction as follows: "I asked him whether he was telling me that Governor Rockefeller was replacing me. And he said no, he didn't meant that at all. I said, 'Well, I just wanted to be clear on that because I am letting them in.' "[56]

In addition to Commissioner Oswald and the Governor's representatives, there were two groups of people who played key roles in negotiations. They were a committee of observers and the inmates in D yard and their spokesmen. Consisting of some "volunteers," other persons invited by Douglass, and some recruited at the specific request of inmate spokesmen, the group included more than thirty members ranging from radical leaders of political groups such as the Black Panther Party to "establishment" journalists, ministers, legislators, and lawyers. Among those who played prominent roles were Herman Badillo, U.S. Congressman; Clarence Jones, publisher of the black newspaper, *The Amsterdam News*; William Kunstler, civil liberties lawyer and prominent defender of leading radicals in numerous trials; Arthur Eve, a black minister and Buffalo assemblyman active in the field of prison reform; John Dunne, chairman of the state senate's committee on crime and correction; and Tom Wicker, prominent *New York Times* columnist.

Although the process of selecting spokesmen for the inmates is not entirely clear, a group of inmate spokesmen did exist. Initially the group consisted of about a dozen inmates formed on Thursday afternoon, catalyzed in part by the need to agree on a list of demands. "Elected" by those inmates most active in "organizing" the yard and most interested in pressing demands upon the state, this group was augmented when an "official" election was held the next day, one with voting organized on the basis of cellblocks. All those who were members of the original group were among those elected.[57]

A summary of the key events and key decision prior to the retaking of the prison would start with the arrival of Commissioner Oswald at the prison early Thursday afternoon. During the remainder of the day, negotiations began with various people, including the commissioner, meeting in D yard with inmate leaders in a total of four meetings.[58] Most prominent during these early meetings with inmate leaders were Assemblyman Eve and Herman Schwartz, a law professor from Buffalo who had successfully represented Attica inmates in several cases involving prisoner rights. The results of the first day's negotiations were three. The first was that the possibility of using force to retake the prison was momentarily put aside.[59] The second was that inmate leaders advanced a series of demands that included "radical" demands such as transportation to a "non-imperialistic country," and "complete amnesty" as well as more conventional demands such as "religious freedom," improved food, more education, and increased recreation. It was during these negotiations that the inmates also asked that outside observers be involved in the negotiation process. The third result was that by the end of the day Professor Schwartz was on his way to obtain the signature of a federal judge on an injunction guaranteeing that state officials, including prison officials, would not take reprisals against inmates for their roles in the uprising. (As was made clear to the inmates, the injunction would have no force against criminal prosecutions.)[60]

Negotiations continued intermittently through Sunday afternoon, but chances for a successful outcome diminished daily. Following a confrontation between Oswald and inmate leaders in D yard late Friday morning, members of the committee of observers assumed the major role in negotiations. During the confrontation, the federal injunction obtained by Professor Schwartz was torn in two by an inmate leader because it did not address the issue of amnesty from criminal prosecutions and because it lacked an official seal.[61] During the course of negotiations the issue of criminal amnesty was to remain the major stumbling block to a settlement.

After meeting with inmate leaders twice on Friday, with the second meeting lasting far into Saturday morning, the observers held a long session with Oswald in which they secured his agreement to a list of "28 points" covering many proposals that were designed to satisfy demands by the inmates.[62] However, the commissioner maintained his position that complete "amnesty from prosecution for criminal acts was not a negotiable item." However, he did agree to a pledge of no administrative reprisals, such as adverse parole actions, and no prosecutions for crimes against property.[63] Although agreement on the list of twenty-eight points rekindled some degree of optimism, this optimism was dissipated with news that a corrections officer injured in the takeover had died. Because a murder charge was now likely, the "non-negotiable" issue of criminal amnesty loomed even larger. A long meeting between several of the observers and inmate leaders Saturday evening in D yard led to rejection of the twenty-eight points, primarily on the grounds that amnesty was not included.[64]

On Sunday morning the committee of observers issued a public appeal for Rockefeller to come to Attica to meet with them. They also met with the Governor's secretary, Robert Douglass, and urged him in the strongest possible terms to ask the Governor to come to Attica. Although Douglass was affronted by what he viewed as the hostile tone of the meeting, he called Rockefeller and reported the views of the observers. He also stated that he felt the "real issues" remained amnesty, asylum in a "non-imperialistic country," and the removal of the superintendent of the prison, Vincent Mancusi.[65] (Although the second of these issues had been part of the first list of demands presented by the inmates, it is not likely that the inmates would have pressed it had the other two been satisfied.) In response, the Governor directed Douglass to draft a statement announcing that he would not come to Attica, but Douglass did not notify the observers of Rockefeller's decision.[66]

The Governor postponed a planned assault on Sunday, but he nonetheless rejected two more pleas that he come to Attica. Without the knowledge of anyone else, four observers (Senator Dunne, Congressman Badillo, Clarence Jones, and Tom Wicker) called Rockefeller at his home on Pocantico Hills and pleaded with him for an hour. As the Governor later stated, he had felt that the observers committee wanted his presence at Attica merely because "they wanted to 'buy time' and avoid having to admit to their failure and to the reality that was becoming increasingly clear, namely, that the intransigence and impossible demands of the prisoners were forcing the state toward undertaking a mission to rescue the hostages."[67] During the observers' conversation with Rockefeller, the latter revealed that he had instructed Oswald to "reopen the institution."[68] Commissioner Oswald also made a last-minute attempt to get the Governor to come to Attica. Later admitting that he felt such a visit would have no effect on resolving the crisis, Oswald, nevertheless, recommended it on the grounds that a failure to come "would be harmful to him [Rockefeller] in the public mind."[69] However, the Governor rejected this advice, advice that Oswald admitted was "public relations advice."[70] It is a measure of the loyalty and protectiveness displayed toward Rockefeller by his appointees that amidst his own disappointment and agony, Russell Oswald was still able to think about the preservation of the Governor's public reputation.

Following the rejection by inmates of an ultimatum from Oswald on Monday morning, the stage was set for an assault on the prison by state troopers. In harmony with past state practice, the Division of State Police was to have responsibility for the assault. Although the Governor ordered that corrections officers not participate in the assault because of their emotional involvement, his order never reached state police and correctional services supervisors in charge of the assault.[71] Before rejecting the ultimatum, the inmates brought eight blindfolded hostages to catwalks that spanned the prison yards. Then "executioners held knives to the hostages, taunted state troopers and threatened to kill the hostages."[72]

Tear gas, rifles, shotguns, and handguns were employed in the assault. Most shooting was done by troopers, but some corrections officers took part. After several minutes of shooting, ten hostages and twenty-nine inmates were dead or dying. In addition, three hostages and eighty-five inmates had received gunshot wounds.[73] Although no hostages had been killed by inmates, two hostages who survived the shooting had suffered severe slashes to the neck, and others bore the marks of beatings. (In addition, two hostages killed by gunfire had also suffered minor knife wounds.)[74] Although the McKay Commission acknowledged that a majority of the assault force acted with restraint, it also concluded that there was much unnecessary shooting and "unnecessary deaths and injuries owing to the use of shotguns."[75]

Partly as a result of severe failures in planning, treatment of the injured was badly botched. Sufficient medical personnel, drugs, and supplies were unavailable until several hours after the assault. In addition, severe physical and verbal abuse was administered to inmates, primarily by corrections officers.[76] Finally, prison officials and state officials, including even Governor Rockefeller, gave credence to the rumors and misstatements regarding the causes of death of the hostages and allegations of atrocities such as castration of a hostage by inmates.[77] Not until two New York City pathologists had confirmed the findings of the Monroe County Medical Examiner who had performed autopsies on the dead hostages did state officials admit that the hostages had not all been killed by inmates.[78] The McKay Commission attributed to officials who prematurely released information that hostages had been murdered or maimed in a desire to provide some justification for the assault and its toll in lives and injuries.[79] (Corrections Department officials seemed eager to discredit the work of the Monroe County Medical Examiner. While awaiting the arrival of New York City pathologists, the public information officer of the Corrections Department said to another official, "a top official was being flown up to check the findings of this clown up here.")[80]

Nelson Rockefeller's role in the Attica has been subject to lengthy discussions and analysis by a variety of persons and bodies including columnists, scholars, and governmental bodies. Perhaps the most appropriate point with which to begin our analysis of his role is the McKay Commission's conclusions.[81] Acknowledging that there is no way to know whether Rockefeller's coming to Attica would have produced a settlement that others had been unable to achieve, the McKay Commission, nevertheless, was critical of his rejection of Oswald's request that he come. The commission's view is expressed as follows:

> Recognizing that the decision was not an easy one for the Governor to make, the Commission nevertheless believes that conditions made it appropriate for the Governor to go to Attica. At the time of the uprising, the Governor realized that the

> prison system had long been neglected and was in need of major reform. Many of the inmates' grievances were acknowledged to be legitimate by both the Commissioner and the Governor. In such circumstances, where state neglect was a major contributing factor to the uprising, the Commission feels that the Governor should not have contributed the state's armed forces against the rebels without first appearing on the scene and satisfying himself that there was no other alternative and that all precautions against excessive force had been taken.[82]

The commission underlined its concern that the Governor had the responsibility to assure a proper retaking of the prison, by adding that "the presence of the Governor would have had a stabilizing effect on the troopers and correction oficers taking part in the assault and rehousing of inmates, many of whom were bitter toward Commissioner Oswald for his negotiations with the inmates, but respectful of the Governor."[83]

Any close observer of Nelson Rockefeller's behavior as a public official should be aware that his behavior in the Attica uprising was in one important way very atypical of his style as executive. Given his "nothing is impossible" attitude and his eagerness to try his hand at solving the toughest of problems, the Governor almost never hesitated to take personal charge of difficult situations. Commenting on Attica, one of Rockefeller's key staff people notes that "Attica was the *one instance* in which the Governor did not take charge."[84] Rockefeller's unwillingness to take charge of the Attica situation is dramatically illustrated by his refusal to come to Attica in response to the desperate Sunday afternoon plea by the four observers and Oswald's plea earlier that day. Inasmuch as both these pleas included acknowledgements that the inmates were still unwilling to budge from their "unconditional demands" for amnesty, one could understand, if not accept, the Governor's position that he should not come to Attica. However, his rejection of a later plea that he agree to come to Attica *after release of the hostages* to negotiate further on the twenty-eight points that the inmates had previously rejected as a basis for settlement is almost impossible to defend. This plea, made late Sunday night in a phone conversation between the Governor and Oswald, other key officials, and the observers, was also turned down by Rockefeller. (According to Assemblyman Wemple, all those in the room except for members of the Governor's staff were strongly urging that the Governor come.)[85] Although neither Rockefeller nor Oswald felt there was much chance of the inmates accepting this "after release" proposal, and although the McKay Commission said there was "no evidence before the Governor" that the inmates were prepared to accept anything less than complete amnesty, it is hard to disagree with the Commission's conclusion that the Governor "had nothing to lose by making this proposal."[86] Certainly it is hard to understand why a man who would "move mountains" to achieve a goal would reject this last, most reasonable, of pleas.

The Governor's refusal to accede to the last, most minimal, request made of him is perhaps better understood in light of his last-minute proposal (on

Sunday afternoon) that Commissioner Oswald "make another appeal that night, personally by communication with the prisoners stating that if they laid down their handmade weapons and released the hostages that we would then set up a negotiating group in connection with the carrying out of the terms of the agreed reform and that I would be there to supervise that implementation after they had surrendered."[87] What Rockefeller was demanding at this point was not just release of the hostages but total surrender on the part of the inmates. Not only that, he was not even willing to indicate that he would be part of a "negotiating group" even *after* such a total surrender. The only personal involvement he was willing to concede was to come to Attica to supervise implementation of the "agreed reform," presumably after the negotiating group had completed its negotiations with inmates.[88] A conclusion that the Governor was determined to stay away from Attica under any but totally unlikely circumstances seems inescapable.

As noted above, the McKay Commission's report was especially critical of Rockefeller's failure to exercise on-the-scene supervision of retaking the prison and restoring order. Perhaps even more remarkable was the Governor's failure to make certain that one of his top aides was in charge of coordinating and monitoring the operation. In the absence of such an initiative by the Governor, the major responsibility for the operation rested in the hands of low-level staff, Major John Monahan, commander of Troop A of the State Police stationed in Batavia, New York, and Vincent Mancusi, superintendent of Attica Prison. (These two agreed that Monahan would have responsibility for "command of police matters," such as the assault, and that Mancusi would have responsibility for "custodial decisions.")[89] Concerned about possible harm to the inmates, the Governor had asked his Secretary, Robert Douglass, to make sure that corrections officers did not take part in the assault on the prison. Although many others, including state police officials and corrections officials, also feared that corrections officers were too emotionally involved to act in a responsible way, Rockefeller's orders were never communicated down to the operating levels. Furthermore, few precautions were taken against the possibility of corrections officers taking physical reprisals against inmates.

The McKay Commission's comments on the failure of state officials to prevent reprisals against inmates, reprisals that were witnessed by a variety of objective observers including Senator Dunne and National Guard personnel, reveal the failure of state officials to adequately plan and coordinate the rehousing of inmates. "When questioned concerning their role in preventing reprisals, state officials inevitably testified that another official bore that responsibility."[90] The commission added, "state officials . . . represented the legal order at Attica, and their subsequent explanations only made it apparent that they had failed to meet their responsibilities. The same officials who ordered the invasion of D yard to restore law and order did nothing to prevent law enforcement officers from violating these same principles in the aftermath."[91] Not only was Nelson Rockefeller absent from the scene of operations at Attica, there is some indication that he lacked crucial information about what was to take place in the assault that he ordered. For example, the Governor claimed that he did not know that the state police would use rifles and shotguns in their assault.[92] He claimed that his military representative, General O'Hara, did not brief him about the details of the assault. O'Hara confirmed this, but noted that the Governor never asked him about weapons.[93] The lack of adequate preparation for the medical needs that could be anticipated as a result of an armed assault on the prison drew heavy criticism from the McKay Commission. "The story of the medical treatment of the wounded inmates . . . is a study in total lack of planning and concern."[94]

Although there is no guarantee that the Governor's presence at Attica would have produced better results, he must be assigned a major share of responsibility for the many failures that the McKay Commission cited in planning, coordination, and implementation. One can only conclude that Rockefeller failed to inform himself adequately, that he failed to delegate responsibility clearly, that he failed to monitor the implementation of his decisions, and above all, that he failed to provide the kind of executive leadership essential to assure that those who act in the name of the state act with the highest degree of professionalism and detachment.

The Governor's defense of his conduct relating to Attica was vigorous in the face of the many accusations leveled at him in the course of time, especially those at the hearings on his confirmation as vice-president. A major element in that defense was his claim that he followed his standard procedure of delegating large amounts of authority to his top officials. As he told the House Committee on the Judiciary, "My first decision was, do I support my own appointee in his decision [to negotiate] or do I overrule him? Now I happen to be one of those people who believes in—that you support your people that you appoint. I believe that I try to pick good people and I try to support them. So I supported him."[95] Rockefeller took essentially the same line in defending his decision not to come to Attica against suggestions that his presence *after* the assault decision had been made would have helped prevent deaths and injuries during the assault and its aftermath. "I was Governor, I was responsible, I was on the phone constantly getting reports. I had my key people up there, and I do not think it, [my presence] would have affected the . . . action that was taken."[96] As the McKay Commission points out, Rockefeller did, in fact, delegate substantial authority to Oswald. He drew the line only at forbidding the commissioner from making amnesty from prosecution an item of negotiation with the inmates.[97]

During his testimony at the House hearings, the Governor indicated regret that he had, in fact, allowed such wide discretion to Oswald.

> Now, I would have to say to you that probably the most serious mistake I made . . . was to have not overriden the commissioner's decision to stop the retaking

of the prison by the State police who at that point—this was . . . the first day, within 6 hours—who were in the process of taking back half of the prison already with no arms, only the regular riot equipment, that they should have gone through and completed that action then.

This, in my opinion, is probably the most serious mistake I made, leaving this thing for four days of discussion.[98]

In acknowledging his own "mistake," it is clear that Rockefeller was also indicating his disapproval of the course of action that Oswald had chosen.

The Governor admitted other "mistakes" related to Attica including a failure to extend his sympathy to families of dead inmates when he extended that sympathy to families of dead hostages. However, the mistakes he was willing to admit to did not relate to the central question of his presence at Attica either as a negotiator or as a supervisor of the retaking of the prison. And, in fact, he defended his refusal to go to Attica with an aggressive argument that makes it clear that he saw the Attica uprising as a symbol of developments that threatened the larger framework of order in America and, indeed, the world.

One of the most recent and widely used techniques of modern-day revolutionaries has been the taking of political hostages and using a threat to kill them as blackmail to achieve unconditional demands and to gain wide public attention to further their revolutionary ends. I have followed these developments with great interest and consider that, if tolerated, they pose a serious threat to the ability of free government to preserve order and to protect the security of the individual citizen.

Therefore, I firmly believe that a duly elected official sworn to defend the Constitution and the laws of the state and the nation would be betraying his trust to the people he serves if he were to sanction or condone such criminal act by negotiating under such circumstances.[99]

Rockefeller gave further emphasis to this view of the Attica uprising and his decision to refuse to negotiate with his testimony before the House Committee. He read from what he said was a copy of a speech given by an Attica prisoner. "If you don't come, if you don't stop this, and if you take this prison, all of the United States, every city in this country, there will be riots in the streets, and the cities will burn!" The Governor used the words to indicate what he thought was the significance of Attica. As he said, "This was not just Attica. This was America."[100]

Noting that state officials realized that inmates could kill many hostages during any attempt to storm D yard, the McKay Commission wrote: "The decision to retake the prison was not a quixotic effort to rescue hostages in the midst of 1,200 inmates; it was a decisive reassertion of the state of its sovereignty and power."[101] Having been alerted by Oswald earlier in the summer about the dangers stemming from "revolutionaries" in the prison population of the state, Rockefeller defended his decision to retake the prison by force on the grounds that agreeing to negotiate would encourage further incidents of hostage-taking as part of revolutionary tactics. Inmate demands for amnesty and safe passage to "third-world countries" solidified the Governor's view that he was dealing with more than a "normal" prison riot. Commissioner Oswald states that when he first recommended that Rockefeller come to Attica, adding that I told him "I did not think there was anything he could accomplish given the present intransigence of the rebel leaders," the Governor had "replied that he had dealt in the past with people who were this intransigent, and it was his experience that they did not change and that nothing really substantive would be acomplished by his coming."[102]

Nelson Rockefeller's explanations for his decision not to come to Attica either for negotiations or supervising the retaking of the prison were met with skepticism by many. One of those most critical of the Governor's behavior, Tom Wicker, has offered his own explanation of the Governor's refusal to come to Attica. That explanation is in large part consistent with Rockefeller's own expressions about the importance of a framework of order. Wicker has said that he did not doubt Rockefeller's personal courage nor did he "believe that Rockefeller was so calloused and careless of human life that he simply did not care who and how many might die at Attica."[103] But as he and others pleaded with Rockefeller to come to Attica on Sunday, Wicker found himself explaining the Governor's reluctance in terms of the latter's commitment to the order of society, a commitment that Rockefeller was later to express in his defense. Speaking of himself in the third person, Wicker described that view.

> Institutions must not only function, whatever the end result; the order of things must be preserved. The powerful must not be at the beck and call of the powerless . . . for the powerful are obliged to meet great responsibilities to the order of things. . . .
>
> Governors must not deal as equals with lawbreakers; that would endanger the order of things. . . .
>
> Wicker believed that the Governor was moved primarily by his faith in the order of things, and he was offended by the inmates challenge to that order.[104]

A second possible factor in the Governor's refusal to come to Attica, a combative element in his personality and a reluctance to be defeated in a confrontation, was raised by a former department head who had been close to Rockefeller. Pointing out that he felt Attica was an example of the Governor's reacting to what he perceived as a challenge to him and his authority, this official felt that Rockefeller became caught up in the "turbulence" of Attica when he should have been able to step back from the situation. As he put it, Rockefeller could in the short run become "overly concerned with backing down."[105]

Two other possible factors in Rockefeller's decision not to come to Attica deserve special attention. The first is the distinct possibility that he may have suffered a kind of "crisis of confidence" in regard to Attica. There is at least some reason to believe that this was, in fact, the case. For example, Budget Director Richard Dunham, the only man who was with Rockefeller while the assault at Attica was taking place, remarked, "Personally I think . . . [the reason he did not take charge at Attica] was the Governor's memory of his father's tragedy in Colorado."[106] The "tragedy in Colorado" was the so-called Ludlow massacre which took place at Ludlow, Colorado, in 1913. At the climax of the efforts of Colorado Fuel and Iron, a Rockefeller-controlled company, to disrupt organizing activities by the United Mine Workers, National Guard Troops shot into a tent colony of striking miners and their families. Gunshots and resulting fires caused the deaths of over fifty persons including thirteen women and children. Thereupon, widespread outrage and protest brought the Rockefeller family to its lowest point in national esteem and threatened to ruin the health and reputation of Nelson's father. Although he managed to bear up well in grueling congressional hearings, Junior was deeply affected by the experience. So vitriolic were attacks on the family that special security arrangements were made to protect the family in general and the children in particular.[107]

Perhaps the most intriguing aspect of the possible relevance of his father's experience with Ludlow is that Nelson Rockefeller's "delegation of authority defense" of his failure to take personal charge at Attica is very similar to his father's explanation for his own failure to personally involve himself in affairs preceding the Ludlow massacre. One of the questions put to his father was, "Do you not think you might have paid some attention to those bloody strike conditions out in Colorado, where you have one thousand employees in whose welfare you seem not to have taken any deep personal interest?"[108] Rockefeller replied, "I have done what I regard as the very best thing in the interest of those employees and the larger investment I represent. We have gotten the best men obtainable and are relying on their judgment."[109] And after he stated that he would not go to Colorado to supervise the situation or give in to striker demands for a union shop and that he would stand by company officers "at any cost," he was asked, "and you will do that if it costs all your property and kills all your employees?" "It is a great principle," he replied.[110]

The second possible factor deserving special attention, one closely linked to the crisis-of-confidence argument, involves what must have been Rockefeller's own sense of his personal and political stake in Attica, a personal and political stake involving his reputation and stature as a major national leader. For if reaching the presidency was becoming less likely by 1971, it was still not out of the question, and a major cabinet position was always a possibility.[111] This is not to suggest that Nelson Rockefeller sat back and made a conscious calculation of the personal and political risks that "going to Attica" held for him. Rather it is to suggest that a political animal like the Governor who was proud of his reputation as a problem solver would have instinctively assessed the risks of going to Attica as being greater than those of leaving the resolution of events there in the hands of other people and the hands of fate. For in a real sense Attica was a no-win situation for Rockefeller. The McKay Commission makes it clear that negotiating a peaceful settlement at Attica would have been a very challenging job for anyone, including Nelson Rockefeller. Furthermore, once a decision had been made to retake the prison by force, the odds that some hostages and inmates would be killed were very high. To become directly involved in either negotiation or the retaking of the prison had the potential of bringing down criticism from both liberals and conservatives. Were the Governor to negotiate and fail to win settlement or gain a settlement through promises of some form of amnesty, criticisms from conservatives would have been immediate and strong. Were he to negotiate and fail because he was unwilling to make any compromises on the issue of amnesty or if he were to fail to gain a settlement and then personally supervise a retaking of the prison which resulted in a substantial loss of life, he would spark a high degree of criticism from liberals. That the Governor was, in fact, most concerned about the personal consequences of failure if he had gone to Attica is forcefully revealed in the midst of an emotional defense that he made at his confirmation hearings.

> I am almost finished, just the last words on this point why I didn't go.
>
> We have agreed to the 28 points. . . . there were two points left.
>
> Every one of the men on the phone whom I talked to, including the Commissioner, said we can't see what your presence here can do. But it was not said by any of them, we have failed in this negotiation. If you came something might happen. Well, I am not a messiah. A miracle might happen, you see. This is great. What would happen would be that Nelson Rockefeller would be there and then if it did not succeed, he is there on the world television cameras, et cetera, as the man who failed in this thing, orders the troops in.[112]

The statement removes any doubt that the prospect of being viewed as having failed at Attica was clearly a frightening one for Nelson Rockefeller the problem solver.

Mass Transit: Paying Attention to Program Administration

As Governor, Rockefeller devoted a great deal of time and attention to problems of mass transit, primarily those in New York City.[113] As noted in Chapter 7, a number of his pet programs and projects were in this area. An examination of Rockefeller's handling of problems in the mass transit area is revealing in a number of respects. Although some of the Governor's actions in this area were achieved primarily through his role as legislative leader, his actions included a good number that involved initiatives which he took not just as legislative leader but as "manager of the executive branch." For example, he took the initiative in dealing with an impending crisis brought about by the collapse of an important commuter railroad that was part of the private sector. The case of mass transit also provides a view of Rockefeller's role in following through on decisions in an instance in which his personal and political prestige was at stake. Finally, the Governor's skill at personal politics when dealing with a powerful foe, in this case the legendary Robert Moses, is clearly illustrated in the example of mass transportation.

Two of the reasons that Rockefeller was heavily involved in mass transportation were the growing inability of private railway companies to maintain adequate services at a profit and the perennial political issue of the price of subway fares in New York City. Another was William Ronan's keen personal interest in transportation problems.

As the condition of commuter lines in the New York City area deteriorated in the early 1960s, the state responded with stopgap measures including a variety of subsidies.[114] Reluctant to create state ownership of commuter lines, the Governor avoided any such action until 1965 when, at the recommendation of a task force chaired by Ronan, he proposed state takeover of the near-bankrupt Long Island Rail Road. With legislative approval the state made its purchase for a sum of $65 million.[115] Ever the pragmatist, the Governor had been forced to deal with a crisis by a means which he said was opposed to his basic beliefs. As he later said, "When I was elected Governor in 1958 . . . my attempt was . . . to preserve mass transportation in the hands of private enterprise. We cut the taxes in half. We did all kinds of things to help strengthen the private enterprise operation. Slowly, despite these actions, it deteriorated."[116]

As chairman of the Metropolitan Transportation Authority, former Secretary to the Governor William Ronan was responsible for the rehabilitation and operation of the state's new enterprise. But plagued by commuter complaints and labor management issues, Ronan found himself under siege throughout 1966 and 1967. Not only did Rockefeller vigorously defend his friend and adviser, in August of 1967 he intervened directly to provide assistance. First he took the initiative in creating the advisory council on the Long Island Rail Road, a body to which were appointed many of the leading critics of the railroad. Then he met personally with railroad union leaders to assure them that their prerogatives would be respected. Finally, he impulsively pledged that service on the line would be made "the finest in the country" within a few months.[117] Having thus committed himself to a goal that most observers regarded as highly unrealistic, Rockefeller undertook personally to monitor the MTA's efforts to achieve that goal. For example, he required the secretary of the MTA to report to him by memo every day on progress.[118] Although few observers were willing to call it the best commuter road in the country, by 1972 a reporter could write that "both the riders and the state and, in fact, some of the union men who worked on the railroad, believed that the L.I.R.R. had begun to make a solid turnaround, if not financially, at least in terms of service rendered and in public support."[119]

Important as was Rockefeller's initiative in bringing about purchase of the Long Island Rail Road, that initiative was eclipsed by his role in reshaping an existing transportation authority into the Metropolitan Transportation Authority in 1967. Designed as a type of holding company that would have responsibility for public transportation policy in the New York City area, the MTA represented a bold attempt to confront one of the most difficult problems facing any American city. Confronted with the tasks of rehabilitating the run-down L.I.R.R., maintaining and improving an antiquated subway system, and upgrading commuter service that had been part of the Penn Central and the New Haven systems, the MTA was from its beginning involved in a constant search for adequate financial resources.

The first initiative that Rockefeller took was his successful effort to win voter approval for a $2.5 billion capital facilities transportation bond issue in 1967. Proceeds from this bond issue were used for substantial improvements in the commuter transit system.[120]

The second initiative undertaken by Rockefeller and the MTA was a successful attempt to gain access to the surplus revenues of the Triborough Bridge and Tunnel Authority. Because that authority operated major toll bridges and tunnels in the New York City area, it was a money-maker. By 1966 the authority "had $110,000,000 in cash and securities on hand—a surplus that was growing at the rate of almost $30,000,000 a year."[121] If tolls were to be raised, this surplus would, of course, grow at an even faster rate.

One obstacle to making Triborough's revenues available for transportation needs other than bridges and tunnels was overcome when the legislature approved creation of the MTA as coordinator of most transportation programs in the New York City area. The second was the existence of covenants that protected those who held the bonds of the Triborough Authority. Although the MTA had been given the key role in mass transportation, it could be prevented from using Triborough's revenues by a suit brought by the authority itself or by its bondholders or their agent. And, in fact, such a suit was initiated by the Chase Manhattan Bank, trustee for the bondholders, in 1967. According to Robert Caro, "in the opinion of almost every legal expert on municipal and public authority bonds, if the suit had been prosecuted vigorously, it would have been successful."[122] But as Caro points out, the suit was not prosecuted vigorously. Instead it was settled out of court in February of 1968. In a meeting at the Governor's townhouse in New York City, the two parties to the suit, the state as represented by Nelson Rockefeller and William Ronan, and Chase Manhattan Bank as represented by President David Rockefeller and its counsel Thomas Dewey, agreed to a stipulation that ended the suit and removed the last obstacle to MTA's using Triborough's surplus and revenues.[123] In practical terms, the agreement also meant the end of the autonomy that Triborough Bridge and Tunnel Authority had enjoyed. Although the stipulation signed by the two Rockefeller brothers was sealed by the court with jurisdiction over the suit, it is known that the agreement provided for "an increase in interest payments to the Triborough bondholders of an extra quarter of 1 percent, plus a guarantee of the state's credit as backing for the bonds."[124]

With the settlement of the suit concerning Triborough's autonomy, a key personal obstacle to MTA's control over transportation had been removed. That obstacle consisted of the legendary Robert Moses, head of Triborough and once occupant of a whole set of positions which had allowed him to become the dominant figure in parks and recreation, public power, and transportation in New York State.[125] As a *New York Times* reporter noted, one result of the settlement of the bondholder suit was that "Dr. Ronan finally consolidated power as the state's sole transportation chief at the expense of Mr. Moses."[126] A skilled and tenacious battler, Moses had been stripped of his one remaining position of power, head of the Triborough Authority, by a series of adroit maneuvers on the part of Rockefeller, the last of which was the out-of-court settlement of the bondholder suit. Knowing that Moses had the ability to mobilize opposition, especially that of the media, against the 1967 referendum on the transportation bond issue and knowing that Moses could press a suit against the use of Triborough funds by MTA, Rockefeller managed to restrain Moses from both courses of action until the bond issue had won approval and the bondholders' suit had been settled out of court. He had accomplished this by allowing Moses to believe that the latter would continue to have a major role in the transportation field. More specifically, Moses felt that he had been given a commitment that he would have a seat on the board of the MTA, that he would continue to direct the affairs of the Triborough Authority as its chief executive officer, and that he would have responsibility for building a proposed bridge over Long Island Sound.[127] But after the bondholder suit was settled by the stipulation signed in February 1968, Moses was to discover that he was to be given no seat on the MTA board and that he would serve only as a $25,000 per year consultant to the Triborough Authority with his main responsibility being that of "coordinating" existing Triborough construction projects, relatively small projects already well underway, and the proposed bridge across Long Island.[128]

With the passage of the 1967 transportation bond issue and the consolidation of mass transportation entities in the New York City area in the hands of the MTA, Rockefeller had put the state in a position to launch a comprehensive attack on some very difficult problems. And as noted before, the MTA did manage to produce some improvements in the system of mass transportation, improvements made with the continuing interest and involvement of the Governor. The failure of voters to approve proposed transportation bond issues at referenda in 1971 and 1973 and the continuing financial strains encountered by the mass transit system should not be allowed to obscure the reality of Rockefeller's contributions in this area. Not only had he successfully avoided a transportation crisis inherent in the collapse of the L.I.R.R., but he had outmaneuvered a skilled adversary who was a potential source of damaging controversy. Furthermore, he had managed to at least partially redeem a rash promise that could have resulted in great political embarrassment.

Conclusion

The four cases examined here suggest that Nelson Rockefeller shared with many of us a capacity to perform better in situations in which he could meet problems on his own terms as opposed to situations in which problems were thrust upon him in ways that were not of his own choosing. Thus he was relatively more successful in the case of mass transportation problems than in the other three cases examined here.

When Rockefeller hesitated to come to grips with a problem, as he did in the cases of nursing homes, the Attica uprising, and the activities of Republican state chairman Judson Morhouse, his performance seemed to suffer. (As Chapter 3 reveals, Rockefeller's efforts to capture the Republican nomination for president were characterized by a similar inclination toward hesitancy.)

The question remains: Why did the Governor seem to hesitate in coming to grips with the problems involved in three of the cases examined here? In the Morhouse case and the nursing homes case there are at least two possible explanations that seem to have real validity. One is that in both cases he would have had to turn his back on friends and loyal supporters, in the one case Judson Morhouse and in the other, Samuel Hausman, in order to take decisive action. The second is that neither of these cases involved the kind of major societal problem that Nelson Rockefeller had typically attacked as part of his life strategy. For example, the sense of satisfaction and achievement to be gained from providing more auditors to reduce medicaid waste would be unlikely to have motivated the Governor in the same way as would undertaking a major initiative in social policy or construction. Indeed, by the time the problems associated with controlling nursing home reimbursements arose, Rockefeller had already addressed the more glamorous and, to him, the more significant issue in caring for the elderly, namely, financing additional facilities.

Just as the Morhouse case and the nursing home case failed to provide the Governor with an opportunity to address a glamourous societal problem on his own terms, so did the Attica case fail to do so. In fact, because

Rockefeller had already taken the initiative in addressing the issue of prison reform as he had defined that issue, the Attica uprising could offer nothing but frustration and failed hopes for him. Indeed, the uprising threatened to deny him the opportunity to proceed in his normal problem-solving fashion. Prison reform was certainly a cause worthy of Rockefeller's life strategy, but trying to negotiate an end to a violent uprising under duress was certainly not.

In none of the cases does it appear that Rockefeller failed because his executive style failed him by preventing him from acquiring information or exercising control over subordinates. Rather, his failures seem to arise from his reluctance to make choices and to commit his energies to enforcing those choices. Thus he allowed Morhouse to remain in his position in the face of obvious causes for concern. Thus he failed to follow up on the matter of additional auditors for nursing home reimbursements. Thus he allowed events at Attica to run their course.

Although a casual observer might be tempted to conclude that Rockefeller was simply incapable of acting effectively in conditions of crisis and controversy, we think such a conclusion unwarranted. The case of mass transportation lends at least some support to our rejection of such a conclusion. Having created a crisis-like atmosphere by rashly pledging to make the Long Island Rail Road the best commuter line in the nation, Rockefeller performed admirably by making genuine progress toward that goal.

9 Conclusion

Looking closely at Nelson Rockefeller's life and career, one is struck by the sense that in some ways his life and his career were too good to be true. Blessed with great wealth and all the diverse resources that only the Rockefeller family could confer, possessed of great physical and mental vigor, inspired by the example of the legendary John D. Rockefeller, and made self-confident by overcoming the only handicap he had, his childhood learning disability, he had every reason to set high goals for himself. Setting a high goal for himself is exactly what Nelson Rockefeller did, laying aside whatever thoughts he had of pursuing a career as an architect and opting instead for a grander role, one that would not seem insignificant alongside that of the grandfather on whose birthday he was born. Beginning as a young man, Rockefeller took upon himself the task of identifying problems significant for the survival and well-being of American society and offering solutions to those problems. Pursuing this strategy for achieving the significance he demanded of himself led Rockefeller to a pattern of behavior that varied little according to the particular positions in which he found himself. Furthermore, the executive style that he created early in his career was suited admirably to identifying problems and offering solutions to those problems. Taken together, his life strategy and executive style were well-suited to satisfying the deep desire that he had to achieve in a way appropriate to his status as a Rockefeller, to make his mark by dealing with big problems that were related to his concern with "the effective functioning of society."[1]

Although many regarded him as a politician who measured his every move by a calculus of political costs and benefits, there is ample evidence that Rockefeller was, in fact, a passionate man. Clearly, his two great passions in life were art and problem solving, and he pursued both throughout the course of his adult life. Although he was successful in the pursuit of both, it was probably in the pursuit of his passion for art that he met with fulfillment unmarred by disappointment and failed dreams.

Beginning with his membership on the Board of Trustees of the Metropolitan Museum and the major role he played as treasurer and then president of the Museum of Modern Art in the 1930s, Rockefeller was both collector of art and patron of the arts, pursuing the latter role as both private and public figure. For example, it was revealed that he had given a total of more than $6.5 million to the Museum of Primitive Art and more than $2.5 million to the Museum of Modern Art in the period 1957 to 1974.[2] And as Governor he played a key role in the creation and development of a number of programs and projects involving the arts. Among them were the Council on the Arts and its programs of aid to the various arts, the establishment of the Saratoga Performing Arts Center north of Albany, the conception, design, and construction of the South Mall office/cultural complex which eventually came to bear his name, and the expansion and improvement of art education in New York's public schools, a development he had initiated much earlier when he helped found the National Committee on Art Education under the sponsorship of the Museum of Modern Art.[3] Taking into account these activities, including the impact that he had on the physical appearance of both Albany and New York City, both as Governor and as private citizen, it is perhaps not surprising that his friend Wallace Harrison said that Rockefeller "was as good to New York [State] as de Medici was to the life of Florence."[4]

Rockefeller's affection for, and identification with, New York was nearly total. In one sense he treated the state as though it were a piece of his private property. For example, while Governor he spent over half a million dollars in improvements to the executive mansion and its grounds and in furnishings and paintings for the building.[5]

As Governor of the leading state in the nation, a state more populous than most nations of the world, Nelson Rockefeller had an opportunity for problem solving that is available to only a very few members of the political elite. Nevertheless, he died unfulfilled. For the one office that provided the ultimate in opportunities for a problem solver with his life strategy, the presidency, was denied him. Given the absence of historical perspective, an assessment of his performance as Governor is bound to be difficult, but the effort needs to be made. Perhaps the place to begin such an assessment is Rockefeller's performance in electoral politics, as that performance was crucial to his ambitions as a problem solver.

Rockefeller in Electoral Politics

It is possible that no Governor has ever been more resourceful and successful than Rockefeller was in gubernatorial elections. The handicaps with which he operated, for example, being a Republican in a state with a Democratic enrollment advantage and facing a challenge from the right by a vigorous new party, the Conservative party, were more than compensated for by a collection of advantages: his money, his personal energy and appeal as a campaigner, his sophisticated use of public opinion polling and television, his record of having provided "something for everybody" in the way of governmental benefits, and his willingness to use rough tactics against his opponents. Perhaps the best evidence of his skill is the fact that Republican candidates, including his designated successor-to-be, were beaten in the two elections following his retirement. That fact also suggests that while Rockefeller built personal campaign organizations that could help him win office, he did not leave as his legacy a strong Republican party.

Only the presidency could have provided Rockefeller with the opportunity to fully exercise his life strategy, giving him both the resources and the responsibility to confront the problems, especially international problems, that threatened American society. Thus his failure to achieve that position represents his most poignant failure. Although Rockefeller blamed his failure to win the Republican nomination on his failure to work sufficiently hard at the petty political tasks that he felt had brought the nomination to Richard Nixon, one can make a strong case that he failed because he stubbornly insisted on being the sort of activist, big-spending, "wolf-calling" political executive who was anathema to those who controlled his party's nominating machinery. Nelson Rockefeller could no more give up his activist, problem-solving, pragmatic liberal approach than could he pander to the prejudices of the time by refraining from a politically damaging divorce and remarriage to a recently divorced woman with small children. When the financial situation in New York became grim, after the voters had rejected two proposals for massive bond issues for transportation, and after legislative leaders had reacted coolly to his plan to ask voter approval for what would have been the largest state bond issue in American history, one for community development, he was no longer interested in being Governor. But his appetite for problem solving persisted, as evidenced by his willingness to become Gerald Ford's vice-president, a role that provided him with a last slim opportunity to reach the presidency.

Rockefeller as Seller of Solutions

Of all the aspects of Rockefeller's performance, perhaps that of winning approval for programs and projects is easiest to assess. Confident in the belief that it is a chief executive's responsibility, indeed duty, to take the initiative in winning approval for his proposals, Rockefeller was aggressive in selling his solutions to both the legislature and the public. Although generally more successful with the legislature than the voters, he, nevertheless, did win voter approval for three massive bond issues, one for his Pure Waters Program, one for transportation, and one for "the environment." Rarely willing to capitulate to opposition, Rockefeller succeeded in gaining legislature approval for many controversial proposals, including pet programs dear to his heart. He succeeded by utilizing a varied group of tactics including sweet reason, the carrot of patronage, and the stick of raw intimidation in the form of either a public he had aroused or threats that he had the power to carry out.

Perhaps most significantly, Rockefeller almost always found a way around legislative or public reluctance to approve controversial proposals. Burdened by no commitment to the prerogatives of the legislature or the people, committed only to solving problems, he was adept at finding ways to circumvent opposition. The best example of this, of course, is his resort to moral-obligation borrowing and lease-purchase arrangements as ways of acquiring necessary financial resources without the necessity of winning voter approval for full-faith-and-credit borrowing by the state. The fact that these devices helped contribute to a financial crisis for the state suggests that his performance in winning approval for key programs and projects may have been a success in the narrow sense but a failure in terms of utlimate results.

Rockefeller as Financial Manager

Nelson Rockefeller sometimes described himself as liberal concerning people's problems and conservative concerning questions of economic policy and financial management. But despite the fact that he began his tenure as Governor by practicing a policy of pay-as-you-go, it would be a gross mistake to accept his description of himself as a fiscal conservative.

If the criteria which one used were ingenuity, audacity, and the capacity to marshall the resources necessary to use big government as a problem-confronting mechanism, then one would certainly evaluate Rockefeller's financial stewardship as successful. But if one were to evaluate that stewardship against more conservative standards relating to fiscal prudence, including the avoidance of financial overcommitment and adverse long-term impact on the taxpayers of the state, then one would make a harsh judgment. In fact, the eventual outcome of Rockefeller's reliance on devices such as moral-obligation borrowing was little short of disastrous. The situation less than two years after Rockefeller resigned was summarized by one reporter as follows:

> The UDC problem ballooned into a test of the state's willingness to make good on the moral obligation that backed not only $1 million of UDC's borrowings but billions of dollars in similarly-backed bonds and notes of other agencies.
>
> The ultimate solution involved New York State putting up money to show its good faith—approximately $190 million in cash from the 1974-75 and 1975-76 budgets plus an estimated $80 million a year for the next generation.[6]

Some observers maintained that had Rockefeller still been Governor in 1975 he would have been able to prevent the default of the UDC and the ensuing damage to the state's credit.[7] Ironically, as vice-president, Rockefeller presented a critique of the fiscal practices that had led to the collapse of New York City's credit in 1975 that could well have been made of his own performance as Governor. According to Rockefeller, the lesson of the fiscal crisis in New York City was that "We're learning from this that there is no such thing as a free lunch. Somebody pays for it. It may be the most important lesson of our time."[8]

Rockefeller as Program Producer

Consistent with his conception of the role of a political executive as bearing the major responsibility for identifying key problems and offering solutions to those problems and consistent with his commitment to positive government, it is not surprising that Rockefeller focused a great portion of his personal energies on the production of new programs. As we have shown, he was remarkably successful in removing or surmounting most obstacles to producing, selling, and financing his programs. Using his almost unique abilities to attract and motivate others, including members of his highly loyal personal team, being savvy enough to structure the decision process in such a way so as to encourage innovative ideas and minimize objections based on cost and other practical difficulties, Rockefeller presided over what might have been the most efficient program-production machinery in the history of American government. The result was a lot of programs in a variety of policy areas and a group of notable programs, several of which were truly innovative in one or more respects, and most of which were audacious in their goals and aimed at problems that were widely believed to be among the more significant problems facing not only New York State but the nation. The very quantity of new programs, the vast scope and high cost of many of them, and his persistence in trying new approaches to problems when initial ones seemed to fail all reflect the intensity of Rockefeller's belief that all problems could be solved given the application of sufficient determination and resources. Consistent with a life strategy and an executive style that revolved around the goal of producing and selling programs and consistent with certain of his extraordinary personal qualities, this belief was the soul of his administration.

Rockefeller Coping with Crisis and Controversy

Some of the more notable crises and/or controversies in the Rockefeller administration occurred in instances in which the Governor was acting largely or at least partly outside his favorite role of producing and selling new programs. Among such cases examined in various chapters of this book, including chapter 8, are: Rockefeller's practice of making large gifts and loans to members of his personal team; his direct involvement in certain controversial cases involving Republican Speaker of the Assembly Perry Duryea, Republican State Chairman Judson Morhouse, and parks and construction czar Robert Moses respectively; his role in the crushing of the Attica Prison rebellion; his role in creating the Metropolitan Transportation Authority and trying to make the Long Island Rail Road "the best in the nation"; and his role in "the nursing home scandals" involving entrepreneur Bernard Bergman.

A number of important points are suggested by one or more of the above cases. One is that Rockefeller sometimes took insufficient care to prevent scandal and to see that at least the appearance of evil was avoided. Furthermore, he sometimes allowed his sense of personal obligation to those who had helped him, in itself a laudable quality, to cause him to be less vigilent, and more trusting than a chief executive ought to be. In particular, for someone with as much administrative experience as Rockefeller, he was insufficiently alert to the possibility that staff members might be less inclined to speak their minds as a result of receiving financial assistance from him.

A second point is a certain tendency on the part of Rockefeller to let events run their course when such an approach might be politically beneficial or, at the least, less risky than some other approach. A third point is the Governor's toughness and willingness to deal harshly with those who challenged him directly. Although he did not usually go out of his way to seek a fight, he was capable of being ruthless under the right circumstances.[9] A final point is that Rockefeller was indeed capable of devoting great attention, energy, and skill to the task of making sure that a program succeeded. However, when his personal prestige was not at stake and a problem was not of the sort that his life strategy demanded, he was capable of ignoring the task of implementation as he would never ignore the task of producing and selling programs.

Program Results

It is only appropriate that an assessment of Nelson Rockefeller as Governor address the question of the results of his programs and projects, the solutions toward which his energies and those of his administration were directed. Obviously, there are limitations inherent in evaluating the success of his programs. In some cases the outcome of programs is not yet clear. And in the case of most, we lack the historical perspective necessary to separate out the trivial from the substantial. In addition, any assessment of the results of programs involves value judgments which are subject to dispute. No effort is made here to offer a comprehensive and systematic evaluation of the results of Rockefeller programs, an evaluation that in itself would require book-length treatment. However, we can note the extent to which certain leading programs are generally regarded as having succeeded or failed.[10]

Among those leading programs that are regarded as having been successful in at least approaching the goals initially contemplated are the expansion and development of the State University of New York, the Pure Waters Program, the programs of aid to the arts under the Council on the Arts, and the state office/cultural complex that is now officially named the Nelson A. Rockefeller Empire State Plaza. This is not to say that these programs are without their critics; it is merely to say that for whatever shortcomings they may have and whatever unfortunate side effects they may involve, most observers regard them as having achieved much of what it was hoped they would achieve. (Examples of typical criticisms are that the expansion of the State University occurred too fast and failed to anticipate declines in enrollments that began to affect certain campuses as early as 1979 and that the Empire State Plaza is excessively opulent and expensive, more appropriate as a monument to Rockefeller than as an efficient use of space.)[11]

Among leading programs and projects widely regarded as having failed in some crucial respect, either by virtue of failing to achieve their goals or by achieving goals at costs that were clearly unacceptable in terms of side effects such as the financial health of the state, are the state's narcotic programs, the efforts of the Atomic and Space Development Authority as they related to the development of a nuclear industry in the state, and the activities of the Urban Development Corporation.

Although there were elements of success in each of the programs mentioned, each turned out to be deficient in some fundamental respect. For example, the state commission that investigated the problems of public authorities in the wake of the default of the UDC stated that "the UDC was led and staffed by creative and highly motivated persons who conceived and built many projects of which the citizens of the State can be proud."[12] However, the commission's key judgment regarding the UDC is that its failure to exercise adequate financial controls and its assumption that it could support its projects with unlimited borrowing were major factors in leading to the credit crisis that occurred in the state in 1975.

Almost no one judges the Rockefeller narcotic programs to have been very successful. Although the various initiatives represented by the succession of programs that Rockefeller introduced may have had some marginal impact on the incidence of drug addiction and related crime, these programs fell far short of winning the war that he had declared.

The attempt to make New York State the leading state in nuclear-related industry represented Rockefeller's most significant venture in the use of science and technology for state purposes. For a wide variety of reasons, the attempt failed.[13] Some of these reasons involved factors that were beyond the control of Rockefeller or any state officials, for example, economic uncertainties involving the nuclear-power industry, growing public opposition to nuclear power, and changing regulations by the United States Atomic Energy Commission and its successor agency the Nuclear Regulatory Commission. For example, changes in federal requirements were prompted by concerns over possible earthquake dangers near the nuclear fuel reprocessing and storage facility located in western New York. Nonetheless, the fact is that Rockefeller's efforts in this area must be classified as having failed.

There are several notable Rockefeller programs and projects about whose success or failure no sort of general agreement exists. They include the Housing Finance Agency's use of moral-obligation bonds to finance a variety of programs, the mass transit programs of the Metropolitan Transportation Authority, the land-use and planning program of the Adirondack Park Agency, the electric-power development activities under the electric-power program, the watchdog activities carried out by the Office of Welfare Inspector General and the Office of Education Performance Review, and the program of state aid for the construction of nursing homes. In some of these cases, the Adirondack Park Agency, for example, it is just too soon to make any worthwhile assessment. The APA's impact on the Adirondack area will be clear only in the long run. In others, for example, the Office of Education Performance Review and the Welfare Inspector General, the existence of political controversy makes an assessment extremely difficult. (One result of this controversy is that both offices were abolished in the Democratic administration that followed the Rockefeller administration.) In other cases, there seems to be agreement that certain leading programs produced results that were a *mixture* of success and failure. For example, HFA accomplished much in low-income housing and in the role in financing numerous programs in other areas such as the expansion of the state university. However, aside from low-income housing programs, its programs were financed mainly by moral-obligation borrowing. And use of that device contributed to the same credit crisis as did moral-obligation borrowing by the UDC. Similarly, the program of state loans to finance construction of nonprofit nursing homes, another program financed through HFA, resulted in substantial amounts of construction but at what was viewed by many as excessive cost.[14] Finally, an assessment of some programs, for example, the mass transit activities carried out by the Metropolitan Transportation Authority, must be classified as mixed not because the agency did not, in fact, produce substantial improvements in its area of responsibility but because of the great magnitude of the problem and the consequent size of the resources required.[15]

Explaining Failures: Personality and Executive Style

Nelson Rockefeller's ability to construct and energize a system that allowed him to identify significant problems and launch massive, innovative, and well-financed efforts to solve those problems was truly impressive. Indeed, one might well argue that most of his programs that failed or achieved only mixed results did so primarily because of the intractability of the problems at which they were directed or the inadequacy of the resources that even Rockefeller could apply to them. However, one cannot ignore the element of excess in many of his successes as well as his failures, an excess of ambition, an excess of confidence in his ability to find a way, and an excess of confidence in the capacity of government to solve societal problems. "Rockefeller's inability to accept the limits of his circumstances," as Connery and Benjamin put it, can, of course, be explained partly as a function of his belief system. But one must also consider the extent to which Rockefeller's personality and his executive style may have been implicated in some of the leading "failures" of his administration.

In addition to the programs discussed here, there were other elements in the Rockefeller administration which are regarded as failures or mistakes. For example, in 1974 Rockefeller himself listed five events that he "deeply regretted" without implying that he would necessarily have behaved any differently in any of the "events" he listed: a scandal involving his appointee as head of the State Liquor Authority, the involvement of Republican State Chairman and Rockefeller supporter Judson Morhouse in the SLA scandal, his breaking of a 1962 campaign pledge not to raise taxes, the loss of forty-three lives in the Attica rebellion, and the "divisive situation" involving the indictment of Assembly Republican Leader Perry B. Duryea.[16] To his list one would certainly want to add Rockefeller's practice of giving large gifts and loans to members of his personal team, especially staff members, his failure to anticipate opposition to his ambitious proposals for fallout shelters, his failure to anticipate the fiscal crisis of 1971, his continued attempts to force construction of the Rye-Oyster Bay bridge across Long Island Sound in the face of what he should have known would be unsurmountable opposition, and his role with respect to nursing home irregularities involving Bernard Bergman.

We assume that these "errors," as well as those represented by the failures associated with several of his leading programs, are all failures for which Nelson Rockefeller must be assigned a major share of responsibility. The question remains: How does one try to explain these failures?

Although there is no single explanation that can be applied to all the Rockefeller failures, it seems clear to us that most did not result from any fundamental flaw in his executive style. In most cases he did not "fail" because he had inadequate information or because he could not exercise effective control over other political actors or because he was a victim of "groupthink." For example, he pushed ahead with his narcotic programs, the South Mall, and fallout shelter proposals against the advice of some of his staff. Furthermore, he did not make sure that sufficient auditors were added to the Health Department staff to assure against Medicaid fraud even though he personally knew of the need for these auditors, and he pursued moral-obligation borrowing to excess despite a steady stream of warnings from the state comptroller. When he did fail partly as a result of lack of information, for example, in not anticipating the fiscal crisis in 1971, it was partly because top staff officials in the Division of the Budget too readily accepted a definition of their roles as "facilitator" rather than critic. Having encouraged adoption of this role as a means of removing obstacles to producing bold and innovative programs, Rockefeller was in this case victimized by it.[17]

To what degree might Rockefeller's personality help explain his failures? As noted in Chapter 2, we believe that the need to engage in problem solving was of fundamental importance in shaping Rockefeller's behavior. We also believe that his life strategy and executive style were ideally suited to satisfying that need. However, it is also apparent that Rockefeller gained more satisfaction from identifying problems and offering and selling solutions to those problems than he did from paying close attention to the details involved in making sure that programs worked. This preference helps explain some of his failures, for example, his failure to provide for adequate monitoring of programs involving nursing homes. It may also help explain problems that occurred in the management of some programs and projects that are widely regarded as having achieved their basic goals, for example, the horrendous construction delays and cost overruns associated with the state office building/cultural complex.

As noted here, Rockefeller had a strong sense of loyalty and obligation toward friends and those who had helped him. This personal quality alone helps to explain at least some aspects of his behavior in several of the more questionable episodes in his administration.

Although Rockefeller should clearly be classified as a person of high self-esteem, an "active-positive" in James Barber's terms, he was not immune to the effects of stress.[18] For example, in the case of the Attica rebellion, Rockefeller's behavior seemed to suffer from rigidity, and he failed to behave in his normal problem-solving manner.[19] Despite the fact that Rockefeller had his share of failures, he did not generally adhere rigidly to what Barber terms a "failing course of action" in the face of prolonged opposition and resulting stress, as Barber says "active-negative" presidents do.[20] In fact, Rockefeller often demonstrated a capacity to change course before failures became real disasters. Thus, even though he failed to anticipate the fiscal crisis of 1971 and the opposition of assembly Republicans to his proposed budget, he adjusted quickly and "cut his losses." Even in the case of the bridge he proposed from Rye to Oyster Bay and his proposals for fallout shelters, his stubbornness eventually gave way to an admission of defeat.

Nelson Rockefeller and Pragmatic Liberalism

That the Rockefeller administration was strongly expressive of the elements of pragmatic liberalism is evidenced by our description of that administration. Here we focus on what we regard as a few key elements in pragmatic liberalism which were central to both its successes and failures. They are the conviction that all problems can be solved, a belief that activist big government is necesssry for solving societal problems, a belief that the executive branch of government has the key responsibility for leading the attack on public problems, a belief in the efficacy of joint efforts between the public and private sectors in solving societal problems, and a belief in an executive's outflanking public and legislative reistance in order to achieve what one perceives to be in the best interests of society.

In many respects, the high point in Rockefeller's efforts to provide massive state funding for joint public-private efforts to attack a societal problem was his sponsorship in 1970 and 1971 of an amendment to the state constitution which would have permitted the state to finance through both bond funds and tax funds a wide range of projects relating to community development.[21] (Article VII, Section 8 of the state constitution contains a general prohibition against the state's giving or lending money or its credit to private corporations or associations.)

This amendment and the $3.5 billion bond issue that the Governor intended to propose would have made possible state loans, grants, and debt guarantees for public authorities, local governments, and private firms that were engaged in community improvements. Perhaps the most remarkable feature of the activities to be authorized was their variety and scope. The amendment authorized support of programs for housing, urban and community renewal, "economic prosperity," employment opportunities, health, mental health, environmental health, child care and aged care, "transportation and communications," and civic, cultural, recreational, and other community facilities and services. The Urban Development Corporation would have had a major role in the direction and coordination of such efforts. As noted in Chapter 7, the proposed amendment was defeated by the voters in 1971, and Rockefeller refrained from pressing for legislative authorization for the bond issue because of opposition from the Republican leadership in the assembly.

As has been amply demonstrated in previous chapters, a series of actions beginning in 1960 with creation of the Housing Finance Agency with its power to issue moral-obligation bonds enabled Rockefeller to successfully circumvent constitutional provisions prohibiting state borrowing without voter approval and thereby ignore the wishes of the voters. At the same time, he was able to win legislative acquiescence in moral-obligation bonding by avoiding the necessity for massive tax increases that would otherwise have been required and by arguing that creating authorities with the ability to float moral-obligation bonds "would not cost the taxpayer a cent." Although this argument had some validity when applied to projects traditionally financed by so-called revenue bonds, toll roads for example, it had little or no validity for many of the projects financed under moral-obligation bonds, such as some of the UDC's riskier housing projects, projects too risky for any private developer to attempt. The conclusions of the state commission charged with investigating the collapse of the UDC and recommending reforms to restore investor confidence in the state is worth quoting.

> The self-sufficient moral obligation bond conceived by John Mitchell and promoted by Governor Nelson A. Rockefeller to avoid the referendum requirement is a dangerous and misleading illusion and now a totally discredited device.
>
> The principle vice of the moral obligation concept lay in the official view that projects backed by the State's moral obligation were self-sufficient, so that the moral obligation would never have to be called upon.[22]

In retrospect, it seems clear to almost everyone that in his zeal to solve problems Nelson Rockefeller was caught up in illusions, but they were illusions that were shared by many of the rest of us. The fact is that everyone in a position to oppose the illusion surrounding moral-obligation borrowing and other questionable financial practices was reluctant to expose the reality that lay behind the illusion. The Governor's personal team and other advisers helped him invent the devices upon which financing depended and helped him put them into operation. Even top budget advisers defined their role as being that of helping Rockefeller find the means to do what he wanted. Thus, with the exception of State Comptroller Arthur Levitt, the role of financial critic was all but abandoned.

Aside from occasional outcries from minority party leaders and a few mavericks, the legislature "went along."[23] It approved creation of public benefit corporations and gave them the power to issue moral-obligation bonds, it made first-instance appropriations (loans) to them, it willingly increased their debt limits, and it generally failed to exercise effective oversight of their operations.

State Comptroller Arthur Levitt complained long and loud about moral-obligation borrowing and other aspects of the activities of public benefit corporations. However, he never brought his challenge to court in the form of a suit. Neither did Attorney General Louis Lefkowitz, himself, of course, a member of Rockefeller's personal team.

The investment community was in a position to "blow the whistle" on excessive use of moral-obligation bonds. Yet until 1975, when the situation was hopeless, it failed to do so. Although by 1973 they began to be concerned about UDC's risks, "the bankers continued to market the UDC bonds, relying on the 'crutch' of the moral obligation."[24]

The most intriguing question is why everyone acquiesced in a policy involving overcommitment of the state's resources and the specific illusions on the basis of which that policy was rationalized. The explanation would seem to have three components. The first relates to Nelson Rockefeller and his qualities as a leader and an executive. He was, in fact, hard to resist. His tremendous stock of personal resources and skills helped him to persuade and, when it became necessary, to intimidate. And his executive style allowed him to make effective use of those resources and skills. Finally, Rockefeller really did believe that he could prevail, that he could overcome obstacles that would defeat other men. (Thus, he ignored Arthur Levitt's warnings about financial peril.) In many ways this belief had been fed by his life's experiences, beginning with his successful fight to overcome his learning disability. To varying degrees, those around him came to expect that he could do the impossible.

The second component of the explanation for others having acquiesced in, and in some cases embraced, Rockefeller's illusions is that moral-obligation bonding and other devices for "backdoor financing" supported programs that benefited many politically significant groups. Because these programs all involved vast amounts of construction, they had obvious benefits for construction firms and construction unions. Because moral-obligation bonds of public benefit corporations were tax exempt, they were especially attractive to banks, insurance companies, and other institutional investors as well as individual investors who were in high tax brackets.[25] In addition, they paid higher rates of interest than did "regular" full-faith-and-credit bonds issued by the state. "Liberal" groups and causes also benefited from the many construction programs financed by moral-obligation bonds and/or lease-purchase arrangements. For example, in addition to the housing and urban development projects of UDC, these devices helped finance the expansion of the State University and the construction of hospitals, nursing homes, and mental health facilities. Finally, the legislature benefited in a fundamental sense. Legislators were able to participate in solving problems without the necessity of suffering the pain of raising taxes sufficiently high to support attacks on problems through normal financing arrangements.

The third component of an explanation for Rockefeller's success in pursuing financial schemes based on illusions has to do with the strength of certain elements of pragmatic liberalism as a public philosophy. The fact is that Nelson Rockefeller and his personal team were not the only important actors in the state's politics who believed that "all problems could be solved," that the chief executive should have the dominant role in problem solving, that a partnership between the public and private sectors is appropriate in attacking problems, and that it is appropriate to circumvent the voters in the interest of solving problems.

Because he had been a promoter of the tenets of pragmatic liberalism and because he had helped shape the political consensus that nurtured it, Rockefeller and his deeds were perhaps the most accurate reflection of it. We would argue that his failures as well as his many accomplishments were by and large the failures and accomplishments of pragmatic liberalism.

However, we believe that some failures were magnified and some accomplishments diminished because normal restraints fell before a man who represented the "perfect" coincidence of personality, executive style, and beliefs. When he no longer had the means to function as an effective problem solver in the pragmatic liberal style to which he had become accustomed, he left the office of Governor of New York State. More than any other event, his departure symbolized a decline in the currency of pragmatic liberalism in America.[26]

Notes

Chapter 1

1. For discussions of the substance and evolution of liberalism, see: Louis Hartz, *The Liberal Tradition in America* (New York: Harcourt, Brace and World, 1955); Kenneth M. Dolbeare and Patricia Dolbeare, *American Ideologies: The Competing Political Beliefs of the 1970's*, 2d ed. (Chicago: Rand McNally and Co., 1973); Garry Wills, *Nixon Agonistes: The Crises of the Self-Made Man* (Boston: Houghton Mifflin Co., 1969); Theodore Lowi, *The End of Liberalism: Ideology, Policy, and the Crisis of Public Authority* (New York: W. W. Norton and Co., 1969).

2. Dolbeare and Dolbeare, *American Ideologies*, part I, chapter 4.

3. Wills, *Nixon*, part V, chapter 3.

4. One example of the "marriage of convenience" that bound the two segments of the "new" right was represented by the alliance of forces supporting Barry Goldwater in his race for the presidency in 1964. Libertarians such as economist Milton Friedman supported Goldwater as did social conservatives who objected to the new morality. Wills argues that classical liberalism with its emphasis on individualism remains a powerful force in America. Because of this, he sees the new right and new left as being in constant danger of dissolution from a potential reuniting of the two halves of old-fashioned liberalism.

5. The struggle between the two groups actually began when Truman won out over Wallace as Roosevelt's vice-presidential choice at the Democratic National Convention in 1944.

6. Arthur Schlesinger, Jr., *The Vital Center* (Boston: Houghton Mifflin Co., 1949), p. 182.

7. Ibid., p. 37.

8. There has been a vigorous debate among historians and others regarding the degree to which liberals in general and President Truman in particular were responsible both for the origins of the Cold War and the suppression of domestic political dissent which culminated in the McCarthy era. For a discussion of the works of revisionists as well as counterrevisionists see Geoffrey S. Smith, "'Harry, We Hardly Know You': Revisionism, Politics and Diplomacy, 1945-1954 A Review Essay," *American Political Science Review* (June 1976): 560-82.

9. Lowi (*The End of Liberalism*) classifies Eisenhower, as well as Galbraith, as an "interest-group liberal," p. 77.

10. John Kenneth Galbraith, *American Capitalism: The Concept of Countervailing Power* (Boston: Houghton Mifflin Co., 1952), chapter 12. For an excellent discussion of liberals' growing pragmatism and increasing acceptance of capitalism and ideas often thought of as conservative, see Garry Wills; *Nixon*, part V. Wills identifies Schlesinger, Galbraith, Sorensen, and Goodwin as "consensus thinkers" of the 1950s and 1960s who provided the rationale for a liberalism which could accept many ideas which had been thought of as right-wing since the New Deal. He credits these men, plus Moynihan and Kristol, with turning post-New-Deal liberalism back in the direction of a classical liberalism which stresses individualism, the virtues of the free market, and the evils of big government.

11. Rockefeller Brothers Fund, *Prospect for America: The Rockefeller Panel Reports* (Garden City: Doubleday and Co., 1961), pp. 410, 411.

12. Ibid., p. 420.

13. Ibid., p. xvi.

14. Those who eventually served in the Kennedy administration were Adolph Berle Jr., Chester Bowles, Lucius Clay, Harlan Cleveland, Philip H. Coombs, Roswell Gilpatric, Theodore Hesburgh, James Killian, Max Millikan, and Dean Rusk. Information on Kennedy appointees is drawn from Schlesinger, *A Thousand Days* (Boston: Houghton Mifflin Co., 1965).

15. President's Commission on National Goals, *Goals for Americans: Programs for Action in the Sixties* (New York: Prentice-Hall, 1960). Eisenhower's appointment of the Commission on National Goals followed the report of another commission which concluded that it had been unable to achieve its principle objective, to produce recommendations that would bring about the transfer of specific functions and revenue sources from the federal government to state governments. Congressional Quarterly Service, *Congress and the Nation 1945-1964: A Review of Government and Politics in the Postwar Years* (Washington: Congressional Quarterly Service, 1965), pp. 1395, 1396.

16. James L. Sundquist, *Politics and Policy: The Eisenhower, Kennedy, and Johnson Years* (Washington: The Brookings Institution, 1968), pp. 395-96. Democratic party leaders in the Congress were often resentful of the efforts of the alliance, especially Democratic Party Chairman Paul Butler. This was especially true of Lyndon Johnson, their Senate Majority leader. Thus there was considerable intraparty conflict.

17. Ibid., pp. 409, 410.

18. Herbert Stein notes that the "standard economics of 1960" took a pragmatic view of the relationship between government and business. According to Stein the vast majority of economists believed as follows:

> The economy was not in need of any basic structural reform of the character of the NRA, French planning, or nationalization of industry. In general, the free market worked well and should not be tampered with, but particular issues of government intervention had to be considered on their merits and without prejudice. Steps to make the distribution of income more nearly equal were good, but they were not the urgent need and not the main road to improving the economic condition of the mass of the population, and they had to be evaluated with due regard for their effect on economic growth.

Stein includes Kennedy's advisers as having the views he cites. *The Fiscal Revolution in America* (Chicago: University of Chicago Press, 1969), pp. 381, 382.

19. This act represented the triumph of the idea that taxes should be cut in time of budget deficits in order to stimulate expansion of the economy. Sundquist attributes John Kennedy's conversion to this approach to his education by economists who advised him during his campaign, Paul Samuelson, Seymour Harris, and Galbraith, and the members of his Council on Economic Advisers, Walter Heller, James Tobin, and Kermit Gordon. Sundquist, *Politics and Policy*, p. 37.

20. Sundquist, *Politics and Policy*, pp. 47, 48.

21. Ibid., p. 442.

22. Ibid.

23. Key's analysis is based on poll data of the American Institute of Public Opinion. Specifically, it is based on responses to the question "What do you think is the MOST important problem facing this country today?" V. O. Key Jr., *The Responsible Electorate: Rationality in Presidential Voting 1936-1960* (Cambridge: Harvard University Press, 1966), p. 132. (Milton Cummings wrote most of the chapter in which the above quotation appears, Key having died before completing the book.)

24. As Sundquist points out, Herbert McCloskey and his coauthors found that positions on domestic issues in the period from 1956 to 1968 were similar for Democratic and Republican rank-and-file members and Democratic leaders, the latter defined as delegates to the 1956 Democratic National Convention. However, Republican leaders, defined as delegates to the 1956 Republican National Convention, were more "conservative" on domestic issues. To us this simply suggests that "old-guard" Republican leaders did not share the activist bent of modern liberalism, an activist bent shared by many rank-and-file Republicans. It also helps explain why Republican leaders who did share the activist approach of the dominant modern liberalism have had great difficulty in capturing the Republican nomation for president. Herbert McCloskey, Paul J. Hoffman, and Rosemary O'Hara, "Issue Conflict and Consensus Among Party Leaders and Followers," *American Political Science Review* (1960). See especially pp. 422-24. As measured by the number of presidential messages to Congress in the first ten weeks of a term, President Kennedy's level of legislative activity exceeded that of Franklin Roosevelt. Excluding Inaugural and State of the Union messages, Kennedy sent thirteen major messages to Congress during the first ten weeks. During a comparable period F.D.R. sent only five major messages. Kennedy's immediate predecessor Dwight Eisenhower sent only four major messages in a comparable period. David Halberstam, "Kennedy Pushes Early Fast Pace," *New York Times*, April 3, 1961.

25. Many liberals were deeply suspicious of Kennedy, especially because they viewed him as having been "soft" on Senator Joseph McCarthy in the early 1950s. Schlesinger discusses the suspicion toward Kennedy in *A Thousand Days*, Chapter 1. Schlesinger also offers a defense of Kennedy's liberalism. It is worth noting that Kennedy passed over two leading soft liberal candidates for the position of secretary of state, Adlai Stevenson and Chester Bowles, in favor of Dean Rusk, then head of the Rockefeller Foundation.

26. Ibid., p. 36. See also pp. 23, 36.

27. Wills, p. 524. Richard Barnet's analysis of the "moral code" of the "national security managers," men such as Foster Dulles, Dean Rusk, McNamara, McGeorge Bundy, and Walt Rostow is relevant here. Barnet's view is that these men whose role

in national security policy was dominant after World War II shared a Calvinist moral code that emphasized the duty of those who achieved high position on the basis of personal "excellence" to exercise power as a means of maintaining a world order in which America would be dominant. We would argue that the views of the national security managers were quite compatible with modern liberalism, especially as regards their commitment to a style that tended toward elevating "toughness," competence, and the exercise of power into ends in themselves. Barnet sees the "cult of excellence" as reaching a peak in the Kennedy administration. Richard J. Barnet, *Roots of War* (New York: Atheneum Publishers, 1972), Penguin edition, pp. 68-75. Bruce Miroff's study of Kennedy includes an insightful analysis of what he sees as an addiction to power and toughness common to Kennedy and others in his administration. *Pragmatic Illusions* (New York: David McKay Co., 1976).

28. Richard Neustadt, *Presidential Power* (New York: New American Library, 1960), p. 175. Prior to his inauguration, Kennedy read Neustadt's book as part of his preparation for organizing the White House staff. Schlesinger, *A Thousand Days*, pp. 122, 123.

29. Neustadt, *Presidential Power*, pp. 172, 173.

30. Ibid., p. 173.

31. Schlesinger, *Thousand Days*, p. 25.

32. Theodore White, *Breach of Faith: The Fall of Richard Nixon* (New York: Atheneum Publishers, 1975). Chapter 13 contains the heart of White's argument that Nixon's fall was the result of a personal failure. White asserts that Nixon broke the bonds of trust that must exist between a president and the people. White is sanguine regarding the accretion of power in the presidency. As he puts it, the presidency is an office in which "greater and greater power has to be concentrated. . . .", p. 339.

33. Those who were of the "realist" school offered arguments, some impressive, which could be used to help justify standards of conduct in the international arena different from those in domestic political life. See Hans J. Morgenthau, *Politics Among Nations*, 2d ed. (New York: Alfred A. Knopf, 1954) and Ernest W. Lefever, *Ethics and United States Foreign Policy* (Cleveland: World Publishing Co., 1957).

34. We are not arguing with the view that Richard Nixon carried improper practices to a degree far beyond that of Kennedy and Johnson. We merely argue that the groundwork for his deeds was laid by modern liberalism and those two presidents who were "its" presidents. For views not unlike ours see: Joseph Califano, *A Presidential Nation* (New York: W. W. Norton and Co., 1975) and Marcus Raskin, *Notes on the Old System* (New York: David McKay Co., 1974). Arthur Schlesinger agrees that Nixon's presidency "was not an aberration but a culmination." And he adds that "it carried to reckless extremes a compulsion toward presidential power rising out of deep-running changes in the foundations of society." *The Imperial Presidency* (Boston: Houghton Mifflin Co., 1973), p. 417. However, Schlesinger refrains from any discussion of the role of modern liberalism in laying the groundwork for the Nixon presidency. Richard Barnet has a particularly good discussion of techniques for the manipulation of public opinion as they developed in the national security arena after World War II. Barnet, *Roots*, chapter 10, "The Manipulation of Public Opinion."

35. Some aspects of pragmatic liberalism came under strong attack in the late sixties and the seventies. For example, the Vietnam War and Watergate spawned attacks on the strong presidency and on the use of tactics which contravened normal

standards of behavior. Indeed the presidential campaign of Jimmy Carter in 1976 was based largely on the theme of honesty, morality, and openness in government. Another example of a phenomenon which was based in part on a disenchantment with an element of pragmatic liberalism, reliance on big government, was the passage of spending limitations on state government such as California's Proposition 13 (1978). Although it is clear that pragmatic liberalism was not as dominant in the seventies as in the sixties, it retained considerable strength. For example, President Carter's initial reaction to the oil shortage of 1979 showed a heavy reliance on the ideas of increasing the authority of the president, expanding the role of government as a problem solver and forging mutually-supportive links between government and business in developing new supplies of energy, notably synthetic fuels. For details of the president's proposals, see *New York Times*, July 16, 17, 1979.

36. As we have noted, this change occurred in part as a reaction to disillusionment with socialism and communism. One policy area in which liberalism retained substantial idealism is that of civil rights. However, even here, much of the impetus for change came from atypical elements within the liberal camp. Even Schlesinger acknowledges the contribution to civil rights of "the utopian left." Schlesinger refers to himself and politicians such as Hubert Humphrey as "pragmatic liberals." He says that the Kennedy administration itself expressed "the spirit of liberal pragmatism." To Schlesinger the distinction between pragmatic liberals and utopian liberals is that the latter "did not like power." Schlesinger, *Thousand Days*, pp. 678-83. It is clear to us that pragmatic liberalism as we use the term is not identical to Schlesinger's "liberal pragmatism." Although we would classify him as a pragmatic liberal as we define the term, we would not expect him to agree with what we see as the defining characteristics of our pragmatic liberalism. On the other hand, Bruce Miroff's use of the term pragmatic liberal is more similar to our use of the term. Miroff classifies John F. Kennedy and other modern liberal presidents as pragmatic liberals. More specifically he says that "committed to liberal objectives, yet free from liberal sentimentality, the pragmatic liberal sees himself as grappling with the brute and unpleasant facts of political reality in order to humanize and soften those facts." *Pragmatic Illusions*, p. 384. While there are some similarities in the respective ways in which he and we use the term, there are also substantial dissimilarities. In general, our meaning of the term is broader than his. Compare his discussion in Chapter 7 with our list of the components of pragmatic liberalism.

37. Lowi says the following in describing interest group liberalism: "It may be called liberalism because it expects to use government in a positive and expansive role, it is motivated by the highest sentiments, and it possesses strong faith that what is good for government is good for the society. It is 'interest-group liberalism' because it sees as both necessary and good that the policy agenda and the public interest be defined in terms of the organized interests in society.", p. 71. He also noted that the best formulations of interest group liberalism "can be found among the more articulate Democrats, especially the leading Democratic intellectuals, Professors John Kenneth Galbraith and Arthur Schlesinger, Jr." *Interest Group Liberalism*, p. 71. The first component and the last five components in our list are either absent or lacking in prominence in interest group liberalism as Lowi conceives it.

38. Included among any list of relevant books would be: Schlesinger, *Vital Center* and *Thousand Days*; Galbraith, *American Capitalism and the New Industrial State* (Boston: Houghton Mifflin Co., 1967). Daniel Bell, *The End of Ideology* (New

York: The Free Press, 1960); Lowi, *Liberalism*; Barnet, *Roots*; Stephen Hess, *Organizing the Presidency* (Washington: The Brookings Institution, 1976); Alonzo L. Hamby, *Beyond the New Deal: Harry S. Truman and American Liberalism* (New York: Columbia University Press, 1973); Godfrey Hodgson, *America in Our Time* (Garden City: Doubleday and Co., 1976); Emmet John Hughes, *The Ordeal of Power* (New York: Atheneum Publishers, 1963); Doris Kearns, *Lyndon Johnson and the American Dream* (New York: Harper and Row Publishers, 1976); Miroff, *Illusions*; Theodore Sorensen, *Kennedy* (New York: Harper and Row Publishers, 1965); Stein, *Fiscal Revolution*; Sundquist, *Politics and Policy*.

39. Because of the fact that American political leaders typically lack well-developed and clearly articulated systems of political belief, it is especially important that one examine leaders' actions as a means of shedding light on their beliefs. A similar argument has been made by Daniel Boorstin. He argues that because Americans have not produced much in the way of well-articulated political thought, one must infer our political ideas from an examination of our political institutions. Daniel Boorstin, *The Genius of American Politics* (Chicago: University of Chicago Press, 1953). See especially p. 169.

Chapter 2

1. A good example of another political leader who adopted what we would term a life strategy would be Gandhi. See, for example, James MacGregor Burns, *Leadership* (New York: Harper and Row Publishers, 1978), pp. 106-8. The Georges's study of Woodrow Wilson refers to his "strategy" both as president of Princeton University and president of the United States in terms which suggest some similarity to our use of the term life strategy. They say:

> Wilson hit upon the highly constructive strategy—constructive both from his standpoint and that of the nation—of committing his desire for domination and his ambition for great accomplishments only to reform projects which already enjoyed considerable support and were within reasonable possibility of achievement.

However, the Georges imply that Wilson's choice of strategy was less the product of a conscious, "rational" process than the product of the demands of a damaged ego that could satisfy its need for power and domination only in the context of seeking to satisfy other very powerful needs including approval, respect, and feeling virtuous. Although it ultimately failed Wilson, the strategy cited above promised the possibility of satisfying his need for power as well as his other needs. Alexander L. and Juliette L. George, *Woodrow Wilson and Colonel House: A Personality Study* (New York: Dover Publications, 1964), p. 320.

2. Among two of the more notable definitions are those of James Barber and Alexander George. Barber defines style as a political executive's "way of coping with role demands—his collections of habits for performing to meet the demands." "Strategies for Understanding Politicians," *American Journal of Political Science* (May 1974): 462. Without clearly defining the terms, George talks of "leadership style" and "style of decision-making." Implying some agreement with Barber's use of the term, George argues that style involves the way an executive orients himself toward the politics of policymaking, especially "bureaucratic politics." "Adaptation to Stress in Political Decision Making: the Individual, Small Group, and Or-

ganizational Contexts," in George V. Coelo, et al., eds., *Coping and Adaptation* (New York: Basic Books, 1974), p. 210.

3. The definition seems broad enough to encompass at least two of Barber's three components of style, homework and personal relations. With a little stretching it might also encompass the third, rhetoric, insofar as the latter relates to decision-management. See Barber, *The Presidential Character: Predicting Performance in the White House* (Englewood Cliffs: Prentice-Hall, 1972), p. 7. It also would seem to encompass what George seems to see as the core of decision-making style, the handling of information. See George, "Adaptation to Stress."

4. Barber makes distinctions on the basis of the degree to which an executive emphasizes one component of style, for example, homework as opposed to personal relations. Barber, *Presidential Character*, p. 7. See also his "Classifying and Predicting Presidential Styles," *Journal of Social Issues* (July 1968): 51-80. George distinguishes between "collegial styles" and "bureaucratic styles," a distinction based on the degree to which styles allow for "multiple advocacy." George, "Adaptation to Stress," pp. 203-17.

5. Our distinctions resemble those of Alexander George. However, George seems to see degree of structure and degree of collegiality as opposite extremes of the same dimension. George, "Adaptation to Stress," p. 214. By the degree to which an executive works in the company of others, we mean primarily to indicate a concern with the number of people with whom he interacts. Thus an executive who confines his working relationship to a tiny group of trusted associates would be viewed as less collegial in style than one who makes it a practice to interact personally with large numbers of people. Level of involvement includes time, energy, and emotional commitment invested by an executive.

6. Anthony Downs, *Inside Bureaucracy* (Boston: Little Brown and Co., 1967), chapter 12.

7. See Downs, chapter 5, for a discussion of the relationships between a bureau and its environment.

8. Irving L. Janis, *Victims of Groupthink* (Boston: Houghton Mifflin Co., 1972), p. 9. Alexander George advocates multiple advocacy as a technique which political executives can use to avoid the dangers of "groupthink" as well as the problem of the distortion of information identified by Downs. George, "Adaptation to Stress," pp. 232-40.

9. Here again, Barber and George have done relevant work. Barber sees emotional needs, e.g., affection, achievement, "character," "worldview," and "first independent political success" as having some influence over style. *Presidential Character*. George sees emotional and cognitive needs, belief system/operational code, and experience as influencing style. "Adaptation to Stress," p. 209. See also Fred I. Greenstein, "Personality and Politics," chapter 1 in Fred I. Greenstein and Nelson W. Polsby, eds., *Micropolitical Theory* (Reading, Massachusetts: Addison-Wesley, 1975), 2: 1-92.

10. Greenstein, *Micropolitical Theory*, p. 11. For another discussion of politically relevant needs, see Robert E. Lane, *Political Thinking and Consciousness: The Private Life of the Political Mind* (Chicago: Markham Publishing Co., 1969). See especially pp. 25-47. See also Jeanne N. Knutson, "Personality in the Study of Politics," in Knutson, ed., *Handbook of Political Psychology* (San Francisco: Jossey-Bass Publishers, 1973).

11. For Greenstein's discussion of basic personality structures and needs, see *Micropolitical Theory*, pp. 9-13.

12. George and George, *Woodrow Wilson and Colonel House*. See especially pp. 8, 11, 151. For a commentary on the Georges's approach, see Robert Tucker, "The Georges's Wilson Reexamined: An Essay on Psychobiography," *The American Political Science Review* (June 1977): 606-18.

13. Barber, *Presidential Character*, pp. 12, 13.

14. James Payne and Oliver Woshinsky, "Incentives for Political Participation," *World Politics* (July 1972), p. 519.

15. Ibid.

16. Ibid., p. 20. Payne and Woshinsky explicitly reject power and money as constituting incentives. Rather they categorize these concepts as "*instrumental* goals or resources which men wish to obtain in order to satisfy basic drives (incentives)."

17. Ibid., pp. 528, 529. We would not argue that Rockefeller had no needs other than those related to "devising and managing public policy." For example, he seemed to have relatively strong needs to collect and order information, to impose order on his environment, and to interact with others in a group setting. Although all three needs were satisfied in part through his activities in "devising and managing public policy," they seem to have had an independent status as well, a status reflected in activities outside the latter sphere.

18. For example, a former program associate and official of the Metropolitan Transportation Authority, Edward Kresky, testified that the Governor required a daily progress memo and telephoned frequently in trying to redeem his promise that he would make the Long Island Rail Road the best commuter railroad in the nation. Interview with Edward Kresky, New York City, April 27, 1977.

19. Interview with Nelson A. Rockefeller, New York City, November 16, 1977. Rockefeller attributed his love of problem solving in part to his having attended the Lincoln School of Columbia Teachers College. As he put it, Lincoln was a "John Dewey progressive school."

20. *New York Times*, February 10, 1979.

21. On Wilson, see George and George, *Woodrow Wilson and Colonel House*. On Nixon, see Barber, *Presidential Character*, chapter 11.

22. Peter Collier and David Horowitz, *The Rockefellers: An American Dynasty* (New York: Holt, Rinehart, and Winston, 1976), p. 189.

23. Ibid.

24. Ibid.

25. Statement by Howard Knowles as quoted in Collier and Horowitz, *The Rockefellers*, pp. 196-97.

26. Collier and Horowitz, *The Rockefellers*, p. 192.

27. Ibid.

28. For a discussion of Wilson's relationship to his father, see George and George, *Woodrow Wilson and Colonel House*, chapter 1.

29. Collier and Horowitz, *The Rockefellers*, p. 200. From the time he was a child, Nelson had displayed a capacity for annoying his father with all the sorts of activities that very energetic and aggressive young people are prone to engage in, including lively antics at the dinner table.

30. The Georges make this argument regarding Wilson in *Woodrow Wilson and Colonel House*. See especially chapter 1.

31. Nelson A. Rockefeller, "Don't Accept Anyone's Verdict That You Are Lazy, Stupid or Retarded," *TV Guide*, October 16, 1976, p. 14. In this article, Rockefeller also points out that his best subject was math, especially mathematical concepts as opposed to computation.

32. Robert Lane has an excellent discussion of the various elements of what he refers to as "cognitive needs," the need to "know and understand." See *Political Thinking and Consciousness*, pp. 31-33.

The consequence of reading problems in practical terms are dramatized by Howard Gardner in his discussion of dyslexia: "Consider handling one's own business or legal affairs if one has always to ask someone else what has been written; imagine missing the crucial information '½ PRICE SALE—TODAY ONLY' or 'DANGER—LIVE WIRE'; contemplate keeping up with what's happening in the world. . . ." *The Shattered Mind* (New York: Alfred A. Knopf, 1976), p. 120.

33. One of his closest friends, architect Wallace Harrison, has testified that Rockefeller was of genuine help in state construction projects such as the South Mall complex in Albany. Harrison said, "He lived with the buildings. He had a good eye and he could read blueprints. This was his avocation. He was an asset to everybody. He made suggestions." Interview with Wallace Harrison, New York City, June 1, 1978. Although there are competing theories as to the true nature and cause of dyslexia, there is some indication that it involves an abnormality in the relationship between the left and right hemispheres of the brain. One theory is that dyslexia occurs when the "language-controlling" hemisphere, usually the left, fails to achieve dominance over the other hemisphere, and, as a consequence, the division of labor between the hemispheres is unclear. Gardner, *The Shattered Mind*, pp. 126-27.

34. Desmond reports that as a college student, Rockefeller usually participated in bull sessions only if they involved discussions of "ethics or religion." Desmond also sees Rockefeller as having a taste for the "concrete" as opposed to "abstractions." James Desmond, *Nelson Rockefeller: A Political Biography* (New York: Macmillan Co., 1964), p. 38.

35. Interview with George Dudley, Albany, New York, August 18, 1977.

36. Interview with Nelson A. Rockefeller. The Lincoln School, "a model of Deweyite pragmatism," allowed students to learn at their own rate and encouraged them to develop self-discipline. It avoided concentration on memorization and attention to traditional subjects such as Latin and Greek. Collier and Horowitz, *The Rockefellers*, p. 192.

37. Rockefeller, "Don't Accept Anyone's Verdict," p. 14.

38. As quoted in Michael Kramer and Sam Roberts, *I Never Wanted to be Vice-President of Anything: An Investigative Biography of Nelson Rockefeller* (New York: Basic Books, 1976), p. 41.

39. Desmond, *Nelson Rockefeller*, p. 41.

40. Joe Alex Morris, *Nelson Rockefeller: A Biography* (New York: Harper and Row Publishers, 1960), p. 45.

41. Kramer and Roberts, *Vice President*, p. 41, and Desmond, *Nelson Rockefeller*, p. 38.

42. As quoted in Morris, *Nelson Rockefeller*, p. 48.

43. Ibid., p. 43.

44. *New York Times*, January 28, 1979. Rockefeller's concern with order extended to the details of his physical surroundings. A former executive administrator of Rockefeller's estate at Pocantico Hills for two years is quoted as saying, "If

a light over a painting was one-eighth of an inch off, he would notice it. He'd see the grass growing. He was a perfectionist, but then, so am I and perhaps that's why we got on so well." *Greensburg [Pa.] Tribune Review*, March 25, 1979.

45. Collier and Horowitz, *The Rockefellers*, p. 97. His maternal grandfather, Senator Nelson Aldrich, provided a model of political involvement.

46. As quoted in Morris, *Nelson Rockefeller*, p. 44.

47. Collier and Horowitz, *The Rockefellers*, chapters 8, 9.

48. Ibid., chapters 11, 16.

49. As quoted in Kramer and Roberts, *Vice President*, p. 42.

50. Collier and Horowitz, *The Rockefellers*, p. 199.

51. Ibid.

52. Garry Wills, *Nixon Agonistes: The Crisis of the Self-Made Man* (New York: New American Library, 1971), p. 201.

53. Collier and Horowitz, *The Rockefellers*, pp. 201, 207.

54. Ibid., p. 203.

55. Ibid., p. 207.

56. Ibid., p. 204.

57. U.S., Congress, House, Committee on the Judiciary, *Hearings on the Nomination of Nelson A. Rockefeller to be Vice President of the United States*, 93rd Cong., 2d sess., 1974, p. 16.

58. Collier and Horowitz, *The Rockefellers*, p. 210.

59. Ibid.

60. Ibid., p. 210.

61. Ibid., p. 262.

62. The group included Joseph Rovensky, head of Chase Bank's foreign department, Jay Crane of Jersey Standard, Wallace Harrison, head architect of Rockefeller Center, and the noted economist, Beardsley Ruml.

63. Collier and Horowitz, *The Rockefellers*, p. 213.

64. Steward Alsop, *Nixon and Rockefeller: A Double Portrait* (Garden City: Doubleday and Co., 1960), pp. 84-85.

65. Collier and Horowitz, *The Rockefellers*, p. 213.

66. As quoted in Kramer and Roberts, *Vice President*, p. 50.

67. Barber, *Presidential Character*, p. 6.

68. The office was created by an executive order of the Council of National Defense on August 16, 1940. See U.S., Congress, House, Committee on Appropriations, *Hearings on the National War Agencies Appropriations Bill for 1944*, 78th Cong., 1st sess., 1943, p. 335.

69. The statement that the Governor made in his inaugural address in 1959 is typical of his views regarding the basic lines of conflict in the international sphere.

"The world is divided, essentially, between those who believe in the brotherhood of men under the fatherhood of God—and those who scorn this as a pious myth.

It is divided between those who believe in the dignity of free men—and those who believe in the monstrous supremacy of the totalitarian state.

It is divided between those whose most potent force is their faith in individual freedom—and those whose faith is force itself.

It is divided between those who believe in the essential equality of peoples of all nations and races and creeds—and those whose only creed is their own ruthless race for power.

This division of the world—and this time of decision—leave no corner of the earth, no fraction of humanity, untouched. From this basic struggle, there can be no refuge, nor escape."

State of New York, *Public Papers of Nelson A. Rockefeller, Fifty-third Governor of the State of New York, 1959*, p. 11.

70. We do not imply that Rockefeller was motivated primarily by narrow economic self-interest. We believe that he tended to think in larger terms and that his belief in the superiority of the capitalist system were sincerely held. This does not mean that he was unaware of the fact that he and people like him derived disproportionate benefits from the existing economic system.

71. Morris, *Nelson Rockefeller*, p. 129.

72. Rockefeller clearly believed that political leadership must as its first priority deal with those problems that threatened the viability and stability of the existing political and economic system. An unabashed nationalist and capitalist, but one who felt that capitalism must exercise social responsibility and governments must rely on foreign economic and cultural aid as well as military preparedness, Rockefeller was preoccupied with national security from the time of his earliest experiences in Latin America. Realizing the growing dependence of the United States in an increasingly interdependent world, he often concentrated on designing and promoting approaches that would assure the United States access to raw materials as well as foreign markets.

73. As quoted in Collier and Horowitz, *The Rockefellers*, p. 228.

74. The $3 million of initial capital for this company came in one-third shares from the Rockefeller family, three oil companies (Standard of New Jersey, Gulf, and Shell), and some Venezuelan partners. The threat of a German victory in the war posed a danger for the company's investments. Thus, in addition to his earlier fears of nationalization by socialist regimes, Rockefeller had new cause for concern about dangers to "his" and "our" South America. Ibid., pp. 211, 212.

75. Alsop, *Nixon and Rockefeller*, p. 86.

76. Ibid.

77. Interview with George Dudley.

78. Morris, *Nelson Rockefeller*, p. 140.

79. Ibid.

80. As quoted in Morris, *Nelson Rockefeller*, p. 140.

81. Collier and Horowitz, *The Rockefellers*, p. 232.

82. Interview with George Dudley.

83. Ibid.

84. Downs, *Inside Bureaucracy*, p. 105. Good discussions of how agency heads behave can be found in Aaron Wildavsky, *The Politics of the Budgetary Process*, 2d ed. (Boston: Little, Brown and Co., 1975), and Herbert Kaufman, *Administrative Feedback* (Washington: The Brookings Institution, 1973).

85. Morris, *Nelson Rockefeller*, p. 150.

86. As quoted in Morris, *Nelson Rockefeller*, p. 152.

87. Alsop, *Nixon and Rockefeller*, p. 85. By 1944 OIAA had grown from a handful of employees to several thousand. Top level staff alone had grown from five to twenty-one persons. Morris, *Nelson Rockefeller*, p. 138, and U.S. General Services Administration, National Archives and Record Service, Office of the Federal Register, *United States Government Organization Manual*, 1941, pp. 42-44.

88. On one occasion, Senator McKellar had succeeded in restoring to the OIAA

budget $50,000 that the Bureau of the Budget had recommended be cut. Morris, *Nelson Rockefeller*, pp. 15, 151.

89. Morris, *Nelson Rockefeller*, p. 169.

90. Collier and Horowitz, *The Rockefellers*, p. 231.

91. Interview with George Dudley. In fiscal year 1942, OIAA received about $10 million directly from Congress but over $25 million from the President's Emergency Fund. House Committee on Appropriations, *Hearings on the National War Agencies Appropriations Bill*, p. 176.

92. Desmond, *Nelson Rockefeller*, p. 85.

93. Collier and Horowitz, *The Rockefellers*, p. 230. It was undoubtedly clear to Rockefeller and his staff that the Nazi challenge offered economic opportunities for the United States as well as dangers. For example, if United States firms could take over the markets and access to raw materials previously dominated by Britain and Germany, OIAA's efforts could be justified in terms of economic self-interest alone.

94. Ibid., p. 233.

95. Ibid., p. 231.

96. Edward Jay Epstein, "The Great Rockefeller Power Machine," *New York Magazine*, November 24, 1975, p. 52. Among OIAA advisers were leading figures in advertising, journalism, and film. For example, Walt Disney assisted with film-making.

97. Collier and Horowitz, *The Rockefellers*, p. 232.

98. A former staff member of OIAA told one author that prewar activities had concentrated on "organizing the pro-western elites of Venezuela and Brazil into a private network of influence." Epstein, "Rockefeller Power Machine," p. 50.

99. Epstein, "Rockefeller Power Machine," pp. 51, 52.

100. Ibid., p. 52.

101. Ibid.

102. Alsop reports that Dean Acheson demanded that Rockefeller be fired as a condition of his agreeing to become undersecretary of state, *Nixon and Rockefeller*, p. 89.

103. As quoted in Collier and Horowitz, *The Rockefellers*, p. 236. They also quote a Rockefeller associate as saying, "We'll buy these people." p. 236.

104. Roosevelt had agreed to Stalin's demand at Yalta that Argentina be excluded from the U.N. According to Charles Bohlen, Rockefeller took advantage of F.D.R.'s failing health and powers of concentration to obtain his signature on a memo authorizing an invitation to Argentina to be a member of the U.N. Ibid., p. 239.

105. Alsop, *Nixon and Rockefeller*, pp. 88-89. Future regional alliances including NATO and the Warsaw Pact rested their legality on Article 51.

106. Ibid., p. 90.

107. As quoted in Collier and Horowitz, *The Rockefellers*, p. 260. At a meeting of his South American group in 1952, he remarked that "if the capitalist system has any way to get things done, the Rockefellers have access to it." From the notes of a group member, Adolf Berle, as quoted in *The Rockefellers*, p. 270.

108. Ibid., p. 264. Collier and Horowitz credit Nelson Rockefeller with being a "key behind-the-scenes influence in America's anti-communist effort in Latin America in the postwar years," *The Rockefellers*, pp. 262-63. Among other things, they cite the involvement of some of his associates in the AFL-sponsored Free Trade

Union Committee, a CIA-backed organization, and the American Institute for Free Labor Development. Both organizations worked to create an anti-Communist union movement in Latin America. Both offered assistance to the CIA in efforts against leftist governments.

109. Collier and Horowitz, *The Rockefellers*, pp. 269-70. Among opponents of Rockefeller's plan were conservatives who objected to Point Four as a giveaway program. However, the most influential opposition came from Executive Branch officials including Averell Harriman, special assistant to the president and administrator of the Marshall Plan.

110. Ibid., p. 269.

111. Secretary of State Dulles confided to the president's chief-of-staff, Sherman Adams, that he was concerned about Rockefeller's building a big staff which he then took to Quantico shortly before the Geneva summit meeting. Ibid., p. 274.

112. Alsop, *Nixon and Rockefeller*, p. 95.

113. Such enemies included John Foster Dulles and his brother Allen, head of the CIA; Walter Bedell "Beetle" Smith, key guardian of access to Eisenhower; Budget Director Rowland Hughes; Undersecretary of State Herbert Hoover, Jr.; and very close Eisenhower friend, Secretary of the Treasury George Humphrey.

114. Collier and Horowitz, *The Rockefellers*, p. 276. Eisenhower made great efforts to contain defense spending. (He was later criticized by presidential candidate John Kennedy for neglecting the nation's defense). Collier and Horowitz report that a "still highly classified" report from one of Rockefeller's Quantico seminars called for spending $18 million in a six-year period to carry out "a virtual master plan for the conduct of the cold war." p. 276.

115. This project's relationship to pragmatic liberalism is discussed in chapter 1.

116. *Prospect for America: The Rockefeller Panel Reports* (Garden City: Doubleday and Co., 1962), p. i.

117. The selection of Nelson Rockefeller as chairman of the commission (June 8, 1956) was the result of a compromise between Democratic Governor Averell Harriman and leaders of the Republican controlled Legislature. *New York Times*, July 9, 1956.

118. Seven years as director of the state's "little Hoover commission," formally titled the New York State Coordination Commission, had given Ronan a thorough knowledge of the state's governmental structure. *Public Papers, 1959*, p. 787.

119. Morris, *Nelson Rockefeller*, pp. 318-19.

Chapter 3

1. See generally Arnold Steinberg, *Political Campaign Management* (Lexington, Massachusetts: D.C. Heath and Co., 1976).

2. See James M. Perry, *The New Politics: The Expanding Technology of Political Manipulation* (New York: Clarkson N. Potter, 1968), pp. 107-37.

3. Clark D. Ahlberg and Daniel P. Moynihan, "Changing Governors—and Policies," *Public Administration Review* (Fall 1960): 196-97.

4. Joe Alex Morris, *Nelson Rockefeller: A Biography* (New York: Harper and Row Publishers, 1960), p. 310.

5. Ibid., p. 312.

6. Ibid., p. 313.

7. Ibid.

8. Ibid., p. 316.

9. Stewart Alsop, *Nixon and Rockefeller: A Double Portrait* (New York: Doubleday and Co., 1960), pp. 106-7.

10. As quoted in Morris, *Nelson Rockefeller*, p. 317.

11. *New York Times*, July 1, 1958, p. 36.

12. Oren Root, *Persons and Persuasions* (New York: W. W. Norton and Co., 1974), p. 140.

13. *New York Times*, August 26, 1958, p. 20.

14. Ibid.

15. Neal Peirce, *The Megastates of America: People, Politics, and Power in the Ten Great States* (New York: W. W. Norton and Co., 1972), p. 21.

16. Eugene J. Gleason, Jr., and Joseph E. Zimmerman, "Executive Dominance in New York State" (Paper prepared for delivery at the Annual Meeting of the Northeastern Political Science Association, Saratoga Springs, New York, November 9, 1974), p. 2.

17. See references to the study by Joseph Schlesinger in Thad Beyle, "The Governor's Formal Powers: A View from the Governor's Chair," *Public Administration Review* (November-December 1968): 540. The four powers included in the analysis were: budget power, appointive power, tenure potential, and veto power.

18. Joseph A. Schlesinger, "A Comparison of the Relative Positions of Governors" in Thad Beyle and J. Oliver Williams, eds., *The American Governor in Behavioral Perspective* (New York: Harper and Row Publishers, 1972), p. 3.

19. Ibid.

20. See generally Gleason and Zimmerman, "Executive Dominance," p. 16.

21. Peirce, *The Megastates*, p. 16.

22. Ibid.

23. Ibid.

24. Joseph E. Zimmerman, "New York State Government: Retrospect and Prospect" (Paper prepared for delivery at the Twenty-first College Conference on New York History, Albany, New York, April 30, 1977), p. 8.

25. Ibid.

26. See especially Ronald E. Weber, *Public Policy Preferences in the States* (Bloomington: Indiana University Institute of Public Administration, 1971), and Richard L. Sutton, "The States and the People: Measuring and Accounting for State Representativeness," *Polity* (Summer 1973): 452-76.

27. Jack L. Walker, "The Diffusion of Innovations Among the American States," *American Political Science Review* (September 1969): 380.

28. Fred W. Grupp and Alan R. Richards, "Variations in Elite Perceptions of American States as Referents for Public Policy Making," *American Political Science Review* (September 1975): 850-58.

29. Interview with Joseph Persico, Washington, D.C., February 17, 1978.

30. See Doris A. Graber, *Verbal Behavior and Politics* (Urbana: University of Illinois Press, 1976), pp. 181-89.

31. Ibid.

32. Morris, *Nelson Rockefeller*, p. 324. Morris notes that Rockefeller repeated a story about Al Smith holding his ground against Tammany Hall in a similar incident in 1924 and winning, but noted that Harriman did not have the courage to do so and

that his administration could not suppress racketeering if it knuckled under to Tammany Hall.

33. *New York Times*, November 6, 1958, p. 27.

34. James Desmond, *Nelson Rockefeller: A Political Biography* (New York: Macmillan Co., 1964), p. 177. For the same theme, see generally: Morris, *Nelson Rockefeller*, pp. 321-22; and *New York Times*, September 16, 1958, p. 17; September 24, 1958, p. 24; October 26, 1958, p. 36.

35. State of New York, *Public Papers of Nelson A. Rockefeller, Fifty-third Governor of the State of New York*, 1962, rally at White Plains, October 1, 1962, p. 1326.

36. *New York Times*, August 7, 1966, p. 48.

37. However, during the 1958 campaign, when the popularity of the Eisenhower administration was dwindling, Rockefeller did mute his penchant for addressing national issues. He did so because he did not wish to be lured into the position of defending national Republican party policies and diminishing his appeal to Democratic voters. See, for example, James Desmond, *A Political Biography*, p. 185.

38. For a discussion of effective campaign strategies, see generally Steinberg, *Campaign Management*, pp. 47-83.

39. See, for example, Fred Powledge, "The Marketing of Nelson Rockefeller," *New York Magazine* (November 30, 1970), p. 40.

40. Robert H. Connery and Gerald Benjamin, eds., *Governing New York State: The Rockefeller Years* (New York: The Academy of Political Science, 1964), p. 38.

41. Interview with William Pfeiffer, former chairman of the New York State Republican party and campaign manager for the Rockefeller gubernatorial campaigns of 1962 and 1966, Albany, New York, September 24, 1979.

42. Ibid.

43. Ibid. Although Pfeiffer says that Rockefeller told two people that the former was a "goddamned stubborn Dutchman," he avers that his relationship with the Governor was, if anything, better after the incident.

44. Steinberg, *Campaign Management*, p. 51.

45. Perry, *The New Politics*, p. 111-12.

46. The nominating convention was scheduled at this time in advance of the June 23, 1970, primary elections.

47. Robert H. Connery and Gerald Benjamin, *Rockefeller of New York: Executive Power in the Statehouse* (Ithaca, NY: Cornell University Press, 1979), p. 41.

48. *New York Times*, August 26, 1962.

49. "Notes and Comments," *New Yorker* (November 19, 1966), p. 48.

50. Richard Reeves, "This is the Battle of the Titans?" *New York Times Magazine* (November 1, 1970), p. 70.

51. Powledge, "Marketing of Rockefeller," p. 40.

52. Interview with William Pfeiffer.

53. Alsop, *Nixon and Rockefeller*, p. 107-8.

54. *New York Times*, July 27, 1962, p. 8.

55. Ibid., August 26, 1962, p. E5.

56. Ibid., October 28, 1970, p. 34. The four workers identified were A. Marshall, R. Douglass, H. Morrow, and R. Maiorana.

57. As quoted in James M. Perry, *The New Politics: The Expanding Technology*

of Political Manipulation (New York: Clarkson N. Potter, 1968), p. 123.

58. The table was prepared from six county books: Albany, Delaware, New York, Niagara, Rockland, and Tioga. Books provided by Hugh Morrow, former director of communications for Governor Rockefeller.

59. County Data Book for Tioga County.

60. See David Rosenbloom, *The Election Men: Professional Campaign Managers and American Democracy* (New York: Quadrangle Books, 1973), p. 33.

61. Powledge, "Marketing of Rockefeller," p. 42.

62. Telephone interview with Lloyd Free, San Diego, California, May 22, 1978.

63. Powledge, "Marketing of Rockefeller," p. 39.

64. Leo Egan, "Can Rockefeller Save the GOP in New York?" *Reporter* (October 30, 1958): 11.

65. Ibid., p. 10.

66. *New York Times*, October 13, 1962, p. 28.

67. Robert MacNeil, *The People Machine*, (New York: Harper and Row Publishers, 1968), p. 210.

68. Perry, *The New Politics*, p. 115.

69. See generally *New York Times*, August 23, 31, 1970; Reeves, "Battle of the Titans?" p. 75; Powledge, "Marketing of Rockefeller," p. 40.

70. See Leo Egan, "New York: The Hunch that Paid Off for Nelson Rockefeller," *Reporter* (November 27, 1958): 15-16 and *New York Times*, September 24, 1979.

71. Interview with William Pfeiffer.

72. For example, see Connery and Benjamin, eds., *Governing New York State*, p. 38. They report that Rockefeller gave 321 campaign speeches in 1970 rather than the 217 as noted in the *Public Papers*.

73. As noted in Chapter 2, Rockefeller gained valuable experience in using the media during his stint as Coordinator of Inter-American Affairs.

74. Edward Chester, *Radio, Television and American Politics* (New York: Sheed and Ward, 1969), p. 108.

75. Egan, "New York," pp. 15-16.

76. Desmond, *A Political Biography*, p. 184.

77. Egan, "New York," p. 16.

78. Ibid.

79. Chester, *Radio, Television*, p. 108.

80. Reports appeared in *New York Times* on September 23, October 22, October 30, and November 6, 1962.

81. Richard Donnelly, "How to Turn a Race Around," *Television Magazine* (December 1966), p. 23.

82. Interview with William Pfeiffer.

83. Gene Wycoff, *The Image Candidates* (New York: MacMillan Co., 1968), p. 230.

84. Robert MacNeil, *The People Machine*, p. 211.

85. Perry, *The New Politics*, p. 121.

86. Ibid.

87. Ibid., pp. 107-8.

88. Powledge, "Marketing of Rockefeller," p. 43.

89. Ibid., p. 49.

90. Michael Kramer and Sam Roberts, *"I Never Wanted to be 'Vice' President of 'Anything': An Investigative Biography* (New York: Basic Books, 1976), p. 172.

91. See, for example, *New York Times*, September 27, 1962, p. 1; September 29, 1962, p. 48; October 3, 1962, p. 31; and October 9, 1962, p. 24.

92. Daniel J. Mahoney, *Actions Speak Louder Than Words* (New York: Arlington House, 1968), pp. 53-54.

93. See, for example, *New York Times*, September 20, 1966, p. 74; September 27, 1966, p. 1; October 7, 1966, p. 27; October 21, 1966, p. 31.

94. Perry, *The New Politics*, p. 107.

95. Ibid., p. 128.

96. Ibid., pp. 130-31.

97. As quoted in MacNeil, *The People Machine*, p. 217.

98. *Time Magazine*, October 14, 1970, p. 19.

99. *New York Times*, October 13, 1970, p. 10; October 20, 1970, p. 1.

100. *New York Times*, October 17, 1970, p. 14.

101. *New York Times*, October 29, 1970, p. 1.

102. Kramer and Roberts, *Vice President*, pp. 174-77.

103. As quoted in *New York Times*, October 11, 1974.

104. *New York Times*, October 10, 11, 1974.

105. *New York Times*, October 13, 1974, p. 1.

106. U.S. Congress, House, Committee on the Judiciary, *Hearings on the Nomination of Nelson A. Rockefeller to be Vice President of the United States*, 93rd Cong., 2d sess., 1974, p. 95.

107. Kramer and Roberts, *Vice-President*, p. 175.

108. Statement by Basil Patterson, Democratic nominee for Lt. Governor in 1970 as quoted in Powledge, "Marketing of Rockefeller," p. 39.

109. *New York Times*, November 28, 1970, p. 24.

110. The 1958 media expenditures were approximately one-half of Rockefeller's campaign expenses. See *New York Times*, October 25, 1958, p. 23.

111. Perry, *The New Politics*, p. 107.

112. Ibid., pp. 107-8.

113. See, for example, Peirce, *The Megastates*, p. 25.

114. Interview with Thomas Wallace, assistant secretary of state, Schenectady, New York, March 31, 1980.

115. *New York Times*, October 27, 1970, p. 38.

116. *New York Times*, August 5, 1973, p. 1.

117. Connery and Benjamin, *Rockefeller of New York*, p. 59.

118. *New York Times*, August 5, 1973, p. 1, and interview with Thomas Wallace.

119. *New York Times*, August 5, 1973, p. 1.

120. *Empire State Report* (April 1977), p. 142.

121. John J. Gargan, "Nelson Rockefeller and New York State Electoral Politics: 1958-1970," Kent State University, Center for Urban Regionalism, 1972, p. 10.

122. Ira Sharkansky, *The United States: A Study of a Developing Country* (New York: David McKay Co., 1975), p. 55.

123. Connery and Benjamin, *Rockefeller of New York*, p. 41.

124. Richard L. Rubin, *Party Dynamics: The Democratic Coalition and the Politics of Change* (New York: Oxford University Press, 1976), p. 73.

125. Ibid.
126. Ibid., p. 76.
127. See Kramer and Roberts, *Vice President*, pp. 346-50.
128. Ibid.
129. See generally Richard L. Rubin, *Party Dynamics*, p. 76 and Kramer and Roberts, *Vice President*, p. 347.
130. Kramer and Roberts, *Vice-President*, p. 347.
131. Ibid., pp. 348-50.
132. Frank Gervasi, *The Real Rockefeller* (New York: Atheneum Publishers, 1964), p. 19.
133. Connery and Benjamin, *Rockefeller of New York*, p. 44.
134. William B. Hasseltine, *Third Party Movements in American Politics* (Princeton: D. Van Nostrand Co., 1962), p. 99.
135. George Thayer, *The Farther Shores of Politics* (New York: Simon and Schuster, 1967), p. 451.
136. Mahoney, *Actions Speak Louder*, chapter 1.
137. Kevin P. Phillips, *The Emerging Republican Majority* (New Rochelle: Arlington House, 1969), p. 74.
138. Dick Behn, "Liberals and Conservatives: The Importance of New York's Two 'Third' Parties," *Empire State Report* (April 1977), p. 164.
139. Ibid.
140. Ibid., p. 165.
141. *New York Times*, October 30, 1962, p. 1.
142. See, for example, *Newsweek*, May 14, 1962, p. 32.
143. *New York Times*, September 21, 1962, p. 17.
144. *New York Times*, October 24, 1962, p. 33.
145. *Time Magazine*, April 28, 1961, p. 18.
146. *New York Times*, November 2, 1970, p. 1.
147. Kramer and Roberts, *Vice President*, p. 346.
148. John J. Gargan, "Toward an 'Explanation' of New York State Politics" (Paper prepared for delivery at the 1975 meeting of the Northeastern Political Science Association at Rutgers University), p. 9.
149. Ibid.
150. Gargan, "Electoral Politics," p. 13.
151. For example, see Gervasi, *The Real Rockefeller*, and Kramer and Roberts, *Vice President*, p. 3.
152. Gervasi, *The Real Rockefeller*, p. 19.
153. Inaugural Address of Governor Nelson A. Rockefeller, January 12, 1959.
154. Ibid.
155. Resignation speech, December 11, 1973, State of New York, *Public Papers of Nelson A. Rockefeller, Fifty-third Governor of the State of New York, 1973*, p. 1371.
156. Kramer and Roberts, *Vice-President*, p. 364.
157. Behn, "Liberals and Conservatives," p. 146.
158. Theodore H. White, *The Making of the President 1968* (New York: Atheneum Publishers, 1969), p. 227.
159. Connery and Benjamin, *Rockefeller of New York*, pp. 71-76.
160. Ibid.

161. Garry Wills, *Nixon Agonistes: The Crisis of the Self-Made Man* (New York: The New American Library, 1969), p. 227.

162. Ibid., p. 405.

163. White, *Making of the President 1968,* p. 227.

164. Theodore H. White, *The Making of the President 1964* (New York: the New American Library, 1965), p. 81.

165. As quoted in Morris, *Nelson Rockefeller*, p. 318.

166. White, *Making of the President 1968*, pp. 224-25.

167. Garry Wills, *Nixon Agonistes*, p. 226.

168. Theodore H. White, *The Making of the President 1960* (New York: Atheneum House, 1961), p. 76.

169. Steinberg, *Campaign Management*, p. 171.

170. *Congressional Quarterly*, August 9, 1968, p. 2096.

171. White, *Making of the President 1960*, p. 73.

172. Ibid., p. 132.

173. Ibid.

174. Steinberg, *Campaign Management*, p. 171.

175. Kramer and Roberts, *Vice-President*, p. 7.

176. Gervasi, *The Real Rockefeller*, p. 261.

177. *Congressional Quarterly*, May 17, 1968, p. 1141.

178. White, *Making of the President 1960*, pp. 182-83.

179. *Public Papers 1963*, pp. 853-57. Rockefeller lost the nomination to Richard Nixon in 1960 and again in 1968 but offered a nominating speech in Nixon's behalf in August of 1972. In 1958 he had noted that he was seeking the nomination of his party for Governor because New York needed a person who could grasp opportunities, had political courage, ideas, creative talent, and faith in the future. In his speech in 1972, he praised Richard Nixon's first term in office as demonstrating experienced handling of staggering problems, new initiatives, new programs, and bold action. He noted that Nixon's skill at governmental management and leadership had produced high confidence in America at home and abroad.

180. Remarks at a dinner in New Hampshire Highway Hotel, Concord, New Hampshire, January 24, 1964. *Public Papers 1964*, p. 1231-32.

181. Kramer and Roberts, *Vice President*, pp. 375-76.

182. Kennedy, "Rocky is 64," p. 60.

183. *Empire State Report*, p. 146.

184. White, *Making of the President 1964*, p. 73.

185. Kennedy, "Rocky is 64," p. 61.

Chapter 4

1. Interview with Nelson A.Rockefeller, New York City, November 16, 1977.

2. The role of legislative leaders is discussed in Chapter 5 in the context of the Governor's efforts to achieve adoption of his legislative proposals.

3. One close associate of the Governor, Oscar Ruebhausen, commented that "working with people relaxed him." Interview with Oscar Ruebhausen, New York City, June 1, 1978.

4. Interview with Alan Miller, former commissioner of mental hygiene, Albany,

New York, May 17, 1978. Richard Dunham, former director of the budget, said that the Governor's top staff members had immediate access to him by phone at any time, including the middle of the night, except for the period from noon Saturday to Sunday evening. Because that time was reserved for "family," access was restricted to near emergencies. Interview, Albany, New York, July 6, 1979. He also devoted great time and energy to art, primarily to building and managing his invaluable collection. Oscar Ruebhausen testified that the Governor's involvement with art also served to "relax him." But as his later venture into the retailing of art reproductions was to illustrate, his pleasure in art was intertwined with art as work. In September of 1978 his company, the Nelson Rockefeller Collection Inc., began marketing reproductions of approximately 100 art objects in his personal collection. By the time of his death early in 1979, the business was reported to have grossed over $900,000. During the last year or two of his life, Mr. Rockefeller immersed himself deeply in this venture and the publication of four major "art books" plus his memoirs as a collector. For accounts of these activities, see *Albany Knickerbocker News*, October 4, 1978; *New York Daily News*, February 14, 1979; *New York Times*, Feburary 10, 1979; and *Time*, November 13, 1978, p. 101.

5. Lyndon Johnson is a good example of another official who "lived his job" and had few other diversions. However, unlike Rockefeller, Johnson as president increasingly came to complain about his burdens. We uncovered absolutely no evidence that Rockefeller was a complainer or even a compulsive worker. On the contrary, he gave every evidence of genuinely enjoying the job of being Governor. In this respect he fits Barber's "active-positive" category. See James David Barber, *The Presidential Character: Predicting Performance in the White House*,. 2d ed. (Englewood Cliffs: Prentice-Hall, 1977), parts one and four.

6. Interview with Wallace K. Harrison, New York City, June 1, 1978. William Pfeiffer, a close friend of the Governor, and director of Rockefeller's campaign in 1962 and 1966, said that he would not have been willing to work for Rockefeller on a regular basis "because you aren't your own man. You have to be at his beck and call *always*. He did not mean to be unreasonable, but he expected you to come when he asked." Interview with William Pfeiffer, Albany, New York, September 24, 1979. Another close associate, Attorney General Louis Lefkowitz, noted that Rockefeller would often summon top advisers to his home or New York City office to work on major holidays such as Christmas or New Years. Interview, Albany, New York, June 6, 1977.

7. The Governor himself listed the following qualities as the four that he valued most highly in top staff aides and agency heads: integrity, experience, leadership and administrative ability, and loyalty. Interview with Nelson A. Rockefeller.

8. Interview with Richard Wiebe, former assistant secretary for Program and director of the Office of Planning Services, Albany, New York, June 15, 1978.

9. Interview with Nelson A. Rockefeller.

10. U.S., Congress, Senate, Committee on Rules and Administration, *Hearings on Nomination of Nelson A. Rockefeller to be Vice President of the United States*, 93rd Cong., 2d sess., 1974, p. 559.

11. Interview with Milton Musicus, former assistant secretary to the Governor for administration, Albany, New York, March 9, 1975.

12. Interview with Alan Miller.

13. The description is contained in a statement the Governor submitted to the committees considering his nomination to be vice president. That statement listed gifts and loans made to a large number of persons who had been public servants at or near the time the gifts were made. U.S. Congress, House, Committee on the Judiciary, *Hearings on Nomination of Nelson A. Rockefeller to be Vice President of the United States*, 93rd Cong., 2d sess., 1974, pp. 36-39. Between the period 1958 and 1974, William Ronan received a total of $625,000 in gifts and loans. The loans were forgiven in 1974. For relevant materials, see House hearings cited above, Senate Committee on Rules and Administration, *Hearings on Nomination of Nelson A. Rockefeller*, and *New York Times*, October 29, November 19, 24, 1974.

14. Interview with Nelson A. Rockefeller.

15. All but the budget director were located in the organizational unit known as the Executive Chamber, an office roughly comparable to the White House Office at the national level. The Division of the Budget is located in the state agency known as the Executive Department and is directly responsible to the Governor. However, unlike personnel serving within the Executive Chamber, all personnel in the division are civil servants except for a few top-level officials who are appointed by the director, the latter himself an appointee of the Governor.

16. When talking about his five key staff positions, the Governor referred to the secretary as "the chief administrative officer of the staff." Interview with Nelson A. Rockefeller.

There were four secretaries to the Governor during Rockefeller's tenure. William Ronan served first, from 1959 to 1965. Immediately prior to his selection as executive director of the Commission on the New York State Constitutional Convention, Ronan was first deputy administrator for New York City, a post he had held from July of 1965 until his selection as executive director. Earlier he had been dean of N.Y.U.'s Graduate School of Public Administration. He had also been director of the state's little Hoover Commission. He was succeeded by Alton G. Marshall who held the position of secretary from 1966 to 1970. Marshall had been secretary of the Public Service Commission (1953-1960), deputy director of the Division of the Budget (1961-1965), and executive officer to the Governor (1965-1966).

When Marshall resigned in 1970, the responsibilities for internal and external affairs were separated. At this time, Robert Douglass, formerly counsel to the Governor (1965-1970), was designated as secretary to the Governor (for external affairs), and T. Norman Hurd, who had been director of the Division of the Budget (1959-1970), was chosen as the director of Governmental Operations (for internal affairs). Among the duties assigned to Douglass were to monitor and supervise the Governor's relationships with the legislature, local governments, political parties, and New York State's Washington office. Hurd was to be the Governor's link with state agencies and to serve as supervisor of the activities of the program associates.
When Robert Douglass left state service in 1972, the two positions were again merged, and T. Norman Hurd became the fourth secretary to the Governor. However, Hurd's organization of his own staff retained a structure based on the "internal"—"external" distinction.

17. Although independently elected officials, Lieutenant Governor Malcolm Wilson and Attorney General Louis Lefkowitz played important roles in the ad-

ministration. Both attended many formal meetings of top staff in addition to having numerous informal contacts with the Governor. (Wilson spent a lot of time with the Governor on the campaign circuit. Because Lefkowitz lived near the Governor's New York City apartment, he and the Governor spent time together traveling back and forth to airports.) Because of their respective positions, Lefkowitz was called upon for legal advice, and Wilson was utilized in dealing with legislative and budget matters. As lieutenant governor, Wilson was presiding officer of the state senate. Both were consulted on political matters. Interview with Louis Lefkowitz, Albany, New York, June 6, 1977, and interview with Malcolm Wilson, New York City, April 27, 1977. The Governor's calendar for 1966 shows that he held 136 meetings at which his own staff were the principle attendees. The secretary to the Governor was present at all of those meetings, the counsel at approximately 60 percent, the budget director and lieutenant governor at about 20 percent, and the attorney general at about 15 percent. This data confirms the impressions we gained from respondents concerning which officials worked most closely with the Governor. The calendar of appointments was made available to us by Hugh Morrow, former director of communications in the Rockefeller administration.

18. Interview with William Ronan, New York City, June 13, 1972.

19. Interview with Alton Marshall, New York City, August 28, 1971.

20. A man with extensive high-level staff experience both in the state legislature and the Budget Division noted the consequence of having Budget Division personnel analyze program ideas, a practice common in the Harriman administration. "Even though the particular personnel involved were not 'budget types,' they did analyze from a fiscal point of view. The effect of using this budget unit for analysis of program proposals was to help kill ideas." Interview with Howard Miller, deputy director of the Division of the Budget, Albany, New York, May 2, 1972.

21. Interview with a member of the Governor's staff.

22. U.S. Congress, Senate, Committee on Government Operations, Subcommittee on National Policy Machinery, *Hearings on Organizing for National Security*, part 7, 86th Cong., 2d sess., 1960, pp. 964-65.

23. Ibid.

24. Rockefeller's proposal represented the culmination of the work of the President's Advisory Committee on Government Organization, a group which he chaired from its creation in 1953 until he was elected Governor. For a discussion of this group's work as it related to the Executive Office of the President and in particular the Bureau of the Budget, see Larry Berman, "The Office of Management and Budget that Almost Wasn't: How the Bureau of the Budget Fought to Remain the BOB," paper prepared for delivery at the Annual Meeting of the American Political Science Association, Chicago, September 2-5, 1976, 46 pp.

25. Berman, Office of Management and Budget, p. 7.

26. Two officials in the Harriman administration, an administration that operated without a unit comparable to a program staff, later looked back upon their experience with the state's bureaucracy from the following perspective: "The theme running through each of the events [that we discuss] is the difficulty of change: the difficulty of devising new programs, of financing them, of winning support for them, of implementing them," Clark D. Ahlberg and Daniel P. Moynihan, "Chang-

ing Governors and Policies," *Public Administration Review* (Autumn, 1960): 195.

27. During the fifteen years Nelson Rockefeller was Governor of New York, twenty-two persons served as program associates. Sixteen of the twenty-two had been employed in government-related positions immediately prior to their selection. A wide variety of prior government-related experiences was represented among program staff members. For example, three had been members of the Governor's 1958 campaign staff, four had been serving in positions as New York State public administration interns or trainees, three had been staff members under William Ronan on the Temporary State Commission on the New York Constitutional Convention, and three were in entry-level positions with the Division of the Budget. Program associates had responsibility for an "average" of three so-called "functional areas." For example, in the middle 1960s when there were five members of the program staff, the areas of responsibility were divided as follows: program associate A was responsible for the functional area of education (all levels); B, public employment, and banking and industry; C, labor and conservation; D, transportation, and intergovernmental relations; E, health, mental health, social services, and narcotics. As a result of having designated areas of responsibility, program associates did develop expertise in particular functional areas; however, they were not rigidly confined to these areas. This data was developed primarily through interviews with program associates.

28. As already noted, Ronan initially conceived the institution of the program staff with the goal of helping the Governor implement his campaign promises. Becoming secretary in 1966, Alton Marshall was perhaps the most committed believer in the efficacy of big government of those who served as secretary. Having developed a reputation as an aggressive administrator as secretary to the Public Service Commission, he was made deputy director of the budget by the Governor in 1961. The expectation was that he would be an active and positive force in an agency the Governor and William Ronan viewed as biased against innovative and costly programs. The two individuals who served as secretary during the last three years of the administration, Robert Douglass and T. Norman Hurd, were not as strongly oriented toward matters of policy and program. Douglass, previously counsel to the Governor, was more inclined toward a concern with political matters and legislative matters. Previously director of the budget, Hurd was known as an excellent budget technician and efficient administrator, but did not share Ronan and Marshall's bent for policy innovation.

29. Interview with William Ronan.

30. If thorough "staffing-out" of an idea preceded a decision to include a proposal in the Governor's legislative program, the result might be a recommendation that the proposal not be advanced. However, decisions to advance a proposal were sometimes made before a thorough staffing-out was performed. In such cases staffing-out would be performed after the fact and could not form the basis for rejecting a proposal.

31. Interview with William Ronan. Some of those we interviewed noted that in the course of "costing-out" proposed programs, the staff of the Budget Division sometimes contributed ideas on how to go about putting together a program. Also, the initiation of the Program Analysis and Review system in 1970 enlarged the

Budget Division's role in program-related matters. However, the emphasis in PAR was on improving existing programs rather than the development of new ones. For a description of PAR, see State of New York, Executive Department, *Guidelines for Program Analysis and Review*, June 1970.

32. Interview with a senior staff member of the Division of the Budget during the Rockefeller administration, Albany, New York.

33. Telephone interview with a former program associate, August 1, 1975.

34. This was a fairly common occurrence for a program associate. While less common, there were cases in which an assistant counsel in the Office of the Counsel to the Governor played a similar role. Such cases usually involved a program in which legal problems were a prime consideration.

35. John Kessel found the same thing to be true of the role of the Domestic Council, a staff unit similar to the program staff which existed in the Nixon and Ford administrations. See *The Domestic Presidency: Decision-Making in the White House* (North Scituate: Duxbury, 1975), pp. 82, 102.

36. The office was responsible for preparing the memoranda which the Governor issued upon approving or vetoing pieces of legislation.

37. In some cases, drafting legislation was a routine matter. However, policy questions, major legal problems, or questions involving the likelihood of opposition by legislative leaders or the public sometimes emerged. In general, the Counsel's Office was more heavily involved in getting the Governor's program through the legislature than was the program staff. However, the secretary to the Governor played a key role in this task.

38. Interview with Richard Dunham, Albany, New York, July 6, 1979. One policy area in which the Budget Division did play a significant role in policy questions was that of education. This is evident from the testimony of officials both inside and outside the Division.

39. Generally speaking, program associates were not to recommend against programs on the basis of cost. As one program associate said, "We never thought about whether there was money for programs." Interview with John Garrison, Albany, New York, May 1972.

40. Following his overwhelming reelection victory of 1970, the Governor submitted a budget in January of 1971 calling for $8.45 billion in expenditures. Because of legislative opposition, the Governor was eventually forced to accept a budget of only $7.7 billion. Tight financial conditions during the remainder of his term caused him to reduce the rate of growth in state expenditures.

41. Interview with senior staff member, Division of the Budget, Albany, New York, May 2, 1972.

42. Robert Connery and Gerald Benjamin, *Rockefeller of New York: Executive Power in the State House* (Ithaca: Cornell University Press, 1979), p. 136. The Governor also employed speech writers on his personal payroll. For example, Emmet Hughes, a former Eisenhower speech writer, worked for Rockefeller in drafting speeches in connection with the latter's attempts to capture the Republican presidential nomination. See Theodore White, *The Making of the President 1960* (New York: Atheneum House, 1961), chapter 7.

43. Interview with Nelson A. Rockefeller.

44. Connery and Benjamin, *Rockefeller of New York*, p. 71.

45. Rockefeller occasionally chose Democrats to fill key positions. One example is his appointment of Joseph Swidler to be chairman of the Public Service Commission in 1970. However, he generally accepted the need to cooperate with the needs of Republican party officials.

46. Connery and Benjamin note that the Governor conducted as many as eighteen "town meetings" in a single series. *Rockefeller of New York*, p. 146.

47. At about the same time the comprehensive PPBS system was largely abandoned and replaced by a more modest system focusing on the analysis of selected issues. That system was PAR (Program Analysis and Review).

48. The state constitution limits the number of state departments to twenty. *Constitution of the State of New York* Article V, Section Two. However, one of the twenty departments, the Executive Department, is in one sense a "paper" department which serves as a kind of organizational umbrella for a variety of units. This department, headed by the Governor, also includes the Executive Chamber (the Governor's equivalent of the President's White House Office) and key staff units such as the Division of the Budget and the Office of General Services. Among the remaining departments, two—Audit and Control and Civil Service—are more properly classified as staff agencies than as line agencies).

49. Although they concede him some success in revitalizing agencies through reorganization and in making them more responsive to his goals, Connery and Benjamin emphasize the difficulty Rockefeller had in achieving quick results through reorganization. *Rockefeller of New York*, pp. 160-88.

50. Because most authorities were "public benefit corporations" with the power to finance their operations by issuing bonds, they were not dependent on appropriations to the same degree that other state agencies were. See Chapter 6 for a more detailed discussion of the device of the public benefit corporation.

51. Annemarie Hauck Walsh presents a detailed analysis of Rockefeller's appointment of close associates and advisers to authority boards. *The Public's Business: The Politics and Practices of Government Corporations* (Cambridge: The MIT Press, 1978), pp. 267-72.

52. Interview with William Ronan.

53. Interview with Alton Marshall.

54. Interviews with senior staff in the Governor's office and the Health Department.

55. The Department of Education and its legislatively elected governing board, the Board of Regents, often "went public" in order to resist the Governor. For example, they opposed the Governor's proposal for an "education inspector general." In addition, each year they would conduct a media campaign on behalf of the budget requests they submitted to the Governor. No other agency dared to oppose the Governor in such an open fashion.

56. Lewis A. Dexter, "Court Politics: Presidential Staff Relations as a Special Case of a General Phenomenon," *Administration and Society* (November 1977): 268. Among other reasons for the development of a court, Dexter cites the availability of "surplus resources," e.g., contingency funds, flexible hiring authority, as well as the capacity to confer prestige which normally accrue to a chief executive.

However, the key motivation of the chief executive is to build a "personal team" which can assist him in the very difficult task of assuring that his policies really get implemented, p. 269. Anthony Downs has a good discussion of the phenomenon of personal loyalty among top level officials and their immediate staffs. *Inside Bureaucracy* (Boston: Little Brown, 1967), pp. 67-68.

57. Dexter believes it very difficult for a cabinet officer to serve as an effective "courtier," or member of a chief executive's personal team. As he sees it, the danger is that a cabinet official will become excessively oriented toward administration and task performance at the expense of service to the chief executive. "Court Politics," p. 270.

58. Interview with Alan Miller. Realizing this, Miller says that he began to "speak to Rockefeller's head, not to him as a person."

59. Some persons who served in staff positions concluded, mistakenly we believe, that Rockefeller had no real friends. However, it is clear that he was *friendly* with some people out of necessity. As one senior aid put it, "He could put his arms around any SOB who could get him what he wanted. Somewhere he developed a practical tolerance for people. He kept his feelings to himself." Interview with senior aide, Washington, D.C., February 17, 1978. One of Rockefeller's genuine friends noted that the former was "wary of people" and had very few friends he "trusted implicitly." Interview with William Pfeiffer.

60. Marshall confessed that he was not a confidant of the Governor in the "bull-shitting-ride-the-plane sense." Telephone interview, February 16, 1979. Numerous observers have commented on Douglass's warm relationship with the Governor. Kramer and Roberts say that "he practically became a member of the Rockefeller family." Michael Kramer and Sam Roberts, *I Never wanted to be Vice President of Anything: An Investigative Biography of Nelson Rockefeller* (New York: Basic Books, 1976), p. 128. For some time Douglass lived on the Rockefeller estate at Pocantico Hills. When he left his post as secretary, Douglass returned to private practice with a firm that represents the Rockefeller family's bank, Chase Manhattan.

61. Telephone interview with Alton Marshall.

62. The determination of who were personal friends and professional friends was made on the basis of interviews with a variety of persons, some of whom were themselves members of the Governor's personal team and some of whom were merely in a position to closely observe the dimensions of that team, and descriptions of those persons to whom he had made gifts and/or loans while he was Governor. See House Judiciary Committee, *Hearings on the Nomination of Nelson A. Rockefeller*, pp. 36-39.

63. In the majority of cases, the Governor's associates merely served him in an informal capacity. However, in some cases personal friends and advisers served in state jobs or on task forces set up by the Governor. For example, George Dudley served as the head of a number of state agencies, among them the Office of Regional Development. Both Borella and Robinson served on the Governor's staff as special assistants. Some members of the personal team, Free and Kissinger, for example, were paid directly by Rockefeller. In particular, Kissinger was paid consultants fees by Rockefeller "in his personal capacity," as the former stated in an affadavit submitted to the Senate Committee on Rules and Administration. From 1958

through 1968 the fees to Mr. Kissinger came to $141,750. House Judiciary Committee, *Nomination of Nelson A. Rockefeller*, pp. 882-83. Some also served on assorted boards, councils, and commissions, positions which were part-time in nature. For example, Hinman was a trustee of the State University.

64. An examination of the Governor's appointment book for 1966 reveals that Rockefeller had at least one appointment with most of the outside members of his personal team who are cited here.

65. Interview with Nelson A. Rockefeller.

66. Ronan received his first gift, $75,000, in 1958 before he was a state employee. The remaining gifts were made during a short period in 1974 during which he held no state position. In an apparent effort to minimize potential concerns over possible violations of state laws forbidding gifts to public officials, the Governor gave Ronan a gift of $40,000 and forgave outstanding loans of $150,000 on May 3, 1974, two days after the latter's resignation as chairman of the Metropolitan Transportation Authority and less than two weeks before he began a term on the board of the Power Authority of the State of New York. Revelation of the gifts and loans to Ronan and other individuals caused criticism at the hearings on Rockefeller's nomination to be vice-president. See House Judiciary Committee, *Hearings on Nomination of Nelson A. Rockefeller*; Senate Committee on Rules and Administration, *Hearings on Nomination of Nelson A. Rockefeller*; and *New York Times*, October 29, November 19, 24, 1974.

67. *New York Times*, November 19, 1974.

68. Kramer and Roberts, *Vice-President*, pp. 127-28.

69. *New York Times*, October 29, 1974.

70. Senate Committee on Rules and Administration, *Hearings on Nomination of Nelson A. Rockefeller*, pp. 644, 882-83.

71. Kramer and Roberts, *Vice-President*, p. 130.

72. The statutes are Laws of New York 1965, chapter 1030 and Laws of New York 1965, chapter 1012. The legal brief that the Governor submitted, "Legality of Loans and Gifts by Nelson A. Rockefeller to Members of his Staff and to Other State Employees," is found in Senate Committee on Rules and Administration, *Hearings on Nomination of Nelson A. Rockefeller*, pp. 674-87.

73. Senate Committee on Rules and Administration, *Hearings on Nomination of Nelson A. Rockefeller*, p. 928.

74. Mr. Ronan's part-time job with the Power Authority paid $12,000 per year. As of 1974, he was eligible for retirement benefits of $30,000 per year. *New York Times*, November 19, 1974.

75. Interview with Russell Oswald, Albany, New York, August 16, 1977.

76. Interview with senior state official, Albany, New York, May 15, 1978.

77. *Albany Knickerbocker News*, February 3, 1979.

78. Ibid. In these respects also, Rockefeller closely resembles James Barber's "active-positive" president. Such a president "connects with other people, stimulating their interest, invigorating their own positive imaginations. From some he may elicit a 'charismatic' response; for nearly all he supplies a sense that he is at the center of fascinating events and that the center is moving." *Presidential Character*, p. 211.

79. Interview with Oscar Ruebhausen.

80. Interview with Michael Whiteman, Albany, New York, April 28, 1979.

81. Meetings with legislative leaders are discussed in Chapter 5. Those who observed Rockefeller at meetings were sure that he enjoyed his role in them. As one former agency head said, "He liked an audience, he liked to have people see him perform." Interview with Alan Miller.

82. Interview with John Moore, former assistant to the Governor for graphics. Delmar, New York, June 28, 1977. Although Moore's work did not involve the substance of program development, he was given the title of Program Associate when he was hired in 1959. Although he later left the Governor's staff to work in the Office of Regional Development and the Office of Planning Coordination, he continued to serve the Governor personally as his chief graphics specialist until 1972.

83. For example, as noted before, the Governor had 136 meetings in 1966 at which top staff members were the primary attendees.

84. Not included in the latter figure are twenty-one appointments with his personal physician, Kenneth Riland, a man who was a member of the personal team.

85. As noted, Louis Lefkowitz often traveled with the Governor to and from the airport. Both he and Malcolm Wilson spent time campaigning with the Governor. These two and William Ronan had rooms in the executive mansion, the Governor's residence while in Albany. One commissioner, Alan Miller, came to know the Governor while on a trip to Latin America sponsored by the U.S. Department of State. Some commissioners used social gatherings at the executive mansion as a way to get the Governor's ear.

86. Interview with Henry Diamond, Washington, D.C., February 14, 1978.

87. Interview with Nelson A. Rockefeller. Dr. Carrel was a scientist at Rockefeller Institute who won the Nobel Prize for Medicine in 1912. In 1935 he published *Man and the Unknown*, which included his views on the nature of man and the development of his capacities. (New York: Halcyon House, 1935). Rockefeller met Dr. Carrel in 1939. Telephone conversation with Hugh Morrow, April 8, 1980.

88. Interview with Louis Lefkowitz.

89. Interview with Nelson A. Rockefeller.

90. Conversation with T. Norman Hurd, Albany, New York, April 2, 1979.

91. All those departments headed by appointees of the Governor were required to channel legislation they wanted to propose through the legislative clearance procedure operated by the counsel's office. Some departments, usually those with strong constituency support, occasionally did an "end-run" around the counsel's office. For example, while stating for the record that "we do not make end-runs. One can get in trouble that way, you can lose your job," a senior official in the Department of Health acknowledged that the department would give independent assistance to legislators who introduced bills for which the department could not manage to acquire clearance. Interview with a senior official of the Department of Health, Albany, New York, June 8, 1972.

92. Illustrative of the range of agency "productivity" as a source of ideas were the eight agencies for which one program associate had responsibility. He rated two of the agencies as "very good" sources of ideas, three as "fair," and three as "poor." Interview with a former program associate, Albany, New York, May 25, 1978. Because program associates served as an important link between various professional associates and interest groups and the Governor's office, they were familiar with the sorts of ideas that such groups wanted to promote.

93. The description given of the process of developing the substance of the annual message is, we think, accurate as to the broad outlines of the process. However, we realize that the details of procedure vary to some degree over time.

94. The counsel had three options in dealing with legislation proposed by departments. He could: decline a department's request to include a particular bill in its legislative program, grant a department permission to include a particular bill in its legislative program, or recommend to the annual message group that a bill in a department's proposed legislative program be included instead in the Governor's legislative program. In the case of the last option, staff in the counsel's office would be responsible for preparing the program sheets for the annual message group.

95. Several types of temporary study groups were created during the Rockefeller administration. They include temporary state commissions set up by the legislature, publicly announced task forces created by the Governor, and informal task forces. Only those of the last type ever consisted wholly of in-house personnel. Temporary state commissions were created by legislative action, but appointments were made jointly by the Governor and legislative leaders.

96. A former commissioner of the Department of Environmental Conservation said, "he not only used temporary commissions as political devices, he firmly believed in them. He used them as learning devices as well. This practice goes back to the 1950s with the Rockefeller Brothers Panel Reports." Interview with Henry Diamond.

97. Interview with William Ronan. In the first year or two of the administration, heavy use of the task force device backfired by creating hostility among legislative leaders. Some legislators felt that such groups were preempting a traditional legislative role. Our tabulation, based on a wide variety of official and unofficial sources, shows that a total of 107 publicly announced study groups were created over the course of the administration. (This tabulation excludes all "temporary State commissions" except those whose chairman was appointed by the Governor.) Former members of the Governor's staff estimate that more than forty groups, some never publicized, were created in the first year of the administration alone.

98. Interview with William Sharkey, former program associate, Delmar, New York, October 24, 1972.

99. Interview with John Garrison, former program associate, Albany, New York, May 1972. Our impression is that the sentiment underlying this assertion was shared by most program associates. In large part their job was to find solutions that would be acceptable to the Governor.

100. Two program associates played key roles in the Governor's campaign for the Republican party's presidential nomination in 1964.

101. One former Budget Division official referred derisively to the campaign component of the program innovation process as "program planning by press release." Interview with a former senior official of the Division of the Budget, Albany, New York, February 13, 1974.

102. Dr. Norman Hurd has acknowledged that the program staff was a source of more ideas than was the Budget Division. His estimate of the proportion of program ideas contributed by various participants was as follows: Governor—30 percent; program staff—20 percent; temporary state commissions (bodies whose members were usually chosen jointly by the Governor and legislative leaders)—15 percent;

departments—15 percent; counsel's office—10 percent; Budget Division—10 percent. Interview, May 24, 1972. When we speak of the source of a program idea, we refer to whoever advanced an idea for inclusion in the Governor's legislative package.

103. Interview with Nelson A. Rockefeller.

104. Interview with George Dudley.

105. There were at least two kinds of exceptions to this general rule. First, the Governor and his staff pressed hard to ensure that agencies launched the Governor's new programs and produced ideas for new programs.

106. Interview with Nelson A. Rockefeller.

107. Senate Committee on Government Operations, Subcommittee on National Policy Machinery, *Hearings on Organizing for National Security*, pp. 999-1000.

108. Because of his belief in the efficacy of visual aids and because of his personal fascination with them, Rockefeller often became personally involved with the design of charts and graphs. The high priority which he assigned to such work is reflected in the fact that he personally interviewed and selected the man who served as his "chart man." Interview with John Moore. Moore was the only person with the title of program associate who was personally selected by the Governor.

109. The program was funded. Interview with Russell Oswald.

110. Interview with Alan Miller.

111. Interview with a former agency head.

112. Nelson A. Rockefeller, untitled statement in Emmet John Hughes, *The Living Presidency* (New York: Penguin Books, 1974), pp. 356-57.

113. Interview with Ewald Nyquist, former commissioner of education, Albany, New York, August 11, 1977. According to one account, it was apparent that Nyquist and others at the conference had not been well-briefed on the program. See *New York Times*, February 25, 1970.

114. Although the Education Department is formally independent of the Governor, it is subject to his budgetary powers, which are considerable. Requests to the legislature for appropriations for the department are made by the Governor in his Executive Budget. This is one reason why the department must maintain a reasonable working relationship with him. This fact, coupled with the fact that few departments would reject a Governor's offer of a new program and necessary financing, make it very unlikely that the commissioner would have balked at the Governor's lack of advance consultation on his drug proposal.

115. The Governor's position in New York is considered to be one of the very strongest among the states. See Joseph A. Schlesinger, "The Politics of the Executive," in Herbert Jacob and Kenneth N. Vines, *Politics in the American States: A Comparative Analysis* (Boston: Little Brown and Co., 1965), pp. 207-37. Connery and Benjamin note that Rockefeller minimized the potential problems inherent in the independence of the departments of Law and Audit and Control by making the attorney general a member of his team and by using Norman Hurd to establish good working relations with Comptroller Arthur Levitt. Connery and Benjamin, *Rockefeller of New York*, p. 162.

116. Frustration with the Education Department and its perceived failings eventually led Rockefeller to create a "watch dog agency" to evaluate the department's performance. Creation of the agency, the Office of Education Performance Review,

was the subject of heated controversy. As the former commissioner of education admitted, the Governor created the office in spite of vigorous opposition by him and the department's governing body, the Board of Regents. Interview with Ewald Nyquist. When the legislature failed to approved creation of the office, the Governor created it by means of an executive order signed on July 1, 1973. State of New York, *Public Papers of Nelson A. Rockefeller, Fifty-Third Governor of the State of New York, 1973*, p. 996.

117. Interview with Richard Dunham.

118. The Governor attributed McCrate's foot-dragging to the latter's friendship with James Allen, then commissioner of education. Allen and the Board of Regents resisted expansion of the State University partly because the latter had substantial independence from the regents. Unlike the regents, the Board of Trustees of the State University was appointed by the Governor.

119. Interview with Nelson A. Rockefeller.

120. Ibid.

121. Ibid.

122. Interview with former senior members of the Governor's staff. The Governor was capable of springing surprises on Marshall. One former member of the Governor's staff relates that Marshall was outraged when he discovered that the Governor had appointed his long-time associate George Dudley to be head of the Pure Waters Authority. Interview with a former member of the Governor's staff.

123. Lewis Lapham, "Victory for the Big, Dumb Money," *Harpers*, February 1975, p. 40.

124. Kramer and Roberts recount an incident which illustrates this point. At a meeting of the Commission on Critical Choices at which the nation's energy problem was the topic, the chairman of the Council on Environmental Quality urged attention to the conservation of energy as the key to solving energy shortages. Rockefeller called on Edward Teller for a rebuttal. (Teller had helped develop Rockefeller's proposals for increasing energy supplies.) Teller said, "I will give you the gist of what I want to say in the first minute. In fact in two words: can do." Mr. Rockefeller seconded Teller with "Hear, hear." As quoted in Kramer and Roberts, *Vice-President*, p. 373.

125. Interview with a member of the Governor's staff.

126. Interview with two senior members of the Governor's staff.

127. Although he felt that Ronan had the most influence over the Governor, Malcolm Wilson credited Alton Marshall with having some influence. Partly because Marshall was aggressive and spoke in "very direct language," Wilson felt that he could sometimes "overwhelm" the Governor. Interview with Malcolm Wilson, New York City, April 27, 1977.

128. For example, one top staff official felt that the Governor had unfairly dressed him down at a staff meeting for what Rockefeller saw as his deliberately drafting a bill that was not in line with what the Governor wanted for his hard-line narcotics program of 1973. When the staff member later confronted the Governor privately in a protest at the latter's accusations, he and Rockefeller had a frank discussion in which the latter took pains to understand the basis for the official's objection to the implication that he had acted in bad faith. Interview with a former member of the Governor's staff.

129. Interview with Nelson A. Rockefeller.

130. Senate Committee on Rules and Administration, *Nomination of Nelson A. Rockefeller*, p. 616.

131. Ibid., p. 497. Most members of the Governor's staff received neither gifts, nor loans from him. According to the testimony of the Governor and recipients, loans and gifts were usually made following an initiative taken by the staff member.

132. The structure that Rockefeller created in New York was not identical to the model that he advocated for the federal government. Central to Rockefeller's model was an executive assistant to the president who would be able to fairly weigh the competing viewpoints of a budget unit and a program planning unit and make an "unbiased" judgment as to their respective merits. However, the position of secretary to the Governor in the Rockefeller administration was not "organizationally neutral" with regard to the program staff and the Division of the Budget. Rather, the program staff was the secretary's staff and operated more or less as his personal extension. Given that situation, the secretary could hardly be expected to act as a neutral arbiter of the sometimes competing viewpoints of the two units. Thus the structure the Governor created could have been expected to lessen the influence of a budget unit even more than would the structure be proposed for the federal government.

133. Interview with T. Norman Hurd, Albany, New York, May 24, 1972.

134. James Barber has noted that some chief executives, Calvin Coolidge, for example, were content to let others do most of the work associated with their jobs. *Presidential Character*, p. 147.

135. Interview with Louis Lefkowitz.

136. Interview with Nelson A. Rockefeller.

137. A former staff member who played the major role in producing a comprehensive report on a proposed reorganization of state agencies noted that the Governor never read the report although he recommended several of its proposals to the legislature. Rather, he absorbed its contents quickly through specially prepared "flip charts" that contained the essence of the report's major conclusions and recommendations. (The report was popularly known as the Ronan Report). Interview with Milton Musicus.

138. Conversation with William Sharkey, Albany, New York, April 6, 1979.

139. Interview with Nelson A. Rockefeller. Like Harry Truman, the Governor seemed to take pride in "making decisions." Noting that he agreed with Truman's oftquoted remark "The buck stops here," he credited his willingness to accept responsibility and make decisions to a capacity for self-responsibility that he believed he developed as a result of attending the Lincoln School.

140. For example, when responding to the same question, William Ronan said, "The governor became the catalyst for the forces related to program innovation in the state. The Governor was in the center of things." Interview with William Ronan.

141. As noted earlier, Kenneth Riland, an osteopathic physician who was the Governor's personal physician and confidant, is credited with influencing the Governor to act in this matter.

142. William Kennedy, "Rocky is 64, Going on 35," *New York Times Magazine*, April 29, 1973, p. 17.

143. Telephone interview with Alton Marshall, March 16, 1979. Other staff members were not always as generous in their views of outsiders. For example, a former staff member expressed himself in the following terms: "There were dilettantes who

did not know what was going on and who thought that the government could do nothing right. We called these people 'ear pissers.' The staff resented the fact that the government 'could do nothing right'.... The staff felt some outsiders were primarily interested in giving the Governor what he wanted to hear." Interview with a former senior staff member. Marshall was not above cooperating with an agency head to block one of the Governor's pet ideas. A former agency head recounted the great efforts that he and Marshall had to exert to convince Rockefeller not to build a heliport on top of one of the buildings in the new South Mall complex. When Marshall informed the commissioner of the plan, the latter sent a letter to the Governor saying a heliport would be a bad idea. Temporarily dissuaded, the Governor later brought up the idea again. This time the commissioner told Marshall he thought he had an idea that would surely stop Rockefeller. It worked. He sent a letter to the Governor pointing out that many school children visit the mall. He added, "What would happen if a helicopter crashed on top of a school bus?" Interview with a former agency head.

144. Interview with a former senior staff member.

145. Interview with Nelson A. Rockefeller.

146. One staff member who attended the first meeting at which a gigantic scale model of the South mall was shown to the Governor by Wallace Harrison related the following incident that illustrates the extent of Rockefeller's involvement in what would normally be regarded as decisions to be made by the relevant professionals. The scale model was dominated by a forty-four story skyscraper and a row of six buildings about half that size. To a trained eye, it was obvious that the skyscraper was positioned so that its tapering sides related in a particular way to the six other tall buildings, also with tapering sides. Eyeing the tallest building, the Governor said to Harrison, "That building is facing the wrong way." Harrison stared at the skyscraper for a minute. Then he said, "O.K. Governor," and he picked up the model and turned it around. Interview with a former member of the Governor's staff. Wallace Harrison confirmed this story. Interview. (The planned total of six "agency buildings" was later reduced to four.)

147. See Chapter eight.

Chapter 5

1. Table 5.1 includes all bills that the Governor submitted as part of his legislative program. (It does not include bills submitted by state agencies as part of their legislative programs.) The Governor's "program bills" were given special treatment by legislative leaders in each house after being given to appropriate committee chairman for introduction. Records of introduction and other action on program bills were provided to us by the Office of the Minority Leader of the New York State Assembly, Perry B. Duryea. Records for the first term of the administration were not available. As best as we can determine, the Governor's staff kept no comprehensive records of program bills until sometime in the mid-1960s. We were unable to track down the present location of such records. Because the Governor's program bills sometimes included bills primarily for purposes of "show," some would argue that lists of program bills can never be meaningful. Although such objections have some validity, they apply to the analysis of the legislative success of any chief executive. In any event, we have assumed that Rockefeller had some degree of commitment to all his program bills.

2. We have made no systematic study of the success rates of other governors. However, we do have figures available for Governor Malcolm Wilson's one year tenure. (Lieutenant governor under Rockefeller, Wilson became governor when Rockefeller resigned late in 1973.) Having a Republican legislature, as did Rockefeller for most of his administration, Wilson achieved a success rate of 77 percent in 1974. This is a higher rate than any achieved by Rockefeller in all except one of the eleven years for which we have data. However, it should be noted that Wilson proposed only 56 program bills, a total that is smaller than Rockefeller proposed in all but three of the eleven years. Two other factors contributed to Wilson's success. The first is that he had good personal relationships with many legislators and a history of dealing with legislators during his many years as lieutenant governor and, prior to that, as a legislator. The second is that recognizing his weakness as a candidate for governor in 1974, Republican legislators made special efforts to help him. Gary Haber reports that Governor Hugh Carey, a Democrat who was elected governor in 1974, achieved a success rate of only 36 percent in the 1976 legislative session. In that session Carey faced a legislature in which the Democratic and Republican parties each controlled one house. For a detailed comparison of Rockefeller and Carey as legislative leaders, see Gary M. Haber, "Hugh Carey, Nelson Rockefeller and the New York Legislature: The State of Executive-Legislative Relations in New York," senior thesis, Union College, March, 1978.

3. Of the four men who served as secretary, William Ronan and Robert Douglass devoted relatively more time and energy to legislative relations. Lt. Gov. Malcolm Wilson also assisted in dealing with legislators.

4. Interview with Nelson A. Rockefeller, New York City, November 16, 1977.

5. Ibid.

6. Ibid.

7. Interview with Joseph Carlino, Mineola, New York, December 19, 1977.

8. In the early years of the administration the meetings were held on Sunday evenings.

9. Data compiled from the Governor's appointments calendar for 1966.

10. Meetings held on an "as-needed" basis were often attended only by the Governor, one or two aides, and the leaders themselves.

11. Interview with Nelson A. Rockefeller.

12. Ibid. In general, the Governor's statement is accepted as accurate by most observers. However, it is clear that he was sometimes willing to circumvent the Democratic leaders and go directly for votes to rank-and-file Democrats when their party was in the minority. For an example, see Alan. G. Hevesi, *Legislative Politics in New York State: A Comparative Analysis* (New York: Praeger Publishers, 1975), pp. 105-6.

13. In an attempt to respond to the legislature's feelings of being overwhelmed by the fast pace of the Governor's legislative submissions in 1959, Rockefeller and his staff attempted to better organize the submission both of bills that were part of his 1960 legislative program and bills that were submitted by departments. (The actual introduction of bills into the legislature is done by legislators themselves. The Governor's program bills were assigned by legislative leaders to legislators for introduction as were departmental bills). Among the steps taken were the "prefiling" of 150 pieces of departmental legislation and many program bills and the Governor's announcing of six of his major program proposals in November and

December of 1959. However, these steps failed to totally eliminate legislative dissatisfaction. Some legislators, especially committee chairmen, complained that the Governor's presession activity put the legislature at a disadvantage in exercising legislative initiative because it was generally in session for only about four months and its committees did not operate on a year-round basis. Robert McCrate, "Some Observations of the 1960 Legislative Session," *New York State Legislative Annual 1960* (Albany: New York Legislative Service, 1960), pp. ix-xvii. McCrate was counsel to the Governor in 1960.

14. Interview with Joseph Carlino.

15. Ibid.

16. Hevesi, *Legislative Politics*, p. 109. Hevesi also credits Mahoney with blocking a number of important Rockefeller proposals including a bill to prohibit discrimination in the sale of housing, a bill creating new state Supreme Court judgeships for New York City, a bill to combine school districts, and a bill providing tax relief for Manhattan commuters, pp. 109-12.

17. Ibid., p. 112.

18. Edward Teller is widely acknowledged to have been a major force behind the Governor's interest in the nuclear fallout issue. The key report on which Rockefeller relied to make his case was produced by the Special Task Force on Radioactive Fallout, a group chaired by one of the Governor's cloest associates, Oscar Ruebhausen. The group also included the heads of eight state agencies including four who were among Rockefeller's closer advisors: Budget Director T. Norman Hurd; James Gaynor, commissioner of housing; Joseph H. Murphy, commissioner of taxation and finance; and Herman E. Hilleboe, commissioner of health. Among the groups' recommendations were the following: "a law requiring all new construction within the state to provide shielding from fallout up to a minimum specified standard," and a law requiring "owners of all existing buildings by a specified future date either to modify them or otherwise to provide fallout protection for their occupants." State of New York, Special Task Force on Protection from Radioactive Fallout, *Report on Protection from Radioactive Fallout* July 6, 1959. A follow-up report produced by a wholly in-house group produced plans for fallout shelters and related measures which could be employed by citizens as protections against radioactive fallout. State of New York, Committee on Fallout Protection, *Survival in a Nuclear Attack: Plan for Protection from Radioactive Fallout*, February 15, 1960.

19. A leading opponent of the Governor, then State Senator Jack Bronston, recalls one of the meetings at which the Governor promoted his plans for protection from nuclear fallout. "I remember one afternoon when he invited a bunch of us into the red room at the mansion in Albany, and he had all these maps on the wall. And these maps had nuclear bombs exploding all over them in color. And he gave us a long, emotional lecture on how many lives the shelters could save in case of nuclear attack." As quoted in Jack Newfield, "The Case Against Nelson," *New York Magazine* (March 9, 1970): 31.

20. Interview with an individual present at the meeting.

21. New York Legislative Service. *New York State Legislative Annual 1960* (Albany: New York Legislative Service, 1960), p. 464.

22. Memoranda of approval filed with three bills passed by the legislature in 1961 (A.I. 4753, A.I. 4755, and A.I. 4757) as included in State of New York, *Public Papers of Nelson A. Rockefeller, Fifty-third Governor of the State of New York, 1961*, p. 511. One of the bills provided a $100 per person exemption from any

increase in real property taxes caused by an assessment increase made as a result of shelter installation.

23. Hevesi, *Legislative Politics*, p. 107.

24. Interview with Joseph Carlino.

25. Republicans in the senate were an especially cohesive group with a well-developed sense of party. This was especially true of upstate Republicans, those who constituted the bulk of the party's membership. As Hevesi points out, Mahoney prided himself on "standing up for his party members." Hevesi, *Legislative Politics*, p. 109. He also offers an example in which Mahoney succeeded in reversing a senate vote against one of the Governor's program bills, a vote taken while Mahoney was out of the chamber. After his plea to the senate to reconsider, the body reversed itself and voted unanimously in favor of the bill. pp. 36-37.

26. Interview with Walter Mahoney, former majority leader of the New York State senate, Albany, New York, February 5, 1979. Mahoney indicated that his personal relationship with the Governor was good and avers that Rockefeller was an easy man to work with. And while he can recall the Governor being "irked" when a particular bill did not pass, he cannot recall seeing him "really mad."

27. Following Joseph Carlino's defeat in the 1964 election, Republican Perry Duryea became minority leader of the assembly. He became speaker in 1969 after his party regained control of the assembly in the 1968 election. Mahoney was also defeated in 1964, the election in which the Republicans also lost control of the senate. He was succeeded as Republican leader by Earl Brydges. The latter maintained a high level of cooperation with the Governor. Mr. Brydges moved from minority leader to majority leader when the Republicans recaptured control of the senate in a special election in 1965, an election held in an odd year as a consequence of court-ordered redistricting. For a discussion of Brydges as majority leader, see Hevesi, *Legislative Politics*, pp. 37-41.

28. For an account of the battle for the leadership positions, see Hevesi, *Legislative Politics*, pp. 171-79.

29. Republican intervention was possible because the leaders of each house must be elected by a majority of all votes, not merely a majority of votes in a party conference.

30. Interview with Joseph Zaretski, former majority leader and minority leader of the senate, New York City, June 1, 1978. Zaretski states that the reason senate Democrats appeared to be "playing ball" with the Governor was that the Governor's programs were the sorts of programs that Democrats favored.

31. Statement by Albert Abrams, former secretary of the New York State senate, as quoted in Gary Haber, "Hugh Carey, Nelson Rockefeller and the New York Legislature," p. 46.

32. Interview with Joseph Zaretski.

33. Interview with Malcolm Wilson, New York City, April 27, 1977.

34. For a description of Travia as Speaker see Hevesi, pp. 49-52.

35. A former top aide to the speaker voiced the opinion that taking everything into account, Travia was "the Governor's greatest supporter." He also indicated that the speaker was very reluctant to oppose the Governor "in a crunch." Personal interview.

36. Interview with Nelson A. Rockefeller.

37. Telephone interview with Perry Duryea, former speaker and minority leader of the New York State assembly, September 5, 1979.

38. Interview with Perry Duryea, Albany, New York, June 27, 1977.

39. The Governor himself apparently agreed with Mr. Carlino's assessment. At House hearings on his nomination to be vice-president, he stated that the fact of his working closely with Speaker Travia "upset Mr. Duryea a little bit because as minority leader he felt there should have been a closer relationship." U.S., Congress, House, Committee on the Judiciary, *Hearing on the Nomination of Nelson A. Rockefeller to be Vice President of the United States*, 93rd Cong., 2d sess., 1974, p. 127. However, Duryea states that the Governor did not seek Democratic votes without first consulting with him. Telephone interview with Perry Duryea.

40. The Conservative party was a real force in the state's politics by 1970, the year in which it elected James Buckley to the U.S. Senate and made major gains in the assembly.

41. Interview with a staff official of the New York State assembly, December 18, 1974.

42. Interview with Perry Duryea, June 27, 1977. A good example of a proposal that was withdrawn because of leaders' arguments that their members would not buy the idea was a proposal for a huge community development bond issue which the Governor wanted the legislature to approve in 1971. *Albany Knickerbocker News*, June 10, 1971.

43. Hevesi, *Legislative Politics*, p. 54.

44. Perhaps the most notable incident of this kind occurred in 1969 when two Democratic assemblymen broke away from a solid rank of Democratic opposition to a Rockefeller proposal for an increase in the state's sales tax. Their votes enabled the proposal to pass. After the legislative session had ended, one of the two, Assemblyman Albert Stockmeister, was appointed by the Governor to the state's Civil Service Commission, a position paying the then-substantial salary of $26,000. Although the Governor explained that Stockmeister had been recommended for the position by the Rochester Republican party, most observers believed that the appointment was the Governor's way of rewarding Stockmeister for his vote. For a discussion of the incident, see Hevesi, *Legislative Politics*, p. 106, and Newfield, "The Case Against Nelson," p. 30.

45. Clay Richards, "GOP Disenchantment Swells to Rebellion," *Albany Knickerbocker News*, April 1, 1971.

46. For an account of one conference, see the *New York Times*, February 25, 1971.

47. Syracuse area lawmakers were the most extreme "cutters." Led by Senator John Hughes, who had voted against every budget the Governor had ever proposed, they demanded that the budget be cut so deeply that no new taxes would be required.

48. For statements by Alan Miller, commissioner of mental hygiene, and Henry Diamond, commissioner of environmental conservation, see *Albany Knickerbocker News*, March 10, 1971. Legislators reacted angrily to Miller's alleged statements that patients might die if proposed budget cuts were made. *Albany Knickerbocker News*, March 11, 1971. Miller notes that his department helped mobilize some constituencies to oppose the proposed cuts. When Rockefeller learned of the proposals, he called Miller and said "get out the troops." Interview with Alan Miller, Albany, New York, July 10, 1979.

49. As quoted in the *Albany Knickerbocker News*, March 16, 1971.

50. As quoted in the *Albany Times Union*, March 21, 1971.

51. In late March the Governor lamented the lack of Democratic cooperation before a meeting of Republican county chairmen. "It's no secret to you that up until now I have always enjoyed a good working relationship with the Democratic party in the state legislature. Whenever it came time to pass a budget, they were willing to cooperate for the best interest of the people of the state. The present Democratic leadership isn't willing to cooperate except on its own terms." As quoted in the *Albany Knickerbocker News*, April 1, 1971.

52. *Public Papers 1971*, pp. 228-35.

53. See his remarks at the annual dinner of the State Republican Committee, *Public Papers 1971*, p. 1752.

54. "Mystery mailings" made on behalf of a bogus "Action Committee for the Liberal Party" were alleged to have been made by the assembly campaign committee as a means of drawing votes away from Democratic candidates in marginal districts. For a discussion, see Michael Kramer and Sam Roberts, *I Never Wanted to be Vice-President of Anything* (New York: Basic Books, 1976), pp. 114-17. The indictment was dismissed on the grounds that the law on which it was based was an unconstitutional restriction of freedoms guaranteed by the first amendment to the United States Constitution. The law required identification of sponsors of campaign literature, *New York Times*, January 25, 1974.

55. The Governor strongly denied that he had any role in bringing about the indictment of Mr. Duryea. House Judiciary Committee, *Hearings on the Nomination of Nelson A. Rockefeller 1974*, p. 127.

56. Telephone interview with Perry Duryea.

57. *Albany Knickerbocker News*, October 7, 1978. Duryea has stated that "I am the only person in Albany who ever opposed the Governor and he never forgave me. The gubernatorial campaign showed that." Telephone interview with Perry Duryea.

58. A good example of an instance in which the Governor simply overwhelmed minority party leaders was related by a reliable source who was involved in the case. Needing the votes of a half-dozen Democratic senators to pass a controversial banking bill, the Governor somehow managed to win the support of the Democratic state chairman and the Democratic leaders in New York City. Senate minority leader Joseph Zaretski was confronted with a surprise visit from the state chairman. Going from Zaretski's office to a Democratic caucus, the chairman informed the Democrats on behalf of the city's party leaders that the senators must produce the necessary votes. A chagrined Zaretski was powerless to resist and the Governor got the necessary votes. Personal interview with a former leader of the New York State Senate.

59. Hevesi, *Legislative Politics*, p. 111.

60. Kramer and Roberts, *Vice President*, pp. 78-81.

61. According to Hevesi, this wide margin was created when numerous assemblymen switched their votes to "no" upon seeing that the bill had been defeated on the roll call by a vote of 69 to 63. Hevesi, *Legislative Politics*, p. 50. The *Assembly Journal* includes only the official count of 85 to 48. State of New York, the Assembly, *Journal of the Assembly*, 191st sess., 1968, 2: 2495. Had black legislators been present, the bill would have passed.

62. Interview with Nelson A. Rockefeller. The actual tally of the vote on passage was 86 to 45. New York State, *Assembly Journal*, pp. 2497-98. Perry Duryea characterizes the Governor's account of the passage of the UDC bill as "a total

misrepresentation." Duryea says that he provided all the votes that he had agreed to provide, but that the absence of black and liberal legislators caused the bill to fail. According to Duryea, Rockefeller did call and request the minority leader to provide additional Republican votes so that the bill could pass the same day. Although Duryea did manage to win additional Republican votes, he vehemently denies that any threats of punishment from the Governor were responsible for vote changes. His explanation for the changes in position by Republicans is that minor changes in the bill made it more acceptable and that some legislators voted for it because they believed that they would thereby receive some favors from the Governor that they would not otherwise get. Telephone interview with Perry Duryea.

The official record shows that on April 9 the senate passed a piece of legislation (S.5643) amending the Urban Development Corporation Act before forwarding that act to the assembly for approval. S.5642 required that "community advisory committees" be established to advise the Urban Development Corporation concerning projects in their areas. The assembly approved this same bill before approving the UDC bill itself. Thus the official record confirms Duryea's statement that changes were made between the first and second votes in the assembly. For the record of senate action on the bill creating UDC, S4840A, see State of New York, *Journal of the Senate*, 191st sess., 1968, 1: 776-77. For the record of assembly action, see New York State, *Assembly Journal*, pp. 2490-99, 2474.

63. For an account of his remarks, see the *New York Times*, April 11, 1968.

64. While he acknowledged the importance of using "political muscle," as he put it, and seemed to genuinely enjoy using it, the Governor did not want to give the impression that he relied on it as his basic approach. As he said to us, "I tried to do it on the basis of merits. But in the last analysis if the program was good and if I had a commitment and then they didn't come through then I had no hesitation about using it, political muscle." Interview with Nelson A. Rockefeller.

65. Governor Rockefeller normally vetoed more than 20 percent of the bills passed by the legislature. Joseph Zimmerman notes that the Governor holds the record of 567 vetoes in one session, a figure constituting 34.5 percent of all bills passed in 1965. Joseph F. Zimmerman, "New York State Government: Retrospect and Prospect" (Paper prepared for delivery at the Twenty-First College Conference on New York History, Albany, New York, April 30, 1977), p. 9. The legislature has the power to override vetoes by the Governor, but none of Rockefeller's vetoes was ever overridden. (The first override of a gubernatorial veto of a piece of legislation in this century occurred in 1976 in the first administration of Governor Hugh Carey.) One major reason for this is that the bulk of bills are passed near the end of the legislative session. Thus the legislature is not in a position to even attempt to override vetoes issued by a governor during the thirty-day period allowed him for action after the close of the session.

66. The story was related by Clark Wemple, an assemblyman from Schenectady. Interview, Schenectady, New York, January 17, 1979.

67. Joseph Zimmerman states that Rockefeller issued 978 messages of necessity during regular legislative sessions. Of the total, 346 were issued on the last day of a session. Zimmerman, *New York*, p. 21.

68. For a discussion of the supposed connection between the UDC bill and the pension bill, see the *Albany Knickerbocker News*, September 2, 1971.

69. *New York Times*, April 11, 1968.

70. For a discussion of the Governor's proposals, see the *New York Times*, January 4, 5, 1973.

71. *New York Times*, Feburary 11, 1973. During February and March Rockefeller devoted substantial portions of speeches to the subject of drugs. Besides speaking in Albany, he spoke in Chicago, Tennessee, and Virginia. See *Public Papers 1973*.

72. *New York Times*, March 5, 1973.

73. As quoted in Edward Jay Epstein, "The Great Rockefeller Power Machine," *New York Magazine* (November 24, 1975): 71.

74. Another index of the Governor's single-minded determination to do something about the drug problem is the previously mentioned fact that he had overridden strong objections from top staff to the proposals he decided to submit to the legislature in 1973.

75. Epstein, "Rockefeller Power Machine," pp. 67-71. Mr. Epstein is also author of *Agency of Fear: Opiates and Political Power in America* (New York: G. P. Putnam's Sons, 1977).

76. Epstein, "Rockefeller Power Machine," p. 68. The author also quotes a Hudson Institute report to the Governor as acknowledging that the cost of addict theft was only a fraction of $5 billion: "No matter how we generate estimates of total value of property stolen in New York City, we cannot find any way of getting these estimates above $500 million per year," pp. 68-69. Also according to Epstein, the Governor's statements that addicts accounted for a high proportion of all crimes committed was belied by the Hudson Institute study. The study concluded that less than 2 percent of addicts financed their habit by robbery or muggings. Epstein, *Agency*, p. 44. In testimony before the Codes Committees of the state senate and assembly, Rockefeller claimed that 120,000 addicts in New York City stole $18 million each day for a total of $6.5 billion per year. He cited the state's Narcotics Addiction Control Commission as the source of his data. *Public Papers 1973*, p. 1263.

77. For a list of provisions of modifications in Rockefeller's proposals, see *Public Papers 1973*, pp. 832-34. Among other significant modifications were provisions for parole after mandatory periods of imprisonment for sale of hard drugs. Thus although conviction would result in lifetime supervision of those convicted, not all would actually spend a lifetime in prison. Even with changes the proposal was regarded as harsh. Its passage was one reason that the New York Civil Liberties Union's rating of the Governor dropped from 78 percent in 1972 to 33 percent in 1973. *Albany Knickerbocker News*, July 21, 1973.

78. Dick Behn, "The Future of the Republican Party," *Empire State Report* (April 1977): 160.

79. Senate Committee on Rules and Administration, *Hearing on the Nomination of Nelson A. Rockefeller*, p. 479.

80. Ibid.

81. The Governor once appointed Democratic Assemblyman Andrew Stein, a mortal enemy of Stanley Steingut, as chairman of the Temporary State Commission on Living Costs and the Economy. Stein was the son of Jerry Finklestein, a wealthy and influential friend of the Governor. (A Democrat, the latter was a director of Rockefeller Center and a Rockefeller appointee to the board of directors of the New York Port Authority.) *Albany Knickerbocker News*, February 24, 1975. A maverick

who was very unpopular within his own party, Stein was a constant critic of Steingut. Stein's commission conducted investigations of nursing homes which focused in large part on Steingut's alleged role in blocking investigations of certain homes. *Albany Knickerbocker News*, April 1, 1975.

82. Although the Governor did not threaten Wemple or offer him any "deal," the assemblyman noted that the Governor alternated between being "friendly" and "rather caustic." However, Wemple refused to change his mind on new taxes. *Albany Knickerbocker News*, January 30, 1976.

83. Interview with Nelson A. Rockefeller.

84. Kramer and Roberts, *Vice-President*, p. 118.

85. Ibid., pp. 119, 120.

86. *New York Times*, March 21, 1973.

87. Interview with Henry Diamond, Washington, D.C., February 14, 1978.

88. U.S., Congress, House, Committee on the Judiciary, *Analysis of the Philosophy and Public Record of Nelson A. Rockefeller, Nominee for Vice President of the United States*, Committee print, 93rd Cong., 2d sess., pp. 99-100.

89. *Albany Knickerbocker News*, May 30, 1973. The bill that was passed contained some more-or-less cosmetic changes designed to mollify opponents.

90. In 1967 the Governor had succeeded in winning voter approval for a $2.5 billion bond issue for both highway construction and mass transit. A special nongovernmental committee called Action for Transportation had spearheaded a successful public relations campaign and spent substantial sums of money in the process. Joseph Zimmerman, "Public Transportation" in Robert Connery and Gerald Benjamin, *Governing New York State: The Rockefeller Years* (New York: The Academy of Political Science, 1974), p. 221.

91. *Albany Knickerbocker News*, September 13, 1972.

92. Zimmerman, "Public Transportation," p. 222.

93. In light of the fact that the Governor resigned near the end of 1973, it is notable that he fought hard against heavy odds on the proposal for this bond issue. He had not asked for legislative authorization for the bond issue at the regular session of the legislature in 1973. Rather, he pressured legislative leaders into adding the proposal to the agenda of a special session they had asked him to call so that they might deal with the topic of public pension reforms. Former Speaker Perry Duryea believed that the proposal for a transportation bond issue had received very little staff work prior to the Governor's putting it forth. Interview with Perry Duryea.

94. Robert H. Connery and Gerald Benjamin, *Rockefeller of New York: Executive Power in the State House* (Ithaca: Cornell University Press, 1979), pp. 359-60.

95. Ibid., p. 360.

96. Ibid., p. 361.

97. *Albany Knickerbocker News*, April 26, 1973.

98. Ibid.

99. Interview with Henry L. Diamond.

100. Telephone conversation with T. Norman Hurd, former secretary to the Governor, May 4, 1979.

101. Interview with Nelson A. Rockefeller.

102. Interview with Joseph Carlino.

103. *New York Times*, January 4, 1973.

104. Interview with Nelson A. Rockefeller.

105. Donald Axelrod, "Higher Education," in Connery and Benjamin, *Governing New York State*, p. 138.

106. Interview with Nelson A. Rockefeller.

107. Beginning in 1967, a program associate was hired to devote full-time to the area of federal-state relations. Then in 1971 the Governor established an office in Washington as a base for his attempts to win additional federal assistance.

108. Connery and Benjamin, *Rockefeller of New York*, pp. 341-43.

109. Donald H. Haider, *When Governments Come to Washington* (New York: The Free Press, 1974).

110. Donald Haider, "The State of the Federal Government," in Connery and Benjamin, *Governing New York State*, p. 91.

111. Ibid., pp. 91-92.

112. Ibid., p. 92.

113. Haider credits the Governor with personally persuading Wilbur Mills, chairman of the House Ways and Means Committee, to reverse a position that new federal aid should bypass the states and go directly to cities and rural communities. *When Governments Come to Washington*, p. 249-50.

114. Connery and Benjamin credit the Governor with providing the basis for at least two key compromises that made possible the passage of a revenue-sharing measure. The first involved a change in a House-passed formula that based allocation of revenue-sharing payments in substantial part on state income tax collections. Because this feature gave an advantage to large states with income taxes, New York being the leading example, governors of some states objected. Only by proposing that combined state-local tax effort be substituted for income tax effort was Rockefeller able to maintain unanimous support from the dozen governors who were slated to testify before the Senate Finance Committee. The second compromise was based on the Governor's suggestion that each state could choose to have its allocation based on either the House-favored formula, one favoring urban states, or the Senate-favored formula, one favoring less urban states. It is clear that the Governor's success in helping to build a consensus on a particular revenue-sharing measure was based in part upon the staff assistance he could command, especially that of James Cannon, head of the Washington office that the Governor had established in 1971. For a good discussion of the Governor's role in helping shape the exact form of the revenue-sharing measure that eventually was signed into law, see Connery and Benjamin, *Rockefeller of New York*, pp. 398-416.

115. *New York Times*, May 15, 1972.

116. Connery and Benjamin, *Rockefeller of New York*, pp. 408-9. The authors point out that the Governor courted Mills extensively and took advantage of Mills' ambition for the presidential nomination. For example, they note that the Governor sent his close friend, osteopath Ken Riland, to Arkansas to examine Mills' injured back and offer his assistance.

117. Ibid., p. 408.

118. It should be noted that the legislation would not benefit the state as much as an approach that the Governor had advocated prior to, as well as after, his campaign for revenue sharing. That approach was federal assumption of welfare expenses, a proposal the Governor came to realize had less chance of passage than did revenue-sharing. House Judiciary Committee, *Analysis of the Philosophy*, pp. 11-12.

Chapter 6

1. Ira Sharkansky, *The Politics of Taxing and Spending* (New York: Bobbs-Merrill Co., 1969), p. 6.
2. Ibid. See generally chapter 1.
3. *New York Times*, August 26, 1958, p. 20.
4. State of New York, *Public Papers of Governor Nelson A. Rockefeller, Fifty-third Governor of the State of New York, 1959*, p. 13.
5. Ibid., p. 4.
6. Ibid.
7. Ibid., p. 35.
8. Ibid., p. 18.
9. Ibid., p. 19.
10. Ibid.
11. *Public Papers 1960*, p. 63.
12. Ibid.
13. Ibid.
14. Ibid., p. 64.
15. See, for example, *Public Papers 1961*, p. 55.
16. *Public Papers 1963*, pp. 51, 54.
17. *Public Papers 1959*, p. 18.
18. *Public Papers 1963*, p. 72.
19. *Public Papers 1964*, pp. 31, 32.
20. Ibid.
21. *Public Papers 1964*, pp. 1199-1200. John Gargan points out that 1965 marked a watershed in the Rockefeller administration. Having failed to capture the Republican nomination for president in 1964, Rockefeller, Gargan suggests, felt free to abandon tightfisted conservative fiscal policies in the interest of launching major attacks on problems such as water pollution, education, and financing municipal services. See John G. Gargan, *The Politics of Water Pollution in New York State: The Development and Adoption of the 1965 Pure Waters Program*, Ph.D. diss., Syracuse University, June 1, 1968, pp. 269-81.
22. *Public Papers 1966*, p. 54.
23. Ibid., p. 87.
24. Ibid., "Annual Message," p. 10.
25. "Annual Message" in *Public Papers 1967*, p. 17.
26. "Executive Budget" in *Public Papers 1967*, pp. 74-75.
27. "Annual Message" in *Public Papers 1968*, pp. 11-12.
28. "Annual Message" in *Public Papers 1969*, p. 38.
29. Ibid., p. 40.
30. Ibid.
31. "Annual Message" in *Public Papers 1970*, p. 14.
32. "Inaugural Address" in *Public Papers 1971*, p. 11.
33. Ibid., p. 33.
34. "Annual Message" in *Public Papers 1971*, p. 22.
35. Ibid., p. 62.
36. "Executive Budget" in *Public Papers 1971*, p. 103.

37. Terms borrowed from the Executive Budget, in *Public Papers 1973*, p. 43.

38. "Annual Message" in *Public Papers 1972*, p. 134.

39. Ibid., p. 154.

40. "Annual Message" in *Public Papers 1973*, p. 12.

41. Ibid., p. 13.

42. Ibid., p. 14.

43. Ibid., p. 42.

44. The specific percentages of business tax contributions to the total income for the state by terms were: 21 percent for the first term; 20.9 percent for the second; and 15.0 percent and 15.3 percent for the third and fourth terms respectively.

45. Annmarie H. Walsh, *The Public's Business: The Politics and Practices of Government Corporations* (Cambridge: The MIT Press, 1978), p. 267. Walsh cites the preface by Nelson A. Rockefeller to Sidney D. Goldbert and Harold Seidman, *The Government Corporation: Elements of a Model Charter* (Chicago: Public Administration Service, 1953), p. viii.

46. New York State, Office of the Comptroller, *1974 Annual Report*, n.d., p. 26.

47. Walsh, *The Public's Business*, p. 24.

48. See Robert Smith, *Public Authorities, Special Districts, and Local Government* (Washington, D.C., 1964), p. 147.

49. Walsh, *The Public's Business*, p. 266.

50. Ibid., pp. 265-66, and data from New York State Department of State.

51. Ibid.

52. Ibid., p. 267.

53. Three of the twenty-six authorities authorized as of 1960 had never been activated: Albany Light Heat and Power Authority (1935), Brooklyn Sports Center Authority (1956), and New York State World War Memorial Authority (1957).

54. Walsh, *The Public's Business*, p. 22.

55. Humphrey S. Tyler, "The Steady Growth of Backdoor Financing," *Empire State Report* (June 1975): 213.

56. Ibid. Annmarie Walsh notes that "Bonds sold on the strength of project revenues are most acceptable to critics of backdoor financing." also, "Because public authorities repay their bonds out of their own revenues during the life of their projects, banking commentators tend to agree with the proposition that authorities are self-supporting. In fact, authorities derive their revenues not only from sales of goods and services to private consumers but also from lease payments from governments that do levy taxes, and from various loans and grants from city, state, and federal agencies. If authority bonds impose no direct lien on the general tax power of a government, they are called revenue bonds, regardless of the volume of government subsidies that may be backing them. A general obligation bond directly invokes the legal liability of a taxing government, but a revenue bond is often repaid from tax revenues." Walsh, *The Public's Business*, p. 57 n.44.

57. State of New York, Office of the Comptroller, *Debt-Like Commitments of the State of New York*, January, 1973, p. 1.

58. State comptroller, *1973 Annual Report*, p. 19.

59. *Albany Times Union*, August 17, 1975; March 22, 1981.

60. Private Housing Finance Law, McKinney's Consolidated Laws of New York Annotated, chapter 41, section 47 (1)(d).

61. Tyler, "Backdoor Financing," p. 222.

62. Walsh, *The Public's Business*, p. 133.

63. Ibid.

64. Ibid., p. 134.

65. Tyler, "Backdoor Financing," p. 212.

66. Ibid., p. 212. When Nelson Rockefeller assumed office, there were 7,482 employees in the State University System and 142,081 students enrolled in public colleges in the state. At the conclusion of his term as Governor, the total number of employees had grown to 34,342 (358 percent increase), and student enrollments had increased to 517,536 (264 percent increase).

67. Walsh, *The Public's Business*, p. 134.

68. Ibid., p. 135.

69. Ibid., p. 138.

70. Ibid., p. 139.

71. New York State, Moreland Act Commission on the Urban Development Corporation and other State Financing Agencies, *Restoring Credit and Confidence: A Reform Program for New York State and its Public Authorities*, March 31, 1976, p. 16.

72. *Public Papers 1973*, p. 51.

73. State comptroller, *1969 Annual Report*, p. 31.

74. Walsh, *The Public's Business*, p. 298.

75. State comptroller, *1970 Annual Report*, p. 30.

76. See Robert H. Connery and Gerald Benjamin, *Rockefeller of New York: Executive Power in the Statehouse* (Ithaca: Cornell University Press, 1979), pp. 218-20.

77. Ibid., p. 199.

78. State comptroller, *1974 Annual Report*, p. 12.

79. Connery and Benjamin, *Rockefeller of New York*, pp. 201-2.

80. Ibid., p. 210.

81. Ibid., pp. 211 and 212.

82. *Public Papers 1972*, pp. 128-47.

83. Interview with Joseph Persico, Washington, D.C., February 17, 1978.

84. Connery and Benjamin, *Rockefeller of New York*, pp. 414-16.

85. State of New York, Office of the Comptroller, *Statewide Public Authorities: A Fourth Branch of Government*, November, 1972.

86. Ibid., p. 3.

87. Ibid.

88. Walsh, *The Public's Business*, p. 386. Presumably Levitt also had available the alternative of refusing to pay over state monies to public authorities that used moral obligation bonding. Such a move would have forced state officials to sue Levitt to force payment.

89. Ibid., p. 276.

90. March 30, 1964 in Ontario, Oregon. *Public Papers 1964*,. p. 1247.

91. Neal R. Peirce, *The Megastates of America: People, Politics and Power in the Ten Great States* (New York: W. W. Horton and Company, Inc., 1972), p. 36.

92. Interview with Nelson A. Rockefeller, New York City, November 16, 1977.

Chapter 7

1. For example, see Neal R. Peirce, *The Megastates of America: People, Power and Politics in the Ten Great States* (New York: W. W. Norton and Co., 1972), pp. 27-35.

2. Because a "program" sometimes required more than one piece of legislation, the number of programs put into effect during the course of the administration would be substantially less than the number of bills passed. For example, the Governor's Pure Waters Program of 1965 was based on five separate pieces of legislation. See Governor's memorandum of approval in New York Legislative Service, *New York State Legislative Annual 1965* (New York: New York Legislative Service, 1965), p. 504.

3. The total number of bills passed in the fourth term is higher than the number passed in the second term even though the Governor served only three years of his fourth term. Had he served the fourth year, it seems reasonable to assume that the total number of bills passed during that term would have reached at least 165. (The lowest number of bills passed in any of the three years of the term that he did serve was 30.) Although smaller than the number passed in the first and third terms, 165 would be far above the number passed in the second term.

4. "Report to the Governor on the Proposed Reorganization of the Executive Branch of New York State Government," in State of New York, *Public Papers of Nelson A. Rockefeller, Fifty-third Governor of the State of New York*, 1960, pp. 1131-1394.

5. Presented with a "working list" of programs by us, the Governor agreed that all were among the most significant of his administration. He added one to our list, state loans for the construction of municipal hospitals and nursing homes. Subsequent to the interview with the Governor, we added the electric-power program to the list, partly on the basis of the assurance of the chief staff person who worked on the program that Rockefeller indeed had a strong commitment to that program. We also added the development of Stewart Air Force Base into a commercial jetport, the creation of the Office of Welfare Inspector General and the Office of Education Performance Review, and the bridge across Long Island Sound to connect Rye and Oyster Bay on the basis of a variety of indications that Rockefeller was, in fact, strongly committed to all four.

6. Peirce, *Megastates*, p. 26.

7. In 1968 the Governor authored *Unity, Freedom and Peace*, a book that, in essence, advertised his qualifications for the presidency. In seeking to show that he had addressed issues that were national problems, he cited five of his pet programs, including the Urban Development Corporation, his 1966 narcotics control program, his proposal for universal health insurance, his expansion of the State University, and the program of loans for the construction and rehabilitation of municipal hospitals. *Unity, Freedom and Peace: A Blueprint for Tomorrow* (New York: Random House, 1968), pp. 49, 56-59, 72, 74-76, 79-80.

8. Dick Netzer, *The Subsidized Muse: Public Support for the Arts in the United States* (London: Cambridge University Press, 1978), p. 80.

9. Ibid., p. 90.

10. Governor's memorandum of approval on five bills constituting the Pure

Waters Program, New York Legislative Service, *New York State Legislative Annual 1965* (Albany: New York Legislative Service, 1965), pp. 504-5.

11. By June, 1972, financing of these activities had led to an outstanding debt of more than $2 billion. This figure is compiled from State of New York, Office of the Comptroller, *Debt-like Commitments of the State of New York*, January, 1973, p. 4.

12. Ibid., p. 9. In fiscal year 1971-72 alone, rental payments from SUCF to HFA amounted to $47.3 million, p. 16. Dormitory construction is financed separately from academic facilities. Dormitories are financed by the issuance of bonds by the Dormitory Authority, with debt service being maintained by use of rental fees charged to students. Ibid., p. 41.

13. Address at the Annual Meeting of the American Political Science Association, New Orleans, Louisiana, September 5, 1973, p. 5.

14. William J. Quirk, "Standing to Sue in New York," *St. John's Law Review* (March 1973), pp. 431-34, 438-48. Quirk notes that a decision by the Court of Appeals in the St. Clair case denying legal standing to sue to one who sought to challenge the constitutionality of the statute creating and empowering the Housing Finance Agency allowed the state to enter "a ten year period during which the executive customarily disregarded the Constitution," (pp. 446-47). Quirk also notes that this decision left state officials, the attorney general or the comptroller, for example, as the only possible source of a challenge to the devices of moral-obligation bonding and lease purchase. However, such a challenge never came. For example, the attorney general defended the HFA statute in the St. Clair case (p. 448). He notes that in 1972 the Court of Appeals affirmed a lower court decision that UDC's moral-obligation bonds "might be classified as contingent liabilities on the part of the State of New York." As quoted in Quirk, "Standing to Sue," p. 435.

15. One result of the heavy reliance on the HFA is that by June of 1972, it had debt outstanding of $3,812.1 billion. This is more than the state's total full-faith-and-credit debt outstanding on that date. State comptroller, *Debt-like Commitments*, p. 11.

16. A ninth program, construction of the South Mall office/cultural complex, was also based on a lease-purchase arrangement, but in this case the borrowing agency was not an authority, but rather Albany County. For a discussion of the mall and its finances, see Maureen D. Griess, "Empire State Plaza: Does Nelson's Folly Have a Future?" *Empire State Report* February 1977, pp. 43-47.

17. New York State, Urban Development Corporation, *Annual Report*, 1972, pp. 68-69. As a result of objections to proposed low- and middle-income projects in Westchester County in 1973, the legislature passed a bill giving local governments the power to veto UDC projects. Connery and Benjamin state that Rockefeller signed the bill because the legislature might otherwise have refused to increase the authority's borrowing authorization. Robert Connery and Gerald Benjamin, *Rockefeller of New York: Executive Power in the Statehouse* (Ithaca: Cornell University Press, 1979), p. 264.

18. The APA has been a constant target of attacks by residents of, and legislators from, the park and other upstate areas. Residents protest that the land-use plan formulated by the agency and approved by the legislature is far too restrictive. According to one summary of the plan, "it will, in effect, bar large second-home

developments, discourage uniform lot sizes, and promote cluster-type housing within new average density rules [and it will permit] no more than one building for each 42 acres, on the average . . . on more than half of the private land and industrial activities would be largely confined to areas that are now built up." *New York Times*, May 23, 1973. For the plan itself as approved by the legislature, see *Laws of New York 1973*, chapter 348.

19. Eugene J. Gleason, Jr., and Joseph F. Zimmerman, "Executive Dominance in New York State" (Paper prepared for delivery at the Annual Meeting of the Northeastern Political Science Association, November 9, 1974), p. 25. See also chapter 8.

20. Ibid., p. 24.

21. In addition to creating a Welfare Inspector General, the legislature approved the Governor's proposal to transfer the power to appoint the Commissioner of Social Welfare from the State Board of Social Welfare to the Governor. *New York Times*, June 10, 1971.

22. Gleason and Zimmerman, "Executive Dominance," pp. 27-28.

23. State of New York, The Assembly, Committee on Ways and Means. "Funding the Arts in New York State," *The Ways and Means Report*, Summer, 1979, p. 1.

24. Ibid., p. 2.

25. Interview with a former program associate, Albany, New York, February 20, 1975.

26. For example, see his statement that he gave approval to state purchase of the Long Island Rail Road only after trying all other possible measures, state subsidies, for example, in an attempt to prevent its collapse. Address at Meeting of American Political Science Association, p. 9-10.

27. Governor's memorandum filed with Senate Bill Number 5746, *Public Papers 1968*, p. 518-20.

28. Ibid.

29. *Laws of New York 1968*, chapter 174.

30. As we note in Chapter 2 in our discussion of the Governor's early search for a significant role in life, he did, in fact, have a strong interest in architecture, even to the point of considering it as a possible career.

31. As quoted in Mark Libbon, ed., *City of Marble: A Look into the Empire State Plaza* (Albany: *City of Marble*, 1977), p. 16.

32. As quoted in Michael Kramer and Sam Roberts, *I Never Wanted to be Vice-President of Anything: An Investigative Biography of Nelson Rockefeller* (New York: Basic Books, 1976), p. 347. Labor union support for programs involving construction was a key element for the Governor. For example, construction unions were vigorous supporters of passage of three transportation bond issues and the proposal to construct the bridge over Long Island Sound to connect Rye and Oyster Bay.

33. Although Table 7.2 lists the Governor's proposal for protection from nuclear attack as having failed, portions of the program, those calling for construction of an attackproof center for government operations and civil defense activities in time of enemy attack, state aid for construction of shelters at schools, colleges, and universities, and construction of shelters for state workers and state university students, gained legislative approval. The total amount appropriate toward such construction

items in 1960 and 1961 was approximately $100 million. See *Public Papers 1961*, pp. 74, 157-61, 567-68.

34. Each proposed bond issue was to provide funds for both highway construction and mass transit. However, the mix between the two forms of transportation differed. For example, of the 1967 bond issue, half of the total was to go for highways, two-fifths for mass transit, and one-tenth for aviation. But under the 1973 proposal, three-fifths was to go for mass transit and only two-fifths for highways. See Joseph Zimmerman, "Public Transportation" in Robert H. Connery and Gerald Benjamin, eds., *Governing New York State: The Rockefeller Years* (New York: The Academy of Political Science, 1974), p. 222.

35. Renamed the Governor Nelson A. Rockefeller Empire State Plaza during the administration of Democrat Hugh Carey, the ninety-eight acre complex includes several massive state office buildings, the state museum and library, a theatre, a convention hall, a recital hall, underground parking, restaurants and shops, acres of landscaped space, and three large reflecting pools. By June of 1975, $985 million in bonds had been sold to finance construction itself, and by 1981 total costs were estimated at $1.7 billion. (*Albany Knickerbocker News*, November 21, 1975 and *Albany Times Union*, March 22, 1981). As noted in Chapter 6, Albany County sold the bonds for the complex and the state leases the buildings from the county.

36. U.S., Congress, Senate, Committee on Rules and Administration, *Hearings on the Nomination of Nelson A. Rockefeller to be Vice President of the United States*, 93rd Cong., 2d Session, 1974, p. 217.

37. *Albany Times Union*, January 28, 1979. Corning added that Rockefeller changed initial plans for the mall by adding the museum, convention center, and a restaurant in response to Corning's criticism that the initial plans called for a "sterile nine-to-five complex that would be dead and deserted at night."

38. Interview with Ewald Nyquist, former commissioner of education, Albany, New York, August 11, 1977.

39. Although it was not a key part of the narcotic addiction control programs he proposed in 1966, 1970, and 1973, Rockefeller did lead the state into a major commitment to one form of treatment heavily dependent on medical science. That form of treatment involved maintaining heroin addicts on the drug methadone. Thus by December of 1970 the state was operating, and supporting, programs which involved more than 6000 addicts. State expenditures for fiscal year 1970-1971 amounted to more than $18 million. State of New York, *Executive Budget for the Fiscal Year 1971-1972*, pp. 493-94.

40. Governor's Memorandum filed with Senate Bill 2446, a bill creating the Atomic Research and Development Authority, in *Public Papers 1962*, pp. 324-35.

41. State of New York, Office of Atomic Development, *An Atomic Development Plan for the State of New York*, 1959.

42. *Public Papers 1959*, pp. 108-9. In 1959 Rockefeller noted that one of his task forces, his Commission on Economic Expansion, had noted that the state needed adequate transportation and electrical power in order to ensure a prosperous economy. He pointed out that the legislature had approved his proposals for creation of an Office of Transportation and an Office of Atomic Development. *Public Papers 1959*, p. 1054.

43. For a discussion of these organizations, see James E. Underwood, *Science/Technology Related Activities in the Government of New York State: the Organiza-*

tional Pattern, the University of the State of New York, Education Department, Office of Science and Technology, 1971.

44. Convinced that he did become more conservative during his last term in office, critics of the Governor attributed this change to his desire to woo conservative Republicans in a desperate attempt to keep alive his hopes for the presidential nomination. For example, Edward Jay Epstein feels that this motive lay behind the Governor's harsh drug proposals in 1973. Edward Jay Epstein, "The Great Rockefeller Power Machine," *New York Magazine*, November 24, 1975. The Governor's attempts to make his peace with the conservative wing of the Republican party caused him to draw attention to those aspects of his fourth term that did, in fact, appear "conservative." For example, in December of 1973 he bragged to the Southern Republican conference about his "get-tough" efforts in the fields of welfare and drugs. *Public Papers 1973*, p. 1370. Conservative columnist George Will felt that Rockefeller had managed to calm many of "the most truculant doubters." As he put it, "Rockefeller's visit must have convinced even the most hardshelled of them that he has been unjustly suspected of impolitic beliefs." *The Washington Post*, September 5, 1975.

45. Senate Committee on Rules and Administration, *Hearings on the Nomination of Nelson A. Rockefeller*, p. 90.

46. Ibid.

47. Interview with Nelson A. Rockefeller, New York City, November 16, 1977.

48. Senate Committee on Rules and Administration, *Hearings on the Nomination of Nelson A. Rockefeller*, p. 90.

49. Ibid., p. 91.

50. Ibid., p. 92.

51. "Annual Message to the Legislature," in *Public Papers 1966*, pp. 12-14.

52. "Special Message Recommending Complete Reorganization of the State Welfare Program," March 29, 1971. *Public Papers 1971*, pp. 228-35.

53. *Wyman v. Lopez*, 404 U.S. 1055.

54. See Supreme Court "Orders," (71-620) in *Wyman v. Lopez*, 404 U.S. 1055.

55. *Albany Times Union*, October 10, 1979.

56. "Message Recommending Reorganization of Welfare," p. 232.

57. Elizabeth Wickenden, "Notes on HR/H2: New York Demonstration Projects," mimeo, September 28, 1971. This memo contains "Incentive Opportunities for the Employable Adult," Appendix III of "Incentives for Independence," the project application submitted to the Department of Health, Education, and Welfare by the New York State Department of Social Services. Adults could receive incentive points for a wide variety of activities ranging from providing day-care for a public assistance family to assisting in tracking down a deserting parent.

58. Ibid., pp. 5, 6.

59. *Public Papers 1965*, p. 1390.

60. For example, during the campaign to win passage of his 1973 drug program, the Governor said he was considering proposing the death penalty for members of organized crime who were dealing in drugs. *New York Times*, March 6, 1973.

61. *New York Times*, September 12, 1973.

62. *Public Papers 1968*, pp. 1023-25.

63. Senate Committee on Rules and Administration, *Hearings on the Nomination of Nelson A. Rockefeller*, p. 113.

64. *New York Times*, May 15, 1972.

65. *Albany Knickerbocker News*, May 15, 1972.

66. Nelson A. Rockefeller, *Annual Message to the Legislature*, January 6, 1971, pp. 29-31.

67. *Albany Knickerbocker News*, January 21, 1971.

68. In his annual message of 1971, the Governor also urged the legislature to again vote approval of a proposed amendment to the state constitution, an amendment that would empower state as well as local governments to allow private businesses to receive grants and loans from the state and have direct access to the state's credit for the purposes of community development. In the absence of such a change in the constitution, funds from the proposed community development bond issue could not have been used in the way the Governor intended. However, in November 1971, the state's voters rejected the proposed change by a margin of almost two to one. See State of New York, *Manual for the Use of the Legislature of the State of New York 1975*, p. 349.

69. *New York Times*, June 10, 1971.

70. Ibid.

71. *Albany Knickerbocker News*, July 21, 1973.

72. *New York Times*, January 17, 1973.

73. One should recall that the Governor had taken "conservative" stands on some issues in earlier periods of his administration. For example, in 1964 he proposed, and later signed, two anti-crime measures loosening restrictions on police who were searching for evidence. Dubbed the "no-knock" and "stop-and-frisk" proposals, they were subjected to severe criticism on the grounds of an alleged unconstitutionality. For a discussion of these bills and the reaction to them, see U.S. Congress, House, Committee on the Judiciary, *Selected Issues and the Positions of Nelson A. Rockefeller, Nominee for Vice-President of the United States*, Committee Print, 93rd Cong., 2d sess., 1974, pp. 57-58. Other "conservative" policies in earlier years included the pay-as-you-go policy emphasized during his first term and part of the second, and that provision of his 1966 drug program which provided that convicted addicts could avoid jail sentences by agreeing to "voluntary" commitment to rehabilitation facilities.

74. State of New York, Housing Finance Agency, *Annual Report*, 1972, p. 3, and State of New York, Urban Development Corporation, *Annual Report*, 1973, p. 11.

Chapter 8

1. For an excellent discussion of decision making under various sorts of pressures including stress and frustration, see Bruce Buchanan, *The Presidential Experience: What the Office Does to the Man* (Englewood Cliffs: Prentice-Hall, 1978).

2. Governor's Memorandum of Approval on S.I. 4596 and S.I. 5003, July 28, 1966, State of New York, *Public Papers of Nelson A. Rockefeller, Fifty-third Governor of the State of New York 1966*, pp. 447-48.

3. State of New York, Office of the Comptroller, *Debt-Like Commitments of the State of New York*, January, 1973, p. 39.

4. Ibid.

5. State of New York, Moreland Act Commission on Nursing Homes and Residential Facilities, *Regulating Nursing Home Care: The Paper Tigers*, October, 1975, pp. 4-7. Prior to 1973 the city of New York exercised the power to license and inspect proprietary homes within its boundaries.

6. *Albany Knickerbocker News*, June 18, 1976.

7. *Schenectady Gazette*, July 22, 1975.

8. For a thorough discussion of Hausman's role and his relationship with Bergman, see State of New York, Moreland Act Commission on Nursing Homes and Residential Facilities, *Political Influence and Political Accountability: One Foot in the Door*, February, 1976. On Bergman's operations, see Mary Adelaide Mandelson, *Tender Loving Greed* (New York: Alfred A. Knopf, 1974).

9. Ibid., p. 39. This characterization was based on testimony by Hausman, Robert Douglass, and Rockefeller.

10. State of New York, Moreland Act Commission on Nursing Homes and Residential Facilities, *Political Influence and Political Accountability: One Foot in the Door*, February, 1976, p. 40.

11. Ibid.

12. *New York Times*, October 10, 1974. During the same period of time the Governor gave over $80 thousand to the NAACP Legal Defense and Educational Fund and lesser amounts to other black charities. He also gave substantial amounts to various religious organizations and churches including more than $150 thousand to the Archbishopric of New York, more than $100 thousand to the Archdiocese of New York, and over $130 thousand to Ebeneezer Baptist Church in Atlanta, the church of the Reverend Martin Luther King, Sr., the church where his late son once preached.

13. State of New York, Moreland Commission, *Political Influence*, pp. 40-41. The commission states that it found no evidence to support the contention that there was anti-Semitic discrimination against Bergman, p. 41.

14. Ibid., p. 43.

15. *New York Times*, August 29, 1975.

16. State of New York, Moreland Commission, *Political Influence*, p. 127.

17. On May 4, 1973, Samuel Hausman had scheduled a meeting with the Governor at the latter's office in New York City. In testimony before the nursing home commission and a United States House subcommittee, then Speaker of the Assembly Stanley Steingut stated that the purpose of the meeting was to discuss Bergman's nursing home problems. However, Steingut testified that when he arrived outside the Governor's office, an embarrassed Hausman emerged from the Governor's office to say that Rockefeller refused to meet with Steingut because of a fued that the two were having. In any event, the meeting was aborted. Ibid., p. 41. See also, *New York Times*, February 5, 1975.

18. State of New York, Moreland Commission, *Political Influence*, p. 44.

19. Ibid., pp. 45, 47. Although the Commission on Nursing Homes was headed by a Democrat, its approach does not seem to have been one of simply doing a "hatchet job" on Republicans. One piece of evidence of this is that the commission was also critical of the role of Stanley Steingut, a leading Democrat. Ibid., pp. 76-81.

20. It should be noted that the Governor stated in his budget message for fiscal year 1973-74 that the state's financial situation had improved. In light of this he

recommended a number of substantial increases in spending including $57 million for the State University, $99 million for transportation programs, and $1.5 million for increases in the program of tuition assistance for college students. *New York Times*, January 17, 1973.

Rockefeller acknowledged to the Moreland Act Commission that he had learned of the shortage of auditors through the monthly reports which the commissioner of health submitted to him. Further evidence that he did indeed read such reports is that the commission found the Governor's handwritten comments on some of the summaries which Dr. Hurd attached to department reports. During 1972, the commissioner of health had at least twice reminded the Governor of the need for more auditors. Comptroller Levitt had done likewise in 1971. State of New York, Moreland Commission, *Political Influence*, pp. 112-14. Connery and Benjamin defend the Governor by asserting that the Health Department did not make a "strong" request for additional auditors. They do not cite any source upon which this judgment is based. Robert Connery and Gerald Benjamin, *Rockefeller of New York, Executive Power in the State House* (Ithaca: Cornell University Press, 1979), p. 172.

21. This structure was created in 1966 under Article 28 of the Public Health Law. See State of New York, Moreland Commission, *Regulating Nursing Home Care*, pp. 14-21.

22. State of New York, Moreland Commission, *Political Influence*, pp. 115-16. In 1979 the Deputy Attorney General for Medicaid Fraud Control reported that audits of 343 nursing homes had revealed $63 million in overstated expense claims. State of New York, Deputy Attorney General, *Fourth Annual Report*, May 10, 1979, pp. 7-8.

23. *New York Times*, August 29, 1975.

24. Ibid.

25. Interview with a former official in the Division of the Budget, February 13, 1974.

26. *New York Times*, May 21, 1966. Acquitted on two felony counts and two misdemeanor counts, he was convicted on two counts, one alleging he aided Playboy executives in bribing SLA Chairman Martin Epstein and one alleging he had induced Epstein to take a bribe.

27. *New York Times*, November 17, 1974.

28. Ibid.

29. U.S., Congress, Senate, Committee on Rules and Administration, *Hearings on Nomination of Nelson A. Rockefeller to be Vice-President of the United States*, 93rd Cong., 2d sess., 1974, pp. 571-72, 600-2. It should be noted that Morhouse had both a law practice and a large plumbing supply business. *New York Times*, November 17, 1974.

30. *New York Times*, November 13, 1974.

31. Senate Committee on Rules and Administration, *Hearings on Nomination of Nelson A. Rockefeller*, p. 606.

32. Ibid. Connery and Benjamin state that "investigations by Anthony Scotti, New York County District Attorney, demonstrated that Morhouse had been involved in influence peddling well before he established his relationship with the Governor." *Rockefeller of New York*, p. 67.

33. Ibid, pp. 572, 887.

34. Senate Committee on Rules and Administration, *Hearings on Nomination of Nelson A. Rockefeller*, pp. 145-47.

35. *New York Times*, November 17, 1974.

36. The Governor's willingness to "go to the wall" for those who had served him well, especially those who had made personal sacrifices, is also illustrated by the case of Fred Young, a man who gave up his position as presiding judge of the Court of Claims to serve as chairman of the Republican party in 1963. Rockefeller repaid Judge Young's willingness to serve him by reappointing him to the Court of Claims after he had served about two years as party chairman. In 1966 he reappointed him as presiding judge in the face of charges that such an appointment represented a blatant political payoff. But an even more impressive demonstration of Rockefeller's loyalty to Judge Young was his personal pledge to keep Young as presiding judge in the face of criticism from within the judiciary regarding Young's performance, a performance critics argued was weakened by the illness which afflicted Young. The Governor is reported to have told Young that "As long as I am Governor, you will be chief judge." The story of this pledge was conveyed to us in an interview with a former state official who was close to both Rockefeller and Young.

37. State of New York, Special Commission on Attica, *Attica: The Official Report of the New York State Special Commission on Attica* (New York: Bantam Books, 1972), p. xi. This report will hereafter be cited as the *McKay Report*, after its chairman, Robert McKay of New York University.

38. Interview with Leslie Mikalson, Albany, New York, March 13, 1979.

39. Testimony to the McKay Commission as quoted in Tom Wicker, *A Time to Die* (New York, Quadrangle Press, 1975), p. 307.

40. *McKay Report*, p. 19.

41. For a description of Attica State Prison including prisoner routines, see chapter 2 of the *McKay Report*.

42. For example, rules were changed to end censorship of mail from inmates to certain categories of recipients, including attorneys of record and some public officials such as judges and state legislators. On an experimental basis, inmates in certain prisons were to be allowed to shower once each day. State of New York, Departmental of Correctional Services, *Six-Month Operational Digest* (mimeo), July 1971, pp. 3, 4. This digest also set forth elements in the department's new approach. For example, it stated, albeit defensively, that "there is no intention of coddling, but rather a fair, firm commitment to bring about change in those who want to change and a secure, humane confinement for those who are not interested in change." p. 8.

43. Russell Oswald, *Attica: My Story* (Garden City: Doubleday and Co., 1972), p. 202.

44. Ibid., p. 203.

45. U.S. Congress, House, *Hearings on the Nomination of Nelson A. Rockefeller to be Vice President of the United States*, 93rd Cong., 2d sess., 1974, p. 100.

46. Interview with Richard Dunham, Albany, New York, July 6, 1979.

47. *McKay Report*, p. 31.

48. Ibid., pp. 133-39.

49. The inmates did not accept the report that Jackson had been killed in an attempted escape. George Jackson was known as a Soledad Brother. At the trial of the surviving Soledad Brothers in 1976, the defense produced a black undercover

agent who testified that George Jackson was killed by the police in a fabricated escape attempt. See, for example, Michael Parenti, *Democracy for the Few* (New York: St. Martin's Press, 1977), p. 150, and a book by the undercover agent Louis Trackwood, *Glass House Tapes* (New York: Avon, 1973).

50. Ibid., p. 140. Oswald was unable to deliver his talk in person because he had left Attica to be with his wife, who had been hospitalized after a sudden illness.

51. For a description of the takeover and the incidents leading up to it, see the *McKay Report*, pp. 141-65. For the commission's conclusion that the uprising was "not planned or organized in advance," see p. 105.

52. Ibid., chapter 7. It appears that leaders of various inmate organizations and factions put aside their differences in order to "organize" the situation in D yard. They included the Muslims, the Black Panthers, the Young Lords, and the "Five Percenters," a Muslim group whose members were not followers of Elijah Muhammad, pp. 197-98.

53. Ibid., pp. 201-3.

54. House Committee on the Judiciary, *Hearings on the Nomination of Nelson A. Rockefeller*, p. 101.

55. Douglass had advised against admitting Bobby Seale, chairman of the Black Panther party, to Attica and against permitting the observers to return to D yard Sunday afternoon. *McKay Report*, p. 319.

56. *McKay Report*, p. 279.

57. Ibid., pp. 204-5, 239-40.

58. *The McKay Report* notes that by attending two meetings Oswald broke his profession's traditions of not negotiating with inmates before hostages were released. He also broke with tradition by allowing members of the media, including TV cameras, into the yard for one of the meetings. However, the report also notes that a 1953 statement of the Committee on Riots of the American Prison Association approves the use of "discussions" in "an attempt to get the hostages released by peaceful means." Ibid., p. 219.

59. *McKay Report*, p. 226.

60. *McKay Report*, pp. 205-26.

61. The raucous meeting between Oswald and inmate leaders was also attended by five members of the Committee of Observers, still in the process of being formed, and about a dozen members of the media. Oswald never went back into the yard after this meeting nor did Professor Schwartz. *McKay Report*, pp. 229-33.

62. Although there was never a clear consensus among state officials and observers as to the proper role of the Committee of Observers, the group ended up as chief negotiators between inmates and state officials. *McKay Report*, pp. 235-38.

63. *McKay Report*, pp. 251-52.

64. More than half of the observers left the yard after about five minutes. Apparently they feared staying behind when Black Panther leader Bobby Seale left. Inmate leaders and the inmates in D yard never actually voted to reject the 28 points. But the hostile reaction of the more vocal to them made it clear to the observers that further negotiation was unlikely to succeed. Ibid., p. 262-67.

65. *McKay Report*, p. 272-73.

66. Ibid., p. 273.

67. Oswald, *Attica*, p. 231.

68. Tom Wicker, *A Time to Die*, p. 216.

69. Ibid., p. 233.

70. Ibid.

71. State Police Superintendent William Kerwin did not even come to Attica, and thus responsibility for planning the assault fell to the local commander of a troop whose headquarters was in nearby Batavia. By assault time he had 587 troops under his command, and the Attica superintendent had 312 corrections officers under his command. *McKay Report*, pp. 342-43. Because of the frustration that had built up as a result of concern for the hostages, what troopers and corrections regarded as "coddling" of the inmates, and taunting by inmates, tension and hostility was very high. *McKay Report*, pp. 310-13. Apparently the Governor was not sensitive to the fact that racism was a contributing factor to the potentially explosive "emotional involvement" about which he was concerned. One must remember that rebelling inmates were heavily black and Puerto Rican and that the attack force was virtually all white. See Tom Wicker, *A Time To Die*, p. 305.

72. *McKay Report*, p. 334.

73. *McKay Report*, p. 373. One of those present at Attica during the takeover, Assemblyman Clark Wemple, is emphatic in his belief that the shooting lasted no more than two minutes. Interview, Schenectady, New York, January 18, 1980.

74. Ibid., pp. 374, 458.

75. Ibid., p. 335. Russell Oswald is skeptical of the way in which the McKay Commission went about gathering information to support conclusions on questions of fact regarding Attica. He argues that granting confidentiality to prisoners and staff calls the resulting information into question. *Attica*, pp. 325-26.

76. Ibid., p. 338.

77. Ibid., p. 455-62.

78. *McKay Report*, p. 460.

79. Ibid., p. 456.

80. As quoted in the *McKay Report*, p. 459.

81. The McKay Commission consisted of nine members appointed by the chief judge of the New York Court of Appeals and the presiding justices of the four Appellate Division Departments of the New York State Judicial System. In addition to the books by Russell Oswald and Tom Wicker, books cited in footnotes 43 and 39 respectively, the *New York Times*, the *Albany Knickerbocker News*, and the *Albany Times Union* are good sources on Attica. For example, see "Attica," an article by Patrick J. Sloan in the latter paper, September 22, 1974. For other analyses, see Gerald Benjamin and Stephen P. Rappaport, "Attica and Prison Reform" in Robert H. Connery and Gerald Benjamin *Governing New York State: The Rockefeller Years* (New York: The Academy of Political Science, 1974), pp. 200-13 and Frederick Fleron and Lou Jean Fleron, "Attica: Official Vengeance," in Gene L. Mason and Fred Vetter, eds., *The Politics of Exploitation* (New York: Random House, 1973).

82. *McKay Report*, p. 324.

83. Ibid.

84. Interview with Richard Dunham, former director of the Division of the Budget. Dunham gave the New York City sanitation strike as an example of a tough situation into which the Governor had "jumped" even though that situation had been "[Mayor] Lindsay's problem."

85. Interview with Clark Wemple. The McKay Commission refers to the Sunday evening proposal that the Governor come to Attica after release of the hostages as

the "modified proposal." *McKay Report*, p. 324.

86. *McKay Report*, p. 325.

87. Senate Committee on Rules and Administration, *Hearings on Nomination of Nelson A. Rockefeller*, p. 127.

88. Russell Oswald states that *he* decided around noon on Sunday to make a proposal to the inmates that was similar to the one that Rockefeller stated he recommended later in the afternoon. The one major difference in the two proposals was that Oswald's made no mention at all of the Governor's coming to Attica. Oswald, *Attica*, p. 235. Oswald complains that his proposal was later inaccurately termed an ultimatum.

89. *McKay Report*, pp. 343-44. The agreement between the two men did not provide for a "commander-in-chief."

90. *McKay Report*, p. 445.

91. Ibid., p. 449.

92. *Albany Times Union*, September 22, 1974.

93. Ibid.

94. *McKay Report*, p. 404. In defense of medical care in the wake of the retaking of the prison, Russell Oswald asserts that "no hostage, no inmate, lost his life from lack of medical attention." *Attica*, p. 329.

95. House Judiciary Committee, *Hearings on the Nomination of Nelson A. Rockefeller*, p. 101.

96. Ibid., p. 109.

97. *McKay Report*, pp. 319-20.

98. House Judiciary Committee, *Hearings on the Nomination of Nelson A. Rockefeller*, p. 164. According to the *McKay Report*, guns were, in fact, used in retaking certain areas of the prison. It appears very unlikely that the remainder of the prison could have been retaken by men not armed with guns. In fact, before Oswald decided to begin negotiations, the operation to retake the prison had been halted pending arrival of additional state troopers. *McKay Report*, pp. 188-93, 216.

99. As quoted in the *McKay Report*, p. 319.

100. House Judiciary Committee, *Hearings on the Nomination of Nelson A. Rockefeller*, p. 110.

101. *McKay Report*, p. 329.

102. Oswald, *Attica*, pp. 233-34.

103. Wicker, *A Time To Die*, p. 218.

104. Ibid., p. 219.

105. Interview with Alan Miller, former commissioner of the Department of Mental Hygiene, Albany, New York, May 17, 1978.

106. Interview with Richard Dunham.

107. For a discussion of the Ludlow incident and its effect on the Rockefeller family, see Peter Collier and David Horowitz, *The Rockefellers: An American Dynasty* (New York: Holt; Rinehart and Winston, 1976), chapter 8 and p. 186.

108. As quoted in Collier and Horowitz, *The Rockefellers*, p. 114.

109. Ibid., p. 115.

110. Ibid.

111. Republican State Senator John Dunne, one of those observers who pleaded with the Governor to come to Attica, raised the possibility of a narrower political motivation. According to Tom Wicker, Dunne said, "Politically, ... Rocky's not

going to give an inch because there are more of them [voters] out there [beyond Attica] than there are in here." Wicker, *A Time To Die*, p. 208.

112. House Judiciary Committee, *Hearings on the Nomination of Nelson A. Rockefeller*, pp. 165-66. Those who talked to Rockefeller used a variety of different arguments in trying to convince him to come to Attica. However, they did seem to agree that as long as the inmates insisted upon amnesty and the Governor was flatly opposed to it, his coming could not be expected to do much more than provide more time in which "something might happen."

113. For a discussion of this policy area, see Joseph Zimmerman, "Public Transportation," in Robert H. Connery and Gerald Benjamin, eds., *Governing New York State: The Rockefeller Years* (New York: The Academy of Political Science, 1974), pp. 214-24.

114. Zimmerman, "Public Transportation," pp. 215-16.

115. The mechanism by which the purchase was accomplished was a purchase of LIRR stock by the newly created Metropolitan Commuter Transportation Authority, an agency charged with improving commuter transportation in New York City and surrounding counties. Ibid., p. 216.

116. Senate Committee on Rules and Administration, *Hearings on Nomination of Nelson A. Rockefeller*, p. 499.

117. Fred C. Shapiro, "The Wholly Ronan Empire," *New York Times Magazine*, May 17, 1970, p. 44.

118. Interview with Edward Kresky, former secretary of MTA and former program associate, New York City, April 27, 1977. Kresky noted that the Governor also made frequent phone calls to him and William Ronan concerning the efforts to improve the LIRR.

119. *New York Times*, December 10, 1972.

120. For example, Zimmerman lists improvements to the former LIRR system including "the extension of electrification, the purchase of 770 cars, construction of the 63rd Street Tunnel, upgrading of tracks, new high-level platforms, and various station improvements." "Public Transportation," p. 219.

121. Robert Caro, *The Power Broker: Robert Moses and the Fall of New York* (New York: Alfred A. Knopf, 1974), p. 1133.

122. Ibid., p. 1140. The suit also challenged the MTA's administrative authority over Triborough.

123. Ibid.

124. *New York Times*, October 10, 1974.

125. As a result of a dispute with Rockefeller in 1962 involving the Governor's desire to replace Moses as chairman of the State Council of Parks with Laurance Rockefeller, Moses resigned that position as well as his chairmanship of the Long Island State Parks Commission and the State Power Authority. Certain that the Governor would not risk a storm of criticism by accepting the resignations, Moses carried his threats too far by issuing a news release which implied that Rockefeller was motivated by simple nepotism. The end result was that after this and earlier provocations, the Governor accepted Moses's resignations. Caro, *The Power Broker*, p. 1078.

126. *New York Times*, October 10, 1974.

127. For a detailed discussion of the "understandings" between Rockefeller and Moses, see Caro, *The Power Broker*, pp. 1137-43.

128. Ibid., pp. 1142-43. As Caro notes, the offer from William Ronan was a humiliating "slap in the face." In fact, Moses had been stripped of all power of decision. Under the terms of the consolidation of transportation agencies under MTA as details were finally worked out, the autonomy of Triborough and other units disappeared totally. For example, the MTA Board was to serve as ex officio board of all the MTA's constituent agencies, and William Ronan was to serve as ex officio executive officer of all those agencies. See State of New York, Metropolitan Transportation Authority, 1968 Annual Report, p. 6.

Chapter 9

1. See his statement in U.S., Congress, House, Committee on the Judiciary, *Hearings on the Nomination of Nelson A. Rockefeller to be Vice-President of the United States*, 93rd Cong., 2d sess., November 21, 1974, p. 16.

2. *New York Times*, Oct. 10, 1974.

3. The former head of art education for the state Education Department referred to Rockefeller as the "de Medici of the 20th Century in art education." *Albany Times Union*, February 25, 1979.

4. Interview with Wallace Harrison, New York City, June 1, 1978.

5. *New York Times*, October 20, 1974.

6. *Albany Knickerbocker News*, July 15, 1975. Not taking into account the effects of increases in the cost of state borrowing, which came about as a result of the UDC crisis, the direct costs of rescuing UDC and other state authorities relying on moral-obligation bonding has been high. More specifically, substantial state payments, both regular and first instance, have been necessary to support four authorities and the Project Finance Agency, the latter created to channel funds to UDC by purchasing some of its mortgages. During the period covering fiscal years 1975-1976 through 1980-1981, such state payments amounted to more than $456 million. State of New York, Office of the Comptroller, *The State of New York: Credit Problems and Opportunities*, Appendix B, p. 3, December, 1981.

7. Robert H. Connery and Gerald Benjamin, *Rockefeller of New York: Executive Power in the Statehouse* (Ithaca: Cornell University Press, 1979), p. 265.

8. As quoted in the *New York Times*, October 6, 1975.

9. In the course of praising Rockefeller as a good Governor, Robert Moses noted that the former had "branched out boldly, imaginatively, and ruthlessly into long-neglected areas of construction, welfare, education, public business, and the arts." Robert Moses, *Public Works: A Dangerous Trade* (New York: McGraw Hill Book Co., 1970), p. 881. As noted in chapter 8, Moses had personal experience of Rockefeller's "ruthlessness."

10. Assessments of Rockefeller programs are available in a number of different sources. Some of the more valuable sources are government documents such as reports and audits of the Office of the Comptroller of the State of New York, reports of the New York State Legislative Commission on Expenditure Review, and reports of various investigating commissions created under the state's Moreland Act. Other valuable sources include periodicals such as *Empire State Reports*, *New York Magazine*, and *Fortune*, and newspapers, especially the *New York Times*. Books on the Rockefeller administration, the more prominent of which are included in our

bibliographic essay, also contain assessments of programs. Finally, the many interviews we conducted with state officials or former state officials are of invaluable help in forming assessments of programs.

11. Consisting of sixty-four campuses, the university includes four large university centers, research and medical centers, liberal arts colleges, community colleges, and technical institutions. The vast expansion of the system under Rockefeller is illustrated by the fact that the number of degrees granted each year rose from 10,000 at the end of the 1950s to more than 65,000 by the end of the 1970s. Although a recent assessment calls the development of the state university "the most important accomplishment" of Rockefeller's administration, it also concludes that for the most part the units within the system have not achieved the overall excellence that Rockefeller hoped for. See the five-part series in the *New York Times*, June 29-July 2, 1981. Although the Empire State Plaza regularly draws large numbers of people to Albany for special events and for attractions such as exhibits in the New York State Museum, it has drawn some blistering criticism from architects and art critics. For example, *Time Magazine* critic Robert Hughes has been quoted as describing the complex as "without a question, the ugliest, most pretentious, least successful governmental complex-even including Brazilia-that I've seen in 20 years as an art critic." Quoted in *Albany Times Union*, January 25, 1981.

12. State of New York, Moreland Act Commission on the Urban Development Financing Agencies, *Restoring Credit and Confidence: A Reform Program for New York State and Its Public Authorities*, March 31, 1976, p. 19. However, one author who investigated projects argues that some UDC projects were shoddy and even unsafe. His argument is not easily dismissed. See Martin Mayer, *The Builders: Houses, People, Neighborhoods, Governments, Money* (New York: W. W. Norton and Company, 1978), pp. 276-82.

13. An authoritative source notes that by 1974 there had been an almost negligible increase in the number of jobs created as a result of ASDA's nuclear development programs. State of New York, Legislative Commission on Expenditure Review, *Nuclear Development and Radiation Control: Program Audit 8.1.74*, October 1, 1974, p. S-7.

14. For example, see State of New York, Moreland Act Commission on Nursing Homes and Residential Facilities, *Political Influence and Political Accountability: One Foot in the Door*, February, 1976, pp. 120-22.

15. The fact that voters defeated proposed bond issues for transportation in 1971 and 1973 severely retarded improvements in mass transportation.

16. U.S., Congress, Senate, Committee on Rules and Administration, *Hearings on the Nomination of Nelson A. Rockefeller to be Vice-President of the United States*, 93rd Cong., 2d sess., 1974, pp. 69-70.

17. Bruce Buchanan notes that presidents are often victims of their staff's being excessively deferential toward them and thus withholding unpleasant truths. According to Buchanan, staff "will gradually detach him from what he needs to know . . . in their eagerness to serve him." *The Presidential Experience: What the Office Does to the Man* (Englewood Cliffs: Prentice Hall, 1978), p. 157.

18. For a discussion of the active-positive category, see James David Barber, *The Presidential Character* (Englewood Cliffs: Prentice Hall, 1972), pp. 12-14 and part 4. Barber seems to feel that active-positives are almost immune to the effects of stress. For a somewhat different view, see Buchanan, *The Presidential Experience.*

Buchanan argues that even individuals with high self-esteem will begin to engage in behavior typical of low self-esteem persons provided they are subjected to sufficient pressures such as those arising from stress or frustration. See Chapter 7.

19. As we point out in the preceding chapter, there may also have been a "rational" element in his failure to "take charge" at Attica. The political costs of being seen as having failed after personal intervention at the scene may have played a part in Rockefeller's decision.

20. Barber, *Presidential Character*, chapter 2. If Rockefeller had a personality flaw typical of any of Barber's four types of Presidents, it would be that of Barber's active-positive type. Presidents of that type, says Barber, "in their haste to make things happen, may too quickly and easily knock down the 'formalities' that hold the democratic order in place," p. 246. One might argue that Rockefeller's eagerness to circumvent the voters by resorting to devices such as moral-obligation borrowing represents a failure of this kind.

21. For the language of the proposed amendment, see Senate Introductory 1432, January 1971. For a description of the rationale for the huge community development bond issue, see Rockefeller's Annual Message to the Legislature in State of New York, *Public Papers of Nelson A. Rockefeller, Fifty-Third Governor of the State of New York, 1970.* For a description of activities proposed to be carried out, see the proposed amendment and the *Albany Knickerbocker News*, January 21, 1971. In 1965 voters had defeated a constitutional amendment which would have allowed the state to grant the power of eminent domain to private firms in the housing field. State of New York, *Manual for the Use of the Legislature 1975*, p. 346.

22. State of New York, Moreland Act Commission, *Restoring Credit and Confidence*, p. 17.

23. As late as 1973, the legislature approved an increase in the debt authorization of UDC from $1.5 billion to $2 billion. *New York Times*, November 19, 1975.

24. New York State, Moreland Act Commission, *Restoring Credit*, p. 11.

25. The question arises whether bankers and other members of the investment community were naive about the possible risk of UDC and other public benefit corporations defaulting. As the Moreland Commission on UDC noted, "They knew that the moral obligation was not a legal obligation but they nevertheless treated it as equivalent to a guarantee by a state. For as they said, 'New York will never let these bonds go into default.'" Ibid., pp. 10, 11.

26. That Rockefeller remained the pragmatic liberal problem solver after leaving the governorship is demonstrated by later activities. Immediately upon leaving office, he devoted his energies to his Commission on Critical Choices, a study project similar in intent to that of the Special Studies Project that he chaired in the 1950s. See the *Albany Times Union*, March 17, 1974. As vice-president in the Ford administration, he led the effort to achieve a federal "bailout" of New York City in that city's financial crisis of 1975. See *Albany Knickerbocker News*, October 14, 1975. He also "took on" Ford's more conservative advisers in an all-out battle to gain Ford's approval for creation of an "Energy Independence Authority" that would fund up to $100 billion in energy projects and energy research and development. To be funded by a $25 billion subsidy from the Treasury and about $75 billion in Treasury borrowing, the proposed agency was to bear a strong resemblance to some of Rockefeller's creations as Governor. See the *Washington Post*, September 24, 1975.

Bibliographic Essay

The sources we utilized for our research on Nelson Rockefeller and the Rockefeller administration in New York fall into three conventional categories: secondary sources consisting of both books and articles, primary sources consisting of government documents and newspapers, and primary sources consisting of interviews which we conducted. Although any given type of source may have been of particular importance for a specific subject, we judge that the three types were of about equal importance as sources for the totality of our subject. This essay discusses those sources that contributed most heavily to our knowledge of various aspects of that subject.

Pragmatic Liberalism and Post-World War II Politics in America

The literature on the development of modern liberalism and the politics of the postwar era is voluminous. Those sources most helpful to us fall into three categories: works by leading liberal "spokesmen," works describing and interpreting political beliefs, especially the beliefs of elites, and works describing the policies and decisions of political leaders and their administrations.

The most helpful sources by leading liberals were John K. Galbraith, *American Capitalism: The Concept of Countervailing Power* (Boston: Houghton Mifflin Co., 1952) and Arthur Schlesinger, Jr., *The Vital Center* (Boston: Houghton Mifflin Co., 1949). Also helpful as an expression of the outlook and beliefs of a collection of prominent members of the political and economic elite was Rockefeller Brothers Fund. *Prospect for America: The Rockefeller Panel Reports* (Garden City: Doubleday and Co., 1961).

Of those works describing and analyzing the evolution of liberalism, the following were especially helpful: Louis Hartz, *The Liberal Tradition in America* (New York: Harcourt, Brace and World, 1955); Theodore Lowi, *The End of Liberalism: Ideology, Policy and the Crisis of Public Authority* (New York: W. W. Norton and Co., 1969); and Garry Wills, *Nixon Agonistes: The Crises of the Self-Made Man* (Boston: Houghton Mifflin Co., 1969).

Sources describing and analyzing the policies and decisions of postwar political leaders and their administrations include Richard J. Barnet, *Roots of War* (New

York: Atheneum Publishers, 1972); Alonzo L. Hamby, *Beyond the New Deal: Harry S. Truman and American Liberalism* (New York: Columbia University Press, 1973); Godfrey Hodgson, *America in Our Time* (Garden City: Doubleday and Co., 1976); Emmet J. Hughes, *The Ordeal of Power* (New York: Atheneum Publishers, 1963); Doris Kearns, *Lyndon Johnson and the American Dream* (New York: Harper and Row Publishers, 1976); Bruce Miroff, *Pragmatic Illusions* (New York: David McKay Co., 1976); Arthur Schlesinger, Jr., *A Thousand Days* (Boston: Houghton Mifflin Co., 1965); Schlesinger, *The Imperial Presidency* (Boston: Houghton Mifflin Co., 1973); Theodore Sorensen, *Kennedy* (New York: Harper and Row Publishers, 1965); Herbert Stein, *The Fiscal Revolution in America* (Chicago: University of Chicago Press, 1969); James L. Sundquist, *Politics and Policy: The Eisenhower, Kennedy, and Johnson Years* (Washington: The Brookings Institution, 1968).

Personality, Belief System, and Executive Style

The literature on "political personality" and executive decision making is also voluminous. It encompasses a wide range of topics including needs, motives, beliefs, values, and patterns of behavior. Those sources that were most helpful in organizing our approach to understanding Nelson Rockefeller include James David Barber, "Strategies for Understanding Politicians," *American Journal of Political Science* 18 (May 1974) and *The Presidential Character: Predicting Performance in the White House* (Englewood Cliffs: Prentice-Hall, 1972); Bruce Buchanan, *The Presidential Experience: What the Office Does to the Man* (Englewood Cliffs: Prentice-Hall, 1978); Alexander George, "Adaptation to Stress in Political Decision-Making: the Individual, Small Group, and Organizational Contexts," in George V. Coelho, ed., *Coping and Adaptation* (New York: Basic Books, 1974), pp. 176-245; Fred T. Greenstein, "Personality and Politics," in Fred I. Greenstein, ed., *Micropolitical Theory* (Reading, Massachusetts: Addison Wesley, 1975), pp. 1-92; Jeanne N. Knutson, "Personality in the Study of Politics," in Jeanne N. Knutson, ed., *Handbook of Political Psychology* (San Francisco: Jossey-Bass Publishers, 1973), pp. 38-56; Robert E. Lane, *Political Thinking and Consciousness: the Private Life of the Political Mind* (Chicago: Markham Publishing Co., 1969); James Payne and Oliver Woshinsky, "Incentives for Political Participation," *World Politics* 24 (July 1972), pp. 518-546. Among the sources that were most helpful on the organizational milieu within which executives must function were Anthony Downs, *Inside Bureaucracy* (Boston: Little Brown and Co., 1967); George, "Adaptation to Stress"; Irving L. Janis, *Victims of Groupthink* (Boston: Houghton Mifflin Co., 1972).

Rockefeller's Life and Career Before 1958

There is no classic biography of Nelson Rockefeller, and the quality of some available is not especially high. However, the following were helpful in varying degrees: Stewart Alsop, *Nixon and Rockefeller: A Double Portrait* (Garden City: Doubleday and Co., 1960); James Desmond, *Nelson Rockefeller: A Political Biography* (New York: Macmillan Co., 1964); Frank H. Gervasi, *The Real Rockefeller* (New York: Atheneum, 1964); Michael Kramer and Sam Roberts, *I Never Wanted to be Vice-President of Anything: An Investigative Biography of Nelson Rockefeller* (New York: Basic Books, 1976); Joe Alex Morris, *Nelson*

Rockefeller: A Biography (New York: Harper and Row Publishers, 1960). Although it covers four generations of Rockefellers, one work provides especially valuable materials on Nelson Rockefeller. That work is: Peter Collier, *The Rockefellers: An American Dynasty* (New York: Holt, Rinehart, and Winston, 1976).

Some good insights into Rockefeller's career as Coordinator of Interamerican Affairs is contained in the record of congressional appropriations hearings at which he appeared. Each of those hearings is entitled *Hearings on the National War Agencies Appropriation Bill.* They were conducted by the Committees on Appropriations of the U.S. House and Senate respectively.

Campaigns and Elections

The source materials for the campaigns and elections of Nelson A. Rockefeller were drawn from both the general literature on campaigns and campaigning and a wide range of sources that deal specifically with his four successful campaigns for the governorship and his several unsuccessful attempts at securing the nomination of the Republican party for the presidency. The works on campaigning that were most useful are Arnold Steinberg, *Political Campaign Management* (Lexington, Massachusetts: D.C. Heath and Co., 1976); and James Perry, *The New Politics: The Expanding Technology of Political Manipulation* (New York: Clarkson N. Potter, 1968).

For New York State contests the election statistics compiled by the New York Department of State and the campaign speeches of candidate Rockefeller were especially valuable. The latter were included in State of New York, *Public Papers of Nelson A. Rockefeller, Fifty-third Governor of the State of New York, 1959... 1973*. Also of particular importance in our review of the state campaigns were: Robert H. Connery and Gerald Benjamin, *Rockefeller of New York: Executive Power in the Statehouse* (Ithaca: Cornell University Press, 1979); John J. Gargan, "Nelson Rockefeller and New York State Electoral Politics: 1958-1970," Kent State University, Center for Urban Regionalism, 1972; Gargan, "Toward an 'Explanation' of New York State Politics" (Paper prepared for delivery at the 1975 meeting of the Northeastern Political Science Association at Rutgers University, New Brunswick, New Jersey); Fred Powledge, "The Marketing of Nelson Rockefeller," *New York Magazine* (November 30, 1970). Finally, both *Empire State Report* and the *New York Times* were valuable sources of information on gubernatorial elections and campaigns.

Our description of Rockefeller's attempts to win the Republican nomination for president depends most heavily upon coverage found in the Making of the President series by Theodore H. White. Those volumes are *The Making of the President 1960* (New York: Atheneum House, 1961); *The Making of the President 1964* (New York: Atheneum Publishers, 1965); *The Making of the President 1968* (New York: Atheneum Publishers, 1969); and *The Making of the President 1972* (New York: Atheneum Publishers, 1973).

Rockefeller and His Administration in New York

Secondary sources on Nelson Rockefeller and his administration can be divided into those sources that provide a more or less comprehensive view and those that deal with a particular aspect of his performance or a specific element of his administration. In the first category are a number of works, including two of the biographies already listed. They include Collier, *The Rockefellers*; Connery and Benjamin, *Rockefeller of New York*; Kramer and Roberts, *Vice President*. The Connery volume is notable in that the authors claim free access to Rockefeller's official files. We found their book to be a valuable source of facts concerning a range of questions relating to the Rockefeller administration.

Helpful secondary sources which deal with specific aspects of Rockefeller's performance and/or elements of his administration include: Robert Caro, *The Power Broker: Robert Moses and the Fall of New York* (New York: Alfred A. Knopf, 1974)—Includes an analysis of Rockefeller's dealings with the legendary public works king, Robert Moses; Robert Connery and Gerald Benjamin, eds., *Governing New York State: The Rockefeller Years* (New York: The Academy of Political Science, 1974)—Includes contributions which survey a wide range of policies and programs; Donald H. Haider, *When Governments Come to Washington* (New York: Free Press, 1974)—Deals with Rockefeller's efforts to win approval for federal revenue sharing; Alan G. Hevesi, *Legislative Politics in New York State: A Comparative Analysis* (New York: Praeger Publishers, 1975) —Examines Rockefeller's relations with the state legislature; Russell Oswald, *Attica: My Story* (Garden City: Doubleday Co., 1972)—Contains the commissioner of corrections' account of the Attica Prison uprising; Neal Peirce, *The Megastates of America: People, Politics, and Power in the Ten Great States* (New York: W. W. Norton and Co., 1972)—Contains commentary on the Rockefeller administration, especially its policies and programs; Annmarie H. Walsh, *The Public's Business: The Politics and Practice of Government Corporations* (Cambridge: The M.I.T. Press, 1978)—Contains an analysis of Rockefeller's use of semiautonomous authorities to accomplish governmental objectives; Tom Wicker, *A Time To Die* (New York: Quadrangle Press, 1975) —A participant-observer's account of the Attica Prison uprising by New York Times man Tom Wicker. In addition to the books listed here, a variety of articles from three periodicals provided valuable material. Those periodicals were *Empire State Report*, *The New York Times Magazine*, and *New York Magazine*. Especially valuable was Humphrey S. Tyler, "The Steady Growth of Backdoor Financing," *Empire State Report* (June 1975): 211-13, 222-23—Describes key financial practices in the Rockefeller administration; and Edward Jay Epstein, "The Great Rockefeller Power Machine," *New York Magazine* (November 24, 1975): 44-72.—Describes Rockefeller's efforts in narcotic control. Finally, an unpublished paper provided valuable background information on the structure of New York State government and the development of the powers of the Governor; Joseph F. Zimmerman, "New York State Government: Retrospect and Prospect" (Paper prepared for delivery at the Twenty-First College Conference on New York History, Albany, New York, April 30, 1977).

We have relied heavily on three types of primary sources for information on all aspects of Rockefeller's performance as Governor and the record of his administration. Those types of sources are newspapers, government documents, and interviews. The newspapers that proved most helpful were the *Albany Knickerbocker News*, the *Albany Times Union*, and the *New York Times*. A partial list of government documents would include the following state documents: State of New York. *Public Papers of Nelson A. Rockefeller*; State of New York, Division of the Budget.

Executive Budget for the Fiscal Year 1959-60, . . . 1973-74; State of New York, Office of the Comptroller. *1959, . . . 1974 Annual Reports* (Various other publications of the Office of the Comptroller were helpful, especially *Debt-Like Commitments of the State of New York*, January, 1973.); State of New York, Moreland Act Commission on the Urban Development Financing Agencies. *Restoring Credit and Confidence: A Reform Program for New York State and Its Public Authorities*, March 31, 1976; State of New York, Moreland Act Commission on Nursing Homes and Residential Facilities. *Political Influence and Political Accountability: One Foot in the Door*, February 1976, and *Regulating Nursing Home Care: The Paper Tigers*, October 1975; State of New York, Special Commission on Attica. *Attica: The Official Report of the New York State Special Commission on Attica* (New York: Bantam Books, 1972). Various reports of the Legislative Commission on Expenditure Review were also helpful. See, for example, State of New York, Legislative Commission on Expenditure Review. *Nuclear Development and Radiation Control* Program Audit 8.1.74, October 1, 1974. Annual reports and other documents of operating agencies were occasionally helpful. Without question the most valuable of all state documents were the annual volumes of *Public Papers* already cited. The *Papers* provide a comprehensive collection of the Governor's official messages, actions on important bills, appointments, addresses, news conferences, and other statements and actions.

The most helpful federal documents are those related to congressional consideration of the nomination of Nelson Rockefeller to be vice-president of the United States. We relied most heavily on: U.S., Congress, House, Committee on the Judiciary.*Hearings on the Nomination of Nelson A. Rockefeller to be Vice-President of the United States*, 93rd Cong., 2d sess., 1974; and U.S., Congress, Senate, Committee on Rules and Administration. *Hearings on the Nomination of Nelson A. Rockefeller to be Vice-President of the United States*, 93rd Cong., 2d sess., 1974.

About seventy-five interviews provided us with extensive information about the Governor and his administration. Absolutely essential was an interview with Nelson Rockefeller which lasted almost two hours and provided invaluable information, especially that relating to the topics of the Governor's executive style, his relationship with subordinates as well as legislative leaders, and his programs. Additional interviews were conducted with: 1. Most of the Governor's top aides and advisers, including outside members of his personal team, as well as lower-level members of staff units serving the Governor; 2. top officials of a variety of state agencies and semiautonomous authorities; 3. several legislative leaders and key legislative staff.

Index

About the Authors

JAMES E. UNDERWOOD is Professor and Chairman of the Department of Political Science at Union College in Schenectady, New York. He has published work on public policy in relation to the issues of science and technology, and the control of administration by political leadership.

WILLIAM J. DANIELS is Professor of Political Science at Union College and is the author of numerous articles on the U.S. Supreme Court which have appeared in the *Journal of Legal Repression*, the *Western Political Quarterly*, and *The Black Law Journal*.